PEARSON BACCALAUREATE

WORLD HISTORY

The Cold War:
Superpower tensions and rivalries

2nd Edition

KEELY ROGERS • JO THOMAS

Supporting every learner across the IB continuum

D1599694

Published by Pearson Education Limited, 80 Strand, London, WC2R 0RL.

www.pearsonglobalschools.com

Text © Pearson Education Limited 2015
Edited by Jill Morris
Proofread by Jill Morris and Sarah Nisbet
Designed by Astwood Design
Typeset by Phoenix Photosetting, Chatham, Kent
Original illustrations © Pearson Education 2015
Illustrated by Tech-Set Ltd and Phoenix Photosetting
Cover design by Pearson Education Limited

The rights of Joanna Thomas and Keely Rogers to be identified as authors of this work have been asserted by them in accordance with the Copyright, Designs and Patents Act 1988.

First published 2015

20 19 18 17
IMP 10 9 8 7 6 5 4 3

British Library Cataloguing in Publication Data
A catalogue record for this book is available from the British Library

ISBN 978 1 447 98236 4
eBook only ISBN 978 1 447 98237 1

Acknowledgements
The authors and publisher would like to thank Tom Buchanan for his invaluable help with and feedback on this title, and Malcolm Price for his expert help in the structuring and writing of the Theory of Knowledge section in this book.

The authors and publisher would like to thank the following individuals and organisations for permission to reproduce photographs:

Alamy Images: Bill Miller 226, INTERFOTO 28, 59, RIA Novosti 168; **British Cartoon Archive, University of Kent www.cartoons.ac.uk:** 138, Illingworth, Daily Mail, 1946 / Associated Newspapers Ltd / Solo Syndication 26, Michael Cummings, Daily Express 1969 171b, Nicholas Garland, The Independent, 20 May 1988 198; **copyright Peter Leibing, Hamburg:** 104b; **Corbis:** 63, 65, 90, 251, Alain Nogues / Sygma 107, Bettmann 5, 35, 39b, 75r, 80, 84, 91, 94, 104t, 106, 114t, 126, 243, Bruno Ehrs 250, Hulton-Deutsch Collection 58t, Peter Turnley 240, Reuters 193, 196, Wolfgang Kumm / dpa 220, Yevgeny Khaldei 20; **Getty Images:** 117, AFP 110, 247, Allan Jackson 10, BREEDING 74, Emory Kristof 2, Eric Schwab 24, Express Newspapers 132, Franz Aberham 268, Hulton Archive 56, 79, 184, James Burke 256, Jean Vincent 139, John Dominis 150, Keystone 114b, 191, Larry Burrows 72, Lubomir Kotek 217, MONDADORI 127, Print Collector 44, Ronald L. Haeberle 86, SOVFOTO 283, Steve Eason 210, STR 173, Time Life Pictures 162, Yale Joel 58b; **Globe Cartoon:** 148, 163; **Library of Congress:** drawing by Edmund S. Valtman, reproduction number LC-USZ62-130421 155, drawing by Edmund S. Valtman, reproduction number LC-USZ62-130433 140, drawing by Edmund S. Valtman, reproduction number LC-USZ62-130439 158; **Mary Evans Picture Library:** Epic / Tallandier 100, Everett Collection 15; **McCain Library & Archives, The University of Southern Mississippi:** cartoon by Bob Artley 177; **McCord Museum, Montreal:** John Collins, 1947 233, John Collins, 1950 234, John Collins, 1956 259, John Collins, 1962 208l, John Collins, 1963 208r, 244, John Collins, 1968 209; **National Archives and Records Administration (NARA):** 66t; **Press Association Images:** AP 165, 175; **Punch Cartoon Library:** 33, 83, 190t, 273; **The Art Archive:** 200; **The Charlotte Observer:** Doug Marlette 88; **The Herb Block Foundation:** 66b, 76, 93, 97, 98, 141, 192; **TopFoto:** AP 147, copyright 1999 Topham Picturepoint 171tr, copyright 1999, Topham Picturepoint 128, copyright 2003, Topham Picturepoint 115, Lightroom Photos 68, RIA Novosti 146, ullsteinbild 134; **Universal Uclick:** Tony Auth / The Philadelphia Inquirer 219, 221

Cover image: Front: **Getty Images:** Klubovy. Inside front cover: **Shutterstock. com:** Dmitry Lobanov

The authors and publisher would like to thank the following for their kind permission to reproduce their media on the ebook:

Corbis: Bettmann, Hulton-Deutsch Collection, Peter Turnley; **Fotolia.com:** Georgios Kollidas; **Getty Images:** AFP, BACHRACH, David Fenton, Eric Schwab, Hulton Archive, James Burke, John Dominis, Katherine Young, Keystone, Keystone-France, MPI, National Archives, STR, Yale Joel; **Press Association Images:** AP; **Shutterstock.com:** Everett Historical, Steve Broer; **TopFoto:** copyright 1999 Topham Picturepont

All other images © Pearson Education

We are grateful to the following for permission to reproduce copyright material:

Logos
Logo on page 229 reprinted with the permission of the United Nations

Text
Extract on page 13 from Winston Churchill to his personal secretary John Colville the evening before Operation Barbarossa, the German invasion of the Soviet Union with permission from Curtis Brown; Extract on page 22 from Khrushchev Remembers: The Last Testament by Nikita Khrushchev, translated and edited by Strobe Talbott. Copyright © 1974 by Little, Brown and Company (Inc). Reprinted by permission of Little, Brown and Company; Extract on page 25 from Winston Churchill's address at Westminster College, Fulton, Missouri, 05/03/1946, with permission from Curtis Brown; Extract on page 29,30 from America, Russia and the Cold War 1945–1996, McGraw Hill (LaFeber W 1997) p.57-58, McGraw-Hill Education; Extract on page 32 from America, Russia and the Cold War 1945–1996 McGraw Hill (LaFeber W 1997) p.62, McGraw-Hill Education; Extract on page 47 from America, Russia and the Cold War 1945–1996, McGraw Hill (LaFeber W 1997) p.1, McGraw-Hill Education; Extract on page 48 from Postwar: A History of Europe from 1945 , Vintage (Judt, A) p.108; Extract on page 51 from Origins of the Cold War, Foreign Affairs, pp. 49–50 (Arthur M Schlesinger, Jr), reprinted by permission of Foreign Affairs, (1967). Copyright (1967) by the Council on Foreign Relations, Inc. www.ForeignAffairs.com; Extract on page 52 from The United States and Origins of the Cold War 1941–1947, by John Lewis Gaddis. Copyright © 1972 Columbia University Press. Reprinted with permission of the publisher.; Extract on page 69 from The Cambridge History of American Foreign Relations: Volume 4, America in the Age of Soviet Power, 1945-1991, Cambridge University Press p. 66; Extract on page 87 from Yew, Lee Kuan, The Singapore Story: Memoirs of Lee Kuan Yew, 1st Ed., ©1999, p. 66. Reprinted and Electronically reproduced by permission of Pearson Education, Inc., New York, NY.; Extracts on page 92 and page 96 from The Cold War by John Lewis Gaddis (Penguin Books 2005) Copyright (C) John Lewis Gaddis, 2005 and Penguin Books Ltd; Extract on page 101, from Cold War to Détente 1945–1980 1 ed., Heinemann Educational (Brown C, Mooney PJ) p.66, Pearson Education Limited; Extract on page 110 from The Cold War: An International History (The Making of the Contemporary World) ISBN-13: 978-0415153164, Routledge (Painter D 1999) p.53 reproduced by permission of Routledge; Extract on page 110 from The Cold War (Questions and Analysis in History) ISBN-13: 978-0415195263, Routledge (Lightbody B 1999 reproduced by permission of Routledge; Extract on page 123 from Khrushchev Remembers: The Last Testament by Nikita Khrushchev, translated and edited by Strobe Talbott. Copyright © 1974 by Little, Brown and Company (Inc). Reprinted by permission of Little, Brown and Company; Extract on page 128 from The Rise of Modern China, 6 ed, OUP (Hsu I) p.671 with permission from Oxford University Press; Extract on page 130 from The Rise of Modern China, 6 ed, OUP (Hsu I) p.675 with permission from Oxford University Press; Extract on page 131 from The Cold War by John Lewis Gaddis (Penguin Books 2005) Copyright (C) John Lewis Gaddis, 2005 and Penguin Books Ltd; Extract on page 138 from Mao: The Unknown Story by Jung Chang and Jon Halliday. Reprinted by permission of The Random House Group and © 2005 by Globalflair Ltd.. Used by permission of Alfred A. Knopf, an imprint of the Knopf and Doubleday Publishing Group, a division of Penguin Random House LLC. All rights reserved.; Extract on page 133 from Mao: The Unknown Story by Jung Chang and Jon Halliday. Reprinted by permission of The Random House Group copyright © 2005 by Globalflair Ltd.. Used by permission of Alfred A. Knopf, an imprint of the Knopf and Doubleday Publishing Group, a division of Penguin Random House LLC. All rights reserved.; Extract on page 135, from p.67, Mike Sewell, The Cold War (Cambridge Perspectives in History), 2002 © Cambridge University Press 2002, reproduced with permission; Extract on page 135 from Odd Arne Westad, The Global Cold War: Third World Interventions and the Making of Our Times, 2007 © Odd Arne Westad 2007, published by Cambridge University Press, reproduced with permission; Extract on page 135 from The Cold War by John Lewis Gaddis (Penguin Books 2005) Copyright (C) John Lewis Gaddis, 2005 and Penguin Books Ltd; Extract on page 142 from The Cold War by John Lewis Gaddis (Penguin Books 2005) Copyright (C) John Lewis Gaddis, 2005 and Penguin Books Ltd; Extract on page 151 from The Pelican History of the United States of America 2 Rev Ed. Penguin (Brogan H) pp.625–626, Pearson Education Limited; Extract on page 152 from United Nations Document S/1902, 15 November 1950, pp.2–4, © 1950 United Nations. Reprinted with the permission of the United Nations; Extracts on page 153 and page 159 from On China by Henry Kissinger. Copyright © Henry A. Kissinger, 2011, 2012. and Penguin Books Ltd; Extract on page 161

Contents

Introduction

How will this book help you in your IB examination?

This book is designed to be your guide to success in your International Baccalaureate examination in History. It covers the Cold War: Superpower Tensions and Rivalries topic, and aims to equip you with the knowledge and skills that you will need to answer the essay questions that will be in your Paper 2 examination. In addition, although it is specifically for Paper 2, this book also helps you to develop and practise the source-based skills you need to answer questions on Paper 1.

The book identifies the key themes and topics of the Cold War and includes within each chapter:

- analysis of the key events
- a summary of, or reference to, up-to-date **historiography**

- discussion on how to answer essay questions effectively
- essay planning techniques for each topic and the key themes required
- timelines to help you put events into context
- review and research activities to help you develop your understanding of the key issues and concepts
- compared and contrasted key themes.

The regular use of command terms, enquiry-based research tasks, the source-based activities, and the links to Theory of Knowledge (ToK) and reflection will not only prepare you fully for the Paper 2 essay questions, but will also help to prepare you for the requirements of your Paper 1 exam and your Internal Assessments (IAs).

Notes on the second edition

Key concepts

Throughout the book we focus on and develop the six key concepts that have particular prominence in the Diploma History course: change, continuity, causation, consequence, significance, and perspectives. These concepts have always been key components of the History course, but they are specifically highlighted in the new guide. You will now find that each chapter begins with a list of the key concepts covered within it.

New content

The new course topic 12: The Cold War: Superpower Tensions and Rivalries (20th century) has some content continuity with the last curriculum guide. However, whereas previously the subject was mostly approached in order, it is now divided into topic areas. The first topic – Rivalry, mistrust and accord – approaches the course of the Cold War thematically from the breakdown of the Grand Alliance, the development of superpower rivalry through the policies of containment, peaceful co-existence,

and relations with the People's Republic of China, culminating in a consideration of the reasons for the end of the Cold War. Indeed there is more of a thematic and conceptual approach to this topic than in the previous edition. New to the content of the course is the emphasis on comparative and cross-regional case studies. In this edition we have also included a new section to address the second topic – Leaders and nations – in which the role of cross-regional leaders and nations in the development, course, and end of the Cold War are compared. The final section of the book focuses on the third topic – Cold War crises – in which the causes, impact and significance of cross-regional case studies are examined.

Approaches to learning

'Approaches to teaching and learning' (ATL) reflects the IB learner profile attributes, and is designed to enhance your learning and assist preparation for IAs and examinations. ATL runs throughout the IB Middle Years Programme (MYP) and Diploma Programme (DP), and encourages you to think of common skills that are necessary in all subjects. The variety of skills covered will equip you to continue to be actively engaged in learning after you leave your school or college.

There are five categories of ATL skills: thinking skills, communication skills, social skills, self-management skills, and research skills. These skills encompass the key values that underpin an IB education.

ATL skills are addressed in the activity boxes throughout the book. ATL activities can also be found in the eBook that accompanies this book.

International mindedness

The Cold War topic is 'international' in its causes, the way it was waged, and in its impact on international relations at the time and into the 21st century. In addition, the emphasis in this course on looking at different perspectives and on comparing events in different regions of the world will further your understanding of the international nature of the Cold War. As we go through the book we will highlight the interconnected nature of the historical events of the Cold War and events of today.

How this book works

Interesting fact boxes

These boxes contain information which will deepen and widen your knowledge, but which does not fit within the main body of the text.

The Little Red Book
The 'Little Red Book' was a small red book of Mao's thoughts and sayings that became an essential accessory during the Cultural Revolution.

Essay questions

The essay questions at the start of each chapter will offer topic-specific questions for you to think about while working through the chapter. At the end of the chapter there will be additional Paper 2-style questions. Some of these will ask you to compare the case study you have just covered with another case study from an earlier chapter.

As you read this chapter, consider the following essay questions:
- Examine the key causes of Sino-American hostility from 1949–1970.
- Discuss the reasons for the Sino-American détente in the 1970s.

Key terms

Important terms or concepts are highlighted in the main body of the text and explained in the glossary.

International mindedness

Where there is an activity that promotes international mindedness by comparing regional case studies, focusing on different perspectives, or by getting students to link an event with issues of today, an IM box will be shown.

Research activity
Research the PRC's invasion and occupation of Tibet. Look at the international responses, and compare and contrast regional reactions.

Challenge yourself

These boxes contain open questions that encourage you to think about the topic in more depth, or to make detailed connections with other topics. They are designed to be challenging and to make you think.

CHALLENGE YOURSELF

Investigate the response to Marshall aid in Europe in more depth. Which countries in the Eastern bloc showed interest in receiving aid? What was the impact of Marshall aid in countries such as Italy?

Hints for success

These boxes can be found alongside questions, exercises and worked examples, and they provide insight into how to answer a question in order to achieve the highest marks in an examination. They also identify common pitfalls when answering such questions, and suggest approaches that examiners like to see.

When you are asked to look for an answer in a source, underline the relevant points and then focus on the information that you need to answer the question. Do not list everything: only what is relevant.

Weblinks

Relevant websites are recommended in weblinks boxes at the end of each chapter. They can also be found in the Further Reading section at the end of the book.

Theory of Knowledge

There are also Theory of Knowledge (ToK) boxes throughout the book – see page ix for more information about these.

eBook

In the eBook you will find the following:

- additional worksheets containing student activities
- interactive glossary
- practice examination quizzes (testing knowledge and essay-planning skills)
- revision quizzes
- biographies of key figures covered in the book
- links to relevant Internet sites
- enlargeable photos of useful resources, such as maps and source cartoons.

For more details about your eBook, see pages x–xi.

IB History assessment objectives

This book covers the four IB assessment objectives that are relevant both to the core externally examined papers and to the internally assessed paper. So, although this book is essentially designed as a textbook to accompany the Paper 2 Cold War Topic 12, it addresses *all* of the assessment objectives required for the History syllabus. In other words, as you work through this book, you will be learning and practising the skills that are necessary for each of the core papers. Nevertheless, the main focus will be the objectives assessed in Paper 2.

Specifically, these assessment objectives are:

Assessment Objective 1: Knowledge and understanding

- demonstrate detailed, relevant, and accurate historical knowledge
- demonstrate understanding of historical concepts and context
- demonstrate understanding of historical sources (IA and Paper 1).

Assessment Objective 2: Application and analysis

- formulate clear and coherent arguments

- use relevant historical knowledge to effectively support analysis
- analyse different perspectives on historical issues, events, and developments
- analyse and interpret a variety of sources (IA and Paper 1).

Assessment Objective 3: Synthesis and evaluation

- integrate evidence and analysis to produce a coherent response
- evaluate different perspectives on historical issues and events, and integrate this evaluation effectively into a response
- evaluate sources as historical evidence, recognizing their value and limitations (IA and Paper 1)
- synthesize information from a selection of relevant sources (IA and Paper 1).

Assessment Objective 4: Use and application of appropriate skills

- structure and develop focused essays which respond effectively to the demands of the question
- reflect on the methods used by, and challenges facing, the historian (IA)

- formulate an appropriate, focused question to guide a historical inquiry (IA)
- demonstrate evidence of research skills, organization, referencing, and selection of appropriate sources (IA).

Mark schemes

For the externally assessed components – Paper 1, Paper 2, and Paper 3 – there are two different assessment methods used:

- mark bands
- detailed specific mark schemes for each examination paper.

For the internally assessed/moderated IA there are set assessment criteria. You should refer to the Paper 2 mark bands when you attempt the practice essay questions in each chapter. We will also offer some question-specific mark schemes for the essay questions set in the book. These will give indicative content for the set question.

The Cold War: key themes

As you read and work through this book, you will be covering the major themes of the Cold War topic. At the end of each chapter these themes will be reviewed by considering how to answer possible 'thematic' essay questions. Where and when appropriate, there is an emphasis on comparative questions.

Rivalry, mistrust, and accord

This theme covers the origins of the Cold War, and examines the reasons for the breakdown of the **Grand Alliance** and the emergence of superpower rivalry. The **ideological** differences, mutual suspicion and fear, as well as the key events of the years leading up to 1949 in Europe and Asia, are covered in chapters 2 and 3. The roles of the US and the USSR in the origins of the Cold War are compared at the end of this section.

The nature of the Cold War

The core ideological opposition between the **superpowers** is discussed specifically in chapters 2 and 3. However, it is also a feature that is developed in every chapter, as ideological differences are relevant to each area and each event during the Cold War.

The superpowers and their spheres of influence is another dominant theme in this book. Beginning with the development of superpower spheres of influence in Europe in chapters 2 and 3, it then follows the consolidation and spread of these areas of influence around the globe.

There is discussion and analysis of alliances such as **NATO** and the **Warsaw Pact** throughout the book. Diplomacy is addressed not only through the dealings of the superpowers with each other and their allies, but also in their attempts to influence the **United Nations**.

Development and impact of the Cold War

The global spread of the Cold War is analysed in chapter 5 and its cross-regional impact is considered in case studies on Europe, Asia, the Middle East, Africa, and Latin America. Sino-Soviet and Sino-American relations are considered in depth in chapters 10 and 11.

The important Cold War policies of **containment**, **brinkmanship**, **peaceful co-existence**, and **détente** are addressed in chapters 2, 3, 4, 5, 6, 7, and 13.

The role of the United Nations is the subject of chapter 16 while the role and significance of individual Cold War leaders is considered in chapter 17.

The **arms race** is the theme for chapter 14, which considers both proliferation and the attempts to find nuclear strategies during the Cold War. In addition, chapter 12, on détente, analyses the attempts at arms limitations.

The end of the Cold War: confrontation and reconciliation

The longer-term factors undermining Soviet control is the subject of chapter 13, while the end of the Cold War is then analysed in detail in chapter 15. Chapter 15 also considers the events and impact of one pivotal year – 1989 – at the end of the Cold

War. Major themes considered are the ideological challenges to Soviet control and dissent, economic problems, and the impact of the arms race.

Leaders and nations

To draw comparative studies on the impact of two leaders, each chosen from a different region, in the course and development of the Cold War, chapter 17 analyses the roles of:

- Truman and Stalin in the origins of the Cold War
- Khrushchev and Mao during the development of the Cold War
- Brezhnev, Nixon, and Brandt during the period of détente
- the roles of Reagan and Gorbachev during the period that led to the end of the Cold War.

Students need to be prepared to discuss the impact of Cold War tensions on two cross-regional countries and chapter 18 considers four case studies, from which students can choose: Germany, Egypt, Cuba and China.

Cold War crises

This book concludes with comparative studies of the key Cold War crises that students have covered in the course of their study. The case studies that can be used as examples of Cold War crises are flagged up in each chapter with the heading 'Case study in crisis' in order for them to be clearly identified. Chapter 19 reviews, compares, and contrasts the causes, impact, and significance of four cross-regional crises:

Europe	Crises over Berlin [the Blockade] (1948–1949) / Berlin Wall (1958–1961) / USSR and the invasion of Hungary (1956)
Asia	North Korean invasion of South Korea (1950) / Soviet invasion of Afghanistan (1979)
Africa	Crisis over the Suez Canal (1956)
Americas	Cuban Missile Crisis (1962)

Theory of Knowledge

History is a Group 3 subject in the IB Diploma. It is an 'area of knowledge' that considers individuals and societies. In the subject of IB History, many different ways of obtaining knowledge are used.

When working through this book you should reflect on the methods used not only by professional historians, but also by yourself, as a student of history, to gain knowledge. The methods used by historians are important to highlight, as it will be necessary to compare and contrast these with the other 'areas of knowledge', such as the Human Sciences and the Group 4 Sciences (Physics, Chemistry, and Biology). You should think about the role of individuals in history, the difference between **bias** and selection, and the role played by the historian. You will reflect in detail on these types of question in the final section of your Internal Assessment.

Theory of Knowledge boxes

There are ToK boxes throughout the book. These boxes will enable you to consider ToK issues as they arise, and in context. Often they will just contain a question to stimulate your thoughts and discussion.

How do political leaders attempt to maintain their 'credibility'? Which is more important for this – using reason, ethics, or emotion when addressing the public?

This book also includes a chapter on Theory of Knowledge, which has been updated for the latest ToK curriculum with the help of ToK expert Malcolm Price. In it, you will be encouraged to reflect on the methods used by historians by thinking about questions such as:

- What is the role of the historian?
- What methods do historians use to gain knowledge?
- Who decides which events are historically significant?

These types of questions require you to reflect on and engage with how historians work and will help you with the reflection section of the Internal Assessment.

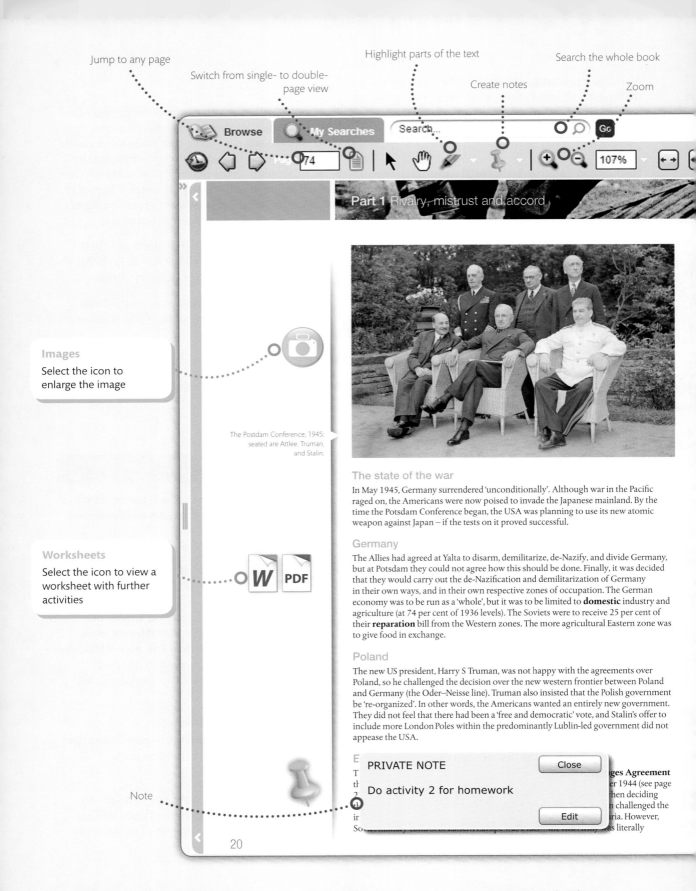

Jump to any page

Switch from single- to double-page view

Highlight parts of the text

Create notes

Search the whole book

Zoom

Browse   My Searches   Search...   Gg

Page 74   107%

Part 1 Rivalry, mistrust and accord

Images
Select the icon to enlarge the image

The Postdam Conference, 1945: seated are Attlee, Truman, and Stalin.

The state of the war

In May 1945, Germany surrendered 'unconditionally'. Although war in the Pacific raged on, the Americans were now poised to invade the Japanese mainland. By the time the Potsdam Conference began, the USA was planning to use its new atomic weapon against Japan – if the tests on it proved successful.

Germany

The Allies had agreed at Yalta to disarm, demilitarize, de-Nazify, and divide Germany, but at Potsdam they could not agree how this should be done. Finally, it was decided that they would carry out the de-Nazification and demilitarization of Germany in their own ways, and in their own respective zones of occupation. The German economy was to be run as a 'whole', but it was to be limited to **domestic** industry and agriculture (at 74 per cent of 1936 levels). The Soviets were to receive 25 per cent of their **reparation** bill from the Western zones. The more agricultural Eastern zone was to give food in exchange.

Poland

The new US president, Harry S Truman, was not happy with the agreements over Poland, so he challenged the decision over the new western frontier between Poland and Germany (the Oder–Neisse line). Truman also insisted that the Polish government be 're-organized'. In other words, the Americans wanted an entirely new government. They did not feel that there had been a 'free and democratic' vote, and Stalin's offer to include more London Poles within the predominantly Lublin-led government did not appease the USA.

Worksheets
Select the icon to view a worksheet with further activities

W   **PDF**

E...
T...   ...ges **Agreement**
th...   ...r 1944 (see page
2...   ...hen deciding
...   ...n challenged the
in...   ...ria. However,
So...   ...as literally

PRIVATE NOTE   [Close]

Do activity 2 for homework

[Edit]

Note

20

See the definitions of key terms in the glossary

Create a bookmark

Switch to whiteboard view

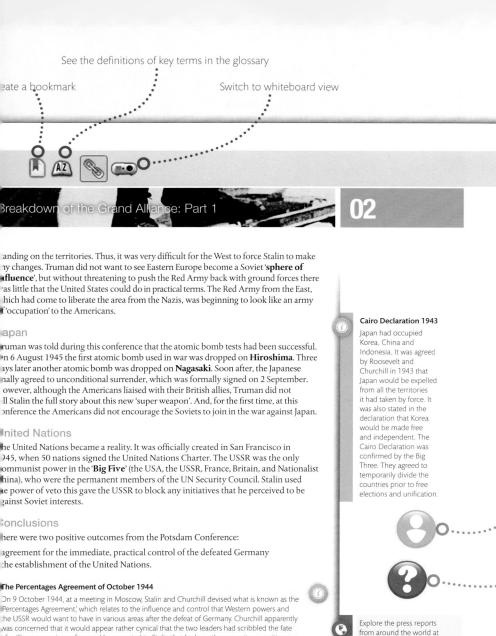

...anding on the territories. Thus, it was very difficult for the West to force Stalin to make any changes. Truman did not want to see Eastern Europe become a Soviet '**sphere of influence**', but without threatening to push the Red Army back with ground forces there was little that the United States could do in practical terms. The Red Army from the East, which had come to liberate the area from the Nazis, was beginning to look like an army of 'occupation' to the Americans.

Japan

Truman was told during this conference that the atomic bomb tests had been successful. On 6 August 1945 the first atomic bomb used in war was dropped on **Hiroshima**. Three days later another atomic bomb was dropped on **Nagasaki**. Soon after, the Japanese finally agreed to unconditional surrender, which was formally signed on 2 September. However, although the Americans liaised with their British allies, Truman did not tell Stalin the full story about this new 'super weapon'. And, for the first time, at this conference the Americans did not encourage the Soviets to join in the war against Japan.

United Nations

The United Nations became a reality. It was officially created in San Francisco in 1945, when 50 nations signed the United Nations Charter. The USSR was the only communist power in the '**Big Five**' (the USA, the USSR, France, Britain, and Nationalist China), who were the permanent members of the UN Security Council. Stalin used the power of veto this gave the USSR to block any initiatives that he perceived to be against Soviet interests.

Conclusions

There were two positive outcomes from the Potsdam Conference:
- agreement for the immediate, practical control of the defeated Germany
- the establishment of the United Nations.

The Percentages Agreement of October 1944
On 9 October 1944, at a meeting in Moscow, Stalin and Churchill devised what is known as the 'Percentages Agreement', which relates to the influence and control that Western powers and the USSR would want to have in various areas after the defeat of Germany. Churchill apparently was concerned that it would appear rather cynical that the two leaders had scribbled the fate of millions on a piece of paper. He suggested to Stalin that he burn the paper it was written on. 'No, you keep it,' said Stalin.

Romania	Greece	Yugoslavia	Hungary	Bulgaria
• Russia 90%	• United Kingdom 90%	• 50%–50%	• 50%–50%	• Russia 75%
• Others 10%	(in accord with USA)			• Others 25%
	• Russia 10%			

Activity 2 — Thinking skills

1. Look over the issues that were discussed at the three conferences. Which issues were satisfactorily resolved?
2. Which decisions were likely to cause tension in the future?
3. From what you have read so far in both chapters 1 and 2, what do you consider to be the 'seeds' of East–West conflict that were sown from 1917 onwards?

Key developments, 1946–1947

Before moving on to Step 2 it is important to look at some key developments that were to have an impact on US–Soviet relations.

Cairo Declaration 1943
Japan had occupied Korea, China and Indonesia. It was agreed by Roosevelt and Churchill in 1943 that Japan would be expelled from all the territories it had taken by force. It was also stated in the declaration that Korea would be made free and independent. The Cairo Declaration was confirmed by the Big Three. They agreed to temporarily divide the countries prior to free elections and unification.

Explore the press reports from around the world at the time of the wartime conferences. What hopes or fears are expressed by different countries with regards to the post-war settlement? What is the perception of a) the USA's aims and b) the Soviet Union's aims?

Biographies
Select the icon to open biographies of key figures mentioned in the text

Quiz
Select the icon to take an interactive quiz to test your knowledge or practise answering exam essay questions

21

01

What was the Cold War?

Key concepts: Significance and causation

This book is concerned with the period 1945–1991: the years recognized as the 'Cold War' era. Cold War is the term used to describe periods of hostility and high tension between states, which stop just short of war. In the period 1945–1991, this was the situation that existed between the two great post-war **superpowers**: the United States and the USSR.

The USA and the USSR had emerged as the two competing superpowers following the defeat of **Nazi** Germany in 1945. Rather than being traditional enemies, expected at some time to enter into conflict, the rapid escalation of nuclear armament by both of these countries made the results of any possible direct conflict unthinkable. It was of paramount importance to find new strategies to avoid escalation to the level of nuclear warfare. This situation led to 45 years of **ideological** conflict, a **conventional** and **nuclear arms race**, and wars fought by **proxy** on the battlefields of Asia, Africa, and Latin America. It also involved economic rivalry and the development of huge espionage networks, as each side tried to infiltrate the other to discover military and strategic secrets.

It was American journalist Walter Lippmann, writing for the *New York Herald Tribune* in 1947, who popularized the term 'Cold War' to describe the relationship that was developing between the USA and the USSR, while the US president of the time, Harry S Truman, preferred the phrase 'the war of nerves'.

Communism versus Capitalism

To understand the fundamental differences that existed between the USA and the USSR in 1945, and why these two countries were perceived by many as inevitable enemies, it is important to understand the key differences between their economic and political philosophies: that is, the opposing ideologies of **Capitalism** and **Communism**.

The **Bolshevik Revolution** in Russia in 1917 saw Vladimir Lenin and the Bolshevik Party establish the world's first Communist state, based on the ideas of the 19th-century economic philosopher Karl Marx. For the leaders of the United States and other countries in the West, these ideas seemed to threaten the very basis of their societies.

TWO RIVAL IDEOLOGIES	
The West	**The USSR**
Economic differences:	**Economic differences:**
Individuals should be able to compete with each other with a minimum of state interference and make as much money as they wish.	Capitalism creates divisions between rich and poor. Thus all businesses and farms should be owned by the state on behalf of the people.
This is known as Capitalism.	This is known as Communism.
Individuals are thus encouraged to work hard with the promise of individual reward.	Goods will be distributed to individuals by the state. Everyone will thus get what is needed and everyone will be working for the collective good.
Political differences:	
Individuals choose the government through voting. There is a range of political parties to choose from.	**Political differences:**
Individuals have certain rights, such as freedom of speech and freedom of the press.	There is no need for a range of political parties, as the Communist Party truly represents the views of all the workers and rules on behalf of the people.
This is known as liberal democracy.	Individual freedoms valued by the West are not necessary.
	This is a one-party state.

Increasing hostility

The mutual suspicion between the West and the Soviet Union manifested itself in various ways between the Bolshevik Revolution (1917) and the start of World War Two (1939):

- the intervention of the West in the **Russian Civil War** (1918–1922), through its support of the conservative forces – the **Whites** – in their attempt to overthrow the new **Bolshevik** government
- the fact that the USSR did not receive diplomatic recognition or join the **League of Nations** until 1934
- the **appeasement** of Adolf Hitler and the Nazis in the 1930s by the West; this was partly motivated by a fear of Soviet Communism, which at the time was stronger than the fear of German **fascism**
- the **Non-Aggression Pact** (**Nazi–Soviet Pact**), between the Soviet Union and Nazi Germany, signed in 1939, which allowed Hitler to concentrate on attacking the West.

Idealism versus self-interest

The USA and the USSR each believed that its particular political philosophy was the 'right' one – that its respective system was the most fair and the best for creating a just society. How they translated these opposing ideologies in practice is outlined below. You can see that each side believed that it offered the only true path to 'peace, freedom, justice, and plenty' for all. However, behind the idealism, the USA and the USSR were also motivated by their own self-interests.

USA	USSR
What ideals underpinned the view of each country?	
• Idealism of Presidents Woodrow Wilson and Franklin D Roosevelt • Struggle for a better world based on collective security, political self-determination, and economic integration • Peace, freedom, justice, and plenty	• Marxist idealism and Stalinism • Struggle for a better world based on international socialism • Peace, freedom, justice, and plenty
How was this to be achieved by each country?	
• Achieved by democracy/Capitalism and international co-operation	• Achieved by spreading Soviet-style Communism
What elements of self-interest lay behind each country's ideals?	
• The need to establish markets and open doors to **free trade** • The desire to avoid another economic crisis of the magnitude of 1929 • President Truman and most of the post-war US administration's belief that what was good for America was good for the world	• The need to secure borders • The need to recover from the effects of World War Two • The need to regain strength as the 'nursery of Communism' • Stalin's belief that what was good for the USSR was good for workers of the world

So, what really motivated the **foreign policies** of the USA and the USSR – idealism, or simply old-fashioned **imperialism**? It could be a matter of perception. As you will see from the events after 1945, it is sometimes very difficult to separate actions based on ideology from those based on self-interest.

What was the significance of Stalinism?

At this juncture it is important to establish what the Soviet leader Josef Stalin's own particular 'brand' of Communism meant. It was a Soviet Union driven by '**Stalinism**' that faced the Capitalist powerhouse of the United States in 1945, and some historians believe that this was a key factor in the development of the Cold War. (For further discussion on the **historiography** of the Cold War, see chapter 4.)

Stalin had taken over the leadership of the Soviet Union after the death of Lenin, becoming sole leader by the late 1920s. His policies included the ruthless **collectivization** of all farms, which led to the deaths of millions of agricultural workers. He also started a series of '**five-year plans**' in industry, which dramatically increased industrial production and put the USSR into a position where it could greatly contribute to the defeat of Nazi Germany in 1945. In the 1930s, Stalin launched the **Great Terror**, which resulted in **purges** of all political opponents, as well as millions of ordinary people, who were executed or sent to the **gulags** (slave labour camps).

By 1945, Stalinism meant:

• the dominance of Stalin over the party, and the party over state institutions
• a powerful state security machine
• the ruthless maintenance of power by the elimination of opposing leaders, groups, or entire sections of the population
• the development of a regime associated with **paranoia** and violence.

Stalin's role in World War Two

Stalin had hoped an attack from Hitler could be delayed indefinitely by signing the Nazi–Soviet Pact in 1939. However, in June 1941, the Germans felt they could no longer hold off action on the Eastern front and, despite the fact that Britain had not yet been defeated, launched **Operation Barbarossa** against the Soviet Union in June 1941.

The **Red Army** was ill-prepared to resist the Nazis, having had most of its experienced and talented officers killed in Stalin's purges. Stalin had also ignored repeated warnings from the West. Ukraine was quickly overrun, and the German army besieged Leningrad and reached the outskirts of Moscow. However, the Soviets were able to prevent the Germans taking Moscow, and after the Soviet victory at Stalingrad the Nazis were slowly pushed back towards Berlin.

Stalin's key role in the final victory over Nazi Germany in Europe not only made him more secure and more powerful in the Soviet Union, but it also put the Soviet Union in a strong position to emerge as one of the leading powers of the post-war world.

Joseph Stalin, leader of the Soviet Union, 1928–1953.

The cost of World War Two

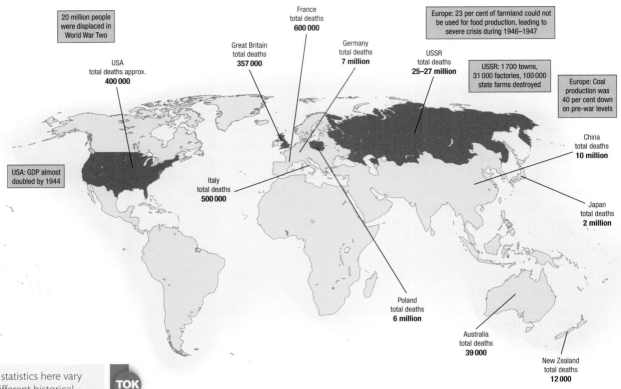

20 million people were displaced in World War Two

USA total deaths approx. **400 000**

USA: GDP almost doubled by 1944

Great Britain total deaths **357 000**

France total deaths **600 000**

Germany total deaths **7 million**

USSR total deaths **25–27 million**

Europe: 23 per cent of farmland could not be used for food production, leading to severe crisis during 1946–1947

USSR: 1 700 towns, 31 000 factories, 100 000 state farms destroyed

Europe: Coal production was 40 per cent down on pre-war levels

China total deaths **10 million**

Italy total deaths **500 000**

Japan total deaths **2 million**

Poland total deaths **6 million**

Australia total deaths **39 000**

New Zealand total deaths **12 000**

 TOK

The statistics here vary in different historical sources. Why might this be the case?

What does this suggest for the historian, with regard to the use of statistics?

Activity 1 · ATL Thinking skills

1. What do the statistics on the map above indicate about the different positions of a) the Soviet Union and b) Europe as a whole compared to that of the USA in 1945?

Why did the USA and the USSR emerge as superpowers after 1945?

American statesman and politician Dean Acheson wrote of the situation in the aftermath of World War Two: 'The whole world structure and order that we had inherited from the 19th century was gone.' In 1945, the 'Old Powers', that is Britain and France, had been shown to be no longer able to maintain peace on their own, while the USA and USSR emerged from World War Two as significantly more powerful than they had been before the war. Why was this?

Military reasons

• To defeat Germany, the USA had become the number-one air-force power in the world.
• To defeat Germany, the USSR had become the number-one land-force power in the world.
• France's and Britain's inability to defeat Germany had changed the balance of power. They had become 'second-rank' powers.
• The USSR now lacked any strong military neighbours. This made it the regional power.

Economic reasons

- The USA's economy was strengthened by the war. It was now able to out-produce all the other powers put together.
- The USA was committed to more 'open trade'. Its politicians and businesspeople wanted to ensure liberal trade, and market competition flourished. The United States was willing to play an active role in avoiding the re-emergence of the disastrous pre-war pattern of trade blocs and tariffs.
- The USA had the economic strength to prevent a return to instability in Europe.
- The small Eastern European countries that had been created after World War One were not economically viable on their own, so they needed the support of a stronger neighbour, and the USSR could replace Germany in this role.

Political reasons

- For the West, the outcome of World War Two showed that the ideals of **democracy** and international collaboration had triumphed over fascism. Thus the political system of the USA was the right path for the future.
- For the Soviet Union, it was Communism that had triumphed over fascism. Indeed, Communism had gained widespread respect in Europe because of its part in resisting the Germans.
- The USSR's huge losses, and the role of the Red Army in defeating the Nazis, gave Stalin a claim to great influence in forming the post-war world.
- The USSR had the political (as well as military) strength to prevent a return to instability in Eastern Europe. Communism could fill the political vacuum there.

Given the new positions of the USA and the USSR in 1945, and their relative strength compared to the weakened European countries, it is not surprising that they were to become the key players in establishing the post-war settlement in Europe that created the new political map. It was during this process, however, that the alliance set up during the war collapsed, and by 1949 – only four years after the end of the war – the state of Cold War had come into existence. This international situation was to last 40 years, until the collapse of the Soviet Union in 1989–1991.

Key stages in the Cold War are outlined in this timeline, which is useful for quick reference when constructing essay plans.

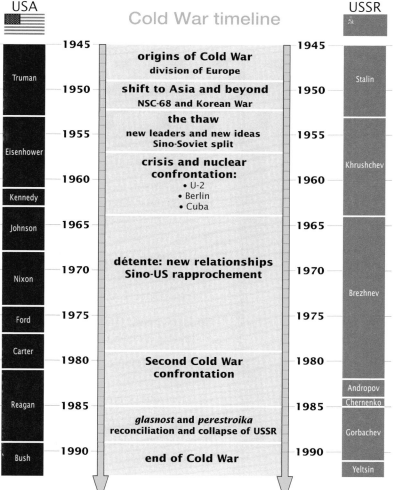

Cold War timeline

USA		USSR
	1945	
Truman	origins of Cold War / division of Europe	Stalin
	1950 shift to Asia and beyond / NSC-68 and Korean War	
Eisenhower	**1955** the thaw / new leaders and new ideas / Sino-Soviet split	Khrushchev
Kennedy	**1960** crisis and nuclear confrontation: • U-2 • Berlin • Cuba	
Johnson	**1965**	
Nixon	**1970** détente: new relationships / Sino-US rapprochement	Brezhnev
Ford	**1975**	
Carter	**1980** Second Cold War confrontation	
Reagan	**1985**	Andropov / Chernenko
	glasnost and *perestroika* / reconciliation and collapse of USSR	Gorbachev
Bush	**1990** end of Cold War	Yeltsin

7

TOK

Consider your answer to question 2 and reflect on how a historian works. Historians select the evidence they identify as the most important and/or relevant, and interpret the value and limitation of different sources. Is historical truth thus really just opinion, or can there be objective historical truth? Are there definitive answers to questions such as question 2?

CHALLENGE YOURSELF

ATL Research skills

Research Karl Marx's theory of revolution and explain the stages through which society must pass. Briefly explain how a society would become Communist, according to Marx.

Do the political parties of your own country fit into any of the definitions given here, or do they contain elements of more than one ideology? Would you label them as left wing or right wing, or somewhere in-between?

To access websites relevant to this chapter, go to www.pearsonhotlinks.com, search for the book title or ISBN, and click on 'chapter 1'.

Activity 2   **ATL Thinking skills**

1. From what you have read so far, identify the main ways by which the superpowers waged the Cold War from 1945.
2. Do you think that ideology or self-interest was likely to be more important as a factor in motivating the USA and the USSR after 1945?
3. To what extent was the USSR a Communist state in 1945?
4. What was the American 'Monroe Doctrine', set down in the early 19th century?
5. What examples exist of US 'economic imperialism' in the century before 1945?

Key political definitions

It is important to understand not only the basic differences in ideology between the USA and the USSR, but also the following political concepts and ideas.

Liberalism: Liberals put their main emphasis on the freedom of the individual. Economically, they believe in minimal interference by the state, and in foreign policy they promote the ideas of **free trade** and co-operation. They strongly believe in:

- civil liberties (freedom of conscience, freedom of speech)
- universal suffrage
- parliamentary constitutional government
- an independent judiciary
- diplomacy rather than force in relations between states.

Fascism: This ideology is rooted in ideas that are the very opposite of liberalism. Fascists believe in:

- limiting individual freedoms in the interest of the state
- extreme **nationalism**
- use of violence to achieve ends
- keeping power in the hands of an elite group or leader
- an aggressive foreign policy.

Socialism: This ideology developed in the early 19th century in the context of the **Industrial Revolution**. (Note that Marxist ideology uses the term socialism to apply to the transitional stage of the revolution before the state withers away.) Socialists believe in:

- a more **egalitarian** social system
- governments providing for the more needy members of society
- international co-operation and solidarity.

Conservatism: This generally implies a belief in maintaining the existing or traditional order. Specifically, conservatives believe in:

- respect for traditional institutions
- limiting government intervention in people's lives
- gradual and/or limited changes in the established order.

Maoism: This is a form of Communism adapted by Mao Zedong to suit China's situation. Mao believed:

- revolution could be achieved by the peasants, not necessarily by the urban **proletariat**, as Marx had envisaged
- class conflict was not as important in revolution as using the human will to make and remake revolution, hence his use of the 'mass movement'
- revolution should be ongoing, or continuous.

Activity 3 Social skills

In pairs, discuss the following questions.

1. Which of these ideologies (also include Communism and Stalinism) can be categorized as left wing and which of them can be categorized as right wing?

2. Where on this line would you place each of the ideologies described above?

   left wing –– right wing

3. What similarities exist between extreme left and extreme right political parties?

4. Is a straight line the best way to represent the positions of the different political ideologies? Could you find another way of doing this?

Right wing and left wing

The origin of the terms 'left' and 'right' dates back to the French Revolution. In the Estates General of 1789, nobles who supported the king sat on his right, while radicals who wanted a change in the political system sat on his left. As a result, 'right' was used to describe people who wanted no change, and 'left' was used to describe those who wanted radical change. **Right wing** now tends to describe groups who favour free-market Capitalism and place an emphasis on law and order, limited state interference, and traditional values in society. **Left wing** now tends to describe those groups who favour more equality in society, and thus more government intervention in the economy in order to try to secure this situation.

02

Breakdown of the Grand Alliance:
Steps to the political, economic and military
division of Europe: Part 1

As you read these two chapters, consider the following essay questions:

- Discuss the reasons for the breakdown of the '**Grand Alliance**' by 1949.
- To what extent was Stalin more responsible than Truman for the onset of a Cold War?
- Examine the key issues in post-war Europe that caused tension between the superpowers.

In 1945, American and Soviet soldiers met at the River Elbe; this signified the final defeat of Germany, which had come about due to successful collaboration between the USA and the **Allies** in the Grand Alliance. However, only four years later, by the end of 1949, Europe had been divided into two separate 'spheres of influence'. In September 1949, following the **Berlin Blockade**, the Federal Republic of Germany (FRG), also known as West Germany, was established. A month later the German Democratic Republic (**GDR**), also known as East Germany, was established and the two Germanys became the heart of the physical dividing line between the two superpower blocs. The eight key steps listed below show the main events that led to this division.

1949
NATO established, April
West Germany established, September
East Germany established, October

Berlin Blockade, June 1948	8
Czech Coup, February 1948	7
Red Army Occupation of Eastern Europe, 1945–1947	6
Marshall Plan, June 1947	5
Truman Doctrine, March 1947 and Cominform, October 1947	4
Churchill's 'Iron Curtain' speech at Fulton, Missouri, March 1946	3
Kennan's Long Telegram, February 1946	2
Wartime conferences: Tehran 1943, Yalta 1945, Potsdam 1945	1

These steps are covered in this and the next chapter.

Timeline of the division of Europe up to 1949

1939	German invasion of Poland: Britain and France declare war on Germany
	Beginning of Winter War between USSR and Finland
1940	Hitler's blitzkrieg through Europe: takeover of Norway, Denmark, the Netherlands, Belgium, and France
	Battle of Britain
1941	Germany begins 'Operation Barbarossa' and invasion of USSR
	Britain and USA sign Atlantic Charter
	Pearl Harbor attack by Japan brings USA into the war
1942	German assault on Stalingrad
	German defeat at El Alamein in North Africa
1943	German defeat at Stalingrad
	Allied invasion of Italy
	Tehran Conference
1944	D-Day landings by Western Allies begin in Normandy
	Rome falls to allied forces
1945	Warsaw falls to Soviet troops
	Yalta Conference
	Russian forces enter Berlin
	President Roosevelt dies and is replaced by Truman
	United Nations meets for the first time in San Francisco
	Germany surrenders
	Potsdam Conference
	Nuclear bombs dropped on Hiroshima and Nagasaki
	Japan surrenders
1946	Kennan's Long Telegram
	Iran crisis
	Churchill's 'Iron Curtain' speech at Fulton, Missouri
1947	Announcement of Truman Doctrine: aid sent to Greece and Turkey
	Marshall Plan for economic recovery of Europe proposed
	Creation of Cominform
1948	Czechoslovakian Coup
	Marshall Plan passed by Congress
	Berlin airlift
1949	COMECON established
	NATO established
	Berlin Blockade ends
	USSR explodes its first atomic bomb
	Federal Republic of Germany established
	German Democratic Republic established

The breakdown of the Grand Alliance

When the Nazis attacked Russia in June 1941, both British Prime Minister Winston Churchill and American President Franklin Roosevelt sent aid to the Soviets. This marked the beginning of the Grand Alliance. However, it did not mark a change in how Stalin's Soviet Union was seen, particularly by the British. Churchill retained his dislike of the Soviet leader, remarking to his secretary, 'If Hitler invaded Hell, I would make at least favourable reference to the Devil in the House of Commons.' Thus, relations between the West and the USSR were still clouded by mutual suspicion, as they had been in the 1920s and 1930s.

Despite the fact that the two Western powers sent a considerable amount of aid to the USSR, Stalin demanded *more* action – nothing less than the opening of a 'second front' in Europe to take some of the pressure off the USSR in the east. The Allies agreed to this 'in principle', but said that they would not be able to open this second front until the time was deemed right. Stalin was suspicious that they were deliberately delaying this offensive in the hope of seeing the Soviet Union permanently weakened by the continuing German onslaught.

At the first of the three wartime conferences, in Tehran in 1943, relations between the USA, the USSR and the UK – the **Big Three** – seemed to improve a little, as the Western leaders proposed a definite date for the Normandy invasion: May 1944. In return, Stalin promised to declare war on Japan once Germany was defeated.

Step 1: The wartime conferences

During the war, the decisions of the Grand Alliance determined the territorial and political structure of post-war Europe. There were three historic conferences between the Allies before the end of World War Two. The key issues under discussion at the conferences fall into the following categories:

• the state of the war
• the status of Germany, Poland, Eastern Europe, and Japan
• the United Nations.

The Tehran Conference, 1943

The first conference was held in Tehran, Iran, in November 1943. Those present were Joseph Stalin representing the USSR, President Franklin Roosevelt representing the USA, and Prime Minister Winston Churchill representing the United Kingdom. This was the first meeting of the Big Three. Their discussions focused on these key areas:

The state of the war

By 1943, the Allies had begun to win the war, following critical turning-point victories in 1942. The Soviets were now pushing the Germans into retreat on the Eastern front, while the Americans and the British had driven the Germans from North Africa and had invaded Mussolini's Italy. However, the UK and the USA had not yet launched the kind of second front in Europe that Stalin had been demanding. Therefore, Stalin continued to press his allies to invade northwestern Europe in order to take on some of the USSR's burden of confronting the German war machine. There was also discussion of the war against Japan in the Pacific, which had entered its brutal 'island hopping' phase.

Germany

The key question for the Allies was what to do with Germany after it had been defeated. The Soviets had very different views about the future of Germany from those of the USA and Britain. Many of these differences stemmed from the varied wartime experiences of the Allies, the 'lessons' that seemed to have been learned from the failure of the **Treaty of Versailles**, and their widely differing ideologies. Thus there was no agreement on the future of a defeated Germany. However, they did confirm that the '**unconditional surrender**' of Germany was their objective. Roosevelt also supported '**Operation Overlord**' (the Allied invasion of northern France that began with D-Day on 6 June 1944) as a priority.

Poland

Stalin's main concern was 'security'. This influenced not only his demands over the future of Germany, but also over the shape of Poland's post-war borders. Stalin wanted to secure his western border by gaining territory from Poland, and by ensuring that Poland had a pro-Soviet government. He argued that Poland had been the traditional launching pad for invasions of Russia. It was thus agreed that the USSR was to keep territory seized in 1939, and Poland in turn would be given territory on its western border with Germany. By agreeing to this, the Allies created a situation that no truly independent Poland could agree to, and also ensured future hostility between Germany and Poland. Thus, a **puppet regime** in Poland looked like a real possibility, and that regime presumably would have to look to the USSR for security. Tensions between the Poles and Soviets were increased in 1943 with the discovery of a mass grave of 10 000 Polish officers in Katyn Forest. These officers had been captured by the Soviets in 1939. The Soviets blamed the Germans for the massacre, but many Poles suspected (rightly) that the Soviets were responsible.

Eastern Europe

The Soviets demanded the right to keep the territories that they had seized between 1939 and 1940 which would give them control of the Baltic States, and parts of Finland and Romania in Eastern Europe. With much reluctance, the Americans and the British agreed to the Soviet annexation of these territories. However, this went against the 1941 '**Atlantic Charter**' agreement between the United States and the United Kingdom.

Japan

The United States and the United Kingdom pressed the USSR to enter the war with Japan. They wanted Stalin to open a Soviet second front in Asia. However, Stalin could not be convinced to do this until the war with Germany was won.

The United Nations

The Americans, in particular, were very keen to establish a replacement for the League of Nations. The British and the Soviets gave their general approval to the idea of a new international organization being established. This would, again, be designed to settle international disputes through **collective security**. The USA hoped that lessons would have been learned from the 'mistakes' that were made in the structure and make-up of the League of Nations and that the proposed **United Nations** organization could more successfully fulfil this brief.

Conclusions

There were two main positive outcomes from the **Tehran Conference**:

• agreement on a new international organization
• agreement on the need for a weak post-war Germany.

The Atlantic Charter of August 1941

The Atlantic Charter was a joint statement made by the USA (before it had entered the war) and the UK, which broadly set down their mutual 'vision' of the shape of the post-war world. The charter focused on the future of occupied territories, which would return to self-rule. Both countries also agreed on free global trade, and the charter's high moral ideas provided the first steps towards the formation of the United Nations.

Roosevelt and Stalin seemed to work reasonably well together. Indeed, on his return to the USA, Roosevelt publicly stated in a radio broadcast: 'I got along fine with Marshal Stalin … I believe that we are going to get along very well with him and the Russian people …' However, as the war continued, the next meeting of the Big Three revealed a growing gap between Stalin's post-war aims and those of the Western powers, though these differences seemed more acute between Stalin and Churchill. Churchill did not trust Stalin, and Roosevelt hoped to play the role of 'mediator' between the British and the Russians. Roosevelt seemed to believe that the more serious problem for post-war stability was British imperialism rather than Soviet strength. Roosevelt is supposed to have told Stanislaw Mikolajczyk, the leader of the Poles who were in exile in London, '… of one thing I am certain, Stalin is not an imperialist'. Roosevelt did not appear overly concerned about the future of Poland, nor was he worried about the Western Allies taking the German capital, Berlin, before the Soviets.

The Yalta Conference, 1945

By the time of the February 1945 **Yalta Conference** on the Black Sea in Russia, Stalin's diplomatic position was greatly strengthened by the physical fact that the Red Army occupied most of Eastern Europe. Once again, the Big Three powers were represented by Stalin, Roosevelt, and Churchill. The topics under discussion were the same as at Tehran.

The Yalta Conference, 1945:
Churchill, Roosevelt, and Stalin.

The state of the war

Germany was now on the verge of being defeated. With the Normandy landings in 1944, a second front had finally been opened. The Soviets had driven the Germans from Eastern Europe, and were now ready to invade Germany itself. The British and Americans had forced the Germans from France, and were now poised to cross the Rhine and invade Germany from the west. Japan was still fighting on, but had been under heavy aerial bombardment from the Americans. The USA was now in control of the air and sea in the Pacific, and the Japanese were preparing for the final desperate defence of their homeland.

Germany

The Allies decided that Germany would be disarmed, **demilitarized**, de-Nazified, and divided. It was agreed that post-war Germany would be divided into four zones of occupation between the USA, the USSR, the UK, and France. This division was to be 'temporary', and Germany was to be run as one country. An **Allied Control Council** (ACC) would be set up to govern Germany. Stalin demanded a large percentage of the **reparations** from Germany after the devastation that the war in the East had wreaked on the Russians. It was agreed that Germany would pay $20 billion, and 50 per cent would go to the USSR.

Poland

Poland presented the greatest problem – where would the lines of its borders be drawn, and what would be the political make-up of her post-war government? At Yalta the new frontiers of Poland were decided. The border between Poland and the USSR was to be drawn at the '**Curzon Line**' (see map below). This put the frontier back to where it had been before the **Russo-Polish War** of 1921. The Poles were to be compensated by gaining territory from Germany. This would be east of the '**Oder–Neisse Line**'. Thus, Stalin had got what he had wanted territorially. In return, he agreed to the establishment of a more democratic government in Poland, following 'free elections'. This developed into the key area of disagreement between the British and the Soviets. The British supported the group known as the 'London Poles', who were the pre-war government that had fled to England in 1939, while the Soviets wanted the Communist-dominated **Lublin Committee** in Poland to form the new post-war government. Stalin's intentions with regard to Poland had already been seen with the **Katyn Forest Massacre** (see page 14) and the failure of the Soviet forces to assist the Polish underground in the **Warsaw Uprising** (see page 17). Both of these actions helped to destroy Poles – led by the London Poles – who were likely to favour a free, independent Poland after the war.

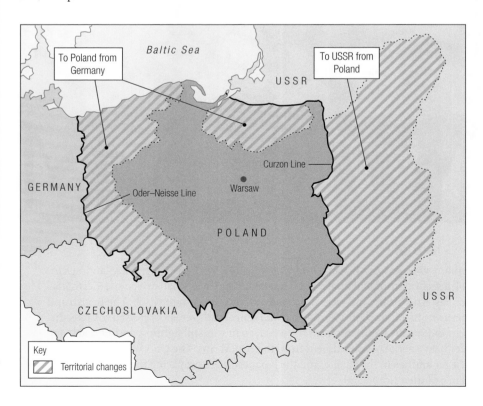

This map shows the new borders of Poland.

Eastern Europe

There seemed to be agreement at **Yalta** over the future nature of the governments of Eastern Europe. Stalin agreed that the countries of Eastern Europe would be able to decide who governed them in free elections. This was perceived as a major victory for the USA and Britain. Indeed, for the British and Americans this was seen as the most significant of the wartime deals made with the Soviet Union.

Japan

Stalin now promised to enter the war with Japan, as soon as the war in Europe was won. However, the Soviets demanded territory in return from Japan as a 'reward'. This would include South Sakhalin and the Kuril Islands. The Americans and the British accepted these terms.

United Nations

Stalin agreed that the Soviet Union would join the United Nations organization. The Allies agreed that there would be five permanent members of the **Security Council**, each with the power of **veto**. Stalin went on to demand that all 16 Soviet republics have separate seats in the UN **General Assembly**. The British and Americans agreed in the end to only three seats for individual republics: Russia, Ukraine, and Belarus.

Conclusions

There were three main positive outcomes of the **Yalta Conference**:

- agreement on the United Nations
- Soviet agreement to join the war in the Pacific against Japan
- the Big Three signing a 'Declaration on Liberated Europe' pledging their support for democratic governments based on free elections in all European countries, including those in Eastern Europe.

Who were the London Poles and the Lublin Poles?

The London Poles: Many thousands of Poles managed to escape from Poland during the two assaults on their country by German and Soviet forces in 1939–1940. These included members of the Polish government and armed forces. Approximately 100 000 refugee Polish troops regrouped in France and contributed to the Allied war effort. Although the exiled Polish government was also in France initially, it moved to London after the fall of France in 1940.

The London Poles were led by General Wladyslaw Sikorski until he died in a plane crash in July 1943. Sikorski had also been commander-in-chief of the Polish armed forces. He was succeeded as prime minister-in-exile by Stanislaw Mikolajczyk, who had been leader of the 'Peasant Party'. Mikolajczyk was fairly left wing, and open to the idea of reaching an agreement with the Soviets. However, the new commander-in-chief of the army, General Kazimierz Sosnkowski, together with other leading Poles, was opposed to any deals with the Soviets.

Churchill had a very tough time persuading the Poles to accept a shift in their border to the west of the Curzon Line (see map on page 16). The Poles insisted that if they were to sacrifice the land they had gained in war (1920–1921), then they must have cast-iron guarantees that Poland's government would be 'free' after the war.

But, as Soviet forces moved west in 1944, it seemed increasingly unlikely that Poland's future government would indeed be free of Soviet interference.

The London Poles played an important part in the doomed Warsaw Uprising of August 1944. At the beginning of August 1944, as the Red Army approached Warsaw and the German occupying forces prepared to retreat, the Polish resistance home army rose up to liberate Poland themselves. They had been encouraged to do so by the Soviets and believed that they would be assisted by the advance of the Red Army. However, Stalin ordered his army to 'rest' on the other side of the Vistula river. The Germans counter-attacked and the Poles

CHALLENGE YOURSELF

 **Research skills**

Research the Warsaw Uprising. What was the impact on the Polish Underground? How have historians interpreted Stalin's motives for delaying the Soviet advance on Warsaw?

were slaughtered. More than 15 000 member of the Polish resistance army were killed and thousands more injured. More than 100 000 civilians (some estimates double this figure) were killed in reprisals. Some saw the Soviet inaction as cynical and deliberate. It was argued that the USSR did not want Poland to 'liberate' itself – it wanted the home army, and any civilian resistance to future Soviet control, crushed. An influential American diplomat in Moscow, George Kennan, later commented that he thought the Soviet's abandonment of the Polish uprising was 'when US policy should have changed' towards the USSR.

The Lublin Poles: Not all Poles were anti-Soviet, and some had felt just as patriotic supporting the Communists. In July 1944, a **Committee of National Liberation** was set up in Soviet-occupied Lublin, a large city in eastern Poland. This group then came to be known as the Lublin Committee, and its members stated that they were a coalition of democratic and patriotic forces who wished to work with the Soviet Union. This group agreed to the Curzon Line boundary and committed itself to a far-reaching programme of social and economic reform. The USSR recognized this group as the only lawful authority in Poland. Indeed, the Red Army was instructed to co-operate only with representatives of the Lublin Committee.

Towards the end of the war, these Lublin Poles became more influential inside Poland than the London group. Although the Lublin Poles were supposed to liaise closely with the London Poles in the post-war Government of National Unity, they dominated post-war politics in Poland. Leading members of the Lublin Committee were Wladyslaw Gomulka and Boleslaw Bierut.

Activity 1  **Thinking skills**

Behind the scenes at Yalta

The letter below was written by President Franklin Roosevelt to Stalin on 6 February 1945, while both were at Yalta. It is about the situation regarding Poland.

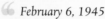 *February 6, 1945*

My dear Marshal Stalin:

I have been giving a great deal of thought to our meeting this afternoon, and I want to tell you in all frankness what is on my mind.

In so far as the Polish Government is concerned, I am greatly disturbed that the three great powers do not have a meeting of minds about the political setup in Poland. It seems to me that it puts all of us in a bad light throughout the world to have you recognizing one government while we and the British are recognizing another in London. I am sure this state of affairs should not continue and that if it does it can only lead our people to think there is a breach between us, which is not the case. I am determined that there shall be no breach between ourselves and the Soviet Union. Surely there is a way to reconcile our differences.

I was very much impressed with some of the things you said today, particularly your determination that your rear must be safeguarded as your army moves into Berlin. You cannot, and we must not, tolerate any temporary government which will give your armed forces any trouble of this sort. I want you to know that I am fully mindful of this.

You must believe me when I tell you that our people at home look with a critical eye on what they consider a disagreement between us at this vital stage of the war. They, in effect, say that if we cannot get a meeting of minds now when our armies are converging on the common enemy, how can we get an understanding on even more vital things in the future.

I have had to make it clear to you that we cannot recognize the Lublin Government as now composed, and the world would regard it as a lamentable outcome of our work here if we parted with an open and obvious divergence between us on this issue.

You said today that you would be prepared to support any suggestions for the solution of this problem which offered a fair chance of success, and you also mentioned the possibility of bringing some members of the Lublin government here.

Realizing that we all have the same anxiety in getting the matter settled, I would like to develop your proposal a little and suggest that we invite here to Yalta at once Mr Beirut [Bierut] and Mr Osubka [Osóbka] Morawski from the Lublin government and also two or three from the following list of Poles, who according to our information would be desirable as representatives of the other elements of the Polish people in development of a new temporary government which all three of us could recognize and support: Bishop Sapieha of Cracow, Vincente [Wincenty] Witos, Mr Zurlowski [Zulawski], Professor Buyak [Bujak], and Professor Kutzeva [Kutzeba]. If, as a result of the presence of these Polish leaders from abroad such as Mr Mikolajczyk, Mr Grabski, and Mr Romer, the United States Government, and I feel sure the British government as well, would be prepared to examine with you conditions in which they would dissociate themselves from the London government and transfer their recognition to the new provisional government.

I hope that I do not have to assure you that the United States will never lend its support in any way to any provisional government in Poland that would be inimical to your interest.

It goes without saying that any interim government formed as a result of our conference with the Poles here would be pledged to the holding of free elections in Poland at the earliest possible date. I know this is completely consistent with your desire to see a new free and democratic Poland emerge from the welter of this war.

Most sincerely yours

Franklin Roosevelt

1. What is the general 'tone' of this letter to Stalin from Roosevelt?
2. Roosevelt shows sympathy for which of Stalin's key concerns?
3. What suggestions are made for resolving the disagreement over the Polish government?
4. What does this suggest about the relationship between Roosevelt and Stalin?

Questions 1 and 4 are asking you to 'read between the lines': that is, to show that you understand what Roosevelt's attitude was towards Stalin. Look carefully at the language he uses and quote any useful words or phrases that support your answer.

What were the crucial developments that took place between the Yalta and Potsdam Conferences?

There were some crucial events that radically changed the atmosphere of, and the influences on, the next meeting of the Allies in 1945.

- President Roosevelt died in April 1945 and was replaced by Truman, who was to adopt a more hardline, or 'get tough', policy towards the Soviets.
- Germany finally surrendered unconditionally on 7 May 1945.
- Winston Churchill's Conservative Party lost the July 1945 UK general election and Churchill was succeeded as prime minister by the Labour Party leader, Clement Attlee.
- As the war in Europe ended, the Soviet Red Army occupied territory as far west as deep inside Germany.
- On 17 July 1945, the day after the **Potsdam Conference** began, the United States successfully tested its first atomic bomb.

The Potsdam Conference, 1945

The Potsdam Conference took place in July 1945 in Potsdam, Germany. Those participating were Joseph Stalin representing the USSR, President Harry S Truman representing the USA, and Prime Minister Clement Attlee representing the UK.

The Postdam Conference, 1945: seated are Attlee, Truman, and Stalin.

The state of the war

In May 1945, Germany surrendered 'unconditionally'. Although war in the Pacific raged on, the Americans were now poised to invade the Japanese mainland. By the time the Potsdam Conference began, the USA was planning to use its new atomic weapon against Japan – if the tests on it proved successful.

Germany

The Allies had agreed at Yalta to disarm, demilitarize, de-Nazify, and divide Germany, but at Potsdam they could not agree how this should be done. Finally, it was decided that they would carry out the de-Nazification and demilitarization of Germany in their own ways, and in their own respective zones of occupation. The German economy was to be run as a 'whole', but it was to be limited to **domestic** industry and agriculture (at 74 per cent of 1936 levels). The Soviets were to receive 25 per cent of their **reparation** bill from the Western zones. The more agricultural Eastern zone was to give food in exchange.

Poland

The new US president, Harry S Truman, was not happy with the agreements over Poland, so he challenged the decision over the new western frontier between Poland and Germany (the Oder–Neisse line). Truman also insisted that the Polish government be 're-organized'. In other words, the Americans wanted an entirely new government. They did not feel that there had been a 'free and democratic' vote, and Stalin's offer to include more London Poles within the predominantly Lublin-led government did not appease the USA.

Eastern Europe

The new US leadership was also unhappy about the so-called **Percentages Agreement** that had been made **bilaterally** between Stalin and Churchill in October 1944 (see page 21). Spheres of influence had been discussed in terms of 'percentages' when deciding the future fate of countries in Eastern and southeastern Europe. Truman challenged the influence that this agreement had given Stalin over Romania and Bulgaria. However, Soviet military control of Eastern Europe was a fact – the Red Army was literally standing on the territories. Thus, it was very difficult for the West to force Stalin to make any changes. Truman did not want to see Eastern Europe become a Soviet '**sphere of influence**', but without threatening to push the Red Army back with ground forces there was little that the United States could do in practical terms. The Red Army from the East, which had come to liberate the area from the Nazis, was beginning to look like an army of 'occupation' to the Americans.

Japan

Truman was told during this conference that the atomic bomb tests had been successful. On 6 August 1945 the first atomic bomb used in war was dropped on **Hiroshima**. Three days later another atomic bomb was dropped on **Nagasaki**. Soon after, the Japanese finally agreed to unconditional surrender, which was formally signed on 2 September. However, although the Americans liaised with their British allies, Truman did not tell Stalin the full story about this new 'super weapon'. And, for the first time, at this conference the Americans did not encourage the Soviets to join in the war against Japan.

United Nations

The United Nations became a reality. It was officially created in San Francisco in 1945, when 50 nations signed the United Nations Charter. The USSR was the only Communist power in the '**Big Five**' (the USA, the USSR, France, Britain, and Nationalist China), who were the permanent members of the UN Security Council. Stalin used the power of veto this gave the USSR to block any initiatives that he perceived to be against Soviet interests.

Conclusions

There were two positive outcomes from the Potsdam Conference:

- agreement for the immediate, practical control of the defeated Germany
- the establishment of the United Nations.

Cairo Declaration 1943

Japan had occupied Korea, China and Indonesia. It was agreed by Roosevelt and Churchill in 1943 that Japan would be expelled from all the territories it had taken by force. It was also stated in the declaration that Korea would be made free and independent. The Cairo Declaration was confirmed by the Big Three. They agreed to temporarily divide the countries prior to free elections and unification.

Explore the press reports from around the world at the time of the wartime conferences. What hopes or fears are expressed by different countries with regards to the post-war settlement? What is the perception of a) the USA's aims and b) the Soviet Union's aims?

The Percentages Agreement of October 1944

On 9 October 1944, at a meeting in Moscow, Stalin and Churchill devised what is known as the 'Percentages Agreement', which relates to the influence and control that Western powers and the USSR would want to have in various areas after the defeat of Germany. Churchill apparently was concerned that it would appear rather cynical that the two leaders had scribbled the fate of millions on a piece of paper. He suggested to Stalin that he burn the paper it was written on. 'No, you keep it,' said Stalin.

Romania	*Greece*	*Yugoslavia*	*Hungary*	*Bulgaria*
• Russia 90%	• United Kingdom 90%	• 50%–50%	• 50%–50%	• Russia 75%
• Others 10%	(in accord with USA)			• Others 25%
	• Russia 10%			

Activity 2
(ATL) Thinking skills

1. Look over the issues that were discussed at the three conferences. Which issues were satisfactorily resolved?

2. Which decisions were likely to cause tension in the future?

3. From what you have read so far in both chapters 1 and 2, what do you consider to be the 'seeds' of East–West conflict that were sown from 1917 onwards?

Key developments, 1946–1947

Before moving on to Step 2 it is important to look at some key developments that were to have an impact on US–Soviet relations.

Salami tactics

One way the Soviet Union gained increasing political control over Eastern Europe was by the method known as '**salami tactics**'. This term is said to have come from a remark made by the Hungarian Communist leader, Matyas Rakosi, who was commenting on how the USSR secured Communist control in Eastern Europe – 'like slicing off salami, piece by piece':

- Stage 1: the Soviets supervised the organization of governments in the Eastern European states, initially establishing a broad alliance of 'anti-fascists'.
- Stage 2: each of the parties was 'sliced off', one after the other.
- Stage 3: the Communist 'core' was left, and then ultimately the local Communists were replaced (if need be) with Moscow-trained people.

By the end of 1946, the so-called **Baggage Train** leaders had returned to Eastern Europe. These were the men who had spent much of the war in Moscow, and were considered by the Soviets to be 'trustworthy': for example, Bierut (who returned to Poland), Kolarov (who returned to Bulgaria), Pauker (who returned to Romania), and Rakosi (who returned to Hungary). These leaders would thus ensure that the post-war governments of their respective countries would be dominated by Moscow-backed, 'Stalinist' Communists.

The 'free elections' promised by Stalin – at Yalta – to occur in a matter of 'weeks' were not held until 19 January 1947. Before the elections there was a campaign of murder, **censorship**, and intimidation. It is estimated that over 50 000 people were deported to **Siberia** prior to the elections.

Case study: Poland

During the elections in Poland in January, Mikolajczyk's **Polish Peasant Party** had 246 candidates disqualified; 149 were arrested and 18 murdered. One million voters were taken off the electoral register for some reason or another. As Desmond Donnelly contends in his book, *Struggle for the World*, 'In these appalling circumstances of intimidation, it was not surprising that Bierut's Communists secured complete control in Poland' (Collins 1965).

The Soviet perspective on these elections was quite different from that of the West, where they were seen as a breach of the Yalta agreements. The Soviets, however, saw them as a victory over 'Western expansionism':

> *The political goals set by Mikolajczyk in cahoots with Churchill required that Warsaw be liberated (by British and American) forces before the Soviet army reached the city. That way a pro-Western government supported by Mikolajczyk would already be in control of the city by the time the Soviets arrived. But it didn't work out that way. Our troops under Rokossovsky got there first.*

Nikita Khrushchev, *Khrushchev Remembers* (Little, Brown & Co. 1970) vol. 2, p.166

This pattern of securing Soviet Communist-style governments was emerging in the other Eastern European countries that the Red Army had occupied at the end of World War Two – Bulgaria, Romania, and Hungary. In Czechoslovakia and Finland there remained only a semblance of democracy.

Soviet pressure on Iran

Another place in which the USSR tried to increase its political control in the aftermath of the war was Iran. At the Tehran Conference, it had been agreed that both the British and the Soviets would withdraw their troops from Iran after the war. The UK took its troops out, but Stalin left 30 000 of his in the north, claiming that they were needed there to help put down internal rebellion.

However, these Soviet troops encouraged a Communist uprising, and the Iranian government complained to the USSR's former allies. The British and Americans demanded that Stalin remove his troops immediately. They also saw this as another breach in the wartime agreements. On 1 January 1946, Stalin refused. He believed that after the war he had as much right to Iranian oil as did his former allies. Four days later, Truman wrote to his **Secretary of State**, James Byrnes. In this letter Truman revealed that he thought the USSR was planning an invasion of Turkey and the Black Sea Straits. He also wrote, '… unless Russia is faced with an iron fist and strong language, war is in the making'.

Iran had made a formal protest to the UN concerning the continued presence of Soviet forces. This was the first crisis the UN had had to deal with. Under this new pressure, Moscow finally pulled its troops out.

Instability in Greece and Turkey

After World War Two there were anti-imperialist, nationalist, and, to a certain extent, 'pro-Communist' rebellions in Greece and Turkey. The British, and to a lesser degree the USA, believed that these rebellions were being directed and supported by the Soviets. Churchill, in particular, was annoyed at Stalin's apparent disregard for the Percentages Agreement (see page 21). Stalin had also asserted that he wanted international control of the Straits of Constantinople rather than Turkish control there.

Communist parties in Italy and France

Communist parties in both of these 'Western democracies' grew stronger in post-war Europe, their membership increasing due to the economic deprivations and hardships experienced at the end of the war. The Americans and the British were suspicious that these newly popular Communist parties were receiving 'encouragement' from Moscow. Indeed there was concern that Italy and France could be 'weak links' in anti-Communist Western Europe.

CHALLENGE YOURSELF

Research skills (ATL)

Research the growth in popularity of Communism in Italy after the war. Why did Communism have so much support? What factors ensured that Communists were not successful in achieving political power?

Activity 3  (ATL) Social skills

1. Consider the events that took place after the wartime conferences. Discuss with a partner when and how the Soviets could be seen to 'break the wartime agreements'.

Step 2: Kennan's Long Telegram, February 1946

George F Kennan, US diplomat in Moscow.

In February 1946, a US diplomat in Moscow, George F Kennan, sent a telegram to the US **State Department** on the nature of Soviet conduct and foreign policy. His views on the motives behind Soviet foreign policy were to have a lasting influence on the State Department. The key idea in this telegram was that the Soviet system was buoyed by the 'threat' of a 'hostile world outside its borders', that the USSR was 'fanatically and implacably' hostile to the West: 'Impervious to the logic of reason Moscow [is] highly sensitive to the logic of force. For this reason it can easily withdraw – and usually does – when strong resistance is encountered at any point.'

Kennan argued that:

- the USSR's view of the world was a traditional one of insecurity
- the Soviets wanted to advance Muscovite Stalinist ideology (not simply 'Marxism')
- the Soviet regime was cruel and repressive and justified this by perceiving nothing but evil in the outside world. That view of a hostile outside environment would sustain the internal Stalinist system
- the USSR was fanatically hostile to the West – but it was not 'suicidal'.

Kennan's 'logic of force' argument helped to harden attitudes in the USA and was to play a key role in the development of the US policy of containment (see chapter 6).

Later the same year, NV Novikov, the Soviet **ambassador** to the US, also sent a telegram. Addressed to Stalin, this set out his concerns about US actions he saw as imperialist and thus a threat to the USSR.

> The foreign policy of the United States, which reflects the imperialist tendencies of American monopolistic capital, is characterized in the postwar period by a striving for world supremacy. This is the real meaning of the many statements by President Truman and other representatives of American ruling circles; that the United States has the right to lead the world. All the forces of American diplomacy – the army, the air force, the navy, industry, and science – are enlisted in the service of this foreign policy. For this purpose broad plans for expansion have been developed and are being implemented through diplomacy and the establishment of a system of naval and air bases stretching far beyond the boundaries of the United States, through the arms race, and through the creation of ever newer types of weapons.

Both the Kennan and the Novikov telegrams indicate the suspicion that was emerging in both the USA and the USSR regarding each other's actions.

Step 3: Churchill's 'Iron Curtain' speech, March 1946

On 5 March 1946, former British Prime Minister Winston Churchill gave a speech at Westminster College in Fulton, Missouri, with President Harry S Truman sitting just behind him on the speakers' platform. This speech is now seen as one of the defining moments in the origins of the Cold War.

Churchill's speech warned of a new danger for Europe:

> A shadow has fallen upon the scenes so lately lighted by the allied victory. Nobody knows what Soviet Russia and its Communist international organization intends to do in the immediate future, or what are the limits, if any, to their expansive proselytizing tendencies. I have a strong admiration and regard for the valiant Russian people and for my war-time comrade, Marshal Stalin. There is sympathy and goodwill … toward the peoples of all the Russias … We understand the Russian need to be secure on her western frontiers from all renewal of German aggression. We welcome her to her rightful place among the leading nations of the world … It is my duty, however, to place before you certain facts about the present position in Europe.
>
> From Stettin in the Baltic to Trieste in the Adriatic, an iron curtain has descended across the Continent. Behind the line lie all the capitals of the ancient states of Central and Eastern Europe – Warsaw, Berlin, Prague, Vienna, Budapest, Belgrade, Bucharest and Sofia. All these famous cities and the populations around them lie in the Soviet sphere and all are subject in one form or another, not only to Soviet influence but to a very high and increasing measure of control from Moscow … The Russian-dominated Polish government has been encouraged to make enormous and wrongful inroads upon Germany, and mass expulsions of millions of Germans on a scale grievous and undreamed of are now taking place. The Communist Parties, which were very small in all these eastern states of Europe, have been raised to pre-eminence and power far beyond their numbers and are seeking everywhere to obtain totalitarian control. Police governments are prevailing in nearly every case …Whatever conclusions may be drawn from these facts … this is certainly not the liberated Europe we fought to build up. Nor is it one which contains the essentials of a permanent peace …
>
> On the other hand I repulse the idea that a new war is inevitable; still more that it is imminent … I do not believe that Soviet Russia desires war. What they desire is the fruits of war and the indefinite expansion of their power and doctrines … Our difficulties and dangers will not be removed by closing our eyes to them. They will not be removed by mere waiting to see what happens; nor will they be relieved by a policy of appeasement … From what I have seen of our Russian friends and allies during the war, I am convinced that there is nothing they admire so much as strength and there is nothing for which they have less respect than for military weakness … If the western democracies stand together in strict adherence to the principles of the United Nations Charter, their influence for furthering these principles will be immense … If, however, they become divided or falter in their duty … then indeed catastrophe may overwhelm us all.

Winston S Churchill, address at Westminster College, Fulton, Missouri, 5 March 1946

Activity 4

 **ATL** Thinking skills

1. Why did Churchill use the phrase 'iron curtain' to describe events in Europe?
2. In what way does Churchill allude to the idea of 'salami tactics' taking place in Eastern Europe?
3. Imagine that you are Stalin reading this speech. What might your reaction be?

What was the basis for the Iron Curtain speech?

In his 'Iron Curtain' speech, Winston Churchill was referring to the fact that, by 1946, Soviet-dominated Communist governments had been set up in Poland, Hungary, Romania, and Bulgaria. This was in spite of the hopes expressed at Yalta that there would be free and democratic elections in Eastern Europe after the war. Communist regimes not linked directly to Moscow had been established in Albania and Yugoslavia as well. Within two to three years this Soviet influence would be extended to East Germany and Czechoslovakia. His remarks were also prompted by the presence of the Red Army in those countries 'liberated' from Germany by the Russians – and by the cloak of secrecy which descended over Eastern Europe within a few months of the end of the war.

Soviet reaction to Churchill's speech

The response from the Soviet leadership was quick – and was one of outrage. Within a week Stalin had compared Churchill to Hitler. He saw the speech as both 'racist' and as 'a call to war with the Soviet Union'. Within three weeks the Soviets had taken several steps:

- they withdrew from the International Monetary Fund (**IMF**)
- they stepped up the tone and intensity of anti-Western **propaganda**
- they initiated a new five-year economic plan of self-strengthening.

Therefore, the 'Iron Curtain' speech led to a further hardening of opinions on both sides. Churchill had publicly defined the new front line in what was now being seen as a new war.

Activity 5   ATL Thinking skills

Source A

'Peep under the iron curtain' by Leslie Illingworth, first published in the *Daily Mail* in 1946.

Source B

    Hitler began his work of unleashing war by proclaiming a 'race theory', declaring that only German-speaking people constituted a superior nation. Mr Churchill sets out to unleash a war with a race theory, asserting that only English-speaking nations are superior nations, who are called upon to decide the destinies of the entire world … There can be no doubt that Mr Churchill's position is a call for war on the USSR.

It is absurd to speak of exclusive control by the USSR in Vienna and Berlin, where there are allied control councils made up of the representatives of four states and where the USSR has only one-quarter of the votes. The Soviet Union's loss of life [in the war] has been several times greater than that of Britain and the USA put together. Possibly in some quarters an inclination is felt to forget about these colossal sacrifices of the Soviet people, which secured the liberation of Europe from the Hitlerite yoke. But the Soviet Union cannot forget about them. And so what can there be surprising about the fact that the Soviet Union, anxious for its future safety, is trying to see to it that governments loyal in their attitude to the Soviet Union should exist in these countries?

Stalin's March 1946 response to Churchill's 'Iron Curtain' speech

1. What arguments does Stalin make in Source B in response to Churchill's speech? What do you consider to be the tone of this speech?
2. What is the message of Illingworth's cartoon (Source A)?
3. How does this cartoon support Churchill's Iron Curtain speech?

How can changes in 'language' affect our understanding of the past? In what ways can our culture affect our interpretation of historical events?

In question 3 you are looking for ways in which the sources say the *same* thing. Be specific in your comparisons: pick out phrases in the speech which you can quote in support of the cartoon.

Activity 6  **ATL Communication skills**

1. Review these key Cold War issues up to 1946. Add brief notes to the bullet point sub-headings. In your notes, consider how each point added to tension between East and West.
   - the opening of a second front
   - the Warsaw Uprising
   - tensions at Yalta
   - clear divisions at Potsdam
   - Hiroshima
   - the Red Army in Eastern Europe
   - Salami tactics
   - Germany
   - Iran
   - Kennan's Long Telegram
   - Churchill's Fulton speech
   - instability in Greece and Turkey
   - Communist Party success in Italy and France
2. Draft a timeline on an A3 sheet of paper, or on your laptop or tablet. You will need to leave a gap between each year to allow enough space to add events and a little detail.

   Origins of the Cold War/superpower tensions
   *USSR actions
   1943 1949
   *USA actions
   - Add events above the line that are actions taken by the USSR in 1945–1946 that led to a breakdown in the Grand Alliance.
   - Add events below the line that are actions taken by the USA in 1945–1946 that led to a breakdown in the Grand Alliance.
   - You will continue to work on this timeline as you read through the next chapter.

   Once you have added your key dates up to 1946, check what you have with a partner. Have you put the same events with the same superpower? Which superpower seems to have acted more provocatively up to 1946?

In pairs, discuss how you have selected the key events to add to your timelines. Which events do you consider more significant in causing the breakdown of the Grand Alliance? Reflect on the challenges faced by historians when identifying which events and evidence are key to their account. How might this selection process be impacted by political or cultural bias?

To access websites relevant to this chapter, go to www.pearsonhotlinks. com, search for the book title or ISBN, and click on 'chapter 2'.

Hünger! Fort mit dem Reichsnährstand!

03

Breakdown of the Grand Alliance:
Steps to the political, economic and military
division of Europe: Part 2

> **Key concepts:** Causation and significance

As you read this chapter, consider the following essay questions:

- Discuss the reasons for the breakdown of the 'Grand Alliance' by 1949.
- To what extent was Stalin more responsible than Truman for the onset of a Cold War?
- Examine the key issues in post-war Europe that caused superpower tension up to 1949.

Confrontation and containment

In Steps 1 to 3 in chapter 2, we examined the breakdown of the Grand Alliance after World War Two. In this chapter, in Steps 4 to 8, the confrontation between the USA and the USSR intensifies as political, economic, and military divisions develop.

Step 4: The Truman Doctrine

Truman made a key speech to the US Congress on 12 March 1947. In this speech he put forward the belief that the United States had the obligation to 'support free peoples who are resisting attempted subjugation by armed minorities or by outside pressures'. This became known as the '**Truman Doctrine**'.

It was a radical change in US foreign policy – a policy which had been traditionally **isolationist**. Truman's new 'doctrine' was in response to the unstable situations in Turkey and, in particular, Greece. At the end of the war, the British had restored the Greek monarchy, but Communist **guerrillas** continued to resist in the countryside. The British government could no longer offer assistance to the Greek government or support the Greek government and army financially, as its own economy had been devastated by the war, leaving it £3000 million in debt.

In February 1947, the British told the USA that they could no longer maintain troops in Greece. The United States did not want to risk a potential Communist takeover of a strategically important European country, so Truman issued his 'doctrine', and, in the name of preserving democracy over Communism, US aid and military advisers were sent to Greece.

The Soviets saw this as evidence of the determination of the United States to expand its sphere of influence, and they did not recognize any legitimacy in this new American involvement in Europe. Truman's decision was affected not only by Churchill's perception of the **expansionist** threat, as outlined in his 'Iron Curtain' speech, but also by George Kennan's Long Telegram. As already mentioned, this doctrine marked a departure from the United States' traditional policy of isolation, and it was the beginning of the American policy of 'containment' of Communism. The philosophy of containment would, in the years to come, draw the USA into the affairs of nations well beyond Europe.

On the longer-term significance of the Truman Doctrine, political historian Walter LaFeber wrote:

 The Truman Doctrine was a milestone in American history … the doctrine became an ideological shield behind which the United States marched to rebuild the Western political and economic system and counter the radical left. From 1947 on, therefore, any threats to that Western system could be easily explained as Communist inspired, not as problems which arose

from difficulties within the system itself. That was the most lasting and tragic result of the Truman Doctrine.

Walter LaFeber, *America, Russia and the Cold War*, 5th ed. (Knopf, 1985) pp.57–58

Activity 1

The Truman Doctrine is announced

 At the present moment in world history nearly every nation must choose between alternative ways of life. The choice is too often not a free one.

One way of life is based upon the will of the majority, and is distinguished by free institutions, representative government, free elections, guarantees of individual liberty, freedom of speech and religion and freedom from political oppression.

The second way of life is based upon the will of a minority forcibly imposed upon the majority. It relies upon terror and oppression, a controlled press and radio, fixed election and the suppression of personal freedom.

I believe that it must be the policy of the United States to support peoples who are resisting attempted subjugation by armed minorities or by outside pressures.

I believe that we must assist free peoples to work out their own destiny in their own way.

President Truman, address to the US Congress, 12 March 1947

1. What justification does Truman give for his doctrine?
2. Identify the key words that Truman uses to describe the West and key words he uses to describe countries under Soviet control. Why do you think he uses this type of language?
3. How important is this document for explaining the development of the Cold War?
4. With reference to the origin, purpose, and content of this source, analyse its values and limitations for historians studying the breakdown of the Grand Alliance.

Step 5: The Marshall Plan

In January 1947, the US Secretary of State, James Byrnes, resigned and was replaced by General George Marshall. Marshall believed that the economies of Western Europe needed immediate help from the USA. In a broadcast to the nation he declared: 'The patient is sinking while the doctors deliberate.' The '**Marshall Plan**' seemed to follow on quite naturally from the Truman Doctrine – it was the economic extension of the ideas outlined by the president. Marshall introduced his plan in a speech at Harvard University on 5 June 1947:

 It is logical that the United States should do whatever it is able to do to assist in the return of normal economic health in the world, without which there can be no political stability and no assured peace. Our policy is not directed against any country or doctrine, but against hunger, poverty, desperation and chaos. Its purpose should be the revival of a working economy in the world so as to permit the emergence of political and social conditions in which free institutions can exist … Any government which is willing to assist in the task of recovery will find full co-operation … on the part of the United States Government.

Before the United States Government can proceed much further in its efforts to alleviate the situation and help start the European world on its way to recovery, there must be some agreement among the countries of Europe as to the requirements of the situation and the part those countries themselves will take in order to give proper effect to whatever action might be undertaken by this Government. It would be neither fitting nor efficacious for this Government to undertake to draw up unilaterally a program designed to place Europe on its feet economically. This is the business of the Europeans. The initiative, I think, must come from Europe.

George C Marshall, address at Harvard University, 5 June 1947, in Department of State Bulletin XXVII, 15 June 1947, pp.1159–1160

Dollar imperialism?

The Marshall Plan was designed to give immediate economic help to Europe. The problem of whether or not to 'allow' the Soviets to join the plan, or indeed to avoid specifically excluding them, was solved by setting down strict criteria to qualify for American economic aid. This involved allowing the United States to investigate the financial records of applicant countries. The USSR would never tolerate this condition.

Thus, the United States invited the USSR to join the Marshall Plan and claimed that this 'aid' was not directed at, or against, any country or doctrine. The stated aims of Marshall Plan aid were to:

• revive European economies so that political and social stability could ensue
• safeguard the future of the US economy.

However, to avoid the interpretation that the United States was in any way coercing European governments to accept the aid plan, it was made clear that 'the initiative must come from Europe'.

The bill allocating the four-year aid programme of $17 billion was not passed by the US Congress until March 1948. The eventual success of the bill was due mainly to the effect of the **Czech Coup** of February 1948 (see Step 7).

 Explore countries that have had or have requested economic assistance from the international community: for example, from the IMF, through the UN, or from another state. What conditions did the state have to meet to receive aid? Has economic assistance benefited states in terms of their political stability? Does the international community have a role in assisting states with economic crises?

Activity 2 — ATL Thinking skills

Country	Amount
Yugoslavia	$109 m
Turkey	$221 m
Denmark	$271 m
Austria	$677 m
Netherlands	$1 079 m
Italy	$1 474 m
United Kingdom	$3 176 m
France	$2 706 m
West Germany	$1 389 m
Greece	$694 m
Belgium/Luxembourg	$556 m
Norway	$254 m
Ireland	$146 m
Sweden	$107 m

1. Study the statistics on which countries received Marshall Aid. Can you explain why so much money went to:
   a. the United Kingdom (refer to chapter 2)
   b. France and Italy (refer to chapter 2)
   c. West Germany (Step 8 may also help you)?

CHALLENGE YOURSELF

Research skills ATL

Investigate the response to Marshall Aid in Europe in more depth. Which countries in the Eastern bloc showed interest in receiving aid? What was the impact of Marshall Aid in countries such as Italy?

Soviet reaction to the Marshall Plan

The Soviets rejected the Marshall Plan – as the USA probably intended them to – because the Americans had asked to see recipients' financial records. The Soviets saw this as a prime example of American '**dollar imperialism**'. In other words, the Soviets felt the USA was establishing a European empire, and that its method was economic domination and dependence, which would ultimately give it political control.

Soviet Foreign Minister Andrej Vyshinsky gave the following speech at the United Nations in September 1947:

> *The so-called Truman Doctrine and the Marshall Plan are particularly glaring examples of the way in which the principles of the United Nations are violated, of the way in which the United Nations is ignored. The United States has moved towards giving up the idea of international co-operation and joint action by the great powers. It has tried to force its will on the other independent countries, whilst at the same time obviously using the money distributed as relief to needy countries as an instrument of political pressure.*
>
> *This is clearly proved by the measures taken by the United States government with regard to Greece and Turkey, which ignore and bypass the United Nations. This policy conflicts sharply with the principle expressed by the General Assembly in its resolution of 11th December 1946, which declares that relief supplies to other countries should, at no time, be used as a political weapon.*
>
> *The Marshall Plan is merely a variant of the Truman Doctrine. It is becoming more and more evident to everyone that the implementation of the Marshall Plan will mean placing European countries under the economic and political control of the United States and direct interference by the latter in those countries.*
>
> *Moreover this plan is an attempt to split Europe into two camps and, with the help of the United Kingdom and France, to complete the formation of a bloc of several European countries hostile to the interests of the democratic countries.*

Previously, the United States had attempted to unite the West with economic tactics; now, it was on a path towards military unity. Historian Walter LaFeber pointed out the significance of the Marshall Plan:

> *The plan's approach … soon evolved into military alliances. Truman proved to be correct in saying that the Truman Doctrine and the Marshall Plan 'are two halves of the same walnut'. Americans willingly acquiesced as the military aspects of the doctrine developed into quite the larger part.*

> **Walter LaFeber, *America, Russia and the Cold War, 1945–1996* (McGraw Hill, 1997) p.62**

Activity 3  (ATL) Thinking skills

1. In pairs, identify where in Vyshinsky's speech he claims the USA is: a) using its economic power to gain political influence; b) breaking a UN resolution by introducing Marshall Aid; c) creating a clear division in Europe.

2. To what extent was the Soviet objection that the Marshall Plan was 'ignoring' or 'bypassing' the United Nations valid?

3. Vyshinsky suggests that the Marshall Plan will lead to the formation of '**two camps**' in Europe. Why?

4. How does Vyshinski's interpretation of Marshall Aid differ from that put forward by George Marshall (see page 30)?

The Soviet response

In response to the Marshall Plan, the Soviets came up with the **Molotov Plan**, which was a series of bilateral trade agreements that aimed to tie the economies of Eastern Europe to the USSR. The outcome was the creation of **COMECON** in January 1949. COMECON was the Council for Mutual Economic Assistance: a centralized agency that linked Eastern bloc countries to Moscow. It was designed to 'stimulate' and control their economic development, and support the collectivization of agriculture and the development of heavy industry.

Activity 4   (ATL) Thinking skills

THE RIVAL BUSES

Punch cartoon, June 1947. Passengers are being given a choice of two buses: one driven by Stalin and the other by Truman.

1. How are a) the USA and b) the USSR portrayed in this cartoon?
2. What is the message of this cartoon regarding Stalin's policy in Eastern Europe?

Cominform and the 'two camps' doctrine

Before moving on to Step 6, it is important to consider two developments on the Soviet side of the Iron Curtain.

Cominform

This was the Communist Information Bureau set up in September 1947. It was created as an instrument to increase Stalin's control over the Communist parties of other countries. It was initially comprised of Communists from the USSR, Yugoslavia, France, Italy, Poland, Bulgaria, Hungary, Czechoslovakia, and Romania. The West was concerned that this organization would actively spread Communism (and destabilize the democratic governments) in the West's own sphere of influence – Western Europe.

Stalin's 'two camps' doctrine

Soviet leader Joseph Stalin developed his idea of a Europe divided into two opposing camps in the 1920s and 1930s. Following World War Two, this idea, in the divisive context of post-war international relations, became a firm foundation for Soviet foreign policy. Indeed, in February 1946 (before Churchill's 'Iron Curtain' speech) Stalin had delivered a speech emphasizing the creation of 'two camps' opposing each other. At the inaugural meeting of **Cominform** in Poland, Soviet delegate Andrei Zhdanov delivered an important speech on Soviet foreign policy. He stated that the Americans had organized an 'anti-Soviet' bloc of countries that were economically dependent upon them – not only those in Western Europe, but also in South America and China. The 'second camp' was the USSR and the 'new democracies' in Eastern Europe. He also included countries he deemed 'associated' or 'sympathetic' to their cause – Indonesia, Vietnam, India, Egypt, and Syria. The Soviet **'two camps' doctrine** was very similar to the 'new world order' outlined by Truman.

Step 6: Red Army occupation of Eastern Europe, 1945–1947

The Soviet Union came to control various Eastern European states by creating what became known as a '**satellite empire**'. These countries kept their separate legal identities – in that they were separate from each other and the USSR – but they were tied into following Moscow's line by the following factors:

- Soviet military power (later formalized in the Warsaw Pact in 1955)
- salami tactics (see Step 1), which transferred the machinery of government into the hands of obedient, pro-Soviet Communists
- state police and security/spy networks
- COMECON (see Step 5).

As discussed under Step 1, Soviet control was in place in most East European countries by 1947. There just remained Czechoslovakia. Salami tactics were taking a little longer there, and Stalin decided that a **coup** to finally oust non-Communist members of the government would be necessary (see Step 7).

Thus, by the end of 1948, the satellite states were economically and militarily under the control of the USSR. The USA and its Western allies saw this 'occupation' of Eastern Europe as a direct breach of the agreements made at Yalta and Potsdam, and, perhaps more importantly, as clear evidence of Soviet expansionist policies in practice.

The 'X article'

Before moving on to Step 7, this is a good point to look at the now infamous '**X article**' written by George F Kennan for *Time Magazine* in 1947. In it Kennan argued that the United States policy towards the Soviet Union had to be one of 'long term' containment of Soviet expansionism. He also suggested that the US should regard the USSR politically as a 'rival' rather than a partner.

Kennan was still a strong influence on President Truman, and his reputation as the United States' key expert on Soviet policy also gave him influence over American public opinion. In view of the Soviet takeover of Eastern Europe, a policy to contain the spread of Communism seemed all the more essential.

CHALLENGE YOURSELF

 **ATL** Research skills

Research the growth of Soviet control in one Eastern bloc country (except for East Germany) in the period 1945–1949. How important were: a) the presence of the Red Army; b) the strength of the local Communist party; c) the use of spy networks and state police; d) control of the economy?

 **ATL** Thinking skills

1. From what you have read so far, discuss who you consider to be most responsible for the growth of hostility between East and West up to 1947 – the USA or the Soviet Union?

Step 7: The Czechoslovakian Coup, February 1948

The Soviets continued, into 1948, to attempt to consolidate their control over Eastern Europe. Czechoslovakia, however, was seen as moving towards the West. What was most worrying to Stalin was that Czechoslovakia had expressed interest in receiving aid from the Marshall Plan. In addition, there was a certain amount of sentimental feeling in the West for the Czechs after their 'abandonment' (or, as some would say, betrayal) in the **Munich Agreements** of 1938.

In February 1948, Stalin organized for pressure to be put on the Czechoslovak coalition government. Twelve non-Communist members were forced to resign. The Czech Communist Party leader demanded the formation of a Communist-led government. Under heavy pressure from Moscow, coupled with loosely veiled threats of armed intervention, Czech President Edvard Beneš agreed. He felt that his country, once again, was isolated.

Two weeks later, the staunchly independent Czech Foreign Minister Jan Masaryk was found dead, in suspicious circumstances. President Truman responded quickly, calling

Czechoslovakians listening to announcement of Communist takeover.

the events in Czechoslovakia a 'coup'. He also said that through the cynical application of force the Soviets had 'sent shock waves throughout the civilized world'.

At this point, the financing for the Marshall Plan had not been passed by Congress. This was mainly due to hesitation over the huge amount of money it would commit the United States to invest. Truman now used the events in Czechoslovakia to push the bill through. Thus, the 'Czech Coup' was directly responsible for the implementation of the Marshall Plan in Europe. Bloody purges of allegedly disloyal Communists continued during 1948: not only in Czechoslovakia, but throughout the Eastern bloc. Nevertheless, there remained a key area of 'weakness' in the heart of Stalin's sphere of influence and control – Berlin.

> **Cold War Crisis:**

Step 8: The Berlin Crisis of 1948

Post-war Germany

The fact that Germany had been invaded on several fronts by Soviet and Western forces meant that, unlike Japan, it was much more difficult to leave it undivided during occupation at the end of World War Two. Accordingly, at Yalta and Potsdam, it was agreed that Germany should be divided temporarily into four zones of occupation, administered by the Allied Control Council (ACC), with Berlin's governance being the responsibility of the Allied *Kommandantur*, which was made up of four military governors. This was all seen as a temporary arrangement while Germany's future was being worked out at a peace conference yet to be arranged. It is important to note, however, that at all times it was the intention to treat Germany as one economic unit, and it was expected that Germany would eventually emerge as a united independent state again. However, by 1949, Germany had become permanently divided into two separate states.

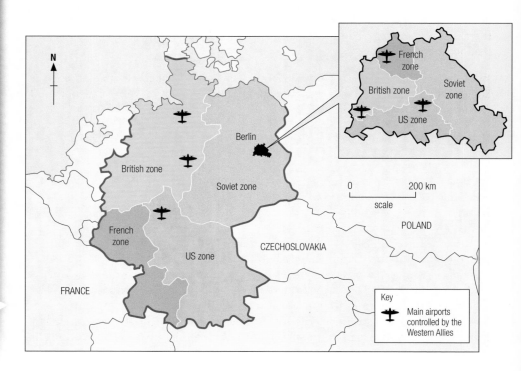

This map shows the division of Germany between the four powers, and also the division of Berlin into sectors.

Why did the post-war powers fail to unify Germany?

This was due to several factors.

Germany's key strategic position and the differing aims of the main powers

Germany's geographic position in the centre of Europe, and its potential economic strength, made it an area of vital concern to all countries, and an area over which they could not agree. The USSR did not wish to see a resurgent united Germany that would pose a threat to its security. At the same time, it wished to get as much out of Germany as possible in terms of reparations. The Soviets were looking for reparations of some US $20 billion. France likewise feared a united Germany rising again on its eastern flank and was not keen to hasten Germany's recovery after the war. The USA had come to see that the best hope for European peace would lie in the rapid economic recovery of Germany, and that the most effective way of containing the spread of Communism would be to bolster the war-torn economies of Western Europe with massive injections of US aid. The UK found it best to endorse the US view: as it was almost bankrupt, it would greatly benefit from American aid.

The increasing lack of trust between East and West as the Cold War developed

The differences in aims and attitudes that the four Allied powers had in 1945 would have been enough on their own to delay any permanent peace settlement for Germany. However, as the Cold War developed, mutual suspicions between the USSR and the Western powers began to harden. Both the West and the Soviet Union became concerned that a powerful Germany could be a threat if it ever joined forces with the other side. By 1946, America felt that it needed to make its position on Germany (and thus Europe) clear. Afraid that Germans would be won over to Communism, Secretary of State James F Byrnes gave a speech in Stuttgart, known as the 'Speech of Hope', in which he promised that Germany would be rebuilt and would not be divided economically, and that Germans would be allowed to govern themselves democratically. Byrnes also committed US troops to Germany, saying: 'As long as there is an occupation army in Germany, the American armed forces will be part of that occupation army.'

With the promise to keep US troops in Europe, this was a clear stand against the Soviets, but its main aim, as Byrnes stated himself, was 'to win the German people … it was a battle between us and Russia over minds.'

The specific disputes between the post-war powers within Germany itself

Specifically, the division intensified for a number of reasons. One major factor was economic conflict. Reparations were the key problem. The arrangements set up at Potsdam, whereby the USSR was to take 25 per cent of German industrial equipment from the Western zones in return for supplying those zones with food and raw materials, did not work. Food was a huge problem in war-torn Germany, especially with the flood of refugees from Eastern Europe swelling the population. The USSR was not delivering enough food to the Western zones and was also being increasingly secretive about what it was taking from the Soviet zone. Thus the United States and the United Kingdom stopped supplies to the Soviet zone. German coal was another important area of disagreement. The Soviets wanted coal from the Western zones, but the Americans wanted to use German coal from these areas to assist in the economic reconstruction of Western Europe. Accordingly, 25 million tons of coal from the Western zones was exported to Europe, rather than to the USSR. Then, early in 1947, the British and US zones were merged into one unit called **Bizonia**.

There was also political conflict. Evidence suggests that Stalin was planning as early as 4 June 1945 to incorporate a reunified Germany within Moscow's sphere of influence. This was to be done by using the Red Army to control the Soviet zone while the Communist Party of Germany **(KPD)** would attempt to get popular support in the other zones. As a first step to achieving this, in April 1946 the Soviets forced through a merger of the Communists and the Social Democrats in their zone to form just one party – the Socialist Unity Party (SED). However, this party was not successful in winning over the West Germans. Several political parties had eventually been established after the war and West Germans were unlikely to vote for a Soviet-controlled party, which, even if it might lead to a unified Germany, would bring minimal economic assistance (compared to the promise of Marshall Aid after 1948) and no chance of democracy. As they saw the impossibility of the situation, the SED leaders began planning their own separate regime in the East.

Similarly, by 1948, the Western powers were beginning to think seriously about consolidating their occupation zones and establishing within them a provisional German government. The **London Conference of Ministers** in 1947, which should have considered the German peace treaty, ended in the Western powers and the Soviets throwing recriminations at each other, indicating that any agreement on Germany's future was remote. Therefore, at the London Conference in 1948, France, Britain, and the United States met to draw up a **constitution** for a new West German state, which would come into existence the following year. As part of the plan to set up a new West German government, it was also agreed to introduce a new currency into the Western sectors. The old German currency had lost its value and in many areas Germans were operating a barter economy. Stalin rightly saw that the introduction of the new currency signalled the establishment of a new Germany in the West. His action, in setting up the blockade of Berlin, was meant to thwart this plan. Stalin probably hoped that this action would also force the West out of Berlin.

The Berlin Blockade, 1948

As agreed at Potsdam, Berlin had been divided between the four occupying powers. The problem for the Western powers was that Berlin lay 100 miles within the Soviet occupation zone, which had been sealed off from the rest of Germany since 1946. The Western forces and the West Germans in Berlin thus had to rely on receiving their food and energy supplies from the West: delivered along road, rail and air 'corridors' (see the map on the next page).

In March 1948, Stalin started putting a stranglehold on Western interests in West Berlin, mainly through transport restrictions. Then, in response to the introduction of the new currency into the Western sectors of Berlin, Stalin began the total blockade of Berlin on 23–24 June 1948. The roads, railways, and waterways linking West Berlin to the Western sector of Germany were all closed; the supply of electricity from East to West was cut; and the USSR left the Berlin *Kommandantur*, having already left the ACC in March.

This was the first crisis of the Cold War and direct military confrontation was always a possibility. However, the West did not try to defeat the blockade by force, but rather supplied Berlin from the air. During the blockade, American and British planes flew more than 200000 flights to Berlin in 320 days, and delivered vital supplies of food and coal to 2.2 million West Berliners. Always, there was the threat of a Soviet military response. By early 1949, it was clear that Stalin's gamble was failing, and he finally ended the blockade in May of that year.

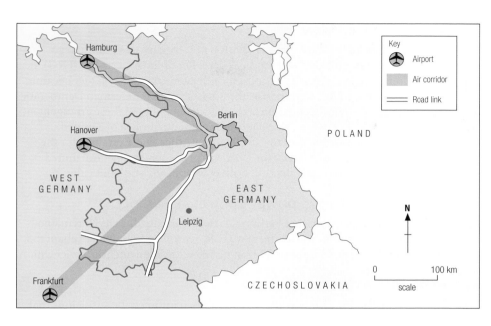

This map shows the position of Berlin and routes in from West Germany.

What were the results of the Berlin Blockade?

This was the first time since 1945 that war had become a possibility – and the blockade had a significant impact on the development of the Cold War. It was now clear that any agreement between the two sides would be difficult, if not impossible. Therefore, the failure of the Berlin Blockade had three important consequences. It led to:

• the division of Germany
• the continuation of four-power control in Berlin
• the formation of the North Atlantic Treaty Organization (NATO).

Berlin children cheering airlift plane.

The division of Germany

The failure of the blockade meant that the division of Germany was bound to go ahead. The West moved quickly to set up the Federal Republic of Germany (**FRG**). It came into existence in September 1949 and a month later Konrad Adenauer became the first chancellor of the FRG. In response, the Soviets set up the German Democratic Republic (GDR) in the Soviet occupation zone. The inevitability of these arrangements stemmed from the fact that neither side could contemplate the idea of a united Germany, which could possibly become an ally to the other side. Certainly, for the West, a divided Germany protected by the USA was preferable to a neutral united Germany. Europe was now clearly divided, both economically and politically.

The continuation of four-power control in Berlin

The division of Germany meant that Berlin also remained a divided city. It remained under four-power occupation within the new GDR. As will be explained in chapter 8, this continued to be a major source of friction between the West and the Soviet Union.

The formation of the NATO

The Soviet threat to Berlin, following the Czech Coup, reinforced the suspicions that the West already had about Stalin and, combined with the resource demands of the **Berlin airlift**, emphasized the need for a US defence commitment to Europe. This resulted in the formation, in April 1949, of NATO by the USA, Canada, the **Brussels Pact** powers, Norway, Denmark, Iceland, Italy and Portugal. At the same time, the US Congress approved a military assistance programme to help build up Europe's armed forces. Thus, from this time, there was a major US military presence in Europe, which was clearly a departure from previous US foreign policy.

In the Paris Pacts, West Germany was to be admitted into NATO. This confirmed the Soviet Union's worst fears concerning the dangers of a return of an armed Germany on its borders. Within a week of West Germany joining NATO in 1955, the Soviet Union had announced the formation of the Warsaw Pact. This brought all the states of Eastern Europe under a single military command. Although it lacked organization, and was initially more of a political than a military alliance, its existence nevertheless meant that Europe was now divided militarily, as well as economically and politically.

TOK

Consider the events leading up to the Berlin Blockade. How does hindsight affect our understanding of the causes of the blockade? How would perspectives differ in the Soviet Union, the USA, and Germany at the time of this crisis, compared to views from other countries around the world?

Activity 6 — **ATL** Self-management and social skills

1. In small groups, put together a review guide/set of flash cards/summary sheets about the Berlin Blockade as a case study of a Cold War crisis. You can use the chart below and add in dates, details, and events.

You will need to add *at least* one more Cold War crisis case study – from a different region – by the end of your course.

Cold War Crisis

Case Study	Causes	Impact	Significance
1. Berlin Blockade 1948–1949 Europe Region			
2. (second case study)			
3. (third case study)			

What conclusions can be drawn about Europe's situation at the end of 1949?

Are there any countries or cities divided into separate sectors or zones today? What events led to their division and how does it impact on the people living there?

- Europe was now clearly divided along political, economic, and military lines (look again at the diagram on page 11).
- Germany was not to be reunited as had been the original aim of the Allies at the end of World War Two. There were now two clear states, although neither side was prepared to recognize the existence of the other (until **Ostpolitik** in the 1970s).
- The USA had abandoned its peacetime policy of avoiding commitments and was now involved economically (through the Marshall Plan) and militarily (through NATO) in Europe.
- No peace treaty had actually been signed with Germany, which meant that the borders of central Europe were not formalized. This was particularly worrying for Poland, as it now included territory taken from Germany in 1945. (This was not finally resolved until 1975.)
- Western countries had developed a greater sense of unity due to the Soviet threat.

What did this situation mean for international relations beyond Europe?

- From this time on, many conflicts, wherever they were in the world, would be seen as part of the struggle between Communism and Capitalism.
- The USA's policy of containment, which had been developed to fight Communism in Europe, was to lead the USA into resisting Communism anywhere in the world that it perceived Communism was a threat. This would involve the USA fighting in both the **Korean War** and the **Vietnam War**.
- The United Nations was never to play the role envisioned in the original discussions between Roosevelt and Churchill at the time of its foundation. With the USA and the USSR now opposing each other and able to use their respective vetoes, the UN could not act effectively to resolve international conflicts.

What is a history essay?

Essays are a central part of your IB course. They are the means by which you demonstrate your historical knowledge and understanding. The diagram below outlines the key points that you must remember each time you write an essay. Use it as a guide every time you have an essay assignment.

How do I write a history essay?

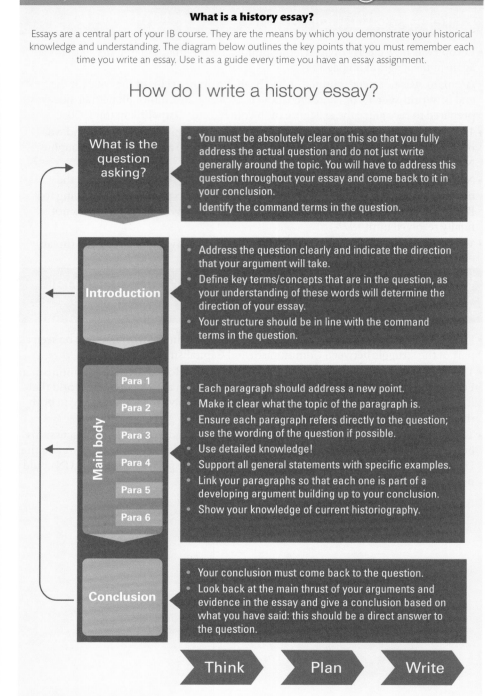

What is the question asking?
- You must be absolutely clear on this so that you fully address the actual question and do not just write generally around the topic. You will have to address this question throughout your essay and come back to it in your conclusion.
- Identify the command terms in the question.

Introduction
- Address the question clearly and indicate the direction that your argument will take.
- Define key terms/concepts that are in the question, as your understanding of these words will determine the direction of your essay.
- Your structure should be in line with the command terms in the question.

Main body (Para 1, Para 2, Para 3, Para 4, Para 5, Para 6)
- Each paragraph should address a new point.
- Make it clear what the topic of the paragraph is.
- Ensure each paragraph refers directly to the question; use the wording of the question if possible.
- Use detailed knowledge!
- Support all general statements with specific examples.
- Link your paragraphs so that each one is part of a developing argument building up to your conclusion.
- Show your knowledge of current historiography.

Conclusion
- Your conclusion must come back to the question.
- Look back at the main thrust of your arguments and evidence in the essay and give a conclusion based on what you have said: this should be a direct answer to the question.

Think ➤ Plan ➤ Write

Creating an essay frame

Essay title: To what extent do you agree that the Grand Alliance had already collapsed by the end of 1946?

Introduction: Always start by identifying/explaining key terms or concepts in the question. You need to explain 'the Grand Alliance' and also show that you understand the significance of the date given in the question – 1946 saw the Kennan Telegram and Churchill's Fulton speech. Also show the direction of your essay and how you are going to respond to the 'To what extent …' part of the question. Set out your argument.

Paragraph 1: *The Grand Alliance was already under strain due to events during World War Two, making a collapse by the end of 1946 likely* ... Here you could go on to explain the issues that caused friction during the war.

Paragraph 2: *The end of the war meant that the aims of the two opposing ideologies were likely to become more obvious and this was likely to cause a breakdown by 1946. This could be seen at Yalta and Potsdam over issues such as Poland* ... Here you could give examples of the tensions that arose over Poland and Eastern Europe following the end of the war.

Paragraph 3: *Events from 1945–1946 strained the Grand Alliance further and actions on both sides indicate that a breakdown had taken place by the end of 1946.* Explain how events in Iran, the Kennan telegram, and the Fulton speech impacted on the Grand Alliance.

Paragraphs 4, 5, and 6: As this is a 'to what extent' question, you need to give an alternative argument. Thus you may want to argue that even at the end of 1946, both sides were still basically working to keep the alliance alive and it was events after 1946 that were key in causing its breakdown: for example, the Truman Doctrine, the Marshall Plan and the Soviet responses to these actions, along with the Berlin Blockade. Make sure you have precise detail to support your points and that you keep referring back to the question by assessing the impact of each event on the Grand Alliance.

Conclusion: Come back to the question and state your overall conclusion based on the evidence that you have presented in your essay.

Practice essay titles – development of the Cold War

- *Discuss the impact of the Truman Doctrine and the Marshall Plan on the emergence of superpower rivalry up to 1949.*
- *Examine the significance of the conferences at Yalta and Potsdam on the development of the Cold War up to 1949.*

NB in chapter 4 we will examine further the roles of Stalin and Truman in causing the Cold War.

To access websites relevant to this chapter, go to www.pearsonhotlinks. com, search for the book title or ISBN, and click on 'chapter 3'.

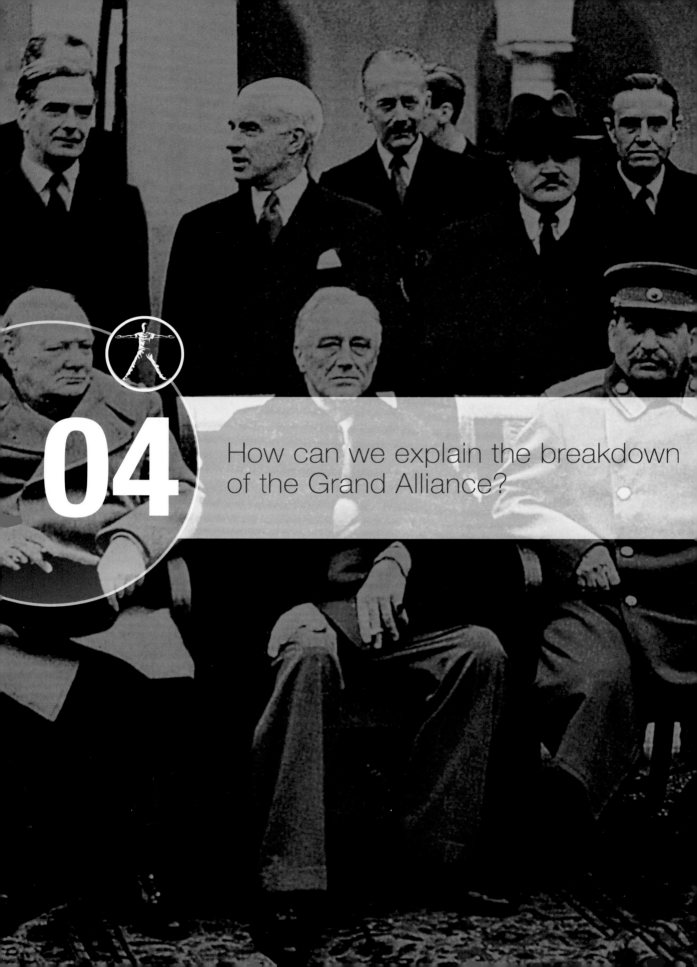

04

How can we explain the breakdown
of the Grand Alliance?

Key concepts: Perspectives

As you read this chapter, consider the following essay questions:

- Examine the role American policies played in the breakdown of the Grand Alliance and the emergence of superpower rivalry in Europe between 1945 and 1949.
- Discuss the role played by ideology in the outbreak and development of the Cold War between 1945 and 1949.

Key

- Communist countries under influence of USSR
- Communist countries not under influence of USSR
- Non-Communist countries
- Iron Curtain
- **1947** Date when Communist government was established

This map shows the East–West divide after 1949.

What was the role of ideology in causing the breakdown of the Grand Alliance?

The breakdown of the Grand Alliance can be seen as a result of the conflict between two competing ideologies. The ideas of Capitalism and Communism were incompatible and both sides felt threatened by the other, believing that their way of life was in danger of attack from an opposing ideology. The seeds of ideological mistrust had been sown in the 1920s (see page 4) following the Bolshevik Revolution of 1917; the **Red Scare** in the USA, following the Communist takeover in Russia, indicates how distrust and fear of Communism was entrenched in **domestic** US politics by 1945. Thus, although there were initially attempts to create a post-war settlement at Yalta and Potsdam, increasingly, both sides viewed the other's actions through an ideological lens.

From the US point of view, the actions of Communists after 1945 looked like a plan to spread Communism worldwide:

- Salami tactics after 1945, the Czech Coup and the Berlin Blockade appeared to be motivated by a desire to spread Communism in Eastern Europe.
- The newly established Cominform was seen as an organization which was designed to promote worldwide revolution.
- The rise of Communist parties in France and Italy after World War Two and the civil war in Greece were all seen as being encouraged and funded by the Soviets.
- Soviet activity in Iran reinforced the belief that Stalin wanted influence outside of Eastern Europe.

However, from the Soviet point of view, the Capitalist ideology of the US also drove the Cold War at the start, and Soviet leaders believed that Capitalist nations were seeking to 'encircle' the Soviet Union and to overthrow its Communist government:

- The Marshall Plan was seen as an example of 'dollar imperialism' and an attempt to extend influence over Europe and lure East European states away from the Soviet Union.
- US economic power, and its drive to establish free trade across the globe and keep markets favourable to US interests, seemed to indicate the possibility of US global economic domination.
- US actions in Germany, particularly its introduction of the new currency in Western zones, appeared to be an attempt to spread US influence.

The fact that the USSR and the USA now faced each other as the two superpowers in a bipolar world also meant the ideological divide that had existed since 1917 was exacerbated. It was further reinforced by the propaganda that started to appear on both sides from 1946, and which was also used as a weapon by each side to undermine the other.

What was the role of Great Power rivalry in causing the breakdown of the Grand Alliance?

Alternatively, it could also be argued that the breakdown in relations between America and the USSR was the result of traditional Great Power rivalries. This can be supported by the insightful, if not prophetic, writings of French historian Alexis de Tocqueville, who wrote the following in 1835:

> *There are at the present time two great nations in the world … I allude to the Russians and the Americans … Their starting point is different, and their courses are not the same; yet each of them seems marked out by the will of Heaven to sway the destinies of half the globe.*

Alexis de Tocqueville, *Democracy in America* (Washington Square Press 1964) pp.124–125

De Tocqueville wrote this before Karl Marx's *Das Capital* or the 'Communist Manifesto', and long before the Bolshevik **Russian Revolution**. So, is it possible that the conflict between the USA and USSR was not really about ideology at all? Walter LaFeber and Louis Halle consider the conflict in similar terms, as both see the USA and the USSR as expansionist powers. Therefore, the hostility that followed 1945 was a continuation of policies they had respectively pursued since the 19th century. LaFeber writes:

> *The two powers did not initially come into conflict because one was Communist and the other Capitalist. Rather, they first confronted one another on the plains of Asia in the late nineteenth century. That meeting climaxed a century in which Americans had expanded westward over half the globe and Russians had moved eastward across Asia.*

Walter LaFeber, *America, Russia and the Cold War 1945–84*, 5th ed. (Knopf 1985) p.1

The end of World War Two heightened the possibility of conflict due to the fact that both the USA and USSR had emerged as superpowers (see pages 6–7); furthermore, the power vacuums created by the decline of smaller states meant that they naturally attempted to expand their influence – and consequently came into conflict.

Former US Secretary of State, Henry Kissinger, writing in the 1980s, also claimed that the USSR's motives were not based on ideology, but were rather a continuum of the long history of **tsarist** empire building.

What was the role of economic interests in causing the breakdown of the Grand Alliance?

The fact that both sides had set up opposing economic systems in Europe by 1949 indicates that economic interests were important in the breakdown of the Grand Alliance.

The economic destruction of Europe following the war gave both sides the opportunity to impose their economic systems on Europe. The USA wanted to establish open markets, and to prevent a return to the economic problems of the inter-war years. To this end they set up the **Bretton Woods system** at the end of the war, which included the International Monetary Fund and the **World Bank**. The USSR was involved in the setting up of these institutions, but the tough conditions placed on applications for loans caused disputes between the USA and the USSR. The emphasis on **free market Capitalism** meant that the USSR withdrew from the Bretton Woods system. To Stalin, the USA's pursuit of the world's markets looked like 'dollar imperialism': the US setting up economic spheres of influence that were based on its own Capitalist aims, and which also promoted American interests in general.

The Marshall Plan further reinforced this perception. As you have read, this was an economic plan designed to save a bankrupt Europe, but it also had a strong ideological motive – to prevent Europe's poverty leading to support for Communism. In response, the Soviets set up COMECON, in which the USSR provided financial assistance to the Eastern European countries. However, the system established by COMECON tended to work to the advantage of the USSR and helped the regimes of Eastern Europe to impose Stalinist economic systems on their countries. Thus, like the US, the Soviets used economic measures to secure their ideological aims.

Economic issues were also important in the superpowers' different views of Germany. The US saw the economic recovery of Germany as key for a general European recovery, and also as an important market for American goods. Marshall Aid was used in West Germany to help generate prosperity. However, Stalin was determined to keep Germany economically weak so that it could not again threaten the Soviet Union. He dismantled much of East Germany's industrial plant and shipped it back to the USSR.

These differing economic aims helped lead to the Berlin Blockade. The West's decision to introduce a new currency in the Western sector highlighted the recovery of economic confidence in West Berlin. This triggered the blockade that led to the permanent division of Germany in 1949.

Thus, the different economic aims and actions of the superpowers played a key role in causing tension between the superpowers.

How far did the actions of the USA and USSR cause the breakdown of the Grand Alliance?

The issue of which country holds most blame for causing the Cold War is an area of debate among historians, as you will see below. Many historians argue that, despite countries' different ideologies, the Cold War was not inevitable and did not have to develop as early as it did, but that the actions of each power played a key role in raising tension.

Was the USSR responsible for the breakdown of the Grand Alliance?

It could be argued that the USA did not intend to stay in Europe after World War Two and that it was only the actions of the USSR that made it reverse its decision to extricate itself from European affairs. Roosevelt made it clear at Yalta that the US did not expect to remain in occupation in Germany, and thus Europe, for more than two years. The US also expected the Soviet Union to remain a part of Bretton Woods and the new economic structures, believing, as Tony Judt writes, that 'the mutual benefits to be had from an increase in international commerce and financial stability would eventually overcome national traditions and political mistrust' (*Postwar: A History of Europe from 1945* [Heinemann 2005] p.108).

Thus, the Americans were taken by surprise by Stalin's withdrawal from Bretton Woods institutions; indeed, many US politicians continued to believe, at least until mid-1946, that the continuation of the alliance was possible.

However, Stalin's actions from 1945 made this increasingly unlikely:

- Stalin did not keep to the agreement made at Yalta regarding Poland. He also did not keep to his agreement to allow free elections in the other East European countries that the Red Army had liberated. Using 'salami tactics', all of these countries were under Communist control by the end of 1948, which meant a Stalinist-style one-party state with no individual freedoms. Thus his actions were perceived by the West as aggressive and expansionist.
- The Soviets exploited wartime agreements to retain a military presence in northern Iran after the war until they were forced to leave in 1946.
- The Berlin Blockade was ill-conceived and seen by the West as a prelude to a possible attack on West Germany.

- The establishment of Cominform was an attempt to control Communist parties throughout Europe, which was also a sign that Stalin wanted to spread Soviet-style Communism.
- Stalin's suspicious approach to the West meant that he interpreted all actions as deliberate attempts to weaken the USSR. His policies inside the Soviet Union indicate that he was not a leader who would support compromise and conciliation; in fact, he promoted hostility to the West within the USSR in order to get support for his policies.

It was Churchill's Fulton speech and the Kennan telegram which highlighted the implications of Stalin's actions and made Truman act to contain Communism from 1947.

Was the USA responsible for the breakdown of the Grand Alliance?

On the other side, it could be argued that Stalin had good reason for his actions after the war and that it was the overreaction of the US to these actions, along with its pursuit of economic interests, that caused the breakdown of the alliance.

The Soviet Union had experienced hostility from the West since the revolution in 1917. World War Two had a devastating effect on the country, with losses of over 20 million people and huge economic destruction. This left it weakened and with a sense of insecurity. Thus, the establishment of Soviet-style governments in the Eastern states and in Poland was an attempt to create a buffer zone to deter any future attacks. In fact, at first Stalin established broad-based coalitions in these countries, as agreed at Yalta. Also, he did not supply weapons to the Greek Communists, but abided by the Percentages Agreement, which recognized Greece as an area of British influence. Thus, Stalin's actions in setting up more Stalinist-style governments in 1947 and 1948 in Eastern Europe, and introducing the Berlin Blockade, can be seen as effects rather than as *causes* of the Cold War, stemming from the actions of the USA:

- The dropping of the **atom bomb**, which, it could be argued, was designed to make clear to Stalin the military superiority of the US.
- The US's determination to impose its own ideas for a new world order after 1945 through open markets, self-determination, democracy and collective security. Increasingly, this was seen as 'dollar diplomacy' – the US imposing its own values and advancing its own interests.
- The US's failure to take account of Soviet anxiety and insecurity, which stemmed from its previous encounters with the West and the immense losses incurred during the war. The US failed to see that Stalin's actions were not about spreading Communism but were about defending the Soviet Union.
- Truman's exaggeration of the threat of Communism in his speech to Congress, in order to get them to support aid for Greece and Turkey.
- The US's determination after 1947 to interpret all actions of the Soviet Union as being ideological; this made the Americans ignore evidence to the contrary. This can be seen particularly with regard to China becoming Communist; the Soviet Union was blamed when it was clear (also to US officials on the ground in China in 1949) that Mao's victory had little to do with Stalin.
- The US's actions with regard to the Marshall Plan, which was seen by the Soviet Union as 'Capitalist interference'.
- The introduction of a new currency into Berlin, which was provocative, and indicated to Stalin that the West was trying to establish an anti-Soviet state on his borders.
- The West's establishment of NATO, which was an aggressive action against the security of the Soviet Union.

Thus, it could be argued that Soviet foreign policy was mainly carried out in response to US actions and was an attempt to defend itself from what it saw as aggressive anti-Soviet actions. The problem was that every action Stalin took in response to the West, in order to *defend the USSR*, was seen by the West as further evidence of Soviet aggression.

What was the role of fear and suspicion in causing the breakdown of the Grand Alliance?

Fear on the part of the USA

This links to the view that ideology was the driver for the Cold War and that the USA in its actions was responding to its *fear* of Communism. This made it interpret Stalin's actions as aggressive. Although it could be argued that Stalin's actions were designed to ensure Soviet security, the USA was afraid that the USSR would go on expanding if it was not resisted by the policy of containment. Kennan in his Long Telegram and subsequent articles presented an analysis of Soviet foreign policy dictated by the pursuit of world revolution on a world scale. The developing Red Scare (see chapter 5) within the US further increased American fear of Soviet actions. Thus, when the Czech Communists seized power, this was the final straw for Congress, who then passed the Marshall Plan as a way of stopping the further spread of Communism. The Berlin Blockade was seen as further evidence of the Soviets' intention to expand aggressively and the establishment of **Comintern** as evidence of its desire to spread revolution.

The detonation of the first Soviet atom bomb in 1949 only increased the fear of the USA, leading to a nuclear arms race and the establishment of NATO.

When China became Communist and North Korea invaded South Korea, the Americans were afraid that the Soviets were expanding their power into Asia.

Fear on the part of the USSR

Similarly, it could be argued that the USSR saw the USA's actions as aggressive and was afraid that the USA was trying to pursue dollar imperialism – to win over the East European states with its economic aid. The USSR was weakened economically after World War Two while the USA had experienced an economic boom. The US's pursuit of open trade policies, the setting up of the Marshall Plan, the introduction of the new currency into the Western zones of Germany, and the establishment of NATO were all seen by the USSR as aggressive actions. The Soviets' fear was that the USA was deliberately undermining the USSR and using its nuclear superiority and economic strength to stake out its primacy.

Historians such as Gaddis have also highlighted the paranoia and fear that dictated Stalin's actions. Given Stalin's suspicious nature, it is not surprising that he viewed the actions of the West as threatening to himself and to the USSR.

Activity 1   **ATL** Communication skills

1. Set up a formal class debate:

   'This house believes that the breakdown of the Grand Alliance was due to the actions of the USA.'

   Divide the class into two. Each side should have two teams of three: first speaker, second speaker, and final speaker. The rest of the team should help write speeches and prepare questions to ask the opposing side.

   The teams take it in turn to speak. Have a break before the closing speeches to allow questions from the floor.

How have historians interpreted the origins of the Cold War?

From the early days of the Cold War, historians have attempted to explain the breakdown of the Grand Alliance. As you will see, their conclusions have largely been determined by the era in which they were writing.

The Orthodox view

The historical position known as the **Orthodox** or **Traditional view** generally holds that the Soviet Union was responsible for the Cold War. This was the position taken by historians writing in the 1950s and early 1960s. It states that the Soviets were inevitably expansionist due to their suspicion of the West and in accordance with their Marxist theory, which advocated the need to spread revolution throughout the world. Thus, Stalin violated the Yalta and Potsdam agreements, occupied and imposed Soviet control in Eastern Europe, and 'plotted' to spread Communism throughout the world, with Moscow at its centre. The United States, therefore, had to act defensively, from the Truman Doctrine and the Marshall Plan to the establishment of NATO.

Political historian Arthur M Schlesinger gives a clear analysis from the Orthodox perspective:

> 66 ***Marxism–Leninism*** *gave the Russian leaders a view of the world in which the existence of any non-Communist state was by definition a threat to the Soviet Union … An analysis of the origins of the Cold War which leaves out these factors – the intransigence of Leninist ideology, the sinister dynamics of a totalitarian society and the madness of Stalin – is obviously incomplete.*
>
> **Arthur M Schlesinger, Jr, 'Origins of the Cold War',** *Foreign Affairs* **(October 1967) pp.49–50**

Other historians who have presented the Orthodox view include WH McNeill and H Feis.

The Revisionist view

The alternative perspective, which flourished when the consensus over foreign policy in the United States was crumbling during the Vietnam War, held the USA responsible for the Cold War. **Revisionists**, such as William Appleman Williams, have explained the onset of the Cold War in terms of 'dollar diplomacy'. Revisionists see the motives behind US foreign policy as inherently linked to the needs of Capitalism. Thus, containment of Communism was driven by the requirement to secure markets and free trade, and penetrate Eastern Europe. This followed on from the United States' traditional **open-door policy** of the late 19th century.

This stance has been taken further by Revisionist historians Gabriel and Joyce Kolko, who view Soviet action as even less relevant to US foreign policy. They see American policy as determined by the nature of its Capitalist system and by fears of recession. Similarly, Thomas Patterson wrote that 'coercion characterized United States reconstruction diplomacy'. Moreover, many Revisionists hold that Stalin himself was a pragmatic leader, and had the Americans been more willing to understand the Soviets' need for security, and offer some compromises, Stalin also would have made concessions.

Perhaps the most radical thesis from the Revisionists has come from the Cambridge political economist Gar Alperovitz. This follows on from an idea put forward by British physicist PMS Blackett, who wrote that the dropping of nuclear bombs on

Hiroshima and Nagasaki was not important as the last military campaign of World War Two, but rather as the first diplomatic move by the United States in the Cold War. Alperovitz suggests that Japan was already defeated, and that this 'new' weapon of awesome power was used to warn and intimidate the Soviets.

Post-revisionist view

This school of thought does not exactly combine the Orthodox and Revisionist views, but **Post-revisionists** do stress that neither the USA nor the USSR can be held solely responsible for the origins of the Cold War. One of the key figures of this group was American historian John Lewis Gaddis. He declared in 1983 that there was a growing 'consensus' of opinion that followed the 'Post-revisionist' line of argument.

> The Cold War grew out of a complicated interaction of external and internal developments inside both the United States and the Soviet Union. The external situation – circumstances beyond the control of either power – left Americans and Russians facing one another across prostrated Europe at the end of World War Two. Internal influences in the Soviet Union – the search for security, the role of ideology, massive post-war reconstruction needs, the personality of Stalin – together with those in the United States – the need for self-determination, fear of Communism, the illusion of omnipotence fostered by American economic strength and the atomic bomb – made the resulting confrontation a hostile one. Leaders of both superpowers sought peace, but in doing so yielded to considerations, which, while they did not precipitate war, made resolution of differences impossible.

John Lewis Gaddis, *The United States and Origins of the Cold War 1941–1947* (Columbia University Press 1972) pp.359–361

John Lewis Gaddis and Walter LaFeber both agreed at this time that misperceptions played an important part at the beginning of the Cold War. Both superpowers overestimated the strength and threat of the other, and much of the growing tension of the 1940s was a result of a pattern of 'action and reaction'. Both sides were 'improvising' rather than following a well-defined 'plan of action'. Stalin's search for security was not deterred initially by strong lines being drawn, while at the same time the West did not fully recognize the Soviets' motives.

Views of the post-Cold War historians

> … as long as Stalin was running the Soviet Union, a Cold War was unavoidable.

John Lewis Gaddis, *We Now Know: Rethinking Cold War History* (OUP 1998) p.292

With the fall of the Soviet Union in 1989–1991, many new Soviet sources were made available. Russian historians were also now free to write their own accounts of the Cold War without Communist Party **censorship**. John Lewis Gaddis, who had formerly been a key spokesperson of the Post-revisionists, also had access to the new material and the initial writings of the post-Soviet-era Russian historians. He used this material to revise his Post-revisionist view, now putting even more focus on the role of Stalin in the origins of the Cold War. He suggests that it was Stalin's policies, coupled with the Soviet totalitarian/authoritarian government, that drew the West into an escalation of hostility and the protracted **arms race**. Gaddis considered the role of all other key leaders and players in the early stages of the Cold War, and concluded that had Stalin (rather than any of the others, from President Truman to Secretary of State John Foster Dulles) been removed from the equation, the Cold War would have been unlikely to develop.

What emerges generally from the post-Cold War 'new' historians is that individuals and their actions, rather than the policies of whole governments, are of vital importance in explaining key events in the Cold War. This is particularly obvious in the origins of the Korean War and in the **Berlin Crisis** of 1961 (see chapters 5 and 8).

Activity 2   (ATL) Thinking skills

1. Summarize the key ideas of the historiographical schools listed below:
   a. Orthodox/Traditional
   b. Revisionist
   c. Post-revisionist
   d. 'New' historians
2. Add examples from Steps 1 to 8 (see chapters 2 and 3) that could be used to support each of the historiographical viewpoints.

European and Soviet perspectives

What was the role of the Europeans in the development of the Cold War?

In the 1980s, mainly due to the end of the 30-year rule period that secured the confidentiality of government records, historians brought Europe and its role in the origins of the Cold War into clearer focus. Many European governments that had been economically devastated by war, harboured deep anxieties about Soviet expansionism, and this had an important impact on US foreign policy. Indeed, some historians now argue that European elites partly engineered the Cold War to lock the USA into military and economic support. The British in particular did much to heighten US awareness/perception of the 'Soviet threat'. Churchill's 'Iron Curtain' speech is an obvious case in point. European contributions suggested that both the Revisionist and the Post-revisionist historians had not satisfactorily considered the complexity of US foreign policy. A Norwegian scholar, Geir Lunestad, in an article in *Diplomatic History*, asserted that the guiding motives for American foreign policy in the early period of the Cold War can only be properly understood by taking into account the influence of external factors, such as European fears and opinions.

What is the Soviet perspective?

The historiography considered so far is all from a 'Western' perspective. Indeed, as a parallel with Western historians, it is possible to call the Soviet historians who wrote during the Cold War (due to the censorship and other controls) the 'Soviet Orthodox' group, and those who began to write following the fall of the Soviet Union, and who focused on the role of Stalin, the 'Soviet Revisionists'.

During the initial stages of the Cold War itself, the Soviet line held that the Americans were pursuing a policy of aggressive 'dollar imperialism' dictated by the needs of Capitalism. The Soviet Foreign Minister Sergei Molotov wrote a book, *Problems of Foreign Policy*, in which he accused the United States of trying to take over Europe economically and put it under the control 'of strong and enriched foreign firms, banks and industrial companies'. Thus, in response to this, Molotov said the Soviets were only attempting to 'find security', to rebuild after the 'Great Patriotic War' (World War Two) and, where and when possible, to aid in the liberation of the exploited working classes of the world.

Since the end of the Cold War and the opening of former Soviet and Eastern European archives, historians on both sides of the Iron Curtain have reconsidered the role of ideology and the search for security in Soviet foreign policy. Many historians believe that the furthering of socialist objectives became tied to the search for security following World War Two. This also meant that in the crucial initial stages of the Cold War the Soviets believed that the triumph of socialism was unavoidable, and that the USSR should aid Communist groups around the world to fulfil this aim. Other historians using the Soviet archives see the greatest motive for the USSR's foreign policy as being the fear of renewed German and Japanese aggression, and of aggression from the rest of the Capitalist world.

In line with the post-Cold War historians mentioned earlier, some Eastern European historians, such as Vojtech Mastny, focus on Stalin's role in the origins of the Cold War. This perspective could be called 'Soviet Revisionism'. Mastny sees Stalin's role as pivotal, and believes that Soviet foreign policy during this period can be explained in terms of 'Stalinism', and Joseph Stalin's own specific **modus operandi** of paranoia and suspicion.

TOK

Consider how and why historical opinion might have changed over time. Writer Margaret Atwood says 'context is all' – does this mean that 'historical truth' does not really exist?

Activity 3

1. Get into small groups or pairs. You have 10–15 minutes to put together the evidence for one of the following cases from your timelines/chapters 1–3. Also, use at least one historian's arguments to support your points.
    - Group 1: you will argue 'ideology caused the Cold War';
    - Group 2: you will argue 'fear caused the Cold War';
    - Group 3: you will argue 'aggression and traditional expansionism' caused the Cold War.

Present your case to the class – this should take about five minutes. Peers will assess which case is the 'strongest', based on the evidence and arguments presented.

Activity 4
ATL Communication skills

Essay writing

Consider the following essay question:

> **Examine the importance of ideological differences in the breakdown of the Grand Alliance.**

Introduction: Establish what the different ideologies were: that is the key differences between Capitalism and Communism. Set down a time frame to work within – perhaps 1945–1949. Make your main argument clear: for example, that the opposing ideologies of the United States and the USSR were likely to lead to conflict, but that traditional 'empire-building' rivalry was just as important. (You may want to argue that it was more important or less important, but remember to make sure that the evidence you provide in your essays supports your line of argument.)

Section 1: Deal first with the factor identified in the essay title, perhaps like this:

To a certain extent ideology can be seen as the driving force behind the breakdown of the Grand Alliance. Give examples of how both sides could view each other's actions through an ideological lens, using examples from chapters 2 and 3.

Section 2: Now look at the other side of the argument: *It can also be argued, however, that 'expansionism' and self-interest were the reasons why the Cold War started ...* Give examples from chapters 2 and 3 that support this hypothesis. You may wish to reconsider some of the examples for ideological expansionism chosen for paragraph 1 and re-analyse them as self-interest: for example, the USSR's control of the buffer states after 1945 could be interpreted in both ways. In addition, consider the view that America's pursuit of economic interests helped to increase tension. Support these points with relevant historiography.

Section 3: Now address other factors or recent viewpoints on this issue. Historians writing since the collapse of the Soviet Union have brought ideology back to the fore and see this as very important to the origins of the Cold War. However, their focus is on the ideology of Stalin in particular, and the Stalinist regime. Find other examples from chapters 2 and 3 to support these ideas.

Conclusion: Review your overall argument. Remember to follow the 'weight' of the evidence given for each argument and refer explicitly to the question: how important was ideology for the superpowers?

CHALLENGE YOURSELF

In small groups investigate the views of historians' from different regions, who have written in different languages on the origins of the Cold War and the breakdown of the Grand Alliance. Is there a consensus of opinion in different regions, or between regions? In your group create a poster that highlights the views of the historians you have researched and where their views are similar and different. Discuss the possible reasons for these similarities and differences.

Practice essay titles – the origins of the Cold War

Here are some other essay titles through which you could explore the historiographical debate on the origins of the Cold War:

- *Discuss the role Soviet policies played in the outbreak and development of the Cold War between 1945 and 1949.*
- *'The Cold War was caused by fear, not aggression.' To what extent do you agree with this statement?*
- *Compare and contrast the roles of Stalin and Truman in causing the breakdown of the Grand Alliance by 1949.*
- *Examine the role of economic interests in causing the breakdown of the Grand Alliance.*
- *To what extent was the collapse of the wartime alliance between the USA and the USSR inevitable after they had defeated their common enemies in World War Two?*

As a class discuss the following questions:

Does your study of the events and analysis of what led to the breakdown in the Grand Alliance give you a better understanding of the hostility between states today? Can we draw lessons from our study of the origins of the Cold War when considering the breakdown in relations between states today? Try to support your views with specific examples from current affairs.

To access websites relevant to this chapter, go to www.pearsonhotlinks.com, search for the book title or ISBN, and click on 'chapter 4'.

05

The Cold War goes global:
Case study in crisis: The Korean War

South Korean marines,
June 1952.

Key concepts: Causation and significance

As you read this chapter, consider the following essay questions:

- Discuss the reasons for the US policy of containment shifting to Asia after 1949.
- Examine the causes of the Korean War.
- Discuss the impact of the Korean War on the Cold War.

Cold War timeline 1949–1953		
1949	Sept	USSR gets the A-bomb
	Dec	Communist victory in Chinese Civil War
1950	April	US National Security Council produces **NSC-68**
	June	North Korea invades South Korea
	Sept	US troops land at Inchon
	Nov	Chinese launch counter-offensive
	Dec	UN troops fall back to 38th parallel
1951	Feb	UN condemns China as aggressor in Korea
	April	Eisenhower dismisses MacArthur
	July	Truce talks start in Korea
	Sept	USA and Japan sign mutual security pact
	Oct	Greece and Turkey join NATO
1952	March	USSR proposes a neutral Germany
	Nov	Eisenhower elected US president
1953	March	Death of Stalin
	July	Military **armistice** to end Korean hostilities signed

US Foreign Policy, 1949–1950

With the establishment of NATO in April 1949, the USA was optimistic that the Communists had been contained in Europe, first by the Truman Doctrine and subsequently by NATO.

In fact, NATO was quite a 'cheap' option for the USA, as its power rested on the atomic bomb. The USA, therefore, did not have to invest huge sums of money into developing conventional forces in Western Europe to match the Soviet Red Army. However, it should be noted that the USA had little choice but to rely on its nuclear threat, as after World War Two the USA had **demobilized** its fighting men, whereas the USSR had not. Thus each side had its 'ace card' – land forces for the Soviets and the atomic bomb for the USA.

However, by the autumn of 1949, two key events occurred that shifted the balance of power in favour of the USSR: the Soviet Union got a nuclear bomb of its own and China fell to the Communist forces of Mao Zedong.

The USSR gets the bomb

As mentioned above, US security, and the key basis of NATO's power, was the nuclear bomb. In August 1949 this security was shattered when the Soviet Union announced that it had developed its own atomic weapon. The USA had lost its 'ace card'. Not

North Atlantic Treaty Organization (NATO)

NATO consisted of the USA, Canada, Ireland, and 13 European states. It was the first peacetime military alliance in US history. Under its terms, an attack on one member of NATO was an attack on all. In 1952, Greece and Turkey joined, and then in 1955, much to the dismay of the USSR, West Germany joined. The USSR responded by setting up the Warsaw Pact (see chapter 3, page 40).

only that, but the USSR had achieved this far more quickly than the Americans had anticipated.

China falls to the Communists

During the **Chinese Civil War** (1945–1949) the USA had given limited support to the Nationalists under Jiang Jieshi (Chiang Kai-shek). When the country ultimately fell to the Communist guerrilla forces of Mao Zedong, the **White Paper** report on this clearly stated that the USA could not substantially have altered the outcome. It suggested that Jiang and his forces were simply too unpopular with the Chinese people, and that it had been more a case of Nationalist 'collapse' than Communist 'victory'. The White Paper saw Mao as somewhat 'independent' from Moscow. Secretary of State Dean Acheson expressed the US government's view in 1949:

> " The reasons for the failure of the Chinese National Government appear … not to stem from any inadequacy of American aid. Our military observers on the spot have reported that the Nationalist armies did not lose a single battle during the crucial year of 1948 through lack of arms or ammunition. The fact was that the decay which our observers had detected in Chongqing early in the war had fatally sapped the powers of resistance of the **Guomindang**. Its leaders had proved incapable of meeting the crisis confronting them, its troops had lost the will to fight, and its government had lost popular support. The Communists, on the other hand, through a ruthless discipline and fanatical zeal, attempted to sell themselves as guardians and liberators of the people. The Nationalist armies did not have to be defeated; they disintegrated. History has proved again and again that a regime without faith in itself and an army without morale cannot survive the test of battle.

Thus, in 1949 the American experts in Asia believed that they had done what they could in China.

The Red Scare: McCarthyism and the anti-Communist crusade in America

Anti-Communist feeling was strong in the USA after World War Two, but it reached fever pitch in the 1950s, encouraged by Senator Joseph R McCarthy of Wisconsin, who alleged that the Soviet Union had a conspiracy to place Communist sympathizers into key positions in American life. McCarthy's accusations led to 'purges' and **show trials** of those accused of 'un-American' behaviour. Some historians have drawn parallels with the show trials in Stalin's purges of the 1930s. They affected every level of US society – no group, institution, or individual was safe from suspicion. Perhaps the most infamous trial of the period was that of Julius and Ethel Rosenberg, who were convicted of spying for the Soviets and executed in 1953.

During the 1950s the 'anti-Red' crusade reached its peak. It helped to shape and intensify public opinion against Communism in America. McCarthy and his followers created an atmosphere of near-hysterical suspicion and fear of 'the enemy within', and McCarthy went as far as to call for a purge of '**comsymps**' (Communist sympathizers) in the State Department. He claimed that the Truman administration was under Communist influence and that all American liberals were Communist sympathizers.

It was in this atmosphere in February 1950 that Dean Acheson was forced to make a speech appeasing the McCarthyites. Acheson and President Truman had been the focus of an attack by McCarthy for being 'soft on Communism' and Acheson decided to 'reconsider' the findings of the 1949 White Paper on China. He went as far as to claim that China under Mao was '… completely subservient to the Moscow regime'. In other words, his view was the reverse of the impression set down in the White Paper.

▲
Mao Zedong.

▲
Joseph McCarthy.

Following this, all but two of the State Department advisers on China who had said that the Guomindang was 'not worth saving' lost their jobs. They had fallen foul of the McCarthy purges. As a result, the US government lost valuable experts on Far East foreign affairs.

Under continued pressure, Truman now called for a far-reaching review of US foreign and defence policy in response to the new threats perceived as resulting from the Chinese Communist victory and the USSR's A-bomb. It seemed now that the USA might be engaged in a Cold War on two fronts and against a Soviet Union that was now a nuclear power.

In this new climate, President Truman refused to recognize the legitimacy of the new Chinese government.

Activity 1

1. Research in more detail some of the key features and victims of the Red Scare in the USA:
   a. the Hollywood Ten
   b. HUAC (House Un-American Activities Committee)
   c. Alger Hiss
   d. the Rosenbergs
   e. the role of the **FBI**
   f. the McCarran Act
2. Why was McCarthy finally discredited?

Activity 2

1. What is the message of this cartoon regarding the impact of McCarthyism on American society?

CHALLENGE YOURSELF

Research skills

Investigate the other domestic tensions faced by the USA at this time, which were caused by segregation in the South and racial inequalities. How might internal divisions have fostered an atmosphere of insecurity within the USA?

A cartoon of McCarthy replacing the American Statue of Liberty, from the British magazine Punch in the 1950s. On the tablet, 'Human rights' has been crossed out and replaced with the words 'Report by the Investigative Commission of the Senate'.

NSC-68: 'Total Commitment'

NSC-68 was a report of the US National Security Council produced in 1950. It is seen by many historians, such as LaFeber, as 'one of the key documents of the Cold War'.

NSC-68 warned of how *all* Communist activity *everywhere* could be traced back to Moscow. It went on to say that recent developments had a 'global theme' and that they indicated the growing strength and influence of the USSR. This was the '**monolithic**' view of Communism – in other words, all Communism fed back to the 'nerve centre' in Moscow.

The report warned of an 'indefinite period of tension and danger'. It advised the US government to be ready to meet each and every challenge promptly. The report suggested an immediate increase in military strength and spending to $35–$50 billion.

The key significance of NSC-68 was that it encouraged military and economic aid to be given to *any* country perceived by the USA to be resisting Communism.

66 *Secret statement in National Security Council Report 68, State and Defense Department, Washington, April 1950:*

[We advocate] an immediate and large scale build-up in our military and general strength and that of our allies with the intention of righting the power balance and in the hope that through means other than all-out war we could induce a change in the nature of the socialist system …

The United States … can strike out on a bold and massive program of rebuilding the West's defensive potential to surpass that of the Soviet world, and of meeting each fresh challenge promptly and unequivocally … This means virtual abandonment by the United States of trying to distinguish between national and global security. It also means the end of subordinating security needs to the traditional budgeting restrictions; of asking 'How much security can we afford?' In other words, security must henceforth become the dominant element in the national budget, and other elements must be accommodated to it …

This new concept of the security needs of the nation calls for annual appropriations of the order of $50 billion, or not much below the former wartime levels.

Activity 3    ATL Thinking skills

1. Read the above extract from NSC-68. Identify key phrases in this document that you think would explain why LaFeber believes it to be one of the most important documents of the Cold War. Give reasons for your choices of particular phrases.

Revisionist historians have criticized American perceptions of Soviet intentions expressed in NSC-68. They see these perceptions as being based on a false premise and as an 'excuse' for US expansionism – the findings had little to do with the 'real' nature of the Soviet threat.

But the question was: would Americans be willing to pay? The recommendations would require a vast increase in expenditure and the American taxpayer would have to foot the bill. As historian William S Taubman comments, Acheson may have overstated the case in order to persuade the US public to 'put their money where their anti-Communist mouths were'.

Cold War Crisis: ▶

North Korea invades South Korea, 1950

President Truman's **Democratic Party** faced difficult congressional elections in November 1950. Truman wanted to shelve the issues of the recognition of China, commitment in Asia, and the recommendations of NSC-68 until afterwards. However, on 25 June 1950, 90 000 North Korean soldiers launched an invasion of South Korea. Truman had no time now for sober consideration as to whether 'total commitment' on a global scale was a wise policy to follow. The North Korean attack was seen as a clear example of Soviet expansionism. Again, it is possible to see here the United States' belief in a monolithic Communist bloc; the North Koreans were assumed to be acting on the orders of Stalin. There was a fear that failure to take action would undermine the credibility of the USA in its determination to resist Communism and would encourage a '**domino effect**' in neighbouring states. As Truman put it in a meeting with congressional leaders in 1950:

> If we let Korea down, the Soviets will keep right on going and swallow up one piece of Asia after another ... If we were to let Asia go, the Near East would collapse and no telling what would happen in Europe ... Korea is like the Greece of the Far East. If we are tough enough now, if we stand up to them like we did in Greece three years ago, they won't take any more steps.

The US response in Korea was thus dictated by the same policy it had used in Europe: containment.

After initially sending aid to South Korea, the USA sponsored a resolution in the United Nations calling for military action against North Korea. Truman saw this as an important test of the UN. If the UN ignored the North Korean invasion, it would be making the same mistake as its predecessor the League of Nations – that is, not standing up to aggressor states. As the USSR was **boycotting** the Security Council, in protest at the refusal of the USA to allow Communist China a seat on the Council, this resolution was passed on 27 June 1950. On 1 July, US troops arrived in Korea, soon to be joined by 15 other nations under a UN commander – American General Douglas MacArthur. Thus the USA once again found itself at war, and this, as Acheson later explained, 'removed the recommendations of NSC-68 from the realm of theory and made them immediate budget issues'.

Activity 4 | Self-management skills

1. Look back over the chapter so far. What a) international considerations and b) domestic considerations would have had an influence on Truman's decision to become involved in the Korean War?

Why did North Korea attack South Korea in 1950?

This first 'hot war' of the Cold War era, which had far-reaching consequences, was not one that the USA had expected to fight at any stage before 1950. Why, then, did it take place?

Background to the conflict

Japan had officially annexed Korea in 1910 and was still in occupation of Korea when World War Two ended. Korean nationalists, who had led a revolution in 1945 and who included many Communists, were not allowed to decide the fate of Korea in 1945 and it was agreed by the USA and the USSR that the two superpowers would take joint responsibility for **repatriating** the Japanese forces there. The **38th parallel** line of latitude was taken as the dividing point, with the USSR occupying Korea north of the line and the USA occupying Korea south of the line.

This was originally intended to be a temporary arrangement and, at the Council of Foreign Ministers' Moscow Conference in December 1945, the United States and the

The Council of Foreign Ministers

The **Council of Foreign Ministers** was an organization agreed upon at the Potsdam Conference in 1945, towards the end of World War Two. It consisted of the foreign ministers of the UK, USSR, China, France, and the United States, and had the job of drawing up peace treaties with various countries, sorting out territorial questions, and making a peace settlement for Germany. At the later **Moscow Conference** it also dealt with how Japan and Korea were to be governed.

Soviet Union agreed on the creation of a Korean provisional government, followed by a short period of international trusteeship or supervision, leading eventually to independence.

This was difficult to achieve, however, because:

- As the Cold War developed, the USA and the USSR became less willing to co-operate.
- Despite the Moscow Agreement, separate administrations emerged on either side of the 38th parallel. In the South, the US military government put forward as leader the elderly Syngman Rhee, a rebel who had fought against the Japanese and spent much of his life in exile. The Soviets supported the Communists and backed a faction headed by Kim Il Sung, a young Russian-trained Korean Communist who had been a guerrilla fighter against the Japanese. Although the two men were very different, they had much in common: both were Korean nationalists, both wanted to end the division of Korea, and each saw himself as the leader of a united Korea.

In the increasingly tense atmosphere of the Cold War, the division of Korea was confirmed in 1947. The Americans persuaded the UN to establish a commission to supervise Korean elections. This commission was refused entry into the North, but observed a separate election in the South in May 1948. Although most Koreans opposed partition, the Republic of Korea (**ROK**) was set up in the South under Syngman Rhee. It was an undemocratic and strongly anti-Communist administration, which was recognized as legitimate by the UN General Assembly. In response, the Democratic People's Republic of Korea (**DPRK**) was founded in the North under Kim Il Sung in September 1948, and was immediately recognized by the Communist bloc.

Although the USA supported Syngman Rhee with economic and military aid, they did not intend to station troops in the ROK, and the US military had left South Korea by mid-1949. Soviet troops left North Korea in 1948. The United States made it clear that they still saw Europe as the most important area in the Cold War, but decided to maintain a line of offshore strong points, stretching from Japan to the Philippines, rather than involve themselves in expensive military commitments on the mainland. This was made clear in Dean Acheson's **'perimeter' speech** of January 1950, in which both South Korea and Taiwan were publicly excluded from the American defensive perimeter in the Western Pacific.

Activity 5

1. What similarities and what differences are there in the way in which Germany and Korea each became divided into two separate countries?

Why did the superpowers get involved?

So, having both withdrawn their troops, why did the superpowers become involved in a war on this peninsula? The thinking of Orthodox historians followed the US views of 1950: that this was an attack initiated and led by Stalin. Revisionist historians later claimed that Stalin had no role in the invasion, and that the North was possibly responding to attacks from the South. Historian Bruce Cumings, writing in 1981, stated that Soviet control over the DPRK was 'flimsy' and that Kim Il Sung could have acted independently of the Soviets since the DPRK was by no means solely reliant on Soviet arms. Fortunately, the opening of the Soviet archives after 1990 made it much easier to unravel the controversial causes of this war and to clarify the roles of Kim Il Sung and of Stalin.

What was the role of Kim Il Sung in starting the war?

Kim Il Sung's role is key to explaining this war. It is clear that both Syngman Rhee and Kim Il Sung wanted to unify the country. Thus a civil war would have begun here in any case, regardless of the involvement of the superpowers. However, neither side could unify the country on its own, and thus the involvement of the Soviets in support of Kim Il Sung, or the Americans in support of Syngman Rhee, was essential for success. Kim Il Sung put a huge amount of effort into persuading Stalin that he should back an attack on the South. Stalin initially had no interest in these plans and Kim Il Sung obtained Stalin's approval only after persistent appeals. Thus it is clear that the impetus for war came from Pyongyang and not from Moscow. The Truman administration's assumption in June 1950 that the war was Stalin's initiative is therefore false, though his support for Kim Il Sung was key in allowing the war to go ahead.

Kim Il Sung.

What was the role of Stalin in starting the war?

Although initially unwilling to agree to Kim Il Sung's plans for a war against the South, the evidence shows that Stalin gave his approval at the beginning of 1950. There are several possible reasons for his change of mind:

- Stalin may have been more hopeful about the chances of world revolution. The fact that the Communists had won the Chinese Civil War, that the Soviets now had the atomic bomb, and that the West was facing economic difficulties, might have convinced Stalin that now was the time to push forward with spreading Soviet influence in Asia.
- The United States' role in Japan could have provided an impetus to gain influence specifically in Korea. Stalin knew that the United States had changed its policy in Japan and was now turning Japan into a strong anti-Communist base (see chapter 6, pages 74–75); if he could gain control of South Korea, this could secure the Soviet position in northeast Asia.
- Historian John Lewis Gaddis points out Stalin's opportunism as another possible factor – his tendency to advance himself in situations where he thought he could do so without provoking too strong a response. Acheson's perimeter speech could have provided Stalin with a 'tempting opportunity'.

Although he had changed his mind about supporting the attack, Stalin nevertheless remained cautious. He warned 'the Korean friends' not to 'expect great assistance and support from the Soviet Union', because it had 'more important challenges to meet than the Korean problem'. He also made it clear that Kim Il Sung would have to gain the approval of Mao Zedong. 'If you get kicked in the teeth, I will not lift a finger. You have to ask Mao for all the help.' Nevertheless, Stalin's support was key to enabling the invasion to take place, and Soviet commanders were involved in all aspects of the preparation and execution of the attack.

What was the role of Mao Zedong in the outbreak of the war?

When Kim Il Sung visited the People's Republic of China, Mao was initially sceptical about the success of the invasion, but gave his approval because Kim fostered the impression that Stalin was more enthusiastic than Mao actually was, and also because Mao was at this time planning an invasion of Taiwan. He needed Soviet support for this and worried that if he expressed reservations about the invasion, Stalin might also show concern about the results of an attack on Taiwan. Having given his approval, he asked Kim if he needed troops stationed on the Korean border in case the Americans intervened, but Kim said that this would not be necessary. Mao then seems to have paid little attention to the actual preparations that were going on in North Korea.

When the attack on the South came, it surprised not only Mao, but also the South Koreans and the Americans. Planning to win the war quickly, the North carried out a massive tank attack, and it was the nature of this attack that caused the United States to take such swift and dramatic action.

Activity 6 Thinking skills

1. John Lewis Gaddis suggests that the Korean War could be called 'A Comedy of Errors'. Discuss what misconceptions guided the thinking of Truman, Stalin, and Mao during the planning and course of the Korean War.

2. You can use the initial crisis period that followed the North Korean invasion of the South as a Case Study in crisis. Instead of using the course of the war itself, focus on the crisis that led to the US-led UN force intervening.

In pairs discuss the following question using the crisis over Korea in June 1950 as your case study:

Examine the causes of one Cold War crisis.

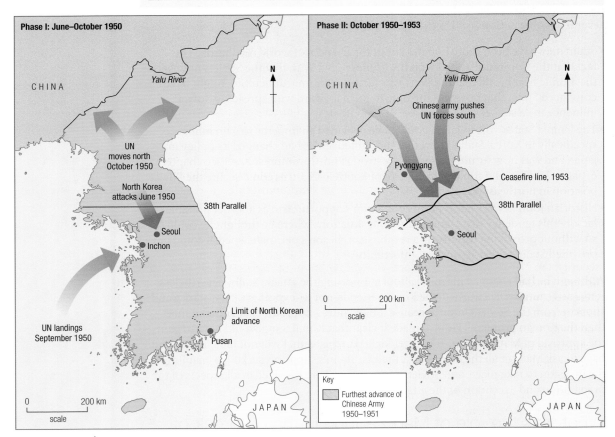

These maps show Phase 1 and Phase 2 of the Korean War.

The course of the war

There were several dramatic changes in the course of the war over the first few months, followed by a stalemate situation, which lasted until the **armistice** in 1953.

- The initial push by the North Koreans took them deep into South Korea, leaving only a corner of the peninsula out of their control. South Korean and American troops were pushed back into a small area around Pusan (now called Busan).

The invasion of Inchon.

- General MacArthur led the UN forces in an amphibious landing at Inchon, in order to bypass the Korean troops and cut them off. Within a month he had retaken Seoul and driven the North Koreans back to the 38th parallel.
- Encouraged by this success, the United States then redefined its war aims, and, rather than just concentrating on 'containment', now decided on a policy of **'roll-back'**. This would mean liberating the North Koreans from Communist rule and reuniting Korea. UN forces crossed the 38th parallel into North Korean territory and began a rapid advance northwards, capturing Pyongyang, the capital of the North, in October.
- The march towards the Yalu river, however, made China concerned about its own security. On 27 November 1950, a force of 200 000 Chinese joined 150 000 North Koreans and sent the UN troops into a rapid retreat. Pyongyang was recaptured in December, and by the end of 1950 the North Koreans and their allies had retaken all land up to the 38th parallel. There were heavy American casualties in the bitter cold, and many were taken prisoner.
- A stalemate then developed around the 38th parallel.
- Truman now realized that the United States needed to go back to the original aim of containing Communism above the 38th parallel. MacArthur disagreed, claiming, 'Here in Asia is where the Communist conspirators have elected to make their play for global conquest. Here we fight Europe's war with arms while the diplomats there still fight it with words.' He was subsequently relieved of his command.
- Peace talks started in 1951 with a focus on the **repatriation** of prisoners of war (POWs).
- The war continued for another two years, during which time fighting continued, causing serious casualties (over 40 per cent of American casualties occurred in this period). The United States put pressure on China by threatening to use atomic weapons.
- A military armistice was finally signed at Panmunjom in July 1953.

General Douglas MacArthur (1880–1964)

MacArthur had fought in World War One and received 13 medals for bravery. He became chief of staff of the US Army in 1930, and during World War Two he was the commander of the war against the Japanese – responsible for the successful island-hopping strategy that pushed the Japanese back from their island strongholds. Following the surrender of the Japanese, he was put in control of rebuilding Japan and developing a new constitution (see chapter 6). At the age of 70 he was put in charge of the UN forces in Korea. However, although he was successful in pushing back the North Koreans, he was dismissed by Truman in 1951 because of his public calls for the use of the atomic bomb against China. He returned to the USA to be greeted as a hero by the American public, but he was unsuccessful in his bid to be nominated as a presidential candidate in 1952.

Activity 7 — ATL Thinking skills

1. What is meant by the reference to using a 'roundish one'?
2. What is the problem with using only a 'squarish one'?

"We've Been Using More Of A Roundish One"

This American cartoon by Herblock appeared in the *Washington Post* newspaper in 1951.

CHALLENGE YOURSELF

ATL Research skills

Research the term 'limited war'. Why was Korea called a 'limited war'? What problems are there with calling Korea a 'limited war'? What other examples of 'limited wars' can you find in the 20th and 21st centuries?

Activity 8 — ATL Thinking and social skills

1. Consider and discuss how the Korean War can be seen as a civil war.

66

Results of the Korean War

Actions of the United States

Fearing that the attack of North Korea on South Korea would be followed by further Soviet aggression elsewhere in the world, the USA carried out the following measures:

- NSC-68's recommendation to triple the defence budget was implemented.
- US land forces in Europe were greatly strengthened.
- NATO was strengthened. Greece and Turkey were brought into NATO and military bases were set up in Turkey (which had a border with the USSR).
- The need for West Germany to become armed and integrated into NATO was given top priority.

Many of these measures had already been under consideration, and the effect of the Korean War was to accelerate these US policies.

In Asia, the United States also took several important steps against what it saw as the threats of Communism (see also chapter 6):

- The Treaty of San Francisco with Japan was signed in 1952. This enabled the United States to maintain military bases in Japan. The United States now also focused on building up Japan economically to make it a bulwark against Communism.
- Taiwan had to be defended as well. At the start of the Korean War, the US **Seventh Fleet** had already been sent to the Taiwan Strait to defend the island against possible Communist invasion. Following the Korean War, the USA supported Taiwan's Jiang Jieshi with military and economic aid and continued to recognize Taiwan as the only official Chinese state until as late as 1971.
- China was now isolated by the United States. It was condemned by the UN as an aggressor and prevented from taking a seat in the UN Security Council.
- The USA also became committed to supporting other regimes in Asia that it believed were resisting Communism. This eventually led to US involvement in the Philippines and in Vietnam.
- **SEATO** (Southeast Asia Treaty Organization) was formed as an anti-Communist containment bloc in the Asian area.

What did the Korean War and the subsequent actions of the USA mean for other countries?

For Korea

The cost in human lives and property was vast; there was also no hope of reunification. This was no longer a local issue, but a superpower issue, and the ceasefire line turned into a heavily armed Cold War frontier. North Korea has subsequently remained under Communist rule. South Korea became a model Capitalist success story with heavy American and Japanese investment.

For China

Although now isolated by the USA, China's reputation grew greatly and it became a major power in the region. It preserved its own revolution, took on the USA, and successfully 'saved' North Korea. This increased Mao Zedong's reputation at home and strengthened the Chinese revolution. However, it also meant that valuable resources at home were diverted away from recovery to the war effort, and in addition China's aim of uniting Taiwan and China had become far more difficult to achieve.

The ceasefire line at the end of the Korean War left Korea divided into two separate states. This 'two-state solution' has meant Korea remains a periodic focus of international tension today. Investigate recent reports and articles about events in North and South Korea. How are the two countries viewed around the world? How do Koreans view the division of their country in the 21st century? To what extent is the situation in Korea stable?

Stalin's reluctance throughout the war to help Mao with any substantial military commitments also meant that in future Mao would be less likely to rely on Soviet help, and would be less concerned about following Moscow's lead (see chapter 11).

For the USSR

Although the USSR had kept out of direct conflict with the USA, the results of the Korean War were not good for the Soviet Union. The USA's decision to triple its defence budget, rearm West Germany, maintain troops in Europe, and fight Communism in Asia, meant that the Soviet Union was now embroiled in an even more intense – and broader – Cold War standoff than had existed in 1950.

For Southeast Asia

The USA's perception of all Communist movements being part of a 'monolithic' movement, and its commitment to intervene wherever it saw the threat of Communism on the move, meant that Southeast Asia became involved in the Cold War. It was now harder for nationalist movements in the region to triumph in the post-colonial era and many of these groups were forced into increasing dependence on the USSR or China. However, it was only in Vietnam that the USA, the USSR, and China became directly involved in the fighting.

Korean civilians flee fighting during the Korean war.

The effects of the Korean War on the Cold War

The Korean War caused the globalization of the superpower rivalry and confrontation. The USA and USSR now found themselves embroiled in conflicts in Asia as well as Europe, and these conflicts would soon spread to other parts of the **developing world**. It also led to the militarization of the Cold War. To maintain the now-greater military commitments, US defence spending increased dramatically, running at around 10 per cent of American **GNP** in the 1950s. In Europe, there was also increased military spending, which helped to boost the economic prosperity of both regions. In the Soviet Union, the Red Army increased from 2.8 million troops in 1950 to almost 5.8 million by 1955. Stalin's successors, however, cut military spending sharply after 1955, though they continued with the development of nuclear armaments.

Warren I Cohen writes the following regarding the impact of the Korean War:

> *Arming the North Koreans and agreeing to the invasion of South Korea proved to be Stalin's most disastrous Cold War gamble. It postponed a thaw in relations with the United States for twenty years. It intensified a confrontation that continued for forty years at enormous cost to the major antagonists. The war shifted the balance of forces within the United States, allowing them to divert the attention and energies of the American people from needed reform to the hunt of Communists at home and abroad. It allowed the creation of a military–industrial complex that consumed the productive power of the American economy and fuelled conflict all over the world. The Korean War altered the nature of the Soviet–American confrontation, changing it from a systematic political competition into an ideologically driven, militarized conflict that threatened the very survival of the globe.*

Warren I Cohen, *America in the Age of Soviet Power 1945–1991* (CUP 1995) p.66

The development of the military–industrial complex

The huge increase in spending triggered by NSC-68 had important effects inside the United States. It gave a boost to the arms production industries through greater opportunities to get government contracts. Many politicians, including Eisenhower, worried about the growing political and economic strength of this sector of industry – or the **military–industrial complex** as Eisenhower termed it in his valedictory address.

Activity 9 — ATL: Thinking and social skills

Case study in crisis: North Korean invasion of South Korea, June 1950

1. You have already examined the causes of this Cold War crisis. Now, in pairs, draft a bullet-point response to the following question, using the Korean Crisis in June 1950 as your case study.

Examine the impact and significance of one Cold War crisis.

Activity 10 — ATL: Communication skills

Using the information in this chapter:

1. Annotate a map of the world to show the impact of the Korean War.

   Or

2. Draw a mind map/spider diagram to show the results of the Korean War.

Interpreting historical sources

On the source-based Paper 1, you will need to show an understanding of a range of different types of historical documents, such as statistics, cartoons, photographs, or written sources.

You will need to be able to show that you understand what the inference or the message of the source is, and, in order to do this well, you will need to use your contextual historical knowledge: for example, your knowledge of the person who created the source, or the historical events that were going on at the time the source was produced. Sometimes there may be several points being made in the source; you need to 'read between the lines' to understand the more subtle message the source conveys.

Assessing sources for their values and limitations

This involves focusing on the origin, the purpose, and the content of the source in order to assess how useful it might be to the historian.

Origin: When using and interpreting sources you need to look first at the nature of the source: that is, what kind of source it is – a photograph, diary, memoir, speech, cartoon, or letter. The type of source will have an influence on how useful it is: for instance, a personal letter can be very useful because the person writing it will usually be giving private views.

You also need to look at where or from whom a source comes and when it was produced. Your knowledge of the person or organization that produced it will help you assess the source's usefulness – for example, was the source written by someone who was likely to have known what was going on?

Purpose: Here you are looking at why the source was produced, written, or drawn, and the audience it was intended for. Was it produced for propaganda purposes? Was it produced to make a person support one particular viewpoint? Was it produced for private, personal purposes? Was it produced to inform people?

Content: The language of the source gives clues as to how useful it is. For instance, is the language exaggerated and clearly slanted in favour of one point of view? Or does the language appear to be objective in tone and language?

- Always come back to the question. It is no good stating what the purpose, origin, and content of a source is if you do not then apply this to answering the question. Use your conclusions about the origin, purpose, and content of the source to answer the question that has been set.
- If a question is asking for both the value and limitations of a source, always start by looking for its value, and then move on to its limitations.
- Don't forget that even if a source has many limitations, it can still be valuable to a historian. It just depends on what question the historian is asking. For example, a propaganda speech by Stalin is not very useful for explaining the true situation in the Soviet Union. However, it can be useful for showing us the nature of Soviet propaganda and the type of information that the Soviet Union wanted the Soviet people of the West to hear.

Cross-referencing historical sources

Cross-referencing questions ask you to look for similarities and differences between two sources. You need to discuss the sources together throughout your response. Write one paragraph on the similarities and one paragraph on the differences. For each point of similarity or difference, include a brief quote or specific reference from each source to back up your argument. You should attempt to find at least six points of comparison and contrast. You may find that there are more points of similarity or more points of difference, not always a 3–3 split, but sometimes a 2–4 or a 4–2. However, you must find similarities *and* differences, even if there are more of one than the other.

Source analysis

Throughout this book there are many activities designed to help you develop the source-analysis skills you will need for Paper 1. The questions on Paper 1 will be looking to test your skills in:

- interpreting historical sources
- cross-referencing historical sources
- analysing sources for their value and limitations
- using sources, in conjunction with your own knowledge, in a historical explanation

Activity 11   ATL Thinking skills

1. Find an example of some of the following historical sources in relation to the Korean War. Assess why each type of source might be useful for a historian studying the nature of this war and how it was fought. What might be the limitations of each of these sources?

   a. private letters/diaries   g. memoirs

   b. poems/novels   h. drawings/paintings

   c. cartoons   i. photographs

   d. newspaper articles   j. statistics

   e. government records   k. eyewitness accounts

   f. speeches by politicians

Activity 12

 ATL Thinking skills

Source A

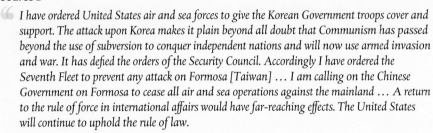

Dear brothers and sisters!

*Great danger threatens our motherland and its people. What is needed to liquidate this menace? In this war which is being waged against the Syngman Rhee **clique**, the Korean people must defend the Korean Democratic People's Republic and its constitution, they must liquidate the unpatriotic fascist puppet regime of Syngman Rhee which has been established in the southern part of the republic; they must liberate the southern part of our motherland from the domination of the Syngman Rhee clique and they must restore the peoples' committees there – the real organs of power. Under the banner of the Korean Democratic People's Republic we must complete the unification of the motherland and create a single, independent, democratic state. The war which we are forced to wage is a just war for the unification and independence of the motherland and for freedom and democracy.*

Broadcast of Kim Il Sung to the nation, 26 June 1950

Source B

I have ordered United States air and sea forces to give the Korean Government troops cover and support. The attack upon Korea makes it plain beyond all doubt that Communism has passed beyond the use of subversion to conquer independent nations and will now use armed invasion and war. It has defied the orders of the Security Council. Accordingly I have ordered the Seventh Fleet to prevent any attack on Formosa [Taiwan] … I am calling on the Chinese Government on Formosa to cease all air and sea operations against the mainland … A return to the rule of force in international affairs would have far-reaching effects. The United States will continue to uphold the rule of law.

Statement by US President Truman, 27 June 1950

1. What are the key points made in Source A regarding the reasons for North Korea's invasion of South Korea?
2. With reference to the origin, purpose and content, assess the values and limitations of Source A for historians studying why the Korean War started.
3. Compare and contrast the two sources' explanations of 25 June 1950.

Activity 13

ATL Thinking skills

Practice essay titles – Korea

- *To what extent do you agree with the view that the main reason for UN action in Korea was US anti-Communism?*
- *Compare and contrast the roles of the USA and the USSR in Korea between 1945 and 1953.*

Review essay questions using chapters 2 to 5

- *Compare and contrast the roles of the superpowers in the causes and course of two Cold War crises, each chosen from a different region.*
- *Compare and contrast the impact and significance of two Cold War crises, each chosen from a different region.*

In question 1 you will need to identify at least three clear points. Avoid repeating the same point!

 TOK

Discuss the following questions as a class or in small groups. Feed back ideas and make notes of your key points in your Theory of Knowledge journals.

- How do historians assess the reliability of different sources? Are some sources innately of more value than others? Consider different types of sources, including speeches, diaries, memoirs, archives, newspaper reports, court hearings, interviews, websites, and the work of historians. Are there any 'general rules' or does it depend specifically on the origin, purpose and content of a source?
- If facts alone cannot prove or disprove something, what else is involved in assessing a historical account?

To access websites relevant to this chapter, go to www.pearsonhotlinks. com, search for the book title or ISBN, and click on 'chapter 5'.

06

The USA and containment in Asia

Key concepts: Significance and continuity

As you read this chapter, consider the following essay questions:

- To what extent was the US policy of containment successful in Asia?
- Examine the impact of the US policy of containment in Asia.

As discussed in chapter 5, the Korean War confirmed to the USA that fighting Communism was not limited to Europe, but was now a worldwide struggle. Containment, therefore, became a key policy in Asia as the United States sought to hold back the spread of Communism. The domino effect had to be avoided at all costs.

Timeline of Asian containment	
1950	Korean War starts
1951	US–Japanese Treaty
1952	US occupation of Japan ends
1953	End of the Korean War
1954	Fall of Dien Bien Phu
	Geneva Accords on French **Indochina**
	Defence pact between USA and Taiwan
	SEATO is established
1955	First Taiwan crisis
1958	Second Taiwan crisis
1963	President Ngo Dinh Diem assassinated
	President John F Kennedy assassinated
1964	Gulf of Tonkin incident
	Congress passes Gulf of Tonkin Resolution
1965	US marines land in Vietnam
	Operation Rolling Thunder starts
1968	**Tet Offensive**
	My Lai Massacre
1969	Paris Peace Talks begin
	President Richard Nixon announces '**Nixon Doctrine**' and **Vietnamization**
1970	Invasion of Cambodia by US and South Vietnamese troops
	Students killed at Kent State University
1972	President Nixon visits China
1973	Paris Peace Agreement signed
	United States withdraws from Vietnam
1975	North Vietnamese troops take over Saigon
	Cambodia falls to **Khmer Rouge**

In this chapter there are four examples of the United States actively seeking to contain Communism in Asia. How successful were the US efforts in each case?

CASE STUDY 1: KOREA

Soldiers being driven to the front line of the Korean War.

On the surface, Korea (see also chapter 5) can be seen as a success for the US policy of containment, as Communism was kept north of the 38th parallel. However, as General Douglas MacArthur had gone further than the original aim of pushing the North Koreans back north of the 38th parallel, and had attempted to 'roll-back' Communism, the end result was something of a 'mutilated' success. The Americans had been routed by the Chinese army, and the losses of both UN forces and Korean civilians were huge. The impact on US foreign policy, with NSC-68 coming into force and thus the militarization and globalization of the Cold War, also needs to be considered when assessing if intervention in Korea can be considered a 'success'. By 1953, Communism had clearly been contained in Korea, but at great cost: both in terms of human and economic losses, and in terms of the impact on future US policy.

CASE STUDY 2: JAPAN

The policy of containment was more clearly a success in Japan.

The United States had occupied Japan following its defeat in 1945. General MacArthur was appointed Supreme Commander of the Allied Powers (**SCAP**), and he was given great powers to devise and execute policies. The American objective was to create a weak and **pacifist** Japan, but this policy was to change radically as the USA decided that Japan was a vital strategic area in Asia for its policy of containment.

MacArthur's initial tasks were to demilitarize the country, bring war criminals to trial, and then devise a new constitution. When completed, this included a **Bill of Rights** and a clause 'renouncing war forever'. Japan's royal family survived these changes, but the emperor's role was reduced from demi-god to being merely a focus of the people's unity.

The emphasis of this new constitution was very much on the rights of the individual, as one of the fundamental beliefs of SCAP was that the most effective way of 'curing' the Japanese of their militarism was by creating a fully democratic society. Around 2500 political prisoners were released from prison – many were Communists – and laws were introduced which were favourable to trade unions and which attempted to break up the hugely powerful elite Japanese families (the **Zaibatsu**).

However, the shift in focus of the Cold War to Asia in 1950 changed many of MacArthur's original policies. Suddenly there was a need for a strong, anti-Communist ally in Asia to counter-balance the new Communist Chinese state: the People's Republic of China. Japan would be that ally, so it was now essential that Communism within Japan should be wiped out. Japan also needed to be economically and militarily capable of resisting Communist threats from other Asian countries. Japanese economic recovery and independence became the most important objective of SCAP. As a result, some trade unions were banned from striking and restrictions were placed on Communists, while the old values of duty and loyalty regained their importance. The *Zaibatsu* were also allowed to continue. This was known as the 'reverse course'. A 'red purge' began, which eliminated thousands of left-wing officials from government and union positions.

The most notable retreat from the idealism of the early occupation was the revised thinking about Japan's defence. It no longer made sense for the United States to seek a weak and pacifist Japan. Therefore, shortly after the outbreak of the Korean War in June 1950, Japan was permitted to establish a 75 000-strong paramilitary force called the 'self-defence force'. American military influence also continued after the end of the occupation in 1952. Together with the Treaty of San Francisco, the **American–Japanese Security Treaty** was signed in 1951, leaving Japan in effect a military protectorate of the USA. The treaty provided for the retention of American bases and allowed the United States to use the American forces stationed there in any way that would contribute to the 'maintenance of international peace and security in the Far East'. It prohibited Japan from granting military bases to any other power without American consent.

Was containment a success in Japan?

The United States achieved the aim of making Japan its bulwark against Communism in the Far East. Japan's economy developed rapidly and, following the so-called economic miracle, it emerged as a great economic power under the control of a Conservative government, which succeeded in forging a strong national consensus in favour of economic growth as Japan's priority. Thus there was never any threat of Communism spreading to Japan. However, historians have challenged how far this was due to the policies of the USA or the efforts of the Japanese themselves. The attitude of the Japanese people, their government's policies, and their approach to hard work were perhaps at least as important as the policies of SCAP.

It should also be noted that the United States would have liked Japan to become much more of a bulwark against Communism. The USA wanted Japan to establish a large military force and to join a regional defence alliance. The Japanese government resisted these demands. The government knew that the US presence in Japan would deter a Soviet attack and it could meanwhile give priority to the pursuit of Japan's economic miracle. With the USA picking up their 'defence bill', the Japanese had money to invest in their economic development.

General MacArthur and Emperor Hirohito.

CASE STUDY 3: TAIWAN

Containment in Taiwan was also seen as a success. US policy towards Taiwan (**Formosa**) changed with the outbreak of the Korean War. Before this time, the USA had no formal plans to help the Nationalists resist an invasion from Communist China. However, when North Korea attacked South Korea, President Truman immediately ordered the US Seventh Fleet to the Taiwan Strait to keep peace between the Nationalist and Communist Chinese. From this point on, the United States recognized Taiwan as the only official Chinese state (this was to remain the situation until 1971) and gave substantial economic and military aid to the island in order to contain Chinese Communism.

Map showing the Taiwan Strait and the islands of Matsu and Quemoy.

American President Dwight D Eisenhower withdrew the Seventh Fleet in 1953 to 'unleash' Taiwan's Nationalist leader, Jiang Jieshi, and allow him to attack mainland China. Nationalists raided the coast of China, which was used as an excuse by the Chinese to bombard the islands of Quemoy and Matsu (see map on page 75) and invade the Tachen Islands. In response, Congress passed the **Formosa Resolution**, which allowed President Eisenhower to take whatever military action he thought was necessary to defend Taiwan. Eisenhower told China that if it took over Taiwan, the United States would use nuclear weapons against a Chinese mainland target. These were Eisenhower's policies of '**massive retaliation**' and 'brinkmanship' in action (see chapter 7). The American president also got the USSR to put pressure on China, and it finally backed down.

When China then bombarded Quemoy and Matsu in 1958, the Seventh Fleet was ordered into the Taiwan Strait and the United States again threatened use of nuclear weapons. China again backed down, though it is worth noting that the United States was unhappy about getting dragged into yet another conflict to protect Taiwan, just as the USSR was unhappy that Mao was taking such risks.

Was containment a success in Taiwan?

Despite the dangers of these crises over Quemoy and Matsu, brinkmanship seemed to have won the day, and Taiwan continued to maintain its independence with American support. (See chapter 11 for more discussion on US action in relation to Taiwan.)

CASE STUDY 4: AN IN-DEPTH STUDY OF THE USA AND CONTAINMENT IN VIETNAM

'Dominoes', a cartoon by Herblock from 1964.

Dominoes

The most striking failure of the US policy of containment was in Vietnam, where the North Vietnamese Communists were not contained. After a decade of military involvement, the loss of hundreds of thousands of American lives, billions of dollars, and the damaging division of US public opinion, the Americans pulled out of Vietnam in 1973. Their fear of other Asian countries 'falling like dominoes' if Communism was not contained seemed to be realized when not only Vietnam but also Cambodia and Laos fell to Communist forces in 1975.

How did the United States become involved?

Indochina (Vietnam, Cambodia, and Laos) was a French **colony** that had been occupied during World War Two by the Japanese. During this time a nationalist movement had grown, and most Vietnamese had no desire to let Vietnam return to the rule of the French after 1945. The most important nationalist was a Communist called Ho Chi Minh, who led a movement called the **Vietminh** that was very active against the Japanese. When the Japanese were defeated in 1945, Ho declared the independence of the Democratic Republic of Vietnam.

The French, however, had no intention of allowing Vietnam to have its independence and hostilities broke

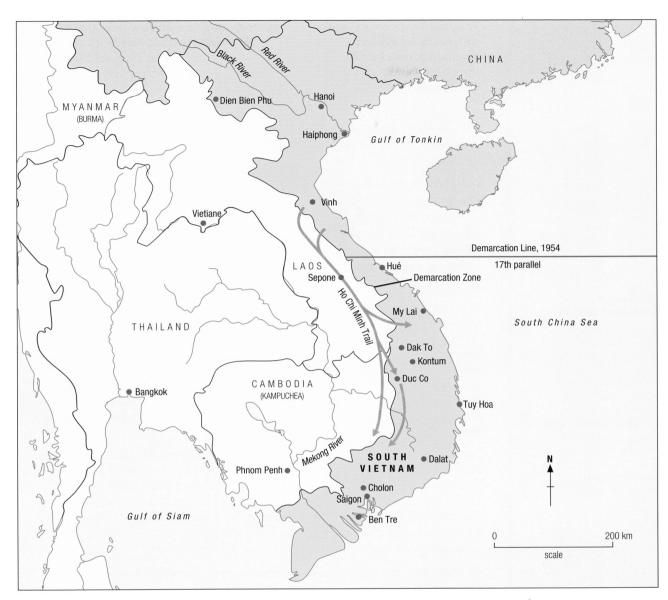

This map of Indochina shows the division of Vietnam after the Geneva Accords, and the Ho Chi Minh Trail.

out between the French and the Vietminh in 1946. Although President Roosevelt had pressured France to relinquish its hold over Vietnam, American opinion towards Ho and the Vietminh hardened once Truman was president. This was due to the developing international situation in Europe and, after 1949, Asia. As the Cold War intensified in both areas, Ho's Communist, rather than nationalist, credentials were emphasized, and the assumption grew that he was being directed from Moscow.

In March 1950, military aid was sent to help France defeat the Vietminh. This aid was continued by Eisenhower, who gave the following reasoning for his government's actions in April 1954:

> You have the specific value of a locality in its production of materials that the world needs. You have the possibility that many human beings pass under a dictatorship that is inimical to the free world. You have the broader considerations that might follow what you would call the 'falling domino' principle ... You have a row of dominoes set up, you knock over the first one, and what will happen to the last one is the certainty that it will go over very quickly.

Thus, the idea of countries turning to Communism like dominoes falling over became entrenched in US government thinking. The domino effect identified Vietnam as the key domino that must not be allowed to fall if Laos, Cambodia, Thailand, Burma, Malaya, Indonesia, and even possibly Singapore and Japan, were to remain safe from Communism.

Although the United States was funding 80 per cent of the war by 1954, President Eisenhower made the decision not to directly intervene, and in that year the French were finally defeated at the battle of Dien Bien Phu. In 1954, at Geneva in Switzerland, a peace agreement (the **Geneva Accords**) was drawn up which decided that:

- The French would withdraw from Indochina.
- There would be a temporary division of Vietnam at the **17th parallel**. Ho Chi Minh would control the north of the country.
- There would be 'free elections' to unite Vietnam in 1956.
- There were to be no foreign bases.
- Laos and Cambodia would be recognized as independent states.

Significantly, the USA did not sign the Geneva Accords. In response to the agreement, they attempted to strengthen the area south of the 17th parallel, supporting a non-Communist government that would be able to resist an invasion from the North. To offset the results of the Geneva Accords, they also established SEATO (the Southeast Asia Treaty Organization). This was signed by Australia, Britain, France, New Zealand, Pakistan, the Philippines, and Thailand. These countries agreed to meet together if there was an armed attack on one of them and, if agreement was unanimous, to take action. In defiance of the Geneva Accords, which said that Laos and Cambodia should remain neutral, SEATO included South Vietnam, Laos, and Cambodia as its 'protected areas'. It thus became a legal basis for future US action in Vietnam.

The man that the United States backed to lead the government in the South was Ngo Dinh Diem, a Catholic who had been educated in the USA. In October 1955, Diem proclaimed the establishment of the Republic of Vietnam (also known as South Vietnam) with himself as president. US aid worth millions of dollars was sent to Diem, and the United States also began its military involvement in the South with the commencement of training of the South Vietnamese army. By 1960 almost 1000 Americans were serving in South Vietnam as military 'advisers'.

Although the United States pressed Diem to carry out reform in the South, Diem turned out to be a ruthless leader who, along with his brother Ngo Dinh Nhu, the chief of police, crushed opposition brutally. Land reforms were not forthcoming, and the Catholic faith was promoted, despite the fact that most Vietnamese were Buddhists. Soon it became clear that a brutal family dictatorship was emerging in South Vietnam.

In 1956 Diem, with US support, refused to hold elections. He claimed that he did not feel bound by the agreements of the Geneva Accords, as he did not believe that the Communists could be trusted to hold fair elections. In reality, Diem and the Americans were afraid that the elections would have resulted in a united, Communist Vietnam. It has been estimated that Ho Chi Minh would have won about 80 per cent of the vote had elections been allowed to go ahead.

With elections not an option, military opposition to Diem became the only alternative in the South. Groups of Communists (referred to by the South Vietnamese government and the USA as the '**Vietcong**', or VC) formed themselves into military units with a political arm known as the National Liberation Front (**NLF**). North Vietnam supported the VC, as did much of the local population in the South, who had become disillusioned with Diem's government.

The Geneva Conference of 1954

From April to July 1954 a conference was held in Geneva in Switzerland in an attempt to end hostilities and create peace in Indo-China. Many countries attended the **Geneva Conference**. The declaration which became known as the Geneva Accords freed Indochina from French colonial control.

The USA became increasingly concerned with its ally Diem, and doubted his ability to maintain its preferred option of the 'two Vietnams' policy.

How did President Kennedy widen the conflict?

After he was elected as president in November 1960, John F Kennedy's policy towards containing Communism was '**flexible response**'. This meant his administration expanded the available means of fighting against Communism. This expansion included the following:

- Increasing the number of US military advisers in the South (there were 17 000 advisers in Vietnam by the time of Kennedy's death).
- Starting **counter-insurgency** operations against Communist guerrillas in the South. This included '**search-and-destroy' missions** against the Vietcong and the spraying of **defoliants**, such as **Agent Orange**, in order to destroy the jungle that gave them cover. The United States also supported the **Strategic Hamlets Program**, which consisted of the resettlement of villagers into fortified villages where they could be kept 'safe' from the Communists.
- Introducing a new US military counter-insurgency force, the '**Green Berets**', trained in guerrilla fighting.
- Encouraging Diem to introduce social and political reforms.

None of these measures succeeded in limiting the growing success of the Vietcong attacks on the South. Indeed, measures such as the Strategic Hamlets Program and the spraying of Agent Orange only alienated the local peasant population further. Meanwhile, rather than winning support by carrying out a reform programme, Diem's unpopular actions continued to generate mass discontent, which reached a head in 1963 with a crisis over his anti-Buddhist policies. When laws were passed banning the celebration of the Buddha's birthday, the Buddhists organized mass protests. These included rallies, hunger strikes, and even **self-immolations**. This unrest caused an international reaction, especially when the response of South Vietnam's First Lady, Madam Nhu (Diem's sister-in-law), was: 'Let them burn and we shall clap our hands.' Kennedy's government now started to cut off its aid to Diem's regime, but, by the end of 1963, Diem and his brother had both been killed in a coup, which was known about in advance by US intelligence services. However, getting rid of Diem did not improve

Thich Qung Duc's self-immolation in Saigon in June 1963. This Buddhist monk was 73 when he set himself on fire in protest against anti-Buddhism laws.

Strategic hamlets or 'agrovilles'

Strategic hamlets were new villages, built by Diem, into which peasants could be placed to 'protect' them from Communist infiltration. They were surrounded by barbed wire and only helped to alienate the peasants, who felt imprisoned and resented having to leave their ancestral lands. This initiative failed to keep villagers from joining the Communists.

the situation, and indeed further served to increase US commitment to subsequent Saigon governments. General William C Westmoreland believed that Diem's assassination 'morally locked us into Vietnam'.

Activity 1   (ATL) **Thinking skills**

President Kennedy resisted sending combat soldiers to Vietnam and on a couple of occasions indicated misgivings about US involvement in this war. Nevertheless, by the time that Kennedy was assassinated, the USA was much more deeply and directly involved in fighting the war in Vietnam.

1. In what ways did Kennedy broaden the USA's commitment to Vietnam?
2. Could the USA have withdrawn from Vietnam in 1963?

Vice President Lyndon Baines Johnson became president after Kennedy was assassinated in November 1963. He inherited a situation in which there was no longer a stable government in South Vietnam, while the strength of the Communists in the region was increasing. He also inherited Kennedy's advisers. These factors pointed towards the likelihood of Johnson continuing the war. Johnson was also as determined as his predecessors to win the 'war against Communism' and prevent the domino effect.

Given the deteriorating situation in South Vietnam by 1964, Johnson needed to be able to increase US commitment to the war; however, he also needed justification for this in order to obtain the support of the US public and Congress. The 'excuse' for the United States to step up its activities in Vietnam came with the so-called **Gulf of Tonkin incident**. On the night of 2 August 1964, the American naval destroyer *Maddox* was fired on by North Vietnamese patrol boats while it was patrolling and gathering intelligence in the Gulf of Tonkin, off the North Vietnamese coast. Two days later, on 4 August 1964, the US destroyers *Maddox* and *Turner Joy* were allegedly fired on. Ship radar apparently showed that they were under attack, but there was much confusion, and no physical evidence of an assault was found. Nevertheless, Johnson called this attack 'open aggression on the high seas', and as a result the United States immediately bombed North Vietnamese installations. The next day, Johnson addressed the US Congress and asked it to pass the **Gulf of Tonkin Resolution**, which authorized the president to 'take all necessary measures to repel any armed attack against the forces of the United States and to prevent further aggression.' For the next six years, the Gulf of Tonkin Resolution was used as the legal basis for the war in Vietnam.

Once the Gulf of Tonkin Resolution had been passed, the USA responded to the situation in Vietnam by:

- Launching a sustained campaign of bombing North Vietnam, which was known as Operation Rolling Thunder.
- Sending 100 000 ground forces to South Vietnam in 1965. Led by General Westmoreland, US soldiers carried out 'search-and-destroy' missions. By 1968, there were 520 000 troops in Vietnam.

Bombing of targets in the South also took place in order to provide support for ground troops and to attack the enemy supply routes and bases. Large numbers of rockets and bombs, plus **napalm**, were dropped on South Vietnam, with devastating effects on the local population.

Activity 2  ATL Research skills

1. Researching the following questions will help your understanding of the type of warfare that went on in Vietnam on both sides, and its effectiveness:

   a. What were the characteristics of US strategy?

   b. What problems did US soldiers face in their fight against the VC?

   c. What impact did the bombing campaign have on North Vietnam?

   d. What were the characteristics of the guerrilla war fought by the VC against the Americans?

   e. Why were the VC successful?

   f. How effective was the South Vietnamese army (ARVN)?

Activity 3 ATL Thinking skills

1. Read the following extract from the US Department of State Bulletin of 1965.

   > The contest in Vietnam is part of a wider pattern of aggressive purpose …
   >
   > Why are we in South Vietnam? We are there because we have a promise to keep. Since 1954 every American president has offered support to the people of South Vietnam. We have helped to build, and we have helped to defend. Thus over many years, we have made a national pledge to help South Vietnam defend its independence. And I intend to keep that promise.
   >
   > To dishonor the pledge, to abandon this small and brave nation to its enemy, and to the terror that must follow, would be an unforgivable wrong.
   >
   > We are also there to strengthen world order. Around the globe from Berlin to Thailand are people whose well-being rests, in part, on the belief that they can count on us if they are attacked. To leave Vietnam to its fate would shake the confidence of all these people in the value of American commitment, the value of America's word. The result would be increased unrest and instability, and even wider war.

Guerrilla tactics are usually chosen by a side that has disadvantages in fighting in terms of weaponry and size of army, but advantages in terms of knowledge of the land and in local support.

Where else have guerrilla tactics been used by one side in a conflict? What similarities can you see between the effectiveness of the guerrilla tactics that were used against the Americans in Vietnam, and the effectiveness of guerrilla tactics used in your own example?

> *We are also there because there are great stakes in the balance. Let no one think for a moment that to retreat from Vietnam would bring an end to conflict. The battle would be renewed in one country and then another. The central lesson of our time is that the appetite for aggression is never satisfied. To withdraw from one battlefield means only to prepare for the next. We must say in South East Asia as we did in Europe, in the words of the Bible: 'Hitherto shalt thou come, but no further'.*

President Johnson in US Department of State Bulletin, 26 April 1965

- **a.** What reasons does President Johnson give to justify US involvement in Vietnam?
- **b.** What evidence is there in this source that the fighting in Vietnam was part of the wider Cold War conflict?

2. Now read the next extract, which was written by an American historian, William Chafe, more than 10 years after the Vietnam War ended:

> ❝ *Without question, the central precondition for American involvement in Vietnam was the set of assumptions that underlay and shaped the entire history of the Cold War. Once committed to the view that the communist world was one, and systematically involved in a worldwide conspiracy to subvert freedom, any effort in other countries that could be interpreted as hostile to the United States automatically became defined as that worldwide conspiracy … containment … became a diffuse, universal rationale for resisting change in the international **status quo**. Given such a definition of the world, and the moralistic rhetoric that accompanied it, distinctions between countries and issues became blurred, and it was America's 'moral' obligation to defend 'freedom' anywhere it was threatened, regardless of how dictatorial, tyrannical or repressive the regimes on 'our' side acted …*

William Chafe, *The Unfinished Journey*, 4th ed. (Oxford University Press 1999) p.298

- **a.** What are Chafe's criticisms of the United States' approach to the situation in Vietnam?
- **b.** Which parts of Johnson's speech would provide evidence for Chafe's criticisms?

The Great Society and the 'credibility gap'

The war that Johnson really wanted to fight was actually at home: a war against poverty and social injustice. He called his programme the '**Great Society**'; it involved improving civil rights, eradicating poverty, increasing access to health and education, and creating a cleaner environment. This encouraged the development of the 'credibility gap'. The credibility gap was the difference in reality between what the Johnson administration told Congress and what was actually happening. 'I was determined', he recalled later, 'to keep the [Vietnam] war from shattering that dream, which meant that I had no choice but to keep my foreign policy in the wings … I knew Congress as well as I know Lady Bird [his wife], and I knew that the day it exploded into a major debate on the war, that day would be the beginning of the end of the Great Society.'

Study the cartoon.

The Train Robbery

This cartoon titled 'The Train Robbery' appeared in 1967 in the British magazine *Punch*.

1. What does the train engine represent? What do the train wagons represent?
2. Who is the man with the axe? What is he doing and why?
3. What is the smoke from the train supposed to represent?
4. What is the overall message (refer back to the title of the cartoon)?

The Tet Offensive

By 1968, the war had reached a turning point. General Westmoreland's policy of 'attrition' had not succeeded in defeating the NLF, and at home an anti-war movement was gaining support, fuelled by the growing number of US casualties. Nevertheless, Johnson told the public at the end of 1967 that there was 'light at the end of the tunnel': that is, the United States was starting to win the war. Then, in the early morning of 30 January 1968, on the Vietnamese new year (known as Tet), 70 000 Communists launched a surprise attack. It was the sheer scale of the assault that was most shocking. The Communists attacked more than 100 cities in the South, including Saigon. It took 11 days for the US and ARVN forces to regain control of Saigon. Even more intense was the battle for the beautiful city of Hué; half the city was destroyed and 5800 civilians were killed. The Communists were gradually pushed back from all the other cities after the use of massive firepower against them. This so-called Tet Offensive was a military failure for the Vietcong. The popular uprising in the South they had hoped to trigger did not happen. They failed to hold on to any of the cities gained at the outset of the offensive and it is estimated that they had casualties of over 40 000.

Anti-war demonstrators. Student protesters would chant outside the White House: 'Hey hey LBJ, how many kids have you killed today?'

However, public opinion in the United States now turned decisively against the war. The American public was sickened by what it saw on television. During what was the first 'televised' war, people were able to watch images in their own homes of the US embassy being attacked by the VC, and they also saw a South Vietnamese police chief execute a VC prisoner in the street.

All this seemed to indicate to the American public not only that they were not winning the war, but that they were also supporting a regime which flouted basic human rights.

Anti-war protests in the United States reached a new peak. The aftermath of the Tet Offensive resulted in a significant change of strategy for the USA. Bombing of the North was halted and peace talks were initiated. On 31 March 1968 President Johnson addressed a stunned US television audience, announcing that he would not be standing for re-election the coming November.

Research images of the Tet Offensive, such as the storming of the US embassy, the battles in Hué and the summary execution of a Communist prisoner. Why did *images* of the Tet Offensive seem to have more credibility and impact on the American public's view of the war in Vietnam than what they were *told* was going on by the US military and US government?

How far is our perception of 'truth' controlled by language?

As a class, discuss images from the Vietnam War, and compare and contrast them with government statements (these could be Vietnamese as well as American) and military press reports from the time. Which of these has more 'truth' about the war and the events in Vietnam?

Activity 5 — (ATL) Thinking and communication skills

1. How did US policies towards the Vietnam War change under President Johnson?

2. Do you agree that the war became Johnson's war? (You may want to set up a formal class debate on this question.)

3. Alternatively, do you agree more with the '**Quagmire Theory**' (that successive presidents took one step after another, thinking each step would be the one to solve the Vietnam problem, but in reality getting deeper and deeper into the quagmire, or muddy marsh)?

Did President Nixon achieve 'peace with honour'?

Richard Nixon was elected president of the United States in November 1968. He wanted American withdrawal from the war, but he was not prepared to accept peace at any price. Rather he wanted 'peace with honour'. There was no way that the United States could merely withdraw from South Vietnam or seem to have been defeated. Nixon wanted a settlement which would guarantee the South a reasonable chance of survival. This was to take another four years, during which time 300 000 Vietnamese and 20 000 Americans died.

To achieve 'peace with honour', Nixon selected Henry Kissinger as his key foreign policy adviser. Kissinger was prepared to use force to get the North to reach a peace agreement. A '**covert**' 14-month bombing campaign was begun along the **Ho Chi Minh Trail** (see map, page 77) inside neutral Cambodia. This did not force the North to agree to peace terms. Nixon also introduced a policy of 'Vietnamization' – the gradual withdrawal of US troops and the handing over of the war to the South Vietnamese government – and so from 1969 to 1973 US troop numbers were steadily scaled down. In June 1969, he issued the Nixon Doctrine, which represented a move away from the policies followed in Asia since Truman. It stated that nations were responsible for their own defence:

> The nations of Asia can and must increasingly shoulder the responsibility for achieving peace and progress in the area with whatever cooperation we can provide. Asian countries must seek their own destiny for if domination by the aggressor can destroy the freedom of a nation, too much dependence on a protector can eventually erode its dignity. But it is not just a matter of dignity, for dependence on foreign aid destroys the incentive to mobilize domestic resources – human, financial and material – in the absence of which no government is capable of dealing effectively with its problems and adversaries.

Activity 6

Refer back to Johnson's state bulletin, on pages 81–82, justifying involvement in Vietnam.

1. What arguments given in the Nixon Doctrine contradict Johnson's arguments for involvement?

2. What does this show about the impact of Vietnam on American global Cold War policy?

Activity 7

Victims of the My Lai massacre.

Revelations about a brutal massacre by US soldiers of unarmed old men, women, and children in the village of **My Lai** began to surface in 1969. The resulting trial of Lieutenant William L Calley added fuel to the anti-war protests and raised deep moral questions about the mass killing of civilians.

Research, in pairs, the My Lai massacre, and attempt to answer the following questions:

1. What happened at My Lai, and what effects did it have on American public opinion?

2. What does this massacre suggest about the attitudes and morale of American troops on the ground in Vietnam?

The Paris peace talks

At the peace talks, which officially opened in Paris on 13 May 1972 and dragged on until January 1973, Henry Kissinger negotiated with the North Vietnamese, who were also determined to achieve 'peace with honour'. Neither side was willing to compromise; the North demanded representation in the government of the South, and all sides continued to try to win an advantage at the negotiating table by achieving an upper hand on the battlefield. For the Americans, this meant using airpower to put pressure on the Communists – even bombing targets in the North that had previously been considered too sensitive. Another strategy used by Nixon and Kissinger was that of pursuing 'détente' with the Soviet Union and China (see chapters 11 and 12). One of the aims of trying to develop better relations with the Soviets and the Chinese was to get them to put pressure on North Vietnam to agree to the peace settlement.

Vietnam War Moratorium Day, 15 October 1969

As public opinion in the United States turned against the Vietnam War, what had been sporadic demonstrations by hippies and left-wing activists spread to students, the middle-aged, and the middle class. Then, on 15 October 1969, across the United States anti-war demonstrations involving over two million people took place. Most wore distinctive black armbands to show their support and to pay tribute to nearly 45 000 Americans who had been killed in the conflict.

Finally, a peace settlement was signed on 27 January 1973. All American troops would withdraw from Vietnam and both North and South would respect the dividing line of the 17th parallel. The last American troops withdrew from Vietnam two weeks after the signing of this peace agreement. However, peace did not come to Vietnam. The North took the initiative, and by April 1975 it had taken Saigon.

By the end of 1975, Vietnam, Cambodia, and Laos had all fallen to the forces of Communism. Containment had failed – the dominoes of Indochina had fallen.

Activity 8 — ATL Thinking skills

Answer the following review questions:

1. Why did Nixon need to end the Vietnam War?
2. What did he mean by 'peace with honour'?
3. What strategies did he use to achieve his aim?
4. To what extent did Nixon achieve 'peace with honour'?

Was Vietnam a failure for the American policy of containment? Historians' views

The image of dominoes falling (see the cartoon at beginning of this chapter), first used by President Eisenhower in 1953, became a reality. It certainly seems obvious that the Vietnam War failed categorically to contain Communism in Indochina. Many historians of the Cold War hold this view. Indeed, as a case study, and in isolation, the Vietnam War is America's biggest and most overt failure. In its attempt to stop the 'cancer of Communism' spreading from the North, across the 17th parallel, and into the South in Vietnam, it indirectly fostered the growth of Communist regimes in Cambodia and Laos.

However, some historians have seen that, in a broader context, the Vietnam War was not a total failure for the United States in terms of containment of Communism. Jim Rohwer in his book *Asia Rising* (Simon & Schuster 1998) writes that 'the broader aims of America's effort in Vietnam were to keep the Capitalist semi-democracies of Southeast Asia from falling to Communism' and that Vietnam allowed other countries in the region, such as Malaysia, Thailand, and Singapore – all of whom faced Communist threats – the breathing space they needed. 'In other words … America … accomplished in a spectacular way the broader aims of Asian stability and prosperity that the intervention was intended to serve.' Indeed, in support of this thesis, the former Singapore premier Lee Kuan Yew noted in his book *The Singapore Story*:

> America's action [in Vietnam] enabled non-Communist Southeast Asia to put their own houses in order. By 1975 they were in better shape to stand up to the Communists. Had there been no US intervention, the will of these countries to resist them would have melted and Southeast Asia would most likely have gone Communist. The prosperous emerging market economies of ASEAN were nurtured during the Vietnam War years.

Lee Kuan Yew, *The Singapore Story* (Prentice Hall 1999) p.66

CHALLENGE YOURSELF

Research skills ATL

Research the Malayan emergency of 1950, and examine the reasons for the failure of the Malayan Communist insurgency.

Activity 9

ATL **Thinking skills**

'Hi, everybody! Look who's here!'

This cartoon by Marlette appeared in 1975 in the US newspaper the *Charlotte Observer*.

1. Explain the meaning of each of the 'myths' in the cartoon.

   (From left to right, the 'myths' are labelled 'Peace with honor', 'Monolithic Communism', 'Light at the end of the tunnel', 'Domino theory', and 'Bloodbath'. A bloodbath is what was supposed to happen if the North invaded the South. Nixon said in an interview with the American Society of Newspaper Editors in 1971 that, 'if the United States were to fail in Vietnam, if the Communists were to take over, the bloodbath that would follow would be a blot on this Nation's history from which we would find it very difficult to return.')

2. What do all of these 'myths' have in common, with regard to US policy in Vietnam?

3. Why has the cartoonist put all the 'myths' in a retirement home?

4. What is the overall message of the cartoon?

Activity 10

ATL **Communication skills**

1. Plot a timeline of key events relevant to the Cold War in Asia from 1945 to 1975. Use a different colour to represent each different Asian country. Add to this 'bullet points' of information explaining when and why the United States became involved, and the outcome of the involvement.

CHALLENGE YOURSELF

ATL **Research skills**

Research why US involvement in Vietnam helped to destabilize the governments of Laos and Cambodia. What impact did the Communist takeover in Cambodia by the Khmer Rouge have on the people of Cambodia? What was the impact of the war on Laos?

Conclusions on the US policy of containment in Asia

Up to 1949, it can be said that the US policy of containment in Europe had been successful. Territorially, Communism had made no gains and the one obvious attempt at Soviet expansion after 1947 had been stopped by the Berlin airlift of 1948. The Marshall Plan had helped to revive European economies and stop the threat of Communist parties gaining control in countries such as Italy and France. Containment in Asia, however, as Vietnam shows, was less successful. This was partly due to the fact that Communism in Asia was much more diverse. Unlike in Europe, it was often linked to strong nationalist movements. Mao Zedong and Ho Chi Minh had so much support in their countries because of local circumstances and their struggles for independence. Although the United States was trying to fight against Soviet imperialism, it actually ended up fighting against local movements and nationalist feeling. This explains why the USA could never be as successful in containing these revolutionary movements as it had been in Europe.

We will review the success of the policy of containment again at the end of chapter 9, when we have looked at superpower rivalry in other regions. We will also consider containment from the perspective of the USSR, particularly when we look at the challenges to Soviet control in chapter 13.

To access websites relevant to this chapter, go to www.pearsonhotlinks. com, search for the book title or ISBN, and click on 'chapter 6'.

Activity 11   **ATL** Self-management and thinking skills

Working on your essay introduction

Once you have worked through this chapter, it should be possible to attempt the essay set at the beginning of the chapter:

> *To what extent was the US policy of containment successful in Asia?*

One of the key parts of an essay is the introduction. Refer back to the essay planning grid at the end of chapter 3 and check what should be included in a good introduction. Then have a look at the introductions below and discuss which you think is the best one and why. How could each one be improved?

Introduction 1: In 1947, the United States adopted a policy of containment in the belief that the Soviet Union would keep trying to extend its power unless stopped. The policy of containment was applied in Europe and was successful in stopping Communism from spreading. When China became Communist in 1949, and with the Red Scare putting pressure on his government at home, President Truman decided to extend this policy of containment to Asia. There were several places where the policy of containment was applied – in Korea, in Vietnam, in Japan, and in Taiwan. Although the USA can be said to have been successful in containing Communism in Korea, Taiwan, and Japan, it failed dramatically in Vietnam.

Introduction 2: The United States faced several threats in Asia in the 1950s and 1960s. China had become Communist in 1949, and then North Korea attacked South Korea in 1950. The island of Formosa (Taiwan) was threatened by mainland China, and Japan was also in danger. The USA believed that it had to deal with these threats. How successful was it?

Introduction 3: Containment became the cornerstone of US policy in 1947 when President Truman issued the Truman Doctrine. This set down the belief that the USA should help any government that was trying to resist Communism, and it led to economic aid in Europe with the Marshall Plan and also a direct confrontation with the Soviets over Berlin in 1948. With China becoming Communist in 1949, the US saw all Communism as a monolithic threat which had to be dealt with in any part of the world. The new ideas for defence were set out in NSC-68, and when North Korea attacked South Korea in 1950, the United States, with UN backing, put containment into action in Asia by sending forces to resist the North Koreans. Following this event, the USA then attempted to contain Communism by building up Japan, protecting Taiwan, and fighting Communist forces in Vietnam.

Practice essay titles – the USA and containment in Asia

• *Discuss the impact of the events in Asia on the development of the Cold War.*
• *Discuss the role played by the Vietnam War in the development of the Cold War.*
• *Examine the reasons for, and the results of, the US policy of containment in Asia.*

07

Peaceful co-existence:
New leaders, new ideas?

USSR

Key concepts: Change

As you read this chapter, consider the following essay questions:

- To what extent was there a thaw in the Cold War after 1953?
- Examine the significance of the policy of 'peaceful co-existence'.

Timeline of US–Soviet relations, 1953–1962

1953		Eisenhower **inaugurated** as US president
	March	Death of Stalin, who is succeeded by Malenkov and Khrushchev
	July	Korean armistice
1954	Jan	US Secretary of State Dulles announces massive retaliation policy
1955	July	Geneva **Summit**
	May	Austrian State Treaty ends four-power occupation of Austria
1956	Feb	Khrushchev denounces Stalin and promotes 'peaceful co-existence' policy
	June	Polish workers revolt
	Oct	**Suez Crisis**
	Oct	Soviets crush Hungarian rising
1957	Oct	USSR announces **Sputnik** satellite success
1958	Nov	Khrushchev issues ultimatum to West over Berlin
1959	Sept	Khrushchev visits USA and meets Eisenhower at **Camp David**
1960	May	**U-2** spy plane shot down and **Paris Summit** collapses
		Kennedy elected US president
1961	June	Khrushchev and Kennedy meet at **Vienna Summit**
		Yuri Gagarin is the first man to make an earth-orbiting space flight
1962	Oct	**Cuban Missile Crisis**

Between 1945 and 1950, developments in the Cold War had been affected by events in Europe. After 1950, the course of the Cold War was influenced by other factors, including:

- events in Asia (see chapters 5 and 6)
- the nuclear arms race (see chapter 14)
- changes in leadership in the United States and USSR, and a move to establish better relations between East and West. These particular changes will be examined in this chapter.

Eisenhower and Dulles in the United States: roll-back, brinkmanship, and the New Look

Republican Dwight D Eisenhower was elected US president in 1952. Nicknamed 'Ike', he had a distinguished military background having commanded the Allied armies in Normandy in 1944. After the end of World War Two he served as the US Army's chief of staff and commander-in-chief of NATO.

Eisenhower's background meant that he was unlikely to be criticized as being 'soft on Communism'. In fact, both he and his Secretary of State, John Foster Dulles, were strongly anti-Communist. Dulles was vociferous in his condemnation of the Soviet system:

Dwight D Eisenhower, US president from 1953 to 1960.

> Soviet Communism believes that human beings are nothing more than ... superior animals ... and that the best kind of a world is that world which is organized as a well managed farm is organized, where certain animals are taken out to pasture, and they are fed and brought back and milked, and they are given a barn as shelter over their heads ... I do not see how, as long as Soviet Communism holds those views ... there can be any permanent reconciliation ... This is an irreconcilable conflict.

US Senate, 83rd Congress, 1st Session, on the nomination of Dulles, 15 January 1953

In the 1952 presidential election campaign, Dulles had also talked about '**roll-back**', by which he meant liberating East European countries that were, at the time, held by the Soviets, but in reality this never happened. No attempt was ever made under Eisenhower to free countries from Soviet control. Although the US quietly encouraged rebellions in Eastern Europe in 1953 and 1956 (see chapter 13), it did not use these opportunities to extend its sphere of influence.

Rather than carrying out roll-back, under Eisenhower the US administration developed a policy of containment called the '**New Look**'. This meant preventing the extension of Soviet Communism outside of the areas where it was already established, in the belief that without any opportunity to expand, the Soviet system would collapse in on itself. Eisenhower put his containment policy into practice by:

- Setting up alliances to encircle the Soviet Union – for example, SEATO.
- Using military power to protect vulnerable areas – for example, West Berlin.
- Assisting forces that were fighting Communism – for example, Diem's government in South Vietnam.
- Using the **CIA** (Central Intelligence Agency) for covert operations more extensively than had been done before (see the box below).
- Initiating an increased reliance on nuclear weapons. A national security document in 1953 stated: 'The US will consider nuclear weapons to be available for use as other munitions.' Conventional weapons would thus play a smaller role in defence.
- Brinkmanship. This involved threats of massive retaliation as an instrument of containment. It entailed going to the brink and threatening nuclear war to intimidate the aggressor into backing down.

Despite the aggressive nature of brinkmanship, Eisenhower was also keenly aware of the dangers of nuclear weapons and was prepared to negotiate with the Soviet Union. Thus there were US–Soviet summits in 1955 and 1959.

CHALLENGE YOURSELF

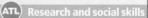 **Research and social skills**

Investigate the overthrow of either Mossadegh in Iran or Guzman in Guatemala. How significant was the role of the CIA? What other factors contributed? With a partner who looked at the other case study, compare the nature and overthrow of these regimes.

The activities of the CIA

The CIA (Central Intelligence Agency) was set up in 1947 by the US government as an intelligence-collecting body, and it undertook extensive covert anti-Communist activities. Historian John Lewis Gaddis wrote of it:

> As the Eisenhower administration took office, the CIA was regularly attempting to infiltrate spies, **saboteurs**, and resistance leaders into the Soviet Union, Eastern Europe, and China. It was financing ostensibly independent radio stations broadcasting to those countries, as well as labor unions, academic conferences, scholarly journals, and student organizations – some of them inside the United States.

John Lewis Gaddis, *The Cold War* (Penguin 2005), pp.163–164

The CIA was also involved in the overthrow of governments it considered too left-wing. In 1953 it helped to overthrow the government of Mohammad Mossadegh in Iran, and in 1954 it played a role in overthrowing Jacobo Arbenz Guzmán in Guatemala.

Activity 1　⟨ATL⟩ Thinking skills

"Don't Be Afraid—I Can Always Pull You Back"

Cartoon by Herblock published in the *Washington Post* in 1956.

1. How is Secretary of State Dulles portrayed in this cartoon? Who is he pushing to The Brink? Why does this character look reluctant?

2. What do you think the cartoonist's attitude is towards the idea of brinkmanship?

3. Find an example from the previous two chapters of where the Americans can be said to have successfully used brinkmanship.

4. How did the new administration's attitude to defence differ from the proposals set out in the Truman administration's NSC-68?

5. How was Eisenhower's New Look a) different from and b) similar to the ideas and policies on containment put forward by Truman?

Khrushchev and co-existence

The fact that US–Soviet summits took place during the 1950s was not only due to Eisenhower's willingness to negotiate, but also due to the attitudes of the new leadership in the Soviet Union.

Following the death of Joseph Stalin in 1953 and the subsequent removal of Stalin's chief of secret police, Lavrentiy Pavlovich Beria, Soviet foreign policy came under the control of Georgy Malenkov who, with Nikita Khrushchev and Nikolai Bulganin, formed a collective leadership. Malenkov formulated the idea of a '**New Course**' with the West. This was later picked up by Khrushchev, who, having won the struggle for leadership, renamed it 'peaceful co-existence'.

This was a move away from the Leninist doctrine of the inevitability of war. 'Peaceful co-existence' meant that Capitalism and Communism should accept the continuing existence of one another rather than use force to destroy each other. Just as the Americans believed that, deprived of opportunities for expansion, Communism would collapse, Khrushchev declared that in any case Capitalism would die out due to its own inherent weaknesses. Thus there was no need to risk nuclear war.

Nikita Khrushchev

Khrushchev had emerged as the leader of the Soviet Union by 1957, having outmanoeuvred his rivals, Beria and Malenkov. Within the Soviet Union, Khrushchev moved away from Stalin's rule by terror, introducing '**de-Stalinization**'. This was first put forward by Khrushchev during a 'secret speech' in February 1956, at a congress of the Soviet Communist Party, in which he criticized Stalin's excessive use of terror and leadership style. This meant an end to mass killings and many prisoners were freed. However, it did not mean a loosening of control over the **satellite states**, as Hungary discovered in 1956 when it tried to introduce more liberal measures (see pages 189–190).

What other factors encouraged a change in international relations?

It was not just Eisenhower and Khrushchev who were keen to avoid a nuclear war. Other world leaders, such as Winston Churchill, also supported the idea of more communication between East and West in order to avoid a **nuclear holocaust**.

Economic factors also played a role in pushing the two superpowers into a friendlier relationship. In the USSR, approximately one third of the economy was directed towards the military, while consumer goods were scarce and living standards very low. The economy of the United States was in much better shape than that of the Soviet Union, but 12 per cent of the **GNP** was still spent on the military. If improved relations could lead to a decrease in military spending, this would be good news for the economies of both countries.

Also, by 1954, the Korean War had ended, removing a major source of conflict between the United States and the Soviet Union.

Activity 2

1. The changed international situation after 1953 has led historians to call this period a 'thaw' in the Cold War. Identify the factors that set the scene for improved relations – or a 'thaw' – between the superpowers after 1953.

East–West relations in the 1950s: the reality

An example of improved US–Soviet relations after 1953 was agreement over Austria. In April 1955, the Soviet Union proposed a formal peace treaty with Austria. The **Austrian State Treaty** ended the four-power occupation of Austria and created an independent and neutral country. Following on from this, the Geneva Summit took place in July 1955. This was the first meeting of the heads of government of the major powers since 1945. However, little of substance was achieved at this meeting, and proposals concerning the arms race, and the issue of Germany, got nowhere. The table below shows the proposals and responses made by the United States and the Soviet Union at this time:

Soviet Proposals:	US Reaction:
• Mutual disbandment of NATO and the Warsaw Pact. • Withdrawal of all foreign troops from Europe followed by the drawing up of a European Security Treaty. • Free elections to be carried out for a reunified German government.	Hostile. These ideas were unacceptable to the West European governments, and no agreement was reached on any of these proposals.
US Proposals:	**Soviet Reaction:**
• An '**Open Skies**' proposal. This meant each side would exchange plans of military installations and allow aerial surveillance of each other's installations.	Hostile. The Soviets did not even bother to make a formal reply. They dismissed it as 'nothing more than a bold espionage plot' and Khrushchev said it would be 'like seeing into our bedrooms'. However, the United States went ahead and used the U-2 **reconnaissance** plane (see pages 98–99).

Was the Geneva Summit a failure?

Despite the failure to achieve any concrete progress on Germany or **disarmament**, the Geneva Summit nevertheless was a breakthrough, in that discussions were carried out in an atmosphere of cordiality. The summit also led to better relations in terms of trade exhibitions, exchanging of certain scientific information, and cultural exchanges. Thus the phrase 'spirit of Geneva' was applied to the events surrounding 1955.

Why did East–West tension increase again after 1955?

In February 1956, Khrushchev gave his de-Stalinization speech, which led to challenges to Soviet control throughout the Eastern bloc (see chapter 13). At the same time as Khrushchev faced problems in Hungary, the West was involved in the Suez Crisis (see chapter 18). Both of these crises helped to dissipate the good feeling achieved at Geneva. The Suez Crisis also raised fears of growing Soviet influence in the Middle East, and this led to the **Eisenhower Doctrine** in January 1957. This clearly stated that the United States would help any country in the Middle East to fight against Communism.

Activity 3
(ATL) Thinking skills

The Eisenhower Doctrine

> There is a general recognition in the Middle East, as elsewhere, that the United States does not seek either political or economic domination over any other people. Our desire is a world environment of freedom, not servitude. On the other hand many, if not all, of the nations of the Middle East are aware of the danger that stems from International Communism and welcome closer co-operation with the United States to realize for themselves the United Nations' goals of independence, economic well-being and spiritual growth. If the Middle East is to continue its geographic role of uniting rather than separating East and West, if its vast economic resources are to serve the well-being of the peoples there, as well as that of others … then the United States must make more evident its willingness to support the independence of the freedom-loving nations of the area …

The action which I propose would have the following features.

It would first of all authorize the United States to co-operate with and assist any nation or group of nations in the general area of the Middle East in the development of economic strength dedicated to the maintenance of national independence.

It would, in the second place, authorize the Executive to undertake in the same region programs of military assistance and co-operation with any nation or group of nations, which desires such aid.

It would in the third place, authorize such assistance and co-operation to include the employment of the armed forces of the United States to secure and protect the territorial integrity and political independence of such nations requesting such aid, against overt armed aggression from any nation controlled by International Communism.

From President Dwight D Eisenhower, 'Special Message to Congress, 5 January 1957', Department of State Bulletin XXXVI, 21 January 1957

1. What message did this Doctrine send to a) the Soviet Union and b) Arab states about American intentions in the Middle East?

The technology race

In addition to this mounting tension between East and West, the Americans now became increasingly worried about a Soviet threat against the United States. On 4 October 1957 the Soviets launched the world's first artificial satellite – Sputnik, 'travelling companion' – to be followed a month later by Sputnik II. This sent the Americans into a state of panic as they became convinced of Soviet superiority in missile technology. This impression was reinforced by Khrushchev, who made the most of the situation:

> *The Sputniks prove that socialism has won the competition between socialist and capitalist countries … that the economy, science, culture and the creative genius of people in all spheres of life develop better and faster under socialism.*

Khrushchev used every opportunity to insist that he could wipe out any American or European city:

> *He would even specify how many missiles and warheads each target might require. But he also tried to be nice about it: at one point, while bullying an American visitor, Hubert Humphrey [a senator from Minnesota, who later became Vice President], he paused to ask where his guest was from. When Humphrey pointed out Minneapolis on the map, Khrushchev circled it with a big blue pencil. 'That's so I don't forget to order them to spare the city when the rockets fly,' he explained amiably.*

As reported in John Lewis Gaddis, *The Cold War* (Penguin 2005) p. 70

The missile gap

The US Congress and the media promoted the idea of a **'missile gap'**. This scenario was confirmed by the **Gaither Report** – the findings of a top-secret investigating committee. The report recommended:

- a vast increase in offensive defence power, especially missile development
- a build-up of conventional forces capable of fighting a limited war
- a massive building programme of **fallout shelters** to protect US citizens from nuclear attack.

The space race

The '**space race**' was another feature of the Cold War which provided plenty of propaganda opportunities on both sides. Not only was it a race for seeing who could be the first to get into space – it was also linked to missile technology, and thus the arms race. Following the success of Sputniks I and II, the United States launched Explorer I. However, the Soviets successfully put the first man into space when Yuri Gagarin orbited Earth in 1961. One month later the first American, Alan Shepard, flew into space. On 20 July 1969, after expenditure of $25 billion, NASA successfully landed American astronaut Neil Armstrong on the moon. It was an enormous propaganda coup.

In actual fact, US Air Force U-2 spy planes flying over the Soviet Union had revealed that, despite Khrushchev's threats, there was no missile gap – the Soviet Union did not have more missiles than the USA. Despite this, Eisenhower had to do something to alleviate public anxiety, and so he supported the establishment of the National Aeronautics and Space Administration (NASA) in 1958 to promote missile development and space exploration. He also provided federal aid to promote science education in schools.

Activity 4

> **ATL Thinking skills**

'Dear Boy, Where Have You Been Keeping Yourself?'

Cartoon by Herblock published in the *Washington Post* in 1957.

1. What is the cartoon suggesting about the American attitudes to science before and after Sputnik?

How did events of 1958–1960 affect East–West relations?

By 1958 Eisenhower was confident about US nuclear superiority and, therefore, could contemplate initiating a ban on atmospheric testing of nuclear weapons. The United States stopped this form of testing in October 1958 and was immediately followed by the Soviet Union. It was hoped that this might lead to a formal **test-ban treaty**. However, Khrushchev heightened East–West tensions at this time by issuing an ultimatum to the West to leave Berlin within 6 months (see chapter 8). In the face of Western determination to stand firm, Khrushchev had to back down. By the early months of 1959, the Berlin Crisis had subsided and talks began about another summit meeting. Khrushchev accepted an invitation to visit the United States in September 1959 – making him the first Soviet leader to visit the USA – and arranged with President Eisenhower for a summit meeting in Paris, scheduled for May 1960.

Discuss recent space projects and programmes. Does the exploration of space in the 21st century foster or hinder international co-operation? Do nations still compete for political or ideological reasons or is there scientific collaboration?

TOK

After reading about the technology race and space race in this chapter, think about the following questions:

- To what extent do you believe that science, and scientific development, is driven by politics and governments?
- How far is scientific knowledge 'objective' rather than 'subjective'?
- What similarities and differences are there between the scientific methods you use in your Group 4 subjects and the methods used by a historian? Are there links in the ways of knowing that both areas of knowledge use?
- You could attempt to draw a 'visual' representation of the similarities and differences between the 'Historical Method' and the 'Scientific Method': for example, a Venn diagram.

This Herblock cartoon shows Eisenhower and Khrushchev together in 1959 in the United States.

1. Why do you think the cartoonist has shown both leaders crossing their fingers? What is the message of this source?

The U-2 incident

Again, although the meeting between Eisenhower and Khrushchev in the United States produced few concrete results, the talks were a success in terms of generating a positive atmosphere, which led people to talk of the 'spirit of Camp David' (Eisenhower's presidential retreat in Maryland). This optimism was short-lived, however, as a few days before the summit meeting convened in Paris, the Soviets announced that an American plane had been shot down over the Soviet Union on 1 May 1960. The Americans tried to claim it was only a weather plane, which had gone off course, but the Soviets were able to reveal that the aircraft was a high-altitude photo-reconnaissance plane. Even more damaging, the pilot, Gary Powers, who had been captured, confessed to the 'spy' nature of his task. Eisenhower then admitted the truth about the U-2 spy planes and took personal responsibility for the incident.

However, at the Paris Summit, Eisenhower refused to apologize for the U-2 incident or to condemn U-2 flights, saying that aerial surveillance was 'a distasteful, but vital necessity'. Khrushchev then cancelled Eisenhower's planned visit to the Soviet Union and the meeting broke up with no further progress being made on a settlement for Berlin or a test-ban treaty. By 1962, any 'thaw' that might have been achieved was shown to be quite definitely at an end when the USA and the USSR had their most intense and dangerous conflict yet, over Cuba (see chapter 9).

Activity 6

 **ATL** Self-management skills

1. What issues/events prevented any lasting Cold War 'thaw' during this period?

2. Explain the meaning of the following: co-existence, massive retaliation, New Look.

3. Who or what was each of the following, and how did each one affect East–West relations during the 1950s?

   a. the Suez Crisis

   b. the Eisenhower Doctrine

   c. the Hungarian Uprising

   d. the Geneva Summit

   e. Sputnik

   f. the Gaither Report

   g. the U-2 incident

NB for some of these, you may need to do extra research. See also chapters 13 and 18.

Activity 7

Structuring the main body of an essay

 **ATL** Communication skills

Here again is an essay question posed at the beginning of this chapter:

> **To what extent was there a thaw in the Cold War between 1953 and 1960?**

Introduction: Look back at the work you did on introductions in the previous chapter and at the guidelines in chapter 3. What would be your starting point with the introduction for this essay?

Main body of the essay: As explained in the essay flow chart in chapter 3, you need to have a clear opening sentence to start each paragraph. This sentence must make it obvious what the point of the paragraph is going to be, and it must clearly link back to the question. The rest of the paragraph should then provide evidence to support your opening statement.

1. Look at the statements below. They can be grouped into three paragraphs to form the main body of the essay. Decide which statements fit better as: a) opening statements for one of the paragraphs of this essay; b) evidence in the main body of the paragraphs.

- The war in Korea was brought to a close.
- There were positive steps towards a reduction of tension and thus a 'thaw' after 1953. The USA continued to see the USSR as a threat in such areas as Asia.
- Tension increased dramatically in the late 1950s due to a series of incidents, which makes it clear that there was in fact no fundamental change in the relationship between the superpowers.
- Austria was finally unified.
- The shooting down of the U-2 spy plane ended any good relations that had been built up during Khrushchev's visit to the United States.
- Nothing concrete was achieved at the Geneva Summit regarding the arms race or the German question.
- There is much evidence that there was still tension between the USA and the USSR after 1953.
- Sputnik raised new fears of superior Soviet technology and of a 'missile gap'. Khrushchev raised tensions over Berlin with an ultimatum to the West to leave.
- There was co-operation in cultural and economic areas following the 'spirit of Geneva'. Cuba brought the Soviet Union and the United States close to a direct nuclear confrontation.

2. In which order would you place the paragraphs? What other evidence might you add in each paragraph?

3. Write a conclusion that supports the arguments that are in the main body of the essay.

NB make sure you have made notes on the role of Khrushchev from this chapter. In chapter 9, we will analyse his policy of 'peaceful co-existence' more fully and develop essay questions on this theme.

 To access websites relevant to this chapter, go to www.pearsonhotlinks. com, search for the book title or ISBN, and click on 'chapter 7'.

08

Peaceful co-existence and containment:
Case study in crisis: Berlin 1958–1961

Key concepts: Causation and consequence

Before reading this chapter, refer back to chapters 2 and 3 and consider the following essay questions:

- Examine the factors that meant Germany was an important country for both the West and the Soviet Union.
- Examine the steps by which the (a) economic, (b) political, and (c) military division of Germany took place after 1945.
- Discuss the factors that prevented an agreement on Germany taking place.

When you have read this chapter you should attempt the following essay question:

- Examine the reasons for, and the results of, the crisis over Berlin in 1958–1961.

Cold War Crisis:

Berlin 1958–1961

66 *… underlying all the questions that separated the Great Powers in the first 16 years of the Cold War was Germany.*

Colin Brown and Peter J Mooney, *Cold War to Détente 1945–1980* (Heinemann Educational 1981) p.66

Timeline of events affecting the post-war development of Germany 1945–1961		
1945	**Feb**	Yalta Conference
	July	Potsdam Conference
1948	**Feb**	Marshall Aid agreed to be Congress
	June	Berlin Blockade
1949	**April**	NATO established
	Sept	Federal Republic of Germany established (FGR – West Germany)
	Oct	German Democratic Republic established (**DDR** – East Germany)
		USSR proposes neutralized Germany
1953	**June**	East German uprising
1954	**Oct**	West Germany admitted to NATO and permitted to rearm
1955	**May**	Warsaw Pact established
	July	Germany discussed at Geneva summit – no agreement
1958		Khrushchev demands German peace treaty and demilitarized West Berlin
1961	**June**	Khrushchev threatens to sign a separate peace treaty with East Germany
	August	Berlin Wall built

The two Germanys

As you have read in chapters 2 and 3, Germany had, by 1949, become two countries. It was this division of Germany that did much to fuel the Cold War in the years up to 1961. Significant differences existed between West Germany and East Germany in the economic and political spheres.

Economic differences between West Germany and East Germany

Economically, West Germany was larger than East Germany with a larger population and greater industrial output. It had also received Marshall Aid. In fact, West Germany in the 1950s and 1960s experienced what became known as the 'economic miracle' and, accordingly, the standard of living of most West Germans rapidly increased. Meanwhile, in East Germany, leader Walter Ulbricht's post-1949 programme of forced collectivization of farms, and of socialization, was disastrous for the economy. With the hardships and drop in living standards that this entailed, many East Germans fled to the West via Berlin.

Political differences between West Germany and East Germany

Politically, West Germany had democracy. In East Germany there had been no free elections since 1946 and, by the 1950s, it was a rigidly Stalinist, authoritarian state. Discontent with the situation in East Germany manifested itself in the riots of June 1953. Workers in East Berlin and elsewhere in the East rose up in revolt. The riots were quickly put down with the help of Soviet tanks. This was the first major rebellion within the Soviet sphere of influence (see chapter 13).

As a result of these differences, there were no further efforts by either side to reunite as one country. Changing the situation seemed more risky than maintaining the status quo. However, the potential for conflict remained – particularly in the increasingly untenable situation of Berlin, which Khrushchev described as 'a fishbone in East Germany's gullet'.

Why did the Berlin Crisis develop?

Khrushchev and the crisis of 1958

After the Berlin Blockade (see chapter 3), Berlin remained divided under joint American–British–French–Soviet occupation, and the economic and political inequalities of the two Germanys could be clearly seen in the differences between West Berlin and East Berlin. West Berlin appeared to be a glittering, dynamic example of what Capitalism could achieve. This factor, along with the political freedoms and open lifestyle of the West Berliners, encouraged East Germans to escape – from the hardships of the East to the prosperity and freedom of the West – through the open frontier in Berlin. All East Berliners had to do was to travel from East Berlin to West Berlin, which could be done by train or subway; from there emigration to West Germany was easy.

This exodus of mainly young and skilled East Germans – which was encouraged by the West – meant that between 1945 and 1961 about one-sixth of the whole

German population took the opportunity to move to the West via Berlin. In addition, the divided city of Berlin allowed the West to maintain a unique propaganda and espionage base 186 kilometres (110 miles) deep into East German territory.

In 1958, Khrushchev proposed a peace treaty that would recognize the existence of the two Germanys. On 27 November 1958, he then demanded that Berlin should be demilitarized, Western troops withdrawn, and Berlin changed into a 'free city'. If the West did not agree to these changes within 6 months, Khrushchev threatened that he would turn over control of access routes to the Western sectors of Berlin to the GDR (East Germany). This was clever diplomacy; it would allow the GDR to interfere at will with traffic using land corridors from the FRG (West Germany). The Western allies would then have to negotiate with East Germany, which would force them to recognize the existence and sovereignty of the GDR. It was a dangerous situation. The West could not contemplate losing face over Berlin or giving up its propaganda and intelligence base, but to resist Khrushchev could mean the possibility of war.

Activity 1   **ATL** Self-management skills

1. What demands did Khrushchev make in 1958? Explain why this was 'clever diplomacy'.

Why was Khrushchev prepared to precipitate this Cold War crisis? Evidence from the Soviet archives points to the fact that the most important influences on Khrushchev's policy-making at this time were:

• Soviet fear of West Germany acquiring nuclear weapons
• concern over the failing East German economy
• pressure from Walter Ulbricht, leader of the GDR.

In the face of Western outrage at his proposal, Khrushchev dropped his ultimatum. He was successful, however, in forcing the Allies to discuss the German question. In February 1959, they agreed that a foreign ministers' conference should meet in Geneva in the summer. At Geneva both sides put forward proposals for German unity, but no agreement was secured. Khrushchev then met in the United States with Eisenhower in September 1959, but again no agreement was reached. A follow-up summit to be held in Paris in May 1960 was called off at the last minute after an American U-2 spy plane was shot down over the Soviet Union (see chapter 7, pages 98–99).

As the numbers of refugees fleeing from East Germany via Berlin continued to grow, Ulbricht grew increasingly frustrated with Khrushchev's failure to solve this problem. He wanted Khrushchev to sort out the Berlin problem immediately – and not in the context of a broader German peace settlement with the West.

Khrushchev, however, hoped that he would have more luck in getting concessions over Berlin with the new president of America, John F Kennedy.

Kennedy and flexible response

John F Kennedy was elected president in 1960. His approach to containment was a policy of 'flexible response', as we have seen in his approach to Vietnam (see page 79). In terms of his wider Cold War policy, it involved:

• more spending on conventional forces
• enlarging the nuclear arsenal
• continuing with CIA covert work

- giving economic aid to developing countries to help them resist Communism
- continuing negotiations with the Soviet Union.

Therefore, Kennedy broadened the range of options for resisting Communism, as it seemed to his administration that the Communist threat was much more diverse than it had been previously. Not only was it more geographically diverse, but Communist forces were now giving assistance to revolutionary movements in the developing world. With flexible response, Kennedy was moving away from Eisenhower's policy of massive retaliation or, as he put it, 'We intend to have a wider choice than humiliation or all-out nuclear war.'

Activity 2  **ATL Thinking skills**

1. Compare Eisenhower's 'New Look' with Kennedy's 'flexible response'. What aspects of their containment policies were similar? What aspects were different?

John F Kennedy, president of the United States from 1961 to 1963.

Khrushchev, Ulbricht, and the crisis of 1960–1961

President Kennedy first met Nikita Khrushchev at the Vienna Summit of 1961. Khrushchev believed that he might be able to exploit Kennedy's relative inexperience in foreign affairs. He also had an advantage in that Kennedy had just suffered the embarrassment of the failed Bay of Pigs invasion (see chapter 9, pages 115–116).

Khrushchev, therefore, decided to renew his ultimatum on Berlin. However, Kennedy, in his determination to appear tough with the Soviets, was not prepared to give any concessions to them. Calling Berlin 'an island of freedom in a Communist sea' and 'a beacon of hope behind the Iron Curtain', he announced in a television broadcast that: 'We cannot and will not permit the Soviets to drive us out of Berlin, either gradually or by force.' He also responded with an increase in military spending and a civil defence programme to build more nuclear fallout shelters.

A 19-year-old East German guard escaping to West Berlin on 15 August 1961, two days after the border was sealed.

The Berlin Wall

With the tension growing over the situation in Berlin, the number of refugees moving from East to West increased. On 12 August 1961 alone, 40 000 refugees fled to the West. Khrushchev had no intention of starting a nuclear war over Berlin, and so, following Kennedy's threat to defend Berlin 'by any means' and the growing crisis in East Germany, he bowed to Ulbricht's pressure and agreed to the closure of the East German border in Berlin. On the morning of 13 August 1961, barbed wire was erected between East and West Berlin. This was followed by a more permanent concrete wall.

What did the building of the wall mean ...

... for Khrushchev?

For Khrushchev, the Berlin Wall was a defeat in the sense that it was a visible admission that the Communist propaganda message had failed: the Soviets had to create a barrier to keep the people in the East. However, it meant that he was able to regain control over the situation and free himself from the continuing pressure from Walter Ulbricht – and the danger that Ulbricht might act independently. Once the wall was built, Khrushchev went back on his promise to Ulbricht and did not sign a separate peace treaty with the GDR that would have given East Germany control over the access routes to Berlin.

This map shows the wall encircling West Berlin.

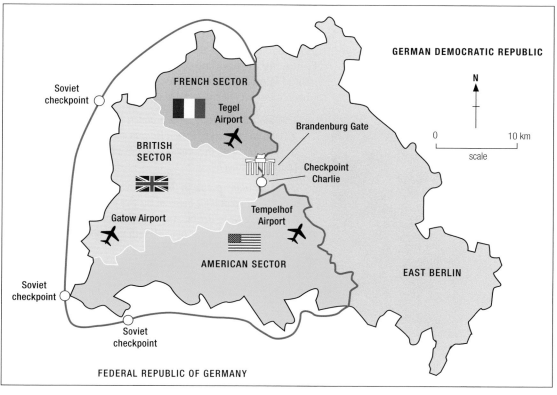

… for Ulbricht?

Although Ulbricht did not get his peace treaty, the closed border in Berlin, combined with Soviet assistance, helped him to consolidate Communist control in the GDR.

… for the citizens of Berlin?

For the citizens of Berlin, the erection of the wall was a horrifying experience. Families and friends were immediately cut off from each other with no hope of reunion. They continued to be on the front line of the Cold War.

… for the Cold War?

In terms of the Cold War, however, the building of the Berlin Wall had the effect of settling the question of Germany and removing it as a key issue in Cold War negotiations (though, as you will read in the next chapter, the Americans did not actually realize this at first).

The Americans complained vigorously about the wall – at one point US tanks confronted Soviet tanks at **Checkpoint Charlie** (the official border post between East and West Berlin) for several hours – but the USA was actually relieved that a war over Berlin had been averted. The focus of the Cold War moved from Europe, although it is important to note that for the Soviet Union the presence of US missile bases in Turkey, on the eastern fringe of Europe, remained an important issue.

East German border guards remove the body of 18-year-old Peter Fechter, shot dead trying to escape into West Berlin in September 1962.

The symbolism of the wall

Between 1961 and 1989, the Berlin Wall stood as a powerful symbol of the division between East and West. Indeed, it seemed as if the idea of an 'Iron Curtain', as put forward by Winston Churchill during his Fulton speech in 1946, had become a reality, in the form of a concrete wall. Following the building of the wall, President Kennedy visited West Berlin and gave his emotive and highly publicized 'Ich bin ein Berliner' speech:

> Two thousand years ago the proudest boast in the world was 'civis Romanus sum' [I am a Roman citizen]. Today, in the world of freedom, the proudest boast is, Ich bin ein Berliner, [I am a Berliner].
>
> There are many people in the world who do not understand what is the great issue between the free world and Communism. Let them come to Berlin. And there are some who say in Europe and elsewhere that we can work with the Communists. Let them come to Berlin.
>
> Freedom has many difficulties and democracy is not perfect: but we have never had to put up a wall to keep our people in. I know of no city which has been besieged for 18 years and still lives with the vitality, force, hope and determination of this city of West Berlin. While the wall is the most obvious and vivid demonstration of the failures of the Communist system, we take no satisfaction in it, for it is an offence not only against history but against humanity …

In 18 years of peace and good faith this generation of Germans has earned the right to be free, including the right to unite their family and nation in lasting peace with the goodwill of all people. When the day finally comes when this city will be joined as one in this great continent of Europe, the people of West Berlin can take great satisfaction in the fact that they were in the front line for almost two decades.

From a speech given in West Berlin by President John F Kennedy on 26 June 1963

Activity 3   (ATL) Thinking skills

1. In what ways does Kennedy use the building of the Berlin Wall as a propaganda weapon against the USSR? Quote directly from his speech to support your arguments.

Over the next three decades, hundreds of people were killed attempting to defect to the West. East German border guards were instructed to shoot to kill. There were also many spectacular and ingenious escapes.

When the collapse of the Soviet Union began in 1989, it was again the wall – or rather the rapid and eager dismantling of it by the people of Berlin – which was the most vivid symbol of political reality: the Cold War was over.

TOK How do political leaders attempt to maintain their 'credibility'? Which is more important for this – using reason or emotion when addressing the public?

 Where else in the world have 'separation barriers' been built to keep people from moving freely, or to keep certain groups out of a particular area or country? Where do 'separation barriers' exist at the moment?

Crowds dismantling the Berlin Wall in 1989.

Read these sources, look back at the Activity section at the end of chapter 5, and then answer the following question.

1. In pairs, compare and contrast Source A, Source B, and Source C in their analysis of the results of the building of the Berlin Wall.

Source A

❝ *The Berlin crisis has been a dreadful moment, but this was followed in Europe by a prolonged period of stability, if not calm. The Soviet Union was not unhappy with the outcome … [There was] a sense of Soviet satisfaction. A problem had been solved. For the 190 people who were to die in the attempt to escape across the Wall, it was solved with grim finality. For the seventeen millions left in the German Democratic Republic, as East Germany called itself, their citizenship was now uncomfortably close to imprisonment. The continent's political permafrost settled deeper … Europe settled down into its two armed camps …*

Martin Walker, *The Cold War* (Vintage Press 1994) p.159

Source B

❝ *The Berlin Wall was an ideological defeat of colossal proportions for the Soviet Union and world Communism. The Wall became a symbol of the Cold War, concrete evidence of the inability of East Germany to win the loyalty of its inhabitants. It was also seen as hard proof that Soviet-style socialism was losing its economic competition with Capitalism. Although the Wall ended the mass emigration that had been destabilizing East Germany and also led to a period of prolonged stability in Europe, no one at the time knew that this would be the outcome. When a crisis arose in October 1962 over Soviet missiles in Cuba, the initial U.S. reaction was that the Soviets had put the missiles there as a way of forcing the West out of Berlin.*

David Painter, *The Cold War: An International History* (Routledge 1999) p.53

Source C

❝ *In August 1961 the Soviet Union was humbled as the Berlin Wall was constructed to save East Germany from ignominious economic collapse. Peaceful coexistence had failed to attract Western concessions, particularly a settlement of divided Germany, and as the Wall was raised peaceful coexistence collapsed.*

Bradley Lightbody, *The Cold War* (Routledge 1999) p.44

2. Individually, draft a response to the following question: Compare and contrast the views expressed in Sources A and B regarding the impact of the Berlin Wall.

Activity 5 **ATL** Self-management and thinking skills?

Essay writing

Consider the following essay question:

> *Examine the reasons for Germany being the focus of Cold War hostility in the 16 years after World War Two.*

Essay frame

An essay like this needs careful planning. The emphasis is on the *reasons* why Germany was a focus for Cold War hostility, so you must be careful that you do not just write a description of the *key events* affecting Germany. Each paragraph should focus on a different reason for the hostility.

Here are some hints for a possible approach to the content and structure. You will still need to develop your own opening sentences for each paragraph. Look back at chapters 3 and 7 for reminders on how to do this.

Introduction: Importance of Germany concerning its strategic position in Europe. Brief overview of main decisions concerning division of Germany made at Yalta and Potsdam. Outline of main tension points to be covered and identification of the main arguments: tension was caused because of differences in aims for Germany, as well as events in Germany itself, and increasingly because of wider developments in the Cold War.

Paragraph 1: Economic reasons: 'Our first break with Soviet policy in Germany came over reparations' – General Lucius Clay in 1946. Why? Agreements unworkable, difference in economic aims for Germany (see chapters 2 and 3).

Paragraph 2: Political reasons: Look at the different political aims that East and West had for Germany by 1948, which triggered the Berlin Blockade. Note that the context of the wider Cold War is also important here for explaining the political aims of each side for Germany by 1948.

Paragraph 3: Military issues and Soviet concern with regard to West Germany entering NATO.

Paragraph 4: The issue of Berlin: the reasons why this city was such an issue of concern for Ulbricht and Khrushchev by 1958.

Conclusion: Note the effect of the building of the wall in removing Germany as a source of tension. Don't forget to come back to the question, but don't summarize everything that you have said in the main body of the essay. Identify the key reason that comes out of your essay as to why Germany was a source of tension during this period. Possibly point to the shift in the focus of tension from Germany in general to Berlin in particular.

Practice essay questions – Germany

Attempt to plan or write these up. You will need to review the material from chapters 2 and 3, with specific reference to Germany.

- *Examine the reasons for and the results of Germany as a centre of Cold War tension between 1945 and 1961.*
- *Examine the role of Germany in the origins and development of the Cold War.*
- *Discuss how far Germany was the cause of superpower confrontation between 1943 and 1961.*

 To access websites relevant to this chapter, go to www.pearsonhotlinks. com, search for the book title or ISBN, and click on 'chapter 8'.

09

Peaceful co-existence and containment:
Case study in crisis: The Cuban Missile Crisis

Key concepts: Consequence, significance, and perspectives

As you read this chapter, consider the following essay questions:

- Examine the causes of the Cuban Missile Crisis in 1962.
- Evaluate how effectively the superpower leaders, Kennedy and Khrushchev, handled the Cuban Missile Crisis.
- Examine the impact of this crisis on the Cold War.
- To what extent has the danger of this crisis been exaggerated?

Cold War Crisis:

The Cuban Missile Crisis

The Cuban Missile Crisis was perhaps the most dramatic Cold War confrontation between the USSR and the USA. During the 13 days of the crisis, the United States and the Soviet Union came close to a direct military showdown for the first time during the Cold War.

Both leaders were under intense domestic pressure to prove themselves, and their individual personalities and perceptions were critical in the development and resolution of the crisis.

The timeline below shows how the USA and the USSR reacted to the sequence of events that followed the 1959 takeover of the government of Cuba by Fidel Castro and his fellow revolutionaries.

Activity 1

 **ATL** Social skills

1. In pairs or small groups, read through the timeline below, which outlines the events. Identify where the actions of one of the superpowers increases the tension over Cuba. How far do the actions of the superpowers provoke a crisis? Identify where Castro's/Cuban policies are provoking a confrontation with the USA or increasing tension between the superpowers. Do you agree on which country seems to be acting most provocatively?

Policies of Cuba	Date	Actions of USA	Actions of USSR
	1959		
Castro seizes power	**Jan 1**		
Batista's supporters executed	**Jan 7**	USA recognizes Cuban government	
	April		
Castro visits USA to discuss package of US aid for his **industrialization** programme			
USA will only give money if Cuba follows guidelines of International Monetary Fund (IMF)			
Request for loan from Organization of American States (**OAS**) also turned down			
Agrarian Reform Law (which appropriates land and bans land ownership by foreigners) introduced	**May**	Convinced that Cuba is Communist: hostility increases	

Policies of Cuba	Date	Actions of USA	Actions of USSR
	1960		
	Feb		First deputy minister of USSR visits Cuba: five-year treaty signed; USSR to buy five million tons of sugar and to give $100 million credit to buy industrial machinery and material Secretly agrees to send arms
First shipment of arms from USSR arrives in Cuba	**March**	Eisenhower orders CIA to train exiles for a future attack on Cuba	
Castro seizes Texaco and Esso oil refineries after they refuse to accept Russian oil	**June**		
	July	Eisenhower reduces Cuban sugar quota by 700 000 tons	Soviets agree to buy the surplus sugar
	August	USA presents a document to OAS charging Cuba with introducing Communism into Western sphere: not supported by OAS	
Castro expropriates US industrial property and nationalizes banks	**Oct 7**	Kennedy in election speech calls Cuba 'a Communist menace'	
	Oct 19	USA proclaims embargo on Cuba except for foodstuffs and medicine	New sugar quota signed
Cuba expropriates 166 more US companies in reply to **embargo**	**Nov** **Dec**	USA suspends sugar quota for 1961	
	1961		
Castro orders US embassy to cut its staff to 11	**Jan 2**	Eisenhower breaks off diplomatic relations	
Castro announces that his regime is a socialist regime	**April 14** **April 15** **April 17**	Air strike against Cuba Bay of Pigs landing	
Cubans victorious over counter-revolutionaries	**April 19**		
	Nov 30	Operation Mongoose put into operation	
Castro declares himself to be a Marxist–Leninist	**Dec 2**	US believes that Castro has now revealed what they knew all along	No comment on Castro's speech
	1962		
	Feb	US **trade embargo** – except for certain foodstuffs and medicine Cuba expelled from OAS	
Economic situation now in crisis; signs trade agreement with China	**May**		
Sugar production is two million tons lower than in 1961	**June**		New trade agreement with Cuba
	Oct 14	US U-2 planes photograph missile sites under construction	

Policies of Cuba	Date	Actions of USA	Actions of USSR
	Oct 16	ExComm set up	
	Oct 22	President Kennedy publicly announces the establishment of Cuban **quarantine**	
	Oct 24		Soviet warships turn back
	Oct 26		Khrushchev sends first telegram U-2 plane shot down
	Oct 27	Robert Kennedy and Anatoly Dobrynin meet	Khrushchev sends second telegram
	Oct 28		Khrushchev agrees to withdraw missiles
Castro refuses to allow UN inspectors into Cuba	**Nov**	Democrats maintain control in mid-term elections	

Background to and causes of the Cuban Missile Crisis

Why was the United States opposed to Castro's revolution?

The origins of the Cuban Missile Crisis can be traced back to the overthrow of the pro-USA Cuban government of General Fulgencio Batista by Fidel Castro in 1959. Cuba lies only 145 kilometres (90 miles) from the coast of Florida. For this reason, the USA considered the island of Cuba to be within its sphere of influence, and it was determined that any government in Cuba should reflect and protect US interests, which were considerable. In the economic arena, the US companies controlled most of the financial, railway, electricity, telegraph, and sugar industries. The United States had an agreement with Cuba allowing it to establish a naval base at **Guantanamo Bay**; furthermore, the **Platt Amendment** of 1901 stipulated that the US would 'exercise the right to intervene for the preservation of Cuban independence' and for 'the maintenance of a government adequate for the protection of life, property, and individual liberty'. It was clear that the US administration intended to decide what constituted Cuban independence and when a government was or was not 'adequate'.

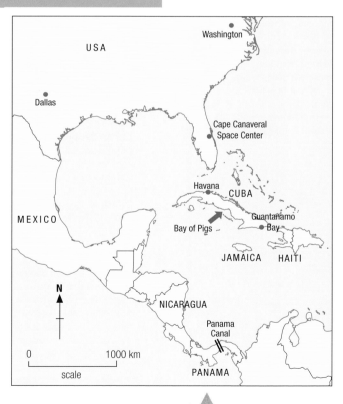

This map shows the geographical position of Cuba in relation to the United States.

Castro takes power

On 7 January 1959, realizing that Batista had lost the support of most Cubans, the United States reluctantly recognized the new government of Fidel Castro, which

Castro and his guerrilla forces take Havana in 1959.

had taken power after fighting a guerrilla war campaign for seven years. The United States still hoped to control events in Cuba through its economic interests and the presence of a large pro-US middle class. Initially, Castro insisted that he was not a Communist, asserting: 'This is not Communism or Marxism, but representative democracy and social justice in a well-planned economy.' In April 1959, he visited the United States in the hope of getting economic assistance for the far-reaching reforms he believed Cuba needed.

However, Castro's revolutionary reforms involved **nationalization** of US economic interests, and most pro-US Cubans chose to move to the United States rather than to stay and resist. The US government tried to moderate Castro's reforms by refusing him economic assistance unless he followed guidelines set out by the International Monetary Fund (IMF). The Organization of American States (OAS) refused to give Castro financial aid for economic development, and so Castro turned to the Soviet Union, which offered economic aid in February 1960 (see timeline on page 112). This direct involvement of the Soviet Union with a Caribbean state was an immediate challenge to the USA, given that Cuba was right on its doorstep.

Organisation of American States (OAS)

The OAS was set up in 1948 by the United States and 20 Latin American nations. It was designed to facilitate co-operation and good economic and political relations between the member states. For the United States it also served as a bulwark against Communist ideas spreading into the Western hemisphere.

Who was Fidel Castro?

Fidel Castro was born into a wealthy land-owning family. He attended a **Jesuit** school and then graduated as a lawyer from Havana University. He took on the legal cases of poor people, and he became very aware of the inequalities in Cuban society. Like all Cubans, he particularly resented the domination of Americans in every aspect of Cuban life. In 1947, Castro joined the **Cuban People's Party**, which campaigned against poverty and injustice. However, although the Cuban People's Party was expected to win the 1952 election (Castro was a candidate), it was not given the opportunity, due to a **military coup** led by General Batista, which took over Cuba's government. Castro then decided that revolution was the only option for gaining power in Cuba and led an attack on the Moncada Army Barracks. This ended in disaster, and Castro was fortunate to survive; he used his trial to make a speech about the problems of Cuba. This was later written up as a book entitled *History Will Absolve Me*. The international recognition and personal popularity that followed his courtroom speech meant that he was released from prison. Castro then planned an attack with other rebels (known as July 26 Movement after the date of the attack on the Moncada Barracks) against the Cuban military **junta**. They based themselves in the Sierra Maestra Mountains, from where they fought a guerrilla war against Batista's regime. This eventually was successful, and Fidel Castro marched into the Cuban capital, Havana, on 9 January 1959 as the country's new leader.

Activity 2 Self-management skills

Study the timeline on pages 111–113, then answer the following questions:

1. What actions taken by Castro would have convinced the United States that he was a Communist?
2. What actions taken by Castro indicate that in fact he may not have been a Communist in 1959?
3. What evidence is there to support the view that the United States helped push Castro into a relationship with the Soviet Union?

1. In order to understand the nature of Castro's revolution, research the following aspects of his struggle:
   - What military tactics did Castro use?
   - How did his army behave towards the local population?
   - What political and economic policies did the Cuban military regime follow with the local population?
   - How do Castro's guerrilla tactics compare with those of other guerrilla armies, such as the Vietminh?
   - What other groups in Cuban society contributed to the final success of Castro?

How did the United States deal with the 'threat' of Castro?

The United States decided to deal with this threatening situation in two ways:

- economically, by proclaiming an embargo on all exports to Cuba except for foodstuffs and medicine
- militarily, by organizing an invasion force of Cuban exiles to overthrow Castro.

The first plan, as can be seen from the timeline, failed in that it drove Castro to sign more economic agreements with the Soviet Union. The second plan, the invasion, ended in a humiliation for the US government.

Why was the Bay of Pigs invasion a failure?

In March 1960, President Eisenhower approved a CIA plan to overthrow Castro's government. Part of this plan involved training Cuban refugees for an invasion of Cuba at the Bay of Pigs. President Kennedy inherited the plan and gave it his approval. However, the invasion was a failure, ending in the capture of 1214 of the original 1400 invaders. These prisoners were later released in return for $53 million worth of food and machines paid for by voluntary groups in the United States.

This was a severe humiliation for Kennedy and his administration. He was blamed by all parties for the failure of this venture and was condemned internationally for allowing it to have taken place. However, it is now clear that the reasons for the failure of the Bay of Pigs invasion were more the fault of the CIA. It underestimated the strength of popular support for Castro within Cuba: it had counted on a popular uprising against Castro, which never materialized – and indeed the whole episode strengthened popular support for his regime. In addition, the actual invasion plans were severely flawed, with the soldier-exiles suffering from a shortage of ammunition and lack of air cover. Castro's air force was much more effective than had been originally supposed. Despite the CIA's assurances to the contrary, the exiles could not survive without the cover from the US Air Force, and this was something that President Kennedy could not sanction if he was to publicly distance himself from the plot.

This photograph shows the growing friendship between Castro and Khrushchev.

What were the results of the failure of the Bay of Pigs invasion?

For Kennedy, the failure of the invasion was humiliating and meant a loss of prestige within the United States and in the rest of the world. It also set back Kennedy's attempts to identify the USA with **anti-colonialism**. Castro's support within Cuba increased and his position was strengthened:

> *What is hidden behind the Yankees' hatred of the Cuban Revolution … a small country of only seven million people, economically underdeveloped, without financial or military means to threaten the security or economy of any other country? What explains it is fear. Not fear of the Cuban revolution, but fear of the Latin American Revolution.*

Fidel Castro, Second Declaration of Havana, 1962

The CIA and Castro

The CIA carried out numerous assassination attempts against Castro. Stories about plots against Castro include exploding cigars, poison in milkshakes, training an ex-girlfriend to shoot him, and, as confirmed in recently published CIA documents, hiring the **Mafia** to kill Castro. However, Fidel Castro has gone on to survive ten US presidents.

The Soviet Union and Khrushchev were further given ammunition to use in criticizing the United States. Other Latin American governments and peoples were outraged and the episode revived fears of US imperialism in the area.

The failure of the Bay of Pigs invasion further strengthened Cuba's ties with the USSR. After the failed attack, Castro declared himself to be a Marxist–Leninist and concluded a defensive alliance with the Soviet Union. Thus, the USA was unable to prevent the flow of Soviet advisers and weapons into Cuba.

The USA continued its efforts to reverse the Cuban revolution through covert action (Operation Mongoose), which involved the sabotage of economic targets, such as sugar plantations and petroleum installations, assassination plots against Castro and other Cuban leaders, and the **diplomatic isolation** of Cuba. For example, Cuba was expelled from the Organization of American States (OAS) in 1962. The USA also put military pressure on Cuba by carrying out training exercises near Puerto Rico.

The Cuban Missile Crisis

Why did Khrushchev put missiles in Cuba?

In 1962, Khrushchev made the decision to put intermediate range **ballistic missiles** (IRBMs) into Cuba. This was a highly provocative act and was bound to cause a reaction from the USA. So, why did Khrushchev make this move?

Khrushchev wrote in his memoirs that the reason was to protect Cuba and also because 'it was high time America learned what it feels like to have her own land and her own people threatened'. The United States had missiles in Turkey, which bordered the Soviet Union, and putting missiles a similar distance away from the United States was seen as a way of redressing the balance.

Equally important was Khrushchev's aim to seize a propaganda advantage after the humiliation of the Berlin Wall (see chapter 8), and to acquire a bargaining chip against the stationing of US nuclear missiles in Europe.

> *By swiftly and secretly installing missiles in Cuba, an island only ninety miles away from the United States, the Russians would have stolen a march on the Americans. It was a gamble with extremely high stakes, but if it had paid off, the Soviets would have immensely improved their prestige in the eyes of the world, not least in Latin America, and by doing so would also have increased their bargaining power in Cold War offensives, for example Berlin.*

Robert Beggs, *Flashpoints: The Cuban Missile Crisis* (Longman 1977) p.91

John Lewis Gaddis, however, believes that Khrushchev put the missiles into Cuba mainly because he feared another invasion of Cuba. Khrushchev may have seen the Bay of Pigs invasion not as a sign of Kennedy's weakness, but rather of his determination to crush the Cuban revolution. Should the US government succeed in this aim, it would be a defeat for Communism worldwide. The fact that the United States had missiles in Turkey, so near to the heart of the Soviet Union, provided a justification for installing missiles in Cuba to protect the island. This viewpoint is supported by the Soviet historians Zubok and Pleshakov, who believe that Khrushchev was primarily concerned with preserving revolutionary Cuba and, thereby, Soviet **hegemony** and the spread of Communism.

Aerial photograph of missile sites in Cuba, issued by the US Embassy in London on 23 October 1962.

Why was the presence of missiles so intolerable to the United States?

On 14 October 1962, Kennedy was presented with photos from a U-2 spy plane which showed evidence that launch pads were being constructed by the Soviets for 64 IRBMs.

It is important to note that in fact the positioning of the missiles in Cuba did not really affect the worldwide nuclear balance. However, it did increase the Soviets' **first strike** capability, and it meant that warning time for missiles fired at the United States would be far less than for missiles fired from within the Soviet Union (see map on page 119). More important, perhaps, is the fact that to the US public it certainly seemed that the balance of power had changed. 'Offensive missiles in Cuba have a very different psychological and political effect in this hemisphere than missiles in the USSR pointed at us,' President Kennedy pointed out at a meeting with his advisers.

Therefore, President Kennedy faced a crisis. The prestige of the USA, and also of Kennedy himself, was again at stake. Cuba was not only a mere 90 miles away from the USA, but it was also the place where the disastrous and – for Kennedy – humiliating Bay of Pigs episode had taken place. Another factor for Kennedy was the impending Congressional elections, which were to take place in early November. For the Democratic Party to face elections with missiles installed in Cuba would be a disaster for the Kennedy administration: so the president had to take action. But how could he resolve the crisis without precipitating a dangerous and world-threatening head-on collision with the USSR?

How was the Cuba crisis linked to the Berlin Crisis?

An added dimension of this crisis was that Kennedy also believed that Khrushchev's actions were part of a Soviet plan to put pressure on America to get out of Berlin. Kennedy said to British Prime Minister Harold Macmillan on 22 October, 'I need not point out to you the possible relation of this secret and dangerous move on the part of Khrushchev to Berlin'; and to his advisers he pointed out that, 'Our problem is not merely Cuba but it is also Berlin.' This, of course, increased the tension further, as Kennedy believed that his decisions would affect not only Cuba, but also Berlin, and thus Europe. Tony Judt concludes that the crisis took the terrifying form that it did because …

> of a simple American misunderstanding that can stand as a metaphor for much of the early cold war. The officials in Washington thought that their Soviet opponents were playing a complicated game of diplomatic chess, with the various pawns on the international board – Czechoslovakia, Korea, Germany, Egypt, Indochina, and now Cuba – being subtly moved around to the calculate advantage of the Moscow principles. In fact, however, the Soviet leaders – first Stalin now Khrushchev – were not playing chess. They were playing poker. They had a weak hand and they knew it … So they bluffed. The outcome of the Cuban crisis would not have been very different if the Americans had realized sooner which game they were in; but the risks encountered along the way would have been much reduced.

Tony Judt, *The Crisis: Kennedy, Khrushchev and Cuba* in *Reappraisals, Reflections on the Forgotten Twentieth Century* (Vintage 2009) pp.334–335

Activity 4   (ATL) **Thinking skills**

1. In pairs draft an essay plan to the following question, using the Cuban Missile Crisis as your case study:

   Discuss the causes of one Cold War crisis.

How was the crisis resolved?

President Kennedy summoned a crisis management team, the Executive Committee (**ExComm**) to deal with the threat of missiles in Cuba. This began what has become known as 'The Thirteen Days'. Kennedy rejected calls from the military for an immediate air strike followed by an invasion of Cuba (General Curtis LeMay actually called for the total elimination of Cuba) and ordered instead a naval blockade of the island. The president made the American position public by going on television to announce the establishment of the '**quarantine**' around Cuba to prevent the delivery of any nuclear warheads to the island. Khrushchev ignored the quarantine, and Soviet ships containing missiles headed for Cuba.

However, on 24 October, six Soviet ships turned back towards the Soviet Union. At this point Dean Rusk, the US Secretary of State, commented, 'We're eyeball to eyeball and I think the other fellow just blinked.' Nevertheless, the crisis continued as the missile sites still remained on Cuba.

On 26 October, Khrushchev sent a telegram to Kennedy saying that the Soviet Union would remove the missiles in return for a US pledge not to invade Cuba. At this point, he was convinced that the United States was on the verge of attacking Cuba:

> … We and you ought not to pull on the ends of the rope in which you have tied the knot of war, because the more the two of us pull, the tighter the knot will be tied. And then it will be necessary to cut that knot, and what that will mean is not for me to explain to you, because you yourself understand perfectly of what terrible forces our countries dispose … I have participated in two wars and know that war ends when it is rolled through cities and villages everywhere sowing death and destruction. For such is the logic of war; if people do not display wisdom they will clash like blind moles.

Letter from Khrushchev to Kennedy, dated 26 October 1962, quoted by the Secretary of Defense Robert McNamara in the television documentary *The Fog of War*

This telegram might have defused the crisis. However, before Kennedy could respond, Khrushchev sent a second, more demanding, letter to the US government insisting on the inclusion of the removal of Turkish missiles in any deal over Cuba. The crisis further escalated after a US U-2 plane was shot down over Cuba. This action had been taken by military leaders in Cuba without authorization from the Soviet Union and seemed a sign that events could easily spiral out of control. The shooting down increased pressure on Kennedy to take military action against Cuba. The consequences of this would have been extremely serious as, unknown to the Americans at the time, short-range nuclear missiles were already on Cuba and ready for use by the Cubans.

Kennedy continued to see military action as a last resort and, on the advice of Llewellyn (Tommy) Thompson, who had been US ambassador to the Soviet Union, he decided to accept Khrushchev's first offer and ignore the second. At the same

This map shows the position and range of missiles based in Cuba compared to those based in Turkey.

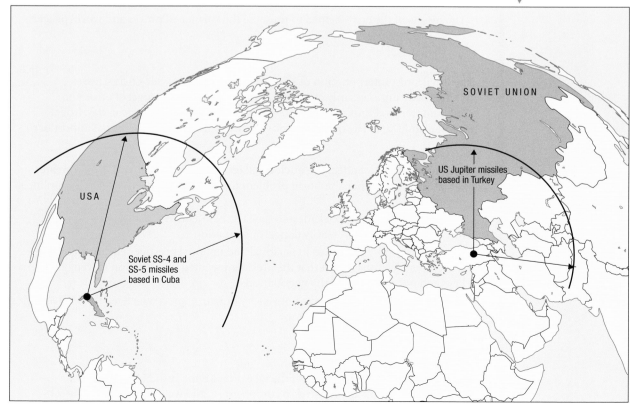

119

time, however, Kennedy's brother, Robert – and then **Attorney General** – met with Anatoly Dobrynin, the Soviet ambassador in Washington, DC, to agree that the United States would remove missiles from Turkey.

On 28 October, Khrushchev cabled President Kennedy and agreed to remove all missiles from Cuba in return for US assurance that it would not invade Cuba. There was no reference to US removal of missiles from Turkey – this part of the deal remained secret.

How effective was Kennedy's handling of the Cuban Missile Crisis?

The Orthodox view

The traditional interpretation of President Kennedy's role in the missile crisis has stressed that this was Kennedy's finest hour, and that he successfully used nuclear brinkmanship to preserve world peace. The writings of Robert Kennedy, Theodore C Sorensen, and Richard E Neustadt all put forward the following arguments in support of this view:

- Kennedy was right to respond to this crisis in a firm and forceful way, as the missiles represented a Soviet threat to alter the balance of power either in actuality or in appearance.
- The idea of imposing a quarantine (blockade) exerted maximum pressure on the Soviet Union while incurring the minimum risk of war.
- Kennedy himself always remained calm and in control of the situation. He resisted pressure for action from the military, he was statesmanlike, and he did not attempt to humiliate Khrushchev.
- The results of the crisis helped to preserve the balance of power and world peace.

The Revisionist view

The Revisionist interpretation of Kennedy's role in the missile crisis stresses that Kennedy unnecessarily raised the Cuban episode to the level of crisis and confrontation and thus subjected the world to the danger of nuclear war. Roger Hagman and David Horowitz put forward the following arguments in support of this view:

- The missiles did not affect the nuclear balance and the USA was under no greater threat. This was rather a political problem that could have been resolved by political means.
- The imposition of the blockade and the fact that Kennedy made the crisis public turned it into an unnecessarily dangerous situation.
- Kennedy was only interested in personal and national prestige. The forthcoming November elections meant that the president wanted the situation solved quickly, so he could not wait for lengthy negotiations.
- The aftermath of the crisis was not victory but arrogance, which led the United States to increase its activity in Vietnam.

New interpretations

Recent evidence seems to support the view that Kennedy did indeed act in a statesmanlike way, was prepared to compromise, and was not motivated by self-interest. The tape recordings of ExComm meetings at the time show Kennedy repeatedly pushing for compromise and point to the fact that he was keenly aware of the dangers of nuclear war. He deceived ExComm by having the secret agreement to remove missiles from Turkey, and it was revealed in 1987 that he had another option up his sleeve: if all else failed, the United Nations **Secretary General** was to suggest a Turkey–Cuba trade-off that Kennedy would then accept.

What conclusions can be reached about Khrushchev's actions?

Khrushchev claimed a victory. He argued that Kennedy had now promised not to invade Cuba, so the continued existence of a socialist Cuba in the Soviet sphere of influence was guaranteed. This is clearly significant, especially if you take Gaddis's view that this was the main reason that Khrushchev put missiles on Cuba in the first place. Khrushchev must also be given credit for being prepared to back down in the face of nuclear war, especially when many saw his handling of the crisis as a humiliation for the Soviet Union. However, the Soviet military were particularly angry. They were already unhappy about Khrushchev's military cuts, and they now had to accept a hasty withdrawal from Cuba, as well as the ultimate humiliation of having US officials inspect the missiles as they were removed.

Castro was also furious with Khrushchev's handling of the affair. He was not consulted about the final deal concerning the missiles – or over his agreement with Kennedy to withdraw the Soviet IL-28 bombers and Soviet troops that had been sent to help the Cuban army. He was also left with the US base at Guantanamo Bay, while US missiles were removed from Turkey in 1963.

Khrushchev had to work hard in the ensuing months to rebuild his relations with Castro and the Cuban regime, and prevent a Sino-Cuban alliance developing. Russian historians Zubok and Pleshakov wrote that during this crisis Khrushchev 'acted in the chillingly "realist" manner of Stalin: walking over the egos and bodies of those who had helped in the implementation of his grandiose designs, but then just happened to be in the way of retreat' ('Khrushchev and Kennedy: The Taming of the Cold War', in *The Cold War*, eds Klaus Larres and Ann Lane (Blackwell 2001) p.130).

Activity 5	 Social and thinking skills

1. In small groups, evaluate the impact of the key leaders on the course of the Cuban Missile Crisis.

What was Castro's role in the crisis?

It is clear now that Castro played a greater role in the development of this crisis than has previously been realized. Particularly significant is the period of time around 24–26 October. Castro was determined to make the most of the situation, and he claims that he would not have hesitated to use the nuclear weapons that were already in Cuba, should the United States have attempted a land invasion. This is despite the fact that it would have led to the destruction of the island. The shooting down of the U-2 plane indicates the difficulties that Khrushchev and Kennedy had in keeping control of the situation on the ground as it developed.

The impact of the Cuban Missile Crisis

What were the results of the crisis …

… for the USA?

Kennedy's personal prestige increased. Cuba shocked the United States into realizing the fragility of its own security, and increased its focus on building up military strength.

… for the USSR?

Despite his claims of victory, the crisis was a humiliation for Khrushchev and contributed to his fall from power in 1964. The USSR did not itself suffer from this humiliation and continued as a superpower for the next three decades.

… for Cuba?

Castro remained in power with the threat of a US invasion removed. However, Cuba became determined not to become a pawn in the East–West struggle, and pursued a foreign policy independent of Moscow (see chapter 18). Havana became a centre of revolutionary activity – such as educating and training activists, and spreading revolution in Africa and Central America – although the Castro regime did continue to rely on the USSR for economic aid and arms.

… for China?

China saw the resolution of the crisis and the USSR's unwillingness to challenge the United States as final proof that the USSR had ceased to be a revolutionary state. Its relationship with the USSR continued to deteriorate from this point, and China opted to carry on developing nuclear weapons independently (see chapter 10).

… for the wider international situation?

The Orthodox view is that the world was made a more secure place because:

- A hotline was established between the USSR and USA to make immediate telephone communication easier.
- Both sides realized the danger of nuclear war. Two important treaties were signed following the crisis: the Limited Test-Ban Treaty of August 1963, which forbade nuclear tests in the atmosphere, space or underwater (not signed by France and China); and the **Nuclear Non-Proliferation Treaty** of 1968, which prevented signatories from transferring weapons, or knowledge of how to make them, to non-nuclear powers.

However, these arms treaties did not in fact prevent the arms race, which intensified after the Cuban Missile Crisis as the Soviets escalated attempts to reach parity with the USA, even if it was conducted within an increasingly precise set of rules. Nevertheless, the world was more secure after the missile crisis in that there was more stability: neither side would now issue challenges to the other side's sphere of influence.

What is the relationship between Cuba and the US today? How far have political and economic relations changed since 1962? Research the news for recent articles on US–Cuban relations and bring to class to share.

Activity 6   **ATL** **Research skills**

1.   Research one of the following:

- One of the results of the Cuban Missile Crisis was that Cuba decided to be more independent of the USSR. It became involved in revolutionary activity in Latin America and also in Africa. Research Cuba's actions, and its success or failure in spreading revolution, in one of these areas: for example, Angola.
- Che Guevara became an icon of socialist revolutionaries. Research Che's role in the Cuban revolution and then his actions in spreading revolution outside of Cuba after 1965.

Activity 7

Essay writing

Consider the following essay question in small groups:

> **'The danger of the Cuban Missile Crisis has been seriously exaggerated.' To what extent do you agree?**

Essay frame

Remember to clarify any key words in the title and show you understand what the question is asking. Here, you need to explain what the 'danger' of the missile crisis was, and set out briefly the areas of debate that you will be discussing in your essay. Also set out your main argument.

Part 1: Points you could consider, regarding whether there was a real danger, are:

- actions of Kennedy and Khrushchev
- pressures on Kennedy and Khrushchev
- aims of Castro
- perceptions of people who were there at the time
- difficulty that Kennedy and Khrushchev had controlling events on the ground: for example, the shooting down of the American U-2

Consider when and how you will bring in the views of historians. The Orthodox historians believe that the danger was very real and that Kennedy saved the situation through his astute management of the crisis. Consider also the view of the Revisionist historians, who argue that Kennedy actually increased the danger through his reckless actions.

Part 2: You now need to look at the other side: that is, the view that the danger was exaggerated. What evidence can you find for this? Would Kennedy or Khrushchev really have been prepared to push the nuclear button, given the consequences (particularly Khrushchev, who knew that the Americans had nuclear superiority over the USSR at this time)?

Part 3: Consider new perspectives: what is the most recent view? Recent analysis would argue that the danger was even more real than supposed at the time. Look back at the chapter to find evidence for this.

Conclusion: Remember to come back to the question and answer it directly.

Activity 8

> The fate of Cuba and the maintenance of Soviet prestige in that part of the world preoccupied me … We had to establish a tangible and effective deterrent to American interference in the Caribbean. But what exactly? The logical answer was missiles. We knew that American missiles were aimed against us in Turkey and Italy, to say nothing of West Germany …
>
> I had the idea of installing missiles with nuclear warheads in Cuba without letting the United States find out if they were there until it was too late to do anything about them …
>
> I want to make one thing absolutely clear: when we put our ballistic missiles in Cuba, we had no desire to start a war. On the contrary, our principal aim was to deter America from starting a war … The climax came after five or six days when our Ambassador to Washington, Anatoly Dobrynin, reported that the President's brother, Robert Kennedy, had come to see him on an unofficial visit. Dobrynin's report went something like this:
>
> 'Robert Kennedy looked exhausted … He said that he had not been home for six days and nights. "The President is in a grave situation," Robert Kennedy said, "and he does not know how to get out of it. We are under very severe stress … from our military to use force against Cuba … We want to ask you, Mr Dobrynin, to pass President Kennedy's message to Chairman Khrushchev through unofficial channels. President Kennedy implores Chairman Khrushchev to accept his offer and to take into consideration the peculiarities of the American system … If the situation continues much longer, the President is not sure that the military will not overthrow him and seize power. The American army could get out of control."'
>
> I hadn't overlooked this possibility. I knew that Kennedy was a young President and that the security of the United States was indeed threatened …

Here are some points to consider when evaluating memoirs as historical evidence.

- Why do people write memoirs? What do you think the purpose of Kennedy or Khrushchev might have been in doing this?
- Did the person writing the memoir have first-hand knowledge of the event/events being described?
- How long after the event/events being described were the memoirs written?

Discuss the following questions in small groups and feed back to the class:

- Our understanding of events in history often changes over time. At the time of the Cuban Missile Crisis, it was perceived by many that the world was on the brink of a nuclear holocaust. How important is it for historians to find out whether this situation was overstated?
- Does a re-evaluation of historical events give us a better understanding of significant events and crises today?
- Will what we believe is the 'truth' about an event today have a different interpretation in 10 or 20 years' time?
- To what extent does historical truth change over time, and how might this affect the ways in which we view primary and secondary sources?

We sent the Americans a note saying that we agreed to remove our missiles and bombers on the condition that the President give us his assurance that there would be no invasion of Cuba by the forces of the United States or anybody else. Finally Kennedy gave in and agreed to make a statement giving us such an assurance …

It had been, to say the least, an interesting and challenging situation. The two most powerful nations in the world had been squared off against each other, each with its finger on the button … It was a great victory for us, though … The Caribbean crisis was a triumph of Soviet foreign policy and a personal triumph in my own career … We achieved, I would say, a spectacular success without having to fire a single shot!

From Nikita Khrushchev's memoirs, *Khrushchev Remembers* (Andrew Nurnberg Associates 1977) p.500

1. What does Khrushchev say about: a) the reasons why he put missiles on Cuba, b) the reasons why he agreed to remove the missiles, c) the outcome of the crisis?
2. With reference to its origin, purpose, and content, assess the values and limitations of this source for historians studying the Cuban Missile Crisis.

Activity 9  **ATL** Thinking skills

Review and essay writing : peaceful co-existence

In order to evaluate the success of the policy of 'peaceful co-existence' up to 1964, look back at the New Leaders chapter (7), the Germany Case Study in Crisis 1958–1961 (chapter 8), and this chapter on the Cuban Missile Crisis.

Review the aims of Khrushchev's policy of peaceful co-existence. Now consider his leadership in the Cold War between 1956 and 1964. Where is there evidence that he pursued his new foreign policy goals? Consider the summit meetings and his visit to the USA, for example. Also consider the key confrontations between the superpowers in this period, specifically the Berlin Crisis (1958–1961) and the Cuban Missile Crisis (1962). Do you agree that although the Soviets initiated peaceful co-existence 'they continued to exploit every opportunity to challenge the West where feasible, whether through propaganda, subversion or even military conflict' and that despite some elements of a thaw in relations there remained a 'profound current of distrust and confrontation' between the Soviet Union and the West? (Dr Gregory Slysz, *20th Century History Review*, 'The Soviet Union's "Peaceful Coexistence"' [April 2011] pp.7–11.)

Now consider the following essay question:

> *To what extent do you agree with the view that peaceful co-existence had failed by 1962 because the USSR was not fully committed to it?*

Essay frame

Introduction: This needs to include a definition of peaceful co-existence and the thinking behind this new approach. You also need some context. Why did the idea of peaceful co-existence look hopeful in 1953? What evidence is there that it had indeed failed by 1961? Also set out your key argument as to why it had failed.

Part 1: What evidence is there that the USSR was not really committed to peaceful co-existence?

- determination to keep competing in the space/arms race
- nature of anti-US propaganda that continued
- Khrushchev's need for a foreign policy victory over the USA, and his attempts to intimidate the USA over nuclear weapons and bully Kennedy over Berlin
- Khrushchev's actions over Cuba

Part 2: What evidence is there that the USSR was interested in peaceful co-existence?

- Geneva Summit; various proposals and agreements
- Austrian State Treaty
- ending of the Korean War
- visit of Khrushchev to the USA

Part 3: What other factors got in the way of peaceful co-existence? You may want to argue here that there were too many unresolved issues to allow for any real peaceful co-existence:

- Berlin
- the arms race
- the US's strong anti-Communist stance fuelled by events inside the US
- the continued distrust of each other's ideologies
- no real change of thinking on either side

Conclusion: Come back to the question; answer it directly, linking back to the argument that you set out in your introduction.

Practice essay questions – the Cuban Missile Crisis

- *Compare and contrast the causes and impact of the Berlin Crisis (1958–1961) and the Cuban Missile Crisis (1962).*
- *Compare and contrast the causes and significance of two Cold War crises, each from a different region.*
- *To what extent did Khrushchev's policy of 'peaceful co-existence' bring about a change in superpower relations between 1956 and 1964?*

Now consider the following essay question:

> *Evaluate the success of the US policy of 'containment' up to 1975.*

This essay question requires you to cover the successes, and failures, of the US policy of containment in:

- Europe – specifically Berlin 1948–1949 and Berlin 1958–1961
- Asia – Japan, Korea, Taiwan, and Vietnam 1945–1975
- the Americas – Cuba 1962.

To prepare for this essay, work in pairs to review each of these geographical areas. Refer back to the relevant chapters and consider the following:

- What examples can you give of where containment was successful and where it failed in each of these areas? What factors affected success?
- Overall, how successful do you consider the policy of containment was for the USA?

After writing your essay, go back and highlight the first sentence of each paragraph. Can you tell from reading the first sentence what the point of the paragraph is going to be? This is vital if the examiner is to follow clearly the direction of your argument.

To access websites relevant to this chapter, go to www.pearsonhotlinks.com, search for the book title or ISBN, and click on 'chapter 9'.

10

Sino-Soviet relations

Key concepts: Change and perspective

As you read this chapter, consider the following essay questions:

- To what extent were Sino-Soviet relations impacted by ideological differences?
- Discuss the reasons for hostility between the USSR and the PRC between 1956 and 1989.
- Examine the reasons for the thaw in Sino-Soviet relations at the end of the 1980s.

China becomes a Communist nation

Chairman Mao proclaiming
the People's Republic of China
in 1949.

Mao Zedong, the Chairman of the victorious **Chinese Communist Party** (CCP), proclaimed the People's Republic of China (PRC) in Beijing on 1 October 1949, saying:

> *Our work will be written down in the history of mankind, and it will clearly demonstrate the fact that the Chinese, who comprise one quarter of humanity, have from now on stood up …*

Chairman Mao Zedong

Background

China and Russia had experienced a troubled history, mainly as a result of their shared 4500-mile border. During Russian **Tsarist** times there was much tension along the border and in the 19th century China lost territories to Russia, amongst others, while it struggled against Western domination. The failure of the ruling **Manchu Dynasty** in China to resist Western exploitation ultimately led to its downfall in the nationalist revolution of 1911. The new regime in China quickly got itself into difficulty by attempting to consolidate control over the whole of the country. It was unable to cajole the Western powers into giving back the territories and rights that they had taken from the Manchu in what were known as the '**unequal treaties**'.

China was impressed and grateful when the new Bolshevik regime, in what was now known as the Union of Soviet Socialist Republics, suggested that it would give up all claims to the former Tsarist empire outside Russia. However, a year later, the Bolsheviks seized Outer Mongolia; and at the end of World War Two, the Soviets stripped $2 billion of equipment and machinery from Manchuria.

Civil war in China

Encouraged by the apparent success of the Bolsheviks in the new USSR, the Chinese Communist Party (CCP) now grew in China. Some of their principal aims for China had similarities with another political group, the Guomindang (GMD), or Nationalist Party. Both wanted to unify China and redress the humiliation it had endured.

The ruling GMD, led by Jiang Jieshi (Chiang Kai-shek), came to see the CCP as its key internal political enemy and waged a campaign to wipe it out. This continued throughout the 1930s until an uneasy truce between the GMD and the CCP was agreed on, in order for the Chinese to unify against Japanese invaders. When Japan withdrew from China in 1945, at the end of World War Two, the GMD and the CCP once again turned on each other, and a brutal civil war ensued. It was not until October 1949 that Mao Zedong, the leader of the Chinese Communist Party, emerged victorious.

Stalin and Mao, 1945–1953

The key differences between the USSR and the Chinese Communists were ideological. Joseph Stalin felt that Mao's interpretation of Marxism, using peasants as the basis for revolution, could not be genuine revolutionary Marxism, which should feature workers leading an urban-based class war.

> *From the infancy of Chinese Communism, Mao's contact with Moscow was neither pleasant nor gratifying. His unorthodox method of revolution, based on peasant mobilization in the countryside, was tolerated by Moscow as legitimate only because all other types of Communist insurrection in China had failed. Mao's approach was never endorsed by Stalin as proper for revolutionizing China.*

Immanuel Hsu, *The Rise of Modern China* (OUP 1999) p.671

China and the Cold War timeline

For a full timeline of events relating to China and the Cold War, see Appendix II.

Mao with Stalin in 1949 at the celebrations in Moscow for Stalin's 70th birthday.

However, this ideological difference was not the only reason Stalin failed to give support to the CCP in the Chinese Civil War. Stalin also:

• feared Mao as a rival for the leadership of the Communist world
• did not want the Cold War to spread to Asia
• knew that Jiang's GMD would recognize Soviet claims to the disputed border territory along frontiers in Manchuria and Xinjiang
• underestimated the CCP and believed the GMD to be the stronger party. He urged the CCP to unite with the GMD, even in the late 1940s, when CCP victory was looking inevitable.

Mao became convinced that Stalin wanted a divided and weak China to leave the USSR dominant in Asia. He saw Stalin's policies as rooted in self-interest rather than true revolutionary doctrine. Mao later said that in 1945 Stalin refused China permission to carry out a revolution and that he told the Chinese: 'Do not have a Civil War: collaborate with Jiang Jieshi. Otherwise the Republic of China will collapse.' Mao, therefore, believed that Stalin saw him as another **Tito** (see chapter 13) rather than a true revolutionary.

The Sino-Soviet Treaty of Alliance

Nevertheless, once the CCP had won the civil war, Mao was invited to visit Moscow in 1950. This trip produced the **Sino-Soviet Treaty of Alliance**, the first treaty between the USSR and China. The USSR became more enthusiastic about the CCP after its victory, and the Soviet press poured praise and admiration on Mao and the new PRC. However, Mao later said of the agreement, 'This was the result of a struggle. Stalin did not wish to sign the treaty; he finally signed it after two months of negotiating.' The US State Department referred to the alliance as 'Moscow making puppets out of the Chinese'. The Treaty offered the PRC the promise of Soviet expertise and low-interest aid:

 Each contracting Party undertakes, in the spirit of friendship … to develop and consolidate economic and cultural ties between China and the Soviet Union, to render the other all possible economic assistance.

The Sino-Soviet Treaty of Alliance

However, the Chinese were offended by the rather 'unfriendly' treatment they received. The Soviets had been superior in their dealings with PRC officials and had not bothered to put on any entertainment for their guests, and Mao thought the accommodation given to the Chinese was poor. In fact, Nikita Khrushchev later said of the treaty, 'It was an insult to the Chinese people. For centuries the French, English, and Americans had been exploiting China, and now the Soviet Union was moving in.' Indeed, it was soon clear that the USSR wanted to exploit the treaty in its own favour – Soviet aid would be loans and the Chinese would have to repay with interest.

Nevertheless, Soviet planners and engineers initially developed 200 Chinese construction projects in the 1950s. Traditional buildings were pulled down for Soviet-style constructions. Soviet scientific technology was prioritized over Western technology in China. Socialist science was seen as best, even if it was less effective. The PRC also accepted that Soviet military assistance was necessary, at least until they had their own nuclear programme.

Activity 1  ATL Thinking skills

1. Why was Stalin reluctant to support Mao and the CCP?

The USSR, the PRC, and the Korean War, 1950–1953

When Americans forces, under the UN flag, came close to the Chinese border near the Yalu river, Stalin encouraged the PRC to send troops into Korea. The Soviets gave material assistance to the one million Chinese troops engaged in battle.

Despite this support for PRC intervention in the Korean War, Mao bitterly complained when the Soviets demanded that China pay for all weapons and materials the USSR had supplied.

> 66 *The cost of Stalin's 'trust' was high: China sent a million 'volunteers' to intervene in the Korean War and had to pay the entire $1.35 billion for the Soviet equipment and supplies necessary for the venture, and Mao lost a son in the war.*
>
> **Immanuel Hsu,** *The Rise of Modern China* **(OUP 1999) p.675**

Sino-Soviet Relations after Stalin, 1953–1956

Although Mao had some respect for the Soviet leader, there had been tensions and suspicions in the relationship between Mao and Stalin. It has even been suggested that Stalin deliberately delayed the end of the Korean War in order to exhaust the PRC. Therefore, when Stalin died in 1953, it was possible that relations would improve. A truce was signed during the Korean War, soon after Stalin's death, and to a certain degree there was a relaxation in the tension, referred to by historian Michael Lynch as something of a 'honeymoon period'. The new Soviet leaders appeared willing to supply further loans and technology to China; they attempted to make their treaties more equal and facilitate easier credit for the PRC.

Mao, Khrushchev, and 'the split', 1956–1964

Despite the chance for improved Sino-Soviet relations during the leadership years of Nikita Khrushchev, three key issues undermined the potential for easing tension between the PRC and the USSR:

- The 'Secret Speech' by Khrushchev in Moscow on 24 February 1956 attacking Stalin's crimes against the party, including comments about the '**cult of personality**', which Mao saw as an attack on his own style of leadership.
- The crushing of the **Hungarian Uprising** in October/November 1956. Mao saw this, and Soviet problems in East Germany and Poland, as failures by the USSR to contain **reactionary** forces (see chapter 13).
- Khrushchev's doctrine of 'peaceful co-existence' with the West (chapter 7), which implied that global revolution could be achieved by means other than armed struggle. Mao saw this as ideological heresy.

Mao and the PRC considered these issues a clear departure from Marxist doctrine, and evidence that the Soviet Union was now dominated by '**revisionists**' (a term used to describe those straying from Marxism). Further evidence in support of this view came in the form of the 1955 Geneva Summit and the Austrian State Treaty of 1955 (see pages 94–95).

Source A

> Mao had concluded that Khrushchev was something of a 'blunderer', who was 'disaster prone'. The awe he had felt for Khrushchev at the time when the Soviet leader denounced Stalin was rapidly fading, replaced by a confidence that he could turn Khrushchev's vulnerability to his own advantage ... Mao was aiming to cut Khrushchev down to size as leader of the Communist bloc, and make his own bid for the leadership which had been his dream since Stalin's death.

Jung Chang and Jon Halliday, *Mao: The Unknown Story* (Random House 2005), pp.421–422

Source B

> Khrushchev and Mao had all the prejudices of nationalists, however much they might be Communists ... Mao treated Khrushchev as a superficial upstart, neglecting no opportunity to confound him with petty humiliations, cryptic pronouncements, and veiled provocations.
>
> Khrushchev could 'never be sure what Mao meant ... I believed in him and he was playing with me'.

John Lewis Gaddis, *The Cold War* (Penguin 2005) p.141

1. According to Chang and Halliday in Source A, how did Mao view Khrushchev?

2. What does Gaddis mean in Source B when he says that 'Khrushchev and Mao had all the prejudices of nationalists'?

> **TOK**
>
> How far is it correct to assume that 'different cultures have different truths'? Can this be applied to the different interpretations of Marxism–Leninism adopted by the Soviets and the Communist Chinese?

Conference of Communist Parties, 1957

Mao attended this conference of the world's Communist parties; this was to be the second and last time he ventured outside China. He had hoped Yugoslavian leader Josip Tito would be in attendance, but he did not appear. Mao called on the USSR to abandon 'revisionism'. He declared that international revolution could not be supported by working alongside 'class enemies': that is, Western Capitalists. In addition, Mao believed that the USSR was initiating détente with the West to further isolate China.

The Chinese chief spokesperson at the meeting was Deng Xiaoping. He was to prove exceptional in putting forward the PRC's ideological stance, and ultimately he was very embarrassing for the Soviets. Deng stated that the **proletarian** world revolution could only come about through force and that Capitalism had to be crushed in violent revolution. The Chinese believed he had out-argued the leading Soviet theorist, Mikhail Suslov.

This had been a sound international platform on which to present the PRC as the 'real' leaders of international revolutionary Communism, which is exactly how Mao and the PRC were beginning to see themselves.

Khrushchev's visit to Beijing, 1958

Khrushchev attempted to ease the growing tension between the USSR and China by visiting Mao in Beijing. However, right from the start things did not go well, and Mao apparently went out of his way to make Khrushchev feel uncomfortable.

For example, it was the height of the summer heat in Beijing, and Khrushchev's hotel had no air conditioning and was plagued by mosquitoes. Mao arranged one round of talks in his swimming pool, which was fine for Mao, who was a regular swimmer, but not so easy for Khrushchev, who hated swimming. To add insult to an already difficult situation, Khrushchev had to wear a pair of shorts that were rather too tight for him, and had to be helped to float by a rubber ring!

The talks, unsurprisingly, were not productive. Again, Deng used the occasion as an opportunity to attack Soviet policy, stating that:

• the Soviets had betrayed the international Communist movement
• the Soviets were guilty of viewing themselves as the only true Marxist–Leninists
• the Soviets had sent spies posing as technical advisers into China.

Taiwan, 1958

As has been explained in chapter 6, the key issue of the PRC's Nationalist enemies in Taiwan was not resolved. The GMD and their leader Jiang Jieshi could not be tolerated as an 'independent' state off the mainland by the PRC. It resolutely wanted reunification with Taiwan and was furious about US support for the Nationalists.

The PRC had bombarded islands off Taiwan in the early 1950s, but had been deterred from further action by US's Seventh Fleet patrols of the straits between Taiwan and the mainland. In 1958, Mao decided to test the United States' resolve again. Without discussing it with the Soviets, he ordered a build-up of troop manoeuvres in the region, giving the impression that the PRC was preparing for a full-scale attack on Taiwan. The United States responded by preparing for war with the PRC.

However, Mao did not launch an attack. He was unprepared to take on the full might of the US war machine, and he did not have the support of the Soviet Union.

Mao Zedong and Nikita Khrushchev in Beijing, 1958.

Khrushchev said that he was not prepared to go to war with the United States to 'test the stability' of the Capitalist system, and he accused Mao's regime of being '**Trotskyist**' in pursuing international revolution at any cost. The Soviets also saw this action as evidence of Mao's lack of understanding of political reality, and his tendency towards **fanaticism**.

The effects of the Taiwan crisis were negative for Sino-Soviet relations. The Soviets withdrew their economic advisers and cancelled commercial contracts with the PRC.

Activity 3

> The second Taiwan Strait crisis was very like the first in 1954–55, which Mao had staged to twist his ally's arm for A-bomb technology … On 23rd August Mao opened up a huge artillery barrage against the tiny island of Quemoy … Washington thought Mao might really be going for Taiwan. No one in the West suspected his true goal: to force the USA to threaten a nuclear war in order to scare his own ally – a ruse unique in the annals of statecraft.

Jung Chang and Jon Halliday, *Mao: The Unknown Story* (Random House 2005) p.430

1. Discuss in pairs what reasons Chang and Halliday give for Mao's initiation of the second Taiwan crisis.

Sino-Soviet relations and the 'Great Leap Forward'

What was the Great Leap Forward?

The **Great Leap Forward** (GLF) was initiated by Mao at a meeting in January 1958. The key idea behind the GLF was to rapidly develop China's agricultural and industrial sectors simultaneously. Mao hoped to harness the energy of the vast population of China, and by so doing dispose of the need for Soviet aid. He believed that sheer force of will would get around the necessity of importing heavy machinery. In the process, Mao also aimed to create the 'proletarian class' required by the Marxist model. He anchored the GLF in the development of two key areas – grain and steel production. His predictions were very ambitious, suggesting that China could out-produce the UK in steel in just 15 years.

In order to achieve increased grain and steel production, Mao promoted the construction of small **backyard steel furnaces** in every commune and in each urban neighbourhood. Peasants and workers set about attempting to produce steel from scrap metal, stripping their local areas of all potential fuel sources to burn in the furnaces. Suspicious of the academic 'intellectuals', Mao ignored their concerns about the economic value of the poor-quality 'pig iron' that these furnaces produced. China's harvests rotted in the fields as peasants focused on making the worthless metal, often out of basic essentials, such as their own pots and pans.

Despite the fact that Mao had seen for himself that high-quality steel could only be produced in proper factories, he continued with the 'backyard furnaces' plan for most of 1959. It is said that behind Mao's reasoning was a desire not to crush the 'revolutionary spirit' of the peasants and workers.

Public works launched during the GLF were also generally unsuccessful, due to the deliberate lack of experienced and expert leadership. As for the broader agricultural picture, some 'revolutionary' techniques were experimented with on the communes.

For example, there was 'close cropping', where seeds were planted very close together (following the false idea that the same crop would not compete with itself), and also the strategy of leaving an area of each field fallow to improve fertility.

Failure and starvation

Peasants in China carrying water to the fields to fight the drought, c. 1960.

At the **Lushan Conference** in July 1959, Marshal Peng Dehuai spoke out against the disastrous impact of the GLF. Mao had Peng removed from his post, and used his denunciation to launch a nationwide campaign against the 'rightists' (right-wing elements). From 1959, China experienced a widespread famine. Even though millions were starving in China, Mao insisted that China continue to export grain – he did not want the humiliation of the outside world knowing the results of his great economic plan. Chinese government sources record horrendous weather conditions affecting China from 1958 to 1962, and there is clear evidence of droughts and floods. But the impact of the GLF exacerbated the problems caused by the weather. As a direct result of the GLF policies, millions of Chinese died. In January 1961, the PRC finally decided to end the GLF revolution. No more grain was exported, and Canadian and Australian grain was imported.

The consequence of the Great Leap Forward was total economic disaster for China. Using recently opened Chinese archives, historian Frank Dikötter in his book *Mao's Great Famine* (Bloomsbury 2010) estimates that there were 'at least' 45 million premature deaths in China during the famine years. Mao stepped down as State Chairman of the PRC in 1959, realizing that he would be held responsible for the disaster that was emerging; he did, however, keep his position as Chairman of the CCP.

Soviets denounce the GLF

In 1959, the Soviets called the rapid industrial change aspect of the GLF 'faulty in design and erroneous in practice'. Mao was personally furious at this criticism. His anger became fuelled by humiliation when it was rumoured that the PRC Chief of Staff, Marshal Peng, had given information to the Soviets about the widespread starvation caused by the agricultural methods of the GLF. The Soviet government declared that the concepts and applications used were 'unorthodox', and the Soviet official press revelled in the failure, denouncing Mao.

Infuriated, Mao was now determined to strike back at the USSR for undermining the position of the PRC in the eyes of the international Communist community. The PRC would now back any Communist country that dissented from Moscow's lead.

Albania

China got its opportunity to attack the USSR and support a 'dissenting Communist state' through Albania. In 1961, the USSR withdrew aid to Albania. Khrushchev made a speech that year, during the Moscow Congress of the Communist Party of the Soviet Union, attacking the Albanian regime for its 'Stalinist' doctrines and backward ways. The PRC observer at the Congress walked out in protest. China interpreted this speech as an attack on their system as well. Soon after, the PRC offered to replace Soviet money and technical assistance given to Albania. This conflict over Albania led to the final severance of diplomatic relations between the Soviets and the Chinese Communists, after more than ten years of growing hostility.

In their war of words, Khrushchev referred to Mao as the 'Asian Hitler' and a 'living corpse'; Mao called Khrushchev 'a redundant old boot'.

Activity 4  ATL Thinking skills

Source A

> By the mid 1950s there were growing problems in the Sino-Soviet alliance. Soviet advisers had caused some resentment in China when their nationalist susceptibilities were ruffled by perceived arrogance. Soviet insistence on payment for material supplied during the Korean War did not help matters. The key to the growing friction was ideology. De-Stalinization and attacks on the cult of personality went down badly in Beijing, as did Soviet critiques of the Great Leap Forward ... Personal relations between the leaders were poor and Mao resented criticism of Molotov and the 'anti-party group' for views that resembled his own.

Mike Sewell, *The Cold War* (CUP 2002) p.67

Source B

> The relationship to China had been lauded as the ultimate proof of Socialism's applicability to the Third World ... With the alliance in tatters, Moscow had to explain what had gone wrong ... [it was] explained by the wrongheadedness of the 'Mao-clique' ... on the other hand, the combination of immense disappointment and no proper cause for failure led many Soviet leaders to racist explanations: the Soviet effort in China was failing because of the inborn deviousness and selfishness of the Chinese.

Odd Arne Westad, *The Global Cold War* (CUP 2007) p.70

Source C

> Despite a degree of mismanagement unparalleled in modern history [the GLF] ... Mao survived as China's 'great helmsman'. What did not survive was the Sino-Soviet alliance which had, as far as Mao was concerned, outlived its usefulness. Khrushchev, fearing the implications, tried desperately to reconstitute it right up to the moment he was deposed in 1964, despite repeated insults, rebuffs and even instances of deliberate sabotage from Mao.

John Lewis Gaddis, *The Cold War* (Penguin 2005) p.142

1. What key points are made in Source B about Sino-Soviet relations?
2. Compare and contrast the views in Sources A and C on what caused the Sino-Soviet split.
3. With reference to its origin, purpose and content, assess the values and limitations of Source B for historians studying Sino-Soviet relations.

TOK

How do historians use a) selection and b) bias to create their historical accounts?

The source question requires you to look at ways in which sources make similar points about the Sino-Soviet split and ways in which they differ.

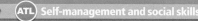

Activity 5   (ATL) **Self-management and social skills**

1. Discuss in pairs/small groups how each of the following led to the split between the USSR and the PRC:

a.	the Chinese Civil War	**f.**	Mao's response to Khrushchev
b.	Stalin's attitude to Mao	**g.**	Taiwan
c.	the Korean War	**h.**	the Great Leap Forward
d.	Stalin's death	**i.**	Albania
e.	Khrushchev's new policies		

2. Attempt to prioritize the events in order of importance. From your discussions, was there a 'turning point' event at which time the Sino-Soviet split became inevitable? Which side seems to be more responsible for causing the split – the Soviets or the Chinese? Remember to support your answers with evidence from the chronology of events and, where possible, the viewpoints of historians.

The Sino-Indian War, 1962

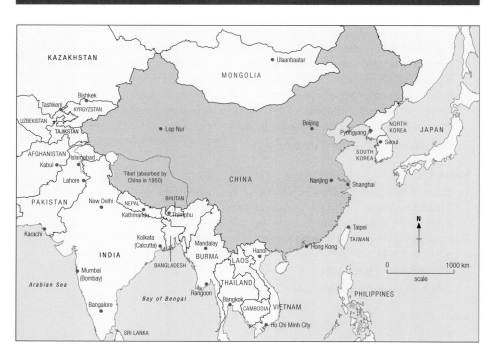

Map of India and China showing national borders.

Another issue that raised tension between the Soviet Union and China was the war with India. In 1962, fighting broke out on the Tibetan border between China and India. In 1950, the PRC had invaded Tibet – an area it wished to bring under Chinese control, and indeed an area it viewed as 'Chinese' and therefore a domestic issue. The continuous brutality of the PRC forces in Tibet aroused international condemnation. The Indian government was also sensitive about troops occupying territory close to its border.

It has been suggested by some historians that Mao had been planning a war with India for some time. China did not recognize the boundary between the two countries that had been drawn up during the British colonial period. Mao demanded that the border be renegotiated by China and India themselves. However, India did not believe there was anything to negotiate about. Its view was that the border was established and settled, and thus the two countries were deadlocked over the issue.

Clashes increased along this border, and from May 1962 the PRC began to prepare for war with India. Although outwardly aggressive, Mao was worried about triggering a war. One of his key concerns was that the nuclear test site at Lop Nur in northwest China was within missile range of India, even though it was beyond the American range from Taiwan.

The war proper erupted on 10 October 1962 between the **Chinese People's Liberation Army** and the Indian military. Part of the fallout from the war was that India allowed American U-2s to fly from bases at Charbatia, from where they were able to photograph China's first A-bomb test. In the war, the Soviets were officially 'neutral'; however, they gave India **MIG fighters**. Therefore, when the Soviet foreign minister offered to act as a mediator, Mao viewed this as outrageous hypocrisy.

The war ended on 20 November 1962. The Chinese had taken the disputed areas and unilaterally declared a ceasefire. Although the PRC had emerged victorious, this was tempered by the fact that the Americans had been able to gain sensitive intelligence and possible access to bases in India. The Soviets had aided the enemy in this war and the PRC's relationship as a key member of the **Non-Aligned Movement** (see chapter 18) alongside Prime Minister Jawaharlal Nehru's India was shattered.

Investigate the relationship between India and China today. Is there a legacy of tension or disputes from the 1962 conflict? In what areas do the two nations co-operate?

The Cuban Missile Crisis, 1962

Sino-Soviet relations reached new depths of division during the Cuban Missile Crisis (see chapter 9 for a discussion of the key events). Mao was openly disparaging about Khrushchev's handling of the crisis. He seized on this perceived mismanagement as an opportunity to expose to the Communist world the USSR's lack of commitment to the revolutionary cause. Mao attacked:

• the placement of *detectable* missiles
• the 'capitulation' (backing down)
• the negative impact it would have on the struggle against US imperialism.

In his book *The Rise of Modern China* Immanuel Hsu claims that 'Mao considered Khrushchev a coward' over his handling of the Cuban Missile Crisis. It could, of course, be argued that Khrushchev had acted like a 'great statesman': that he had applied his policy of peaceful co-existence and thus averted a nuclear catastrophe. But for Mao and the PRC, the idea of existing peacefully with the non-Communist states went against everything their ideology dictated. It seemed to them that the USSR was betraying the revolution, as well as tolerating the exploitation of pre-revolutionary states by Capitalist powers, such as the United States.

Activity 6	 **Thinking skills**

Source A

> *Only after victory in the revolution is it possible and necessary for the proletariat to pursue peaceful co-existence. As for the oppressed peoples and nations, their task is to strive for their own liberation and overthrow the rule of imperialism and its lackeys. They should not practise peaceful co-existence with the imperialists ... It is therefore wrong to apply peaceful co-existence to relations between oppressed and oppressor ... nations.*

Statement made by Mao Zedong in 1963

Source B

> More than three years after he started pushing Maoism onto the world stage ... Mao gave the order to denounce Khrushchev by name as a 'revisionist'. A public slanging match quickly escalated. For Mao, the polemic acted as a sort of international advertising campaign for Maoism ...

Jung Chang and Jon Halliday, *Mao: The Unknown Story* **(Random House 2005), p.489**

Source C

In this cartoon by Vicky, published in the UK in November 1962, Mao is calling 'Chicken!' while Kennedy and Khrushchev face each other across a precipice.

Source D

> We might ask the Chinese comrades, who offer to build a beautiful future on the ruins of the old world destroyed by thermo-nuclear war: did they consult, on this issue, the working class of countries where imperialism is in power? ... What right have you to decide for us questions involving our very existence and our class struggle – we too want socialism, but we want to win it through the class struggle, not by unleashing a world thermo-nuclear war.

The Soviet response to Mao's 1963 statement

1. Explain the propaganda message in Source A.
2. What is the message of Source C?
3. What are the key points being made by the Soviets in Source D?
4. With reference to its origin, purpose and content, analyse the values and limitations of Source D for historians studying Sino-Soviet relations.

Activity 7 — **ATL** Communication skills

1. Consider and plan the following essay questions:

* *To what extent was the Sino-Soviet split caused by the breakdown in the relationship between Mao and Khrushchev?*
* *Examine the importance of 'peaceful co-existence' in the development of Sino-Soviet tension.*

Sino-Soviet relations and the Cultural Revolution, 1966–1976

Mao's '**Great Proletarian Cultural Revolution**' was launched in May 1966. His declared aim was to initiate a revolution at the very heart of traditional Chinese 'culture'. He wanted to eliminate the creeping return of liberal and **bourgeois** thinking and behaviour. Mao believed that this would re-ignite the revolutionary class struggle that had, so he thought, petered out. Most historians agree that this was really Mao's 'relaunch' of himself after the disasters of the Great Leap Forward had forced him to take something of a back seat.

The main tools of the **Cultural Revolution** were the young, who were encouraged to denounce their elders, teachers, and parents and send them for '**re-education**'. This was done with much enthusiasm by Red Guards, wielding Mao's '**Little Red Book**'. Teachers, writers, intellectuals, musicians, older leaders – in fact, all who were viewed as representing 'old thoughts' – were attacked. Power struggles developed at both local and national level.

As there were no clear directives from the party as to how the 'old culture' should be disposed of, many attacks got out of hand. As many as half a million people died. Meanwhile, Mao was able to get rid of his critics and resume supreme control of the PRC. While the excesses of the young Red Guards continued, Mao declared the Cultural Revolution over in 1969. In the hope that society could return to some sort of order from the **anarchy** and chaos that had been unleashed, many of the young **Maoists** were then sent to the countryside themselves, to 'learn from the peasants'.

Khrushchev left office in 1964. However, there was to be no reconciliation between the USSR and the PRC. The Soviet leadership continued to attempt to isolate the PRC. When Mao launched the Great Proletarian Cultural Revolution to eliminate 'revisionists' and China descended yet again into internal crisis, and at certain points to near-civil war, the Soviets denounced the revolution as total fanaticism, and criticized Mao for creating a state of anarchy.

The Soviets also took the opportunity to attack the PRC on a number of other propaganda fronts during the Cutural Revolution, including the following accusations:

- trading illegally with the **apartheid** regime in South Africa
- receiving assistance from West Germany on nuclear research
- developing a worldwide opium trade
- sending supplies to US forces in Vietnam.

Mao responded to these 'false' accusations by calling on other Communist countries to follow the Chinese model rather than the 'revisionist' Soviet system.

The Little Red Book
The 'Little Red Book' was a small red book of Mao's thoughts and sayings that became an essential accessory during the Cultural Revolution.

CHALLENGE YOURSELF

Research and social skills (ATL)

Enquire further into the causes, course, and consequences of the Cultural Revolution. Discuss in small groups or pairs: Mao's reasons for launching this campaign; who the Red Guards were and what their worst excesses were. What were the results of the Cultural Revolution for the PRC? Why did Mao bring it to an end?

Young Red Guards brandishing copies of Mao's 'Little Red Book'.

China, the USSR, and nuclear weapons

Cartoon by Yaltman from 1978 depicting Sino-Soviet relations.

A continuing theme in Sino-Soviet relations was the dispute over aspects of military power, particularly nuclear weapons. In 1957, it appeared that the USSR had gained superiority over the USA with the launch of the Sputnik satellite (see chapter 7). Mao saw this as a tool to engage the USA in brinkmanship and begin to undermine the United States. Unlike the more pragmatic Soviet Union, Mao did not fear nuclear war, as he actually believed it was now an unavoidable part of the revolutionary struggle.

However, Khrushchev had very different views. He wanted to use the apparent technical superiority as leverage to convince the United States to pursue 'co-existence'. This disagreement between the two Communist superpowers on how to engage their Capitalist enemy intensified over the Test-Ban Treaty of 1963. The treaty was an agreement by the USSR and Western nuclear powers to stop atmospheric testing of atomic weapons. Again, Mao viewed this as the USSR abandoning its role as revolutionary leader and instead working with the imperialist powers.

Khrushchev responded to the PRC's criticism of attempts at superpower arms control by accusing the Chinese of wanting to see the USSR and Western powers destroy each other, leaving the PRC as the number-one power.

Mao had been angered by the Soviet response to the PRC's request for nuclear technology. The basic circular argument between them was:

• China: 'If you are our friend, you should want to help us develop our own nuclear programme.'
• USSR: 'As you are our friend, you do not need your own nuclear programme as we will look after you.'

The Soviet position was inflexible. If the PRC wanted help from the USSR in nuclear development then it would have to allow the Soviets to control its defence policy. Typically, Mao stated that this approach betrayed the revolutionary ideal and was also patronizing. He asserted that the Soviets did not view other Communist countries as equals.

Timeline of Chinese technical development	
1960	Soviet scientists' complete withdrawal from China
	China continues with its own research programmes and even uses material from reconstructed shredded documents left by the Soviets
1964	China detonates first atomic bomb
1967	China detonates a hydrogen bomb
1970	China launches its first space satellite

The development of its own nuclear weapons was a huge achievement for China. It not only meant that the PRC would have to be taken seriously as an international power, but it also demonstrated to the USSR that it did not need Soviet support. To push this point, the Chinese code-named their first bomb '59/6', which referred to the year and month the Soviet scientists began to pull out of China. Mao explained the positive results of the Soviet departure:

> Guided missiles and atom bombs are great achievements. This is the result of Khrushchev's 'help'. By withdrawing the experts, he forced us to take our own road. We should give him a big medal.

Mao appeared not to be as wary of nuclear catastrophe as were the USSR and the USA. Indeed, he suggested that nuclear weapons were a useful tool of diplomacy. He also saw them as the key to China usurping the Soviet Union as leader of the international Communist struggle:

> The success of China's hydrogen bomb test has further broken the nuclear monopoly of United States imperialism and Soviet revisionism and dealt a telling blow at their policy of nuclear blackmail. It is very great encouragement … to the revolutionary people of the whole world.

With the launch of the first Chinese space satellite in 1970, the Soviet Union was worried that now the PRC had the potential to develop ICBMs.

Activity 8　　　ATL Thinking skills

Source A

'Mushrooming Cloud' by Herblock, published in the *Washington Post* in 1965.

Discuss what arguments the PRC could have put forward to defend its right to have its own nuclear weapons programme. Consider how these arguments compare and contrast to those made today by countries who want to develop their own nuclear programmes. Discuss this with the rest of your class.

Source B

66 *Defying the logic of balancing power within the international system, Mao sought a different kind of equilibrium: a world filled with danger, whether from the United States or the Soviet Union or both, could minimize the risk that rivals within China might challenge his rule.*

From John Lewis Gaddis, *The Cold War* (Penguin 2005) p.142

1. What is the message of the cartoonist in Source A?
2. What does Source A suggest about China's role in the Cold War at this time?
3. According to Source B, why might Mao want to encourage international hostility towards China?

The PRC and Leonid Brezhnev, 1968–1982

During the Soviet leadership of Leonid Brezhnev there was to be no improvement in Sino-Soviet relations, even though there was a period of détente with the USA.

The invasion of Czechoslovakia, 1968

In the '**Brezhnev Doctrine**' (see chapter 13, page 191), the Soviet Union stated that to maintain order in Eastern Europe, the satellite states had to accept Soviet leadership. When Czechoslovakia attempted to assert some independence, the doctrine was put into practice, and in 1968 Soviet tanks were sent to crush the period of liberalization now known as the '**Prague Spring**'. This invasion undermined the USSR's standing with other Communist states, and this correspondingly damaged its attempts to isolate the PRC.

Mao condemned the use of force against Czechoslovakia. This was not only because the Soviet Union was no longer behaving in a 'truly socialist' manner in his eyes, but also because he was worried that Soviet military might and the Brezhnev Doctrine could be turned against China.

Activity 9	

Source A

66 *A few days ago, the Soviet revisionist leading* **clique** *and its followers dispatched massive armed forces to launch a surprise attack on Czechoslovakia and swiftly occupied it, with the Czechoslovak revisionist leading clique openly calling on the people to resist, thus committing enormous crimes against the Czechoslovak people. This is the most obvious and most typical example of fascist power politics played by the Soviet Union … It marks the total bankruptcy of Soviet revisionism.*

The Chinese Government and people strongly condemn the Soviet revisionist leading clique and its followers for their crime of aggression – the armed occupation of Czechoslovakia – and firmly support the Czechoslovak people in their heroic struggle of resistance to Soviet military occupation.

Extract from a speech by Chinese Premier Zhou Enlai, 23 August 1968 at Romania's National Day Reception

Source B

  Since Brezhnev came to power, the Soviet revisionist clique has stepped up its **collusion** *with US imperialism and its suppression of the revolutionary struggle of the peoples of various countries, intensified its control over and its exploitation of the various east European countries … and intensified its threat of aggression against China. Its dispatch of hundreds of thousands of troops to occupy Czechoslovakia, and its armed provocation against China on our territory are two unacceptable acts staged recently by Soviet revisionism.*

In order to justify its aggression, the Soviet revisionist clique loudly proclaims its so-called theory of 'limited sovereignty' and theory of 'socialist community'. What does all this stuff mean? It means that your own sovereignty is 'limited', while his is unlimited. You won't obey him? He will exercise his 'international dictatorship' over you – dictatorship over the people of other countries, in order to form the 'socialist community' ruled by the new Tsars.

Extract from a speech by Lin Biao to the Ninth Party Congress of the Chinese Communist Party in Beijing, 1 April 1969

1. What criticisms of the USSR's action in Czechoslovakia are made in sources A and B?
2. Why might other Communist states agree with the opinions given in these speeches by Zhou Enlai and Lin Biao?

TOK How far is 'opinion' an asset or an obstacle to the work of a historian?

Sino-Soviet border war, 1969

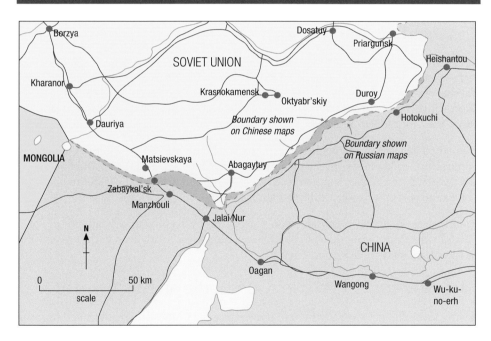

This map shows the Sino-Soviet border conflict.

The hostility between the Soviets and the Chinese Communists came to a head in violent clashes along their mutual border. The PRC denounced the Soviets as 'imperialists', no different from the **tsars** of old, as they still had not returned territory taken from the Chinese in the 19th century. In 1962, border disputes increased to a new level along the Xinjiang frontier and the Amur and Ussuri rivers. Both sides increased the numbers of troops facing one another across the border.

In 1969 the frontier dispute erupted into a proper war. According to the Chinese, the Soviets had violated China's border 4189 times in the period up to 1969. The tension boiled over into actual fighting on 2 March 1969 on Chen-pao or Damansky Island in the Ussuri River. By August, there was clearly the possibility of all-out war between the two Communist states. If this happened, there was a danger of the conflict turning nuclear. Mao feared a Soviet invasion and possible nuclear strikes, so he ordered that tunnels be dug and supplies stored in preparation for this. Fighting continued sporadically for most of the year.

In the end, there was no escalation to all-out nuclear war. However, the war had brought the world's two most powerful Communist countries to the brink.

Some historians view 1969 as the lowest point in Sino-Soviet relations for a number of reasons:

• serious border incidents threatened to turn into full-scale war
• the PRC and Soviet Union realigned missiles to face one another
• there was an intensification of the rivalry to be the leading Communist nation.

The PRC, the USSR, and Indochina

Indochina became a complex focal point for the Sino-Soviet split. China had a strategic interest in Indochina as Vietnam, Cambodia, and Laos were on its border. The PRC had been involved in the peace talks that brought an end to the problems in Indochina in 1954 (see chapter 6). The United States had not wanted the PRC there, and the US Secretary of State, John Foster Dulles, had refused to acknowledge the PRC representative, Zhou Enlai.

The Vietnam War

As explained in chapter 6, when the United States refused to accept the free elections in Vietnam set down in the 1954 agreement, it was drawn further and further into the civil war that developed through its support for the regime in the South. The PRC was not directly involved in the Vietnam War, but gave moral and diplomatic support to Ho Chi Minh. The Chinese also attacked US involvement as 'naked American imperialism'.

There then developed a struggle between the USSR and the PRC to win the Vietnamese Communists to 'their' side in the ideological split. China accused the USSR of being in league with the USA in Vietnam, and the PRC refused to allow the USSR to use Chinese airports for Soviet airlifts to Vietnam.

Nevertheless, the USSR eventually won this contest by keeping up a steady supply of aid and arms throughout the war. In 1978, relations were formalized in the Soviet–Vietnamese Treaty of Peace and Friendship.

Sino-Soviet clashes over Cambodia and Vietnam

Having lost influence over Vietnam to the Soviets, the Chinese then attempted to form closer ties with Cambodia. Cambodia had become Communist in 1975 under Pol Pot's Khmer Rouge party. In many ways, Pol Pot's regime was modelled on 'Maoism'. However, between 1975 and 1979 the brutality of the regime was horrendous and exceeded anything perpetrated in the Cultural Revolution. Although 2.5 million Cambodians died, Pol Pot was hailed as a Maoist hero.

In November 1978, Vietnam signed a military alliance with the USSR. Following a series of clashes on the border, Vietnam invaded Cambodia on 24 December 1978. Its stated aim was **regime change** – to overthrow Pol Pot. The Vietnamese began to expel all Chinese people from the territory they occupied. Pol Pot appealed to the United Nations. China then decided to come to the defence of Pol Pot's regime, arguing that Vietnam's invasion of Cambodia was 'Soviet expansionism'.

Thus, on 17 February 1979, China invaded Vietnam. Its intent was to draw Vietnamese/Soviet forces out of Cambodia. In response, the Soviets increased their backing for the Vietnamese, and both sides claimed the other as the aggressor. In addition, the Vietnamese/Soviets also attempted to present their intervention to the United Nations as being on '**humanitarian**' grounds.

There was no quick victory for the Chinese, and the war dragged on into March. Although Vietnam had clearly won the war, the Chinese People's Liberation Army claimed success. In fact, the PLA had suffered heavy casualties and had been forced to withdraw. The war had been a major setback for PRC propaganda against the USSR, as well as for the PRC's attempt to confirm its role as leader of the Communist world.

Sino-Soviet rapprochement, 1982–2000

There were a number of key reasons for the relaxation of tensions between the Soviet Union and the PRC during the last two decades of the 20th century:

- Mao Zedong's death in 1976
- the overthrow of the anti-Soviet **Gang of Four** in China
- the adoption by the new PRC leader, Deng Xiaoping, of a more tolerant line in relation to the Soviet Union and the West
- Brezhnev's death in 1982.

CHALLENGE YOURSELF

Research skills ATL

Enquire further into the power struggle that followed the death of Mao in 1976. Who were the 'Gang of Four', what happened to Mao's chosen successor Hua Guofeng, and why did Deng Xiaoping emerge as paramount leader? You could also investigate Deng's new policies for China: the **Four Modernizations**.

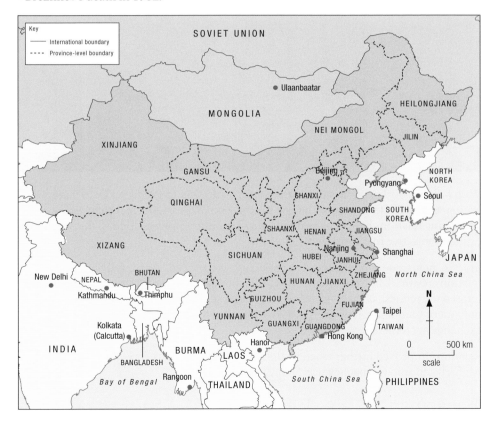

Map of China and its border with the USSR in 1984.

During the comparatively brief Soviet leaderships of Andropov, and then Chernenko, attempts were made to improve relations with China. For example, diplomatic formalities were renewed in 1982, and high-ranking Chinese attended Brezhnev's funeral. But, for most of the 1980s, there were three key issues dividing the PRC and the USSR:

• the Soviet invasion of Afghanistan
• Soviet troops on the border with China
• Soviet support for the Vietnamese occupation of Cambodia.

All moves towards a better relationship during this period came to nothing, primarily because of the Soviet invasion of Afghanistan in 1979. China condemned the invasion as Soviet 'imperial expansionism'. The PRC did not view the invasion as a 'defensive move' as the Soviets claimed, but as an excuse to mass troops on the border with China.

Mikhail Gorbachev and Deng Xiaoping

Mikhail Gorbachev and Deng Xiaoping.

With Mikhail Gorbachev assuming the Soviet leadership in 1985, and Deng Xiaoping leading the PRC, there was, for the first time in over 20 years, the real chance of improving relations between the two Communist superpowers. Indeed, this was a primary objective for Gorbachev.

In 1986, new trade agreements were drawn up, and procedures for full diplomatic relations restored. In November 1987 Gorbachev asked to meet Deng, but the Chinese refused the request as the Soviets had not managed to get their Vietnamese allies to pull out of Cambodia. However, in May 1988, the PRC and the USSR signed a cultural exchange agreement.

Relations improved further when in 1989 the Soviets began their withdrawal from Afghanistan, and Gorbachev was finally invited to Beijing.

Tiananmen Square, 1989

The PRC's decision to brutally crush the Chinese pro-democracy movement demonstrations in Beijing's **Tiananmen Square**, in 1989, highlighted the fundamental differences that had developed by this time between the regime in Communist China and Gorbachev's Soviet Union.

Gorbachev had initiated far-reaching reforms in the USSR and, for the first time since the death of Stalin, a Soviet leader had begun to dismantle Stalin's structural legacy (see chapter 15). ***Perestroika*** addressed economic restructuring, and ***glasnost*** suggested more political freedom and reform.

In China, Deng had also brought about some economic reforms, but there had not been a corresponding policy of political openness. Indeed, Deng believed that economic reform in China was only possible if under the control of the CCP.

Before Gorbachev's visit, on 16 April 1989, students began a peaceful protest for more political freedom, with slogans such as 'Down with bureaucracy!' and 'Long live democracy!' Students in their thousands flooded into the central Tiananmen Square in Beijing. Between 21 and 22 April, up to 100 000 people demonstrated. An official PRC newspaper, the *People's Daily*, condemned the students as a 'small bunch of troublemakers' and called the demonstration 'a counter-revolutionary rebellion'.

On 13 May, 3000 students began a hunger strike in Tiananmen Square. This was highly embarrassing for the leaders of the PRC, particularly as Gorbachev was due to arrive two days later. The protesters welcomed Gorbachev as a hero of reform, chanting his name and incorporating *glasnost* and *perestroika* in their slogans.

The tension rose on 19 May when a million people took to the streets to support the student hunger strikers. On 20 May **martial law** was declared. Deng refused to compromise with the students. Finally, on 4 June 1989, apparently under direct orders from Deng, troops were sent in to disperse the crowd. The students shouted slogans at the army and some threw rocks. The troops opened fire. It remains unclear exactly how many people died. It is likely that the number is in the thousands. Thousands also fled into hiding and were hunted down and arrested by the authorities.

The PRC officially announced that troops had been forced to defend themselves, and that about 100 civilians were dead and 100 more wounded. It denied that thousands had been killed.

Activity 10 | ATL Thinking skills

1. This photograph is one of the most iconic images from the pro-democracy demonstrations in China. Why do you think this image is so powerful?

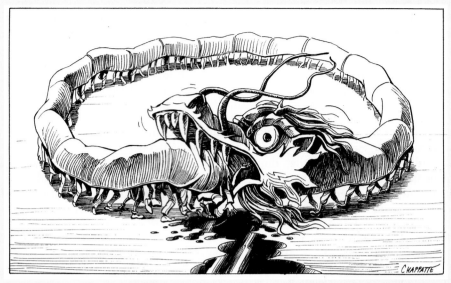

Cartoon by Chappatte, published in the West in 1989, commenting on the Tiananmen Square massacre.

2. What is the cartoonist's message?

The PRC's brutal crushing of the demonstration was condemned around the world. The following appeared in *Time Australia*, on 19 June 1989, allegedly quoting a Chinese worker: 'Tell the United Nations, tell the world what has happened in China. Tell them that the Chinese government is killing the Chinese people.' Despite the violence, there were no crippling sanctions applied to the PRC by the international community, though relations with the USA did suffer (see chapter 11).

The fall of the Soviet Union

When Gorbachev's reforms brought about his downfall, it seemed to Deng and the CCP that their hardline stand against the pro-democracy protests had been the right one. With the new political freedoms came the collapse of Communism in Eastern Europe between 1989 and 1991 (see chapter 15). This included the ending of the monopoly status of the Communist Party of the Soviet Union in 1990. The following year the USSR was dissolved.

The People's Republic of China no longer had a competitor for the leadership of the Communist world. However, the PRC did not seize the international revolutionary initiative. Rather, the regime looked to enhance China's position as a major world player and continue its economic modernization.

How successful has China's quest for economic modernization been? Has it attempted to expand its power in other ways since 1990?

| Activity 11 | (ATL) Self-management skills |

1. Look at the Chinese 'overview' timeline in Appendix II. Identify the 'turning point events' in Sino-Soviet relations. Then, in your own words, explain why these events caused tension between the PRC and the USSR – you could annotate your own version of the timeline.

Essay writing

Consider the following essay question:

> *To what extent were relations between the PRC and the USSR affected by differences over ideology?*

You could adopt a structure that evaluates the effect of ideology on relations between the USSR and the PRC by contrasting it with 'self-interest'.

There is much evidence that the relationship soured into a split due to their differences over ideology, and this can be supported by the evidence of events from your timeline. However, there is also a convincing line of argument that suggests that ideology was really just a cover for a traditional power struggle between the two countries, which were focused more on nationalist self-interest than specific ideology. Again, you will need to select examples of events from your timeline to support your arguments. Some of the events can be used on both sides of the argument – although you will analyse them differently.

Here is another essay question to consider:

> *Examine the reasons for hostility between the USSR and the PRC between 1956 and 1989.*

The danger with this essay question is that you end up writing a narrative account – in other words, simply retelling the chronological story of events without attempting to analyse the question. To avoid this, you could adopt a thematic approach, and structure your essay around the following arguments:

- ideological differences, with examples
- personality clashes, with examples
- self-interest, with examples
- domestic problems, with examples.

This essay would work, but would be given a further dimension if 'external forces' were also discussed. After you have read the next chapter on Sino-American relations, a further theme of 'the role of the USA' could be added.

Here is a third essay question:

> *Examine the reasons for the thaw in Sino-Soviet relations at the end of the 1980s.*

After establishing the key causes of hostility between the USSR and the PRC in your introduction, the main body of the essay could then compare and contrast the changes that precipitated Chinese moves towards a 'thaw' with those of the USSR. As with the previous essay, your plan can be improved by adding the role played by the USA, after you have read the next chapter.

To access websites relevant to this chapter, go to www.pearsonhotlinks.com, search for the book title or ISBN, and click on 'chapter 10'.

11

Sino-American relations

The American flag being raised in China in honor of US President Richard Nixon's visit in February 1972. This was the first time that the US flag had been unfurled in China in over two decades.

China and the Cold War timeline

For a full timeline of the events relating to China and the Cold War, see Appendix II.

Key concepts: Causation and consequence

As you read this chapter, consider the following essay questions:

- Discuss the key causes of Sino-American hostility from 1949 to 1970.
- Examine the reasons for, and the results of, the Sino-American détente in the 1970s.

Background

During World War Two the United States had some direct contact with the Chinese Communist Party (CCP), and had given it some material assistance in the fight against the common enemy, Japan. However, most US aid went to Jiang Jieshi (Chiang Kai-shek) and the Nationalist Guomindang Party (GMD). After the Japanese surrender and withdrawal from China at the end of the war, the CCP and GMD fought each other in the civil war. The Americans pumped material assistance and advice to Jiang's 'anti-Communist' forces, but this did not bring about the Nationalist victory the United States had hoped for.

When Mao Zedong and the CCP came to power in October 1949, the United States refused to recognize the Communist-controlled People's Republic of China (PRC) as a legitimate state. Instead, they backed Jiang Jieshi and the Chinese Nationalists who, at the end of the Chinese Civil War, had fled to the island of Taiwan, about 100 miles off the coast of mainland China. The Americans then ensured that it was the anti-Communists on Taiwan, and *not* the People's Republic of China, that were given China's seat at the United Nations.

Taiwan quickly became the key area of dispute between the USA and the PRC. However, there were other important areas of Sino-American tension: Korea, Japan, and Tibet. The USA was also concerned over the Chinese development of nuclear weapons; Mao decided to start developing his own nuclear weapons during the first Taiwan crisis of 1954–1955.

As Hugh Brogan put it:

> ❝ *The Chinese looked at the Americans through the same sort of telescope as that which the Americans were pointing at them. They too seemed to be a self-confident aggressor power making the first moves in a campaign that, unless unchecked, might lead on to world conquest.*
>
> **Hugh Brogan, *The Pelican History of the United States of America* (Penguin 1986) pp.625–626**

These disputes were the focus for the underlying ideological conflict that initially mirrored the divide between the USA and the USSR. However, by the end of the 1960s there was a radical change, both on the part of the Americans and the Communist Chinese, in their policies towards one another.

The 1950s – increasing tension

Tibet, 1950

In 1950 the Chinese People's Liberation Army (PLA) invaded Tibet. This was not considered by Mao to be an issue of foreign policy, but entirely a domestic concern. After all, the Chinese saw this as part of their consolidation of the CCP's control of the mainland, and the reunification of former Chinese territories.

CHALLENGE YOURSELF

ATL Research skills

Research the PRC's invasion and occupation of Tibet. Look at the international responses, and compare and contrast regional reactions. Also look at international reaction today to China's occupation of Tibet.

However, this was not how much of the outside world viewed the brutality with which the Tibetans were suppressed. There followed a reign of terror in the region, and the United States condemned the People's Republic for what it perceived as expansionism, as well as the horrific bloodshed. The Tibetan spiritual leader, the Dalai Lama, who later fled Tibet, called the actions of the Maoist regime 'cultural genocide'.

The Korean War, 1950–1953

As has been discussed in chapter 5, Korea was divided along the 38th parallel at the end of World War Two. The North was under a Communist regime and the South under an anti-Communist government. The North was supported by the Soviets, and the South by the Americans.

When the North, under Kim Il Sung, invaded the South in 1950, the US State Department believed that this attack was under the direction of Josef Stalin and Mao Zedong. Indeed, they thought that this was a 'joint venture' by the new Communist bloc in Asia. However, as you have read in chapter 5, Mao had been persuaded by Kim Il Sung to agree to the invasion, but was not involved at all in the initial attack. In fact, the PRC had not been particularly concerned with the divided Korea. Its continuing focus was on the issues surrounding Taiwan and Tibet. It was also attempting to consolidate control within mainland China itself and to initiate 'revolutionary' reforms.

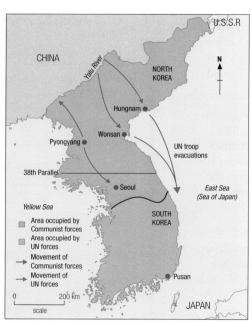

Map showing the Chinese forces pushing back the UN forces in the Korean War.

At the time, the Soviet Union was boycotting the United Nations because of the US's refusal to officially recognize the PRC. Therefore, in the vote to send troops into Korea to defend the South, the Soviet Union did not use its veto (see chapter 5).

Mao condemned American action, but the USA justified its position by claiming that the North had been the 'aggressors'. Mao countered by claiming that the South had been the initial aggressors. Although US forces arrived in South Korea under the UN flag in June 1950, the PRC's Zhou Enlai asserted that the US troops were imperialist invaders.

The Chinese Foreign Ministry issued a public statement to be delivered at the UN by India, indicating its support for North Korea:

> The American aggressors have gone too far. After making a five-thousand-mile journey across the Pacific they invaded the territories of China and Korea. In the language of the American imperialists that is not aggression on their part, whereas the just struggle of the Chinese in defence of their land and their people is aggression. The world knows who is right and who is wrong …
>
> **United Nations Document S/1902, 15 November 1950, pp.2–4**

The PRC organized mass demonstrations in China and warned the Americans that it would be forced to intervene if there was any push into the North. There were already thousands of the People's Liberation Army troops fighting with the North Koreans as 'volunteers'.

In October 1950, UN troops under General Douglas MacArthur crossed north over the 38th parallel and, as they got closer to the Chinese border, the PRC launched its attack across the Yalu river. Over the next three years, millions of Chinese fought in Korea. By the time of the truce in 1953, the PLA had lost nearly a million men.

> *What was most unlikely was Chinese acquiescence in an American presence at a border that was a traditional invasion route into China and specifically the base from which Japan had undertaken the occupation of Manchuria and the invasion of Northern China. China was all the less likely to be passive when such a posture involved a strategic setback on two fronts: The Taiwan Strait and Korea … The misconceptions of both sides compounded each other. The United States did not expect the invasion; China did not expect the reaction. Each side reinforced the other's misconceptions by its own actions. At the end of the process stood two years of war and twenty years of alienation.*

Henry Kissinger, *On China* (Allen Lane 2011) p.132

1. Identify the key points made by Henry Kissinger regarding the reasons for China's response in Korea.

The impact of the Korean War on Sino-American relations

The Korean War led to open conflict between the USA and the PRC. The **Panmunjom Armistice** did not bring about any degree of improvement. The Americans had previously been reluctant to guarantee long-term protection for Taiwan, but after the war they pledged themselves to the defence of the island. Also, Mao was now less in awe of the potential military might of the USA.

The key result of this war in terms of Sino-American relations was that the hostility between the People's Republic of China and the United States now became a key factor in international relations.

In addition, the PRC had been considerably weakened by the Korean conflict, both in terms of the loss of life and the economic cost of the war. However, politically, the war may have strengthened the position of the CCP. The fact that the Soviets had made the Chinese pay the entire bill for the cost of supplies helped to rally the Chinese to their own Communist Party, and made them more determined to stand alone. Mao emphasized that it was Chinese, and not Soviet, blood that had been spilled for the 'international Communist cause'.

> *On the Chinese mainland 600 million people are ruled by the Chinese Communist Party. That party came to power by violence, and, so far, has lived by violence. It retains power not by the will of the Chinese people but by massive, forcible repression. It fought the United Nations in Korea; it supported the Communist War in Indo-China; it took Tibet by force. It fomented the Communist Huk rebellion in the Philippines and the Communist insurrection in Malaya. It does not disguise its expansionist ambitions. It is bitterly hateful of the United States, which it considers a principal obstacle in the way of its path of conquest. As regards China, we have abstained from any act to encourage the Communist regime – morally, politically or materially. Thus: we have not extended diplomatic recognition to the Chinese Communist regime. We have opposed seating in the United Nations. We have not traded with Communist China or sanctioned cultural exchanges with it.*

US Department of State Bulletin, 15 July 1953

1. What claims does the US Department of State make about Chinese actions?

Cold War Crisis:

Taiwan, 1954 and 1958

The Korean War had altered the American perspective towards Asia and the Communist Chinese, and this included its policy on Taiwan. In early 1950, President Truman stated:

> ❝ *The United States has no desire to obtain special rights or privileges or to establish military bases on Formosa [Taiwan] at this time. Nor does it have any intention of utilizing its armed forces to interfere in the present situation. The United States government will not pursue a course which will lead to involvement in the civil strife in China.*

President Harry S Truman, 5 January 1950

However, by 1953, Taiwan had become a key territory in the American policy of containment in Asia (see chapter 6).

The PRC had not attempted to take Taiwan earlier for a number of reasons:

- Taiwan was well defended and the PRC was not confident it had the air power or the landing craft necessary.
- The US Navy Seventh Fleet, which had been based in the area to secure Taiwan for strategic reasons during the Korean War, was now present.
- At the end of the Korean War, the United States stated it would protect Taiwan from aggression.

In 1954, Mao decided to test the commitment of the United States and shelled the islands of Quemoy and Matsu (see map below). Eisenhower responded strongly, even suggesting that nuclear weapons would be used against military targets in China if Taiwan was directly threatened.

This map shows the coast of China with Taiwan, Quemoy, and Matsu.

Why had the United States and Eisenhower responded so forcefully? Firstly, the United States had to show strength to its other allies in the region. It was also confident that the Soviet Union would not go so far as to support the PRC in a war. In addition, John Lewis Gaddis suggests that Nationalist leader Jiang Jieshi had a role in bringing in the USA:

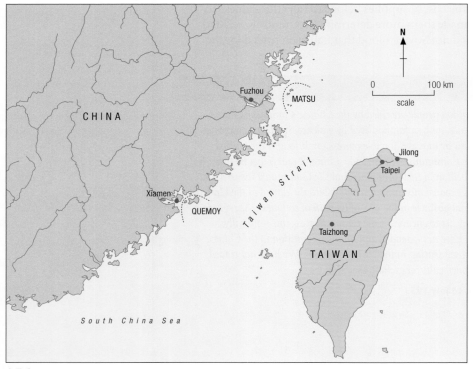

> ❝ *… when Mao began shelling the offshore islands in September 1954 … Chiang [Jiang] claimed the psychological effects of losing them would be so severe that his own regime on Taiwan might collapse. Eisenhower and Dulles responded as they had to Rhee: Chiang got a mutual defence treaty that bound the United States to the defence of Taiwan.*

John Lewis Gaddis, *The Cold War* (Penguin 2005) p.132

In 1958, Mao began shelling Quemoy and Matsu again, and at the same time there was a build-up of PLA troops in the area. US Navy vessels were fired on in the Taiwan Strait. The USA prepared for war with the PRC. In the end, no full-scale attack on Taiwan came. Mao had stepped back from the brink.

The United States believed that the People's Republic of China was an expansionist state and provided leadership for other revolutionary countries. This view of the PRC's aims linked into the American domino effect theory (see chapter 6) and thus China's goals were perceived as a genuine threat to the security of the West. Therefore, the United States pursued the following policies in relation to the containment of China:

- a US trade embargo with the PRC
- obstruction of the PRC's entry to the United Nations
- huge economic and military aid to Taiwan
- an aid programme for the region
- instigation of a regional containment bloc – SEATO
- bilateral defence treaties with Asian states seen as under threat from the PRC.

The Sino-American Cold War in the 1960s

As was discussed in chapter 5, McCarthyism had a significant impact on American policies towards China during the Eisenhower administration. These policies were continued under the administration of John F Kennedy, which maintained the policy of 'containment and isolation' of China.

The US government used the failure of the Great Leap Forward (see chapter 10) to highlight to the public, and the rest of the West, the excesses of this 'Marxist-driven economic experiment' and the PRC's willingness to sacrifice millions of Chinese people in pursuit of its Communist ideology.

Activity 3   ATL **Thinking skills**

Cartoon by Edmund Valtman published in the West in 1961.

1. What is the message of the cartoonist here?
2. How would this message encourage support for American policy towards China at this time?

The key issues of dispute between the PRC and the United States in the 1960s were:

- Taiwan
- Vietnam
- **decolonization** movements
- the Chinese Cultural Revolution.

The United States, the PRC, and Taiwan

Throughout the 1960s the PRC persisted in its demands for the reunification of Taiwan with the mainland. Indeed, as Margaret MacMillan writes: 'The existence of a separate government and another China was an affront to the Chinese nation and to Chinese nationalism' (*Seize the Hour: When Nixon Met Mao* [John Murray 2006] p.228).

Although there was no return to the brink of war that had occurred between the USA and the PRC in the 1958 crisis, the issue was of fundamental importance to the Chinese. This was their overriding preoccupation, and no compromises, such as 'two Chinas', were acceptable to them. Any improvement in Sino-American relations could only be possible, in the PRC's view, when Taiwan no longer existed as a separate state.

The United States, Vietnam, and the People's Republic of China

The war in Vietnam seriously heightened the tension between the USA and the Asia-Pacific region, including America's own allies. The PRC condemned American involvement in Vietnam as 'imperialism' and cited Taiwan as another key example of its expansionism in the region. Mao also claimed that the UN was dominated by the imperialist policies of the West.

Activity 4   (ATL) Thinking skills

Read the lyrics to this Chinese children's song:

> *There is an evil spirit:*
> *His name is Johnson.*
> *His mouth is all sweetness,*
> *But he has a wolf's heart.*
> *He bombs Vietnam cities*
> *And hates the people.*
> *Chinese and Vietnamese are all one family:*
> *We will certainly not agree to this!*
> *I wear a red scarf and join the demonstrations with Daddy.*
> *With small throat but large voice I shout:*
> *'US pirates get out, get out, get out.'*

Quoted in Lois Mitchison, *China* (Bodley Head 1966)

1. How useful is this source as evidence of Chinese public opinion about the Americans during the Vietnam War?

TOK

Think about the following questions:

- As a History student, what criteria do you use to distinguish between knowledge, opinion, and propaganda?
- Would this be more difficult for a child to do?
- What ways of knowing seem to develop as we become more mature? Do these give us a better grasp of truth?

The PRC and decolonization

The PRC's interest in supporting revolutionary/decolonization movements in the developing world was not simply a pursuit of limited ideological goals in those specific countries. It aimed to ultimately replace the USSR as the world leader of international revolution, and to end Western imperialism by supporting anti-colonial movements.

At the **Bandung Conference** in 1955, PRC Premier Zhou Enlai asserted that the USA was the key danger to world peace. The conference had been held in response to the USA's involvement in setting up SEATO, which was an anti-Communist alliance. At this conference, 29 Asian and African states asserted their neutrality.

In 1966, Dean Rusk outlined the USA's policy towards China to the US Congress:

- The USA does not seek to overthrow the PRC.
- The USA objects to PRC involvement in the affairs of other countries: that is, encouraging revolutionary forces worldwide by providing training.
- Although the PRC is more violent in word than action, it still should not be underestimated.

However, despite the rhetoric and the PRC's propaganda in support of 'revolutionary' movements, China did not have the resources to make a definitive difference in the developing world. Even when China had developed its own nuclear weapons, it did not have the delivery systems to use them in wars of decolonization. Therefore, the threat to the developing world posed by the PRC, as perceived by the USA and outlined by Dean Rush in 1966, was probably exaggerated.

The USA and the PRC's Cultural Revolution

As mentioned in chapter 10, the Great Leap Forward and the Cultural Revolution led to a collapse in the PRC's ability to conduct any real foreign policy. The American view of the turmoil going on inside China was similar to the Soviet perception – it was a clear demonstration of the out-of-control fanaticism of the Maoist leadership, which seemed to lack both stability and coherency. The PRC was seen as a danger to the region, and a perpetual threat to the delicate balance envisaged by the American State Department that prevented the 'dominoes' from tipping over.

During the Cultural Revolution, the Chinese increased the ferocity of their attacks on the United States and its allies (calling them 'Capitalist running dogs'). The PRC seriously feared an American attack aimed at bringing about 'regime change'. This, together with the threat of attack by the Soviets, made the PRC leadership incredibly nervous during the first years of the Cultural Revolution.

Activity 5

1. What is the message of the cartoonist here?

'The New Religion' by Edmund Valtman, 1966, published in the West.

Sino-American détente in the 1970s

> *Naturally I personally regret that forces of history have divided and separated the American and Chinese peoples from virtually all communication during the past 15 years. Today the gulf seems broader than ever. However, I myself do not believe it will end in war and one of history's major tragedies.*

Mao Zedong to foreign journalist Edgar Snow, 1965

Four key areas were the focus for Sino-American relations in the 1970s:

- Taiwan
- Vietnam
- the United Nations
- the Soviet Union.

Détente between the two powers started in 1969 when the United States began to ease trade restrictions. In addition, the patrols conducted by the US Seventh Fleet in the Taiwan Strait were halted. However, the major turning point in Sino-American relations came when the United States changed its policy towards the PRC's membership of the United Nations.

This began with what has become known as '**ping-pong diplomacy**', where an American table-tennis team was invited to compete in China and secret talks took place between Henry Kissinger and Zhou Enlai. The climax of this change in relations came with the historic visit in 1972 of President Richard Nixon to Beijing to meet the Communist leadership, including a very sick Mao Zedong. During this meeting a joint **communiqué** was issued, establishing a new relationship between the two superpowers.

Why did the USA want détente with the PRC?

> *Nixon did not believe that one could end a war into which his predecessors had sent 500,000 American soldiers halfway across the world by pulling out unconditionally … Nixon knew that whatever the agony of its involvement in Vietnam, the United States remained the strongest country in the alliance against Communist aggression around the world, and American credibility was critical. The Nixon administration … therefore sought a staged withdrawal from Indochina … In this design China played a key role.*

Henry Kissinger, *On China* (Allen Lane 2011) pp.213–214

There were a number of reasons why the United States found that it was now the right time to move towards détente with the Chinese:

- The situation in Vietnam had led the United States to believe containment was not possible there, and it wanted the PRC's assistance in its exit strategy.
- The USA wanted to put pressure on the Soviet–American attempts at détente.
- Nixon wanted to 'make history'.
- There was public support in the USA for more constructive strategies following the Vietnam War.
- The PRC had developed ICBM capability, so it was now the American view that it was more dangerous *not* to have contact.
- The USA hoped to be able to reduce commitments in Asia, while retaining bases in the Pacific.

These reasons reflect the changing perspectives in the United States on the nature of global Communism. The US administration was beginning to understand that various Communist movements around the world were not as 'monolithic' as it had long suspected, with President Nixon stating: 'Our foreign policy began to differentiate among Communist capitals.' Nixon suggested that the United States would now 'deal with countries on the basis of their actions, not abstract ideological formulas'. The membership of the UN was also changing, and the USA would not be able to control the vote as regards PRC membership for much longer. Both sides now seemed ready to give up attempts to attain hegemony in Asia. This was the key point of the February 1972 joint Sino-American statement, the **Shanghai Communiqué**.

Activity 6	**(ATL)** Thinking and self-management skills

Source A

> *Nixon … was gradually modifying his longstanding opposition to having the People's Republic in the United Nations. This was largely because of his moves towards the People's Republic, but also because it had become clear that the United States was about to lose the vote at the UN.*

Margaret MacMillan, *Seize the Hour: When Nixon Met Mao* (John Murray, 2006) p.211

Source B

> *China exemplified the great changes that had occurred in the Communist world. For years, our guiding principle was containment of what we considered a monolithic challenge. In the 1960s the forces of nationalism dissolved Communist unity into divergent centers of power and doctrine, and our foreign policy began to differentiate among the Communist capitals … We would deal with countries on the basis of their actions not abstract ideological formulas … [The US and China] seemed to have no fundamental interests that need collide in the eager sweep of history.*

President Nixon's Foreign Policy Report to Congress, 1973

Source C

> Once the Soviet Union could no longer count on permanent hostility between the world's most powerful and most populous nations … the scope for Soviet intransigence would narrow and perhaps even evaporate. Soviet leaders would have to hedge their bets because a threatening posture might intensify Sino-American co-operation. In the conditions of the late 1960s, improved Sino-American relations became a key to the Nixon Administration's Soviet strategy.

Henry S Kissinger, *Diplomacy* (Simon & Schuster 1995) p.719

1. Link each of the above sources to one (or more) of the motives listed for why the USA wanted better relations with the PRC.

2. With reference to their origin, purpose and content, assess the values and limitations of using a) Source B and b) Source C to research American motivations at this time.

3. Using these sources, and the information so far in this chapter and in the previous chapters of the book, examine the reasons for the USA's pursuit of better relations with Communist China. Explain your answer thoroughly.

For question 3 you need to integrate both the sources and your own knowledge in your answer. It is important that you include both! Identify key points made in the sources and then develop these with extra information from chapters 10 and 12.

Why did China want détente with the USA?

There were various reasons why China thought it was the right time for détente with the United States.

- In the 1960s and 1970s the PRC saw the USSR as its main rival, so it wanted to reduce tensions with the USA.
- China could gain concessions on key foreign policy issues: for example, UN membership, Taiwan, US withdrawal from Vietnam and Indochina as a whole.
- The PRC was worried about a resurgent Japan, and wanted its power limited.
- The PRC maintained that the détente would be 'temporary', and that it would remain vigilant against US imperialism and aggression. Mao had argued in an article in 1940, 'On Policy', that it was legitimate to play off enemies and to do whatever was necessary to defeat the main enemy at a given time.
- Moderation of its stance against the West could improve the PRC's standing in the developing world.

Activity 7   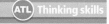 ATL Thinking skills

Source A

> Word went out to party officials to prepare for Nixon's visit by studying Mao's negotiations with the Guomindang after the Second World War. 'Why shouldn't we negotiate with President Nixon?' Zhou asked a visiting British journalist. 'For instance, in the past we talked with Chiang Kai-shek.'

Margaret MacMillan, *Seize the Hour: When Nixon Met Mao* (John Murray 2006) p.203

Source B

> In September, with the fear of a Soviet attack building … Zhou Enlai [was sent] a … report which underlined … earlier conclusions. 'The last thing the U.S. imperialists are willing to see is a victory by the Soviet revisionists in a Sino-Soviet war, as this would [allow the Soviets] to build up a big empire more powerful than the American empire in resources and manpower.' Although in the long term China was struggling against both powers, its strategy should be to use one against the other.

Margaret MacMillan, *Seize the Hour: When Nixon Met Mao* (John Murray 2006) p.143

11

Source C

> While they blamed the United States for Japan's resurgence, they also recognized that the United States could act as a brake on its rearmament and expansion.

Margaret MacMillan, *Seize the Hour: When Nixon Met Mao* (John Murray 2006) p.233

Source D

> It was only in June 1970, after his anti-American manifesto of 20 May had flopped, and when it was inescapably clear that Maoism was getting nowhere in the world, that Mao decided to invite Nixon to China. The motive was not to have a reconciliation with America, but to relaunch himself on the international stage.

Jung Chang and Jon Halliday, *Mao: The Unknown Story* (Random House 2005) p.601

1. Sources A, B, and C are all extracts from Margaret MacMillan's book *Seize the Hour*. Which key motives for the PRC's interest in better relations with the USA are suggested by MacMillan?

2. What extra reason for improved relations is given in Source D?

3. Using these sources, this chapter, and the broader contextual understanding you have gained from chapter 10 in this book, identify the key reasons why Mao and the PRC sought better relations with the USA at this time? (See Hints for success box on page 160.)

What did China gain from détente with the United States?

The People's Republic of China attained some of its objectives and several benefits from pursuing détente with the Americans.

United Nations membership

It was unrealistic of the PRC to hope to become a member of the United Nations in the 1950s, as the General Assembly was dominated by Western countries. To become a member it would need a majority vote in the General Assembly. Every year a vote was taken on PRC membership, and each time it was defeated. In 1961 the United States had sufficient support for the 'important questions' resolution to pass, which meant the question of PRC membership would now need a two-thirds majority.

In 1965, the US ambassador to the UN, Adlai Stevenson, outlined why the United States did not believe the PRC should be a member state:

- The CCP was not the legitimate government of China – it had come to power through force, not by democracy. It also used force to maintain its power.
- It had a record of aggression, and was thus not a 'peace-loving' nation.
- Its sponsorship of revolutionary groups in the developing world would hamper UN work in these areas.
- Taiwan had an honourable record, and should not be expelled.

However, as UN membership grew, it was the non-aligned states and developing countries that began to dominate the General Assembly (see chapter 16). Indeed, in 1970, the General Assembly finally voted in favour of the Chinese UN seat transferring to Beijing. However, the necessary two-thirds majority was not reached. In 1970, the United States initiated the 'two Chinas' policy. This suggested that Beijing took the Security Council seat for China, while Taiwan still maintained representation in the General Assembly. This solution was rejected by both Chinas.

Finally, in the summer of 1971, President Nixon announced his imminent visit to the PRC and also stated that the United States would no longer oppose Beijing's admission to the UN. The USA failed to prevent the expulsion of Taiwan. In reality, the Americans were simply accepting the inevitable.

Result of UN membership for PRC

The PRC now had the power of veto in the UN Security Council. It could be used to block resolutions, an example of which was a PRC veto that prevented the admission of Bangladesh to the UN in 1971. This was done in retaliation for the 'victory' of the USSR and its Indian allies over PRC-backed Pakistan in the **Indo-Pakistan War**. With its wider access to diplomatic contacts through the UN, the PRC also gained better links with countries in the developing world. It was able to increase its prestige and influence, present views on the world stage, and publicly support its allies and denounce its enemies (including the USSR).

Taiwan

It had always been the Chinese Communist view that Taiwan belonged to China, and that this was not a negotiable issue. Indeed, MacMillan suggests that Taiwan was as important to the PRC as their problems with the USSR. When Zhou met Kissinger in July 1971 he said of Taiwan: 'That place is no great use for you, but a great wound for us.'

In 1972 Nixon declared: 'The ultimate relationship between Taiwan and the mainland is not a matter for the US to decide.' This was a key foreign policy objective for the PRC and was a main reason for their pursuit of détente. However, progress towards reunification was very slow – the United States did not want to hurry its transference of official recognition to the PRC, nor was it comfortable with the idea of 'giving up' Taiwan.

The issue dragged on until US President Jimmy Carter finally established full diplomatic relations with China in 1979. At the same time, arms sales to Taiwan were halted. As historian Immanuel Hsu comments, 'The majority of Americans … found it hard to oppose the simple mathematics of … relations with 900 million people on mainland China compared with the 17 million on Taiwan' (*China Without Mao: The Search for a New Order* [OUP 1982] p.63).

However, Jimmy Carter was defeated by the fiercely anti-Communist Republican candidate, Ronald Reagan, in the 1980 presidential election – and a renewed 'Cold War' ensued. Reagan again committed the United States to protecting Taiwan. He resumed arms sales and Sino-American relations deteriorated. Even though the PRC had failed to reunite Taiwan with the mainland, it had to remain relatively diplomatic over the issue. China did not want to provoke the USA at a time when relations with the USSR remained tense.

President Richard Nixon and his Secretary of State, Henry Kissinger, meeting with PRC Chairman Mao Zedong and Premier Zhou Enlai.

Japan

The improved relations with the United States had, as the Chinese hoped, an impact on their relations with Japan. On 12 August 1978, China and Japan signed a friendship treaty. The relationship developed over the next few years, particularly through economic ties. Within 5 years of their friendship treaty, China had become second only to the United States as a trading partner with Japan. This had an additional benefit for the PRC as it was a further pressure on the Soviet Union. The Soviets were concerned at this new friendship between historic enemies, and the situation led to more fears in the USSR of being 'encircled'.

Activity 8

Source A

Cartoon by Chappatte, published in the West in 1979.

Source B

 The détente enabled Peking [Beijing] to purchase American airliners, scientific instruments, and chemical, industrial and agricultural products needed for China's modernization. The exchange of scholars, journalists, athletes, scientists and officials facilitated the mutual flow of ideas and knowledge, reversing the trend of twenty-two years of noncommunication ... [However, it raised] the question of China's credibility before other Communist states, especially those in Asia.

Immanuel Hsu, *The Rise of Modern China* (OUP 1999) p.731

1. Source A is a cartoon published in the West in 1979. What comment is being made about the policies of Deng Xiaoping?
2. In Source B, what key benefits of détente with the Americans does Hsu highlight? What drawbacks are suggested?

What did the US gain from détente with the PRC?

The Americans also gained certain benefits from détente with the PRC.

Vietnam

The Americans attempted to use the PRC to help them get out of Vietnam. Although better relations had been useful in adding weight to the American side in negotiations, it tended to be indirect. In other words, it was more the leverage that the Sino-American détente gave them with the Soviets that assisted in negotiations with the North Vietnamese. As Fitzgerald points out:

 … a truce … was finally signed in January 1973. The Americans firmly believed that Soviet pressure had played an important part in softening Hanoi's negotiating position.

From James Fitzgerald, *The Cold War and Beyond* (Nelson 1995) p.127

This pressure had been achieved, at least in part, by the new US policy towards China.

Wider context

In addition, the new US policy towards China did result in pressure on the USSR to maintain détente with USA. However, the Americans were ultimately unwilling to 'play the China card' in relations with the USSR. They feared creating even more instability, especially if the Soviets began to feel encircled.

America's China policy had some impact on relieving its commitment to mainland Asia. The less aggressive stance pursued by the Americans towards the Asian superpower was popular both in Asia and Europe. To a certain extent, it also made up for the US government's loss of face over its changed policy as regards the PRC's seat at the UN.

Activity 9

For the United States, the reconciliation initiated direct relations with China and reduced the possibility of war between Russia and China, thereby enhancing the prospects of world peace … China's promise to peacefully settle international disputes suggested that Peking would not intervene militarily in Vietnam or forcibly liberate Taiwan. Finally, the possibility of release for Americans detained in China increased … Materially, the most conspicuous gain for the United States was the growing Sino-American trade which helped reduce the American balance-of-payment problems.

Immanuel Hsu, *The Rise of Modern China* (OUP 1990) p.731

1. According to Hsu, what were the key benefits for the Americans of better relations with China?
2. In pairs, consider whether the Sino-Soviet détente was equally beneficial to the USA and the PRC.

The PRC and the Cold War

China emerges as a significant factor in the development of the Cold War. The importance of Communist China's role in the Cold War changed over time. The PRC's influence grew in line with their nuclear power status, their increasingly hostile relationship with the USSR and, ultimately, their growing rapprochement with the USA. This shift in the balance of power resulted in the Cold War becoming a conflict that was more 'tri-polar' (USA, USSR, PRC) than 'bi-polar' (USA, USSR).

Tiananmen Square, the PRC, and the United States, 1989

Following the death of Mao Zedong in 1976, the removal of the fiercely anti-American Gang of Four, and the modernization initiatives of Deng Xiaoping, relations between the PRC and the United States became more co-operative on one level. During the Reagan administration there was some degree of 'cooling off' in terms of the diplomatic developments between the two powers, but there was not a return to the 1960s period of hostility. As MacMillan writes, 'While Sino-American relations did not go back to what they had been before Nixon's visit, they did not move ahead either' (Margaret Macmillan, *Seize the Hour* (John Murray 2006) p.315).

In 1989, the Tiananmen Square pro-democracy protests in Beijing were violently crushed by the government in China (see chapter 11). This flagrant abuse of human rights led to protests on the streets in many Western countries, including the United States. Despite the public demands for a tough response to the actions of the PRC, ultimately Tiananmen Square made little difference to China's international position, including its relations with the United States. There was worldwide condemnation, but no diplomatic isolation or **economic sanctions**. The United States did not want to damage its trade links with the PRC.

Deng Xiaoping

Activity 10 — ATL Thinking skills

> *Peking seeks to disarm U.S. over human rights*
>
> *U.S. Secretary of State James Baker ... the highest ranking American to visit China since the Peking killings on 4 June 1989 ... is approaching China trailing clouds of condemnation ... 'We want to protect human rights and advance liberty'. What especially irks China's leaders, is American criticism of the Tiananmen crackdown, when, according to Baker, 'our hopes for a new democratic China turned to revulsion at the sight of tanks crushing unarmed students'.*

The Observer, British newspaper, 17 November 1991

1. In what way does the source suggest that relations between China and the USA were in fact affected by the events of Tiananmen Square?
2. Why might this 'public' view be different from the reality of relations between the Chinese and American governments?

The United States, the PRC, and the end of the Cold War

In the early 1990s, the new Russian government withdrew its forces from the Pacific. At the same time, the United States did not renew the lease on its naval base in the Philippines. With the ending of the Cold War proper, China was left as the leader of the Communist nations, but this was at a time when Communism was in crisis. The former satellite states in Eastern Europe had all seen their Communist regimes collapse, some quietly and some with bloodshed.

TOK

What are the advantages and disadvantages for historians writing about the history of a country or region which has a different culture from their own?

Instead of seizing its opportunity to export its particular brand of Communism, the new leadership in China focused on its development as a world power. This meant establishing its economic power rather than concentrating on its ideological concerns. In 1992 the United States gave the PRC 'most favoured nation status'. Trade links have boomed and the US and China are now important economic partners. Nevertheless, in recent years tension has again grown between the two countries.

Activity 11 — ATL Thinking skills

Source A

U.S. and China on brink of new Cold War

A new cold war threatens the Pacific ... The overall climate of U.S.–Chinese relations is cooling fast, after Beijing last week denounced a U.S. state department report that labelled China as an authoritarian state which routinely tortured thousands of prisoners of conscience. The U.S. also complains that China has not kept promises to curb exports of ballistic missile technology, nor even replied to complaints about its nuclear co-operation with Iran.

The Guardian, British newspaper, 6 February 1995

Source B

*In April 1997 Jiang Zemin visited Moscow to sign the declaration of a 'new bilateral relationship'. The two countries rejected the claims 'by any one country to the role of absolute leader' ... President Yeltsin, in a hardly veiled reference to President Clinton, claimed 'Someone is longing for a **single polar** world. He wants to decide things for himself.' The Chinese Xinhua newsagency quoted the declaration: 'No country should seek hegemony, practise power politics or monopolize international affairs.'*

Alan Lawrance, *China Under Communism* (Routledge 1998) p.135

Source C

Throughout this process, China and the United States were becoming increasingly intertwined economically. At the beginning of the 1990s the total volume of U.S. trade with mainland China was only half the volume of American trade with Taiwan. By the end of the decade U.S.–China trade had quadrupled, and Chinese exports to the United States had increased sevenfold. American multinationals viewed China as an essential component of their business strategies, both as a locus of production and an increasingly monetary market in its own right. China in turn was using its increasing cash reserves to invest in U.S. Treasury bonds.

Henry Kissinger, *On China* (Allen Lane 2011) p.213

1. What future problems for Sino-American relations are identified in sources A, B, and C?

Activity 12 — ATL Thinking and communication skills

Approaching essay questions on Sino-American relations

Attempt to draw up a 'thermometer' of Sino-American relations using the events covered in this chapter. There are some starting points shown on the next page.

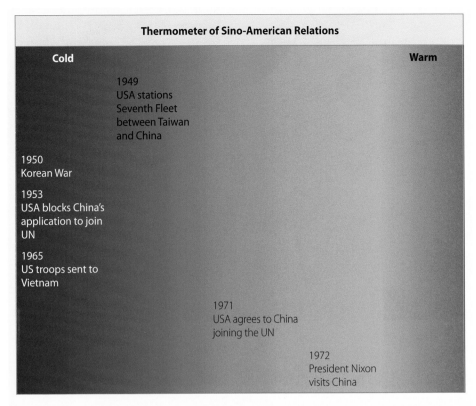

Thermometer of Sino-American Relations

Cold   **Warm**

1949
USA stations
Seventh Fleet
between Taiwan
and China

1950
Korean War

1953
USA blocks China's
application to join
UN

1965
US troops sent to
Vietnam

1971
USA agrees to China
joining the UN

1972
President Nixon
visits China

Now think about how you would approach these two essay questions:

> ***Discuss the reasons for Sino-American détente in the 1970s.***

Consider the long-term and short-term causes, or consider a thematic approach.

> ***Examine the reasons for Sino-American détente in the 1970s, and to what extent was it successful.***

Use your plan for the first question to answer the first part of this second question. You will need to analyse the successes and failures for China, and then for the USA, in the second part of the essay. You should assess the success and failure of détente based on the 'aims' outlined in this chapter, and to what extent they were achieved for each country.

Activity 13

 ATL Thinking and communication skills

Approaching essay questions on China and the Cold War

Consider the following essay question:

> ***Discuss the role of China in the Cold War.***

Using the information in this chapter and in chapter 10, attempt to draw up a thematic approach to this question. This will help you avoid a chronological or narrative response. Consider the changing nature of relations between the PRC and both the USSR and the USA. The rise of Communist China to superpower status, and the importance of 'tri-polar' rather than 'bi-polar' relations in the Cold War, should be included. One thematic approach that could be used for this question is the following:

Main body of essay

Part 1: Argue that Communist China's key role was in increasing tension in the Cold War, and that the PRC made the Cold War more dangerous and war more likely. Include examples of events that support this view.

Part 2: The counter-argument could be that the role of Communist China in the Cold War was actually as a **catalyst** for better relations between the USA and the USSR: that is, the transition of a 'bi-polar' to a 'tri-polar' situation was a key reason for détente between the USSR and the USA.

Include examples of events to support this view.

Conclusion: This could consider how the role of Communist China changed over time during the Cold War.

 To access websites relevant to this chapter, go to www.pearsonhotlinks.com, search for the book title or ISBN, and click on 'chapter 11'.

12

Why did détente end in a second Cold War?

Key concepts: Change and continuity

As you read this chapter, consider the following essay questions:

- Discuss the reasons for détente.
- To what extent did détente result in fundamental changes in the attitudes that the USA and the USSR had towards each other?
- Evaluate the achievements of détente.
- Examine the reasons for the collapse of détente.

The period known as 'détente' started around 1968 and finally ended in 1980 with the victory of Ronald Reagan in the US presidential election. The term détente means 'a relaxation of tension' and during the 1970s it was the word used to describe the attempts of the USA and the USSR to establish a more stable and co-operative relationship. It is also used to describe the improvement in relations between the USA and China, and between Western Europe and the Soviet Union. After 1980, however, détente between the USA and USSR was replaced with a period that became known as the '**Second Cold War**'.

Timeline of détente	
1968	Richard Nixon elected US president
1969	Nuclear Non-Proliferation Treaty signed by over 100 countries
1970	SALT talks open in Vienna
1971	Treaty to denuclearize the seabed signed by 74 countries
	Nixon accepts invitation to visit China
	UN admits China to membership (Taiwan expelled)
1972	Nixon visits China
	Nixon visits USSR for summit with Leonid Brezhnev
	SALT I signed
	East Germany and West Germany sign Basic Treaty
1973	Washington Summit between Nixon and Brezhnev
	Yom Kippur War
1974	Moscow Summit between Nixon and Brezhnev
	Nixon resigns over Watergate; Gerald Ford becomes president
	Vladivostok Summit between Ford and Brezhnev
1975	Helsinki Final Act signed by 35 countries
1976	Jimmy Carter elected as US president
1978	Carter warns USSR against involvement in domestic affairs of other countries
1979	USA and China open diplomatic relations
	Shah flees Iran
	Carter and Brezhnev sign SALT II agreement in Vienna
	US Embassy in Tehran seized and diplomats taken hostage
	USA announces plans to deploy cruise missiles
	Soviet forces invade Afghanistan
1980	US Senate suspends SALT II debate
	Ronald Reagan elected US president

Timeline of détente – *continued*

1981	US hostages released by Iran
1982	Death of Brezhnev; Yuri Andropov becomes Soviet leader
1983	Reagan explains Strategic Defense Initiative (SDI)
	USSR shoots down Korean Airlines flight 007 over its airspace
	First cruise missiles arrive in Europe
1984	Death of Andropov; Konstantin Chernenko becomes Soviet leader
	Reagan re-elected US president

One of the factors pushing the superpowers towards an improvement in relations was the growing awareness of the dangers of nuclear war. As you have seen, the early 1960s saw serious confrontations over Berlin and Cuba, and by the late 1960s both the United States and the Soviet Union were ready to take steps to reduce the risk of nuclear confrontation. This was also made possible by the fact that by 1969 the USSR had reached **nuclear parity** with the United States, meaning it now had a similar nuclear capability to the USA, and so, for the first time, could negotiate from a position of equality. Both superpowers also had their own individual reasons for wanting a relaxation of tensions.

The USSR's reasons for détente

One of the key reasons the USSR needed better relations with the United States was that its economy was stagnating. In order to deal with its economic problems, and also to improve the standard of living for Soviet citizens, it needed to be able to transfer economic resources from the production of armaments to the production of consumer goods. It would also be able to import new technologies from the West.

A second key factor was the USSR's deteriorating relationship with China. As was discussed in chapter 10, the Sino-Soviet split had ended in war in 1969, and it was now crucial for the USSR to keep China isolated from the West by seeking for itself an improved relationship with the West.

The USA's reasons for détente

Détente was initiated by Richard Nixon, who was elected president of the USA in 1968, and his National Security Adviser, Henry Kissinger. Nixon needed to find a way of ending the Vietnam War and he also wanted the United States to follow a more realistic foreign policy, which would take account of the changing international situation – the pursuit of *realpolitik*:

> Henry Kissinger called for a 'philosophical deepening' of American foreign policy. By this he meant adjusting to the changed international order. The Kennedy and Johnson administrations, Kissinger argued, had focused too much on victory in one rather isolated area – Vietnam – at the expense of the global balance of power. The world was shifting from a bipolar balance of power between Washington and Moscow to a multipolar balance shared among five great economic and strategic centres – the United States, the Soviet Union, Western Europe, Japan and China.

John Mason, *The Cold War* (Routledge 1996) p.51

Therefore, Nixon hoped to use détente to get the USSR and China to put pressure on North Vietnam to end the war and, at the same time, to retain and 'deepen' the USA's global role through negotiation rather than confrontation. Arms control would also free up resources that could be used to deal with the faltering American economy.

Henry Kissinger

Henry Kissinger was Richard Nixon's national security adviser and was an expert on international relations. Under Nixon first, and later President Gerald Ford, for whom he was Secretary of State, he travelled all over the world establishing contacts with leaders of different countries. He was a skilled negotiator and played a key role in negotiations to end the Vietnam War, in Arab–Israeli peace negotiations (1973–1978), and in setting up key meetings for Nixon with the USSR and China, as part of the détente process.

Activity 1   (ATL) Thinking skills

A cartoon by Michael Cummings published in the Daily Express in 1969. Brezhnev and Kosygin are on top of the tank; Nixon is climbing down the ladder. The countries in the tank are Rumania, Poland, Hungary, Bulgaria, East Germany and Czechoslovakia.

1. What is the message of this cartoon?

What were the reasons for PRC–USA rapprochement?

Chapters 10 and 11 have discussed in detail Sino-American and Sino-Soviet relations. China's relations with the Soviet Union were at a very low point in the late 1960s. China was worried about international isolation and so saw improved relations with the United States as a way to prevent this and, at the same time, cause concerns in the Soviet Union. For the USA, an improved relationship with China was part of the new *realpolitik* approach to foreign policy. Kissinger, in the CNN television series *The Cold War*, explained that his aim was to 'restore fluidity' to international politics by allowing the USA to deal with China and to move away from its obsession with Vietnam, which he regarded as an 'aberration'.

In addition, the Americans knew that working with the Chinese would give them extra 'leverage', or negotiating power, in their dealings with the Soviets.

What were the reasons for improved East–West relations in Europe?

There was also pressure for détente from Europe. Events in 1968 had shown political instability in both Eastern and Western Europe with the Soviet invasion of Czechoslovakia and student riots and strikes in France, which had seriously undermined President Charles de Gaulle. The new chancellor of West Germany, Willy Brandt, took the lead in trying to improve relations between the two Germanys. He believed that not only West Germany, but also the whole continent, would benefit from a reduction of tensions and greater links between East and West. His policy of encouraging the opening of channels between East and West became known as *Ostpolitik*.

From the Soviet side there was also impetus for improved relations in Europe. A formal peace treaty accepting the new borders of Europe after World War Two had never been signed, and the Soviets wanted to win Western acceptance of the division of Germany and formalize the existing territorial situation in Eastern Europe.

Activity 2   **ATL** Communication skills

1. Summarize the information so far in a spider or pattern diagram to show the different forces working towards détente in the late 1960s.

What were the successes of détente?

Arms agreements between the USA and the USSR: SALT I

After the Cuban Missile Crisis, the USA and the USSR signed several arms control agreements (see page 122). The most significant arms control agreement, however, was **SALT I** (the Strategic Arms Limitation Treaty), signed in 1972. This treaty covered agreement in three areas:

- **The ABM Treaty: ABMs** (Anti-Ballistic Missiles) were allowed at only two sites – each site containing no more than a hundred missiles. As will be discussed in chapter 14, this limitation was key for ensuring the continued emphasis on MAD (mutually assured destruction) and thus the **deterrence** of nuclear war.
- **The Interim Treaty:** This placed limits on the numbers of ICBMs (Inter-Continental Ballistic Missiles) and **SLBMs** (Submarine-Launched Ballistic Missiles).
- **The Basic Principles Agreement:** This laid down rules for the conduct of nuclear war and development of weapons, and committed the two sides to work together to prevent conflict and promote peaceful co-existence. It was followed in 1973 by the Agreement on the Prevention of Nuclear War, which said that if a nuclear conflict looked imminent, both sides would '… immediately enter into urgent consultations with each other and make every effort to avert this risk'.

John Mason writes that SALT I 'began a process of institutionalized arms control, confirmed the Soviet Union's parity with the United States, and reduced tension between the two nuclear powers' (*The Cold War* [Routledge 1996] p.53). It was followed by a spirit of co-operation as Nixon made visits to Moscow in 1972 and 1974, and Brezhnev visited Washington in 1973.

However, there were also severe criticisms of SALT I for not going far enough in limiting nuclear weapons, particularly because it did not mention **MIRV**s (Multiple Independently Targeted Re-entry Vehicles). Stephen Ambrose writes that this omission made the treaty 'about as meaningful as freezing the cavalry of European countries in 1938, but not the tanks' (*Rise to Globalism*, Penguin 2011, p. 231).

SALT II

Many areas for discussion still remained and negotiations for **SALT II** began in 1974, with the treaty finally being signed in 1979. This treaty had agreements on:

- a limit on the number of strategic nuclear delivery vehicles (ICBMs, SLBMs, and heavy bombers) for each side
- a ban on the testing or deployment of new types of ICBMs, heavy mobile ICBMs, and rapid reload systems.

This was the most extensive and complicated arms agreement ever negotiated. However, by the time it was signed, both Democrats and Republicans were criticizing the arms control process as one that accomplished little and which gave advantages to the Soviets. It was never ratified by the US Senate.

Agreements between the two Germanys and the Soviet Union

Willy Brandt in 1970, kneeling at the memorial to the victims of the **Warsaw Ghetto**. Egon Bahr, who was an adviser to Willy Brandt, said in an interview that 'Brandt was a stroke of luck for German history. For the Americans he symbolized reliability – he had proved himself the defender of Berlin against the menace of the East. And for the East, he was a resistance fighter against the Nazis' (Bahr in an interview on the CNN television series *The Cold War*).

A number of treaties were made between the Soviet Union, East Germany, and West Germany in the early 1970s:

- The Moscow Treaty: This was signed in August 1970 between the Soviet Union, Poland, and the Federal Republic of Germany. It recognized the border between East Germany and West Germany and also formally accepted the post-World War Two border in the East with Poland.

- The Final Quadripartite Protocol (1972): This was a major victory for Willy Brandt as it agreed to the maintenance of the 'status quo' in Berlin, confirming that the West had a legal basis for its access routes to the city. Therefore, West Berlin had a much greater degree of security.
- The Basic Treaty (1972): This was signed by East Germany and West Germany. It accepted the existence of two Germanys. West Germany now recognized East Germany and agreed to increase trade links between the two countries.

These agreements did much to reduce tension in Europe, though they were criticized by some in the United States for giving legal recognition to Soviet control over Eastern Europe and formalizing the Cold War divisions in Europe.

Activity 3

> *For many [Germans on both sides of the divide] Brandt's Ostpolitik brought real dividends. Contact and communication between the two Germanys burgeoned. In 1969 a mere half-million phone calls had been placed from West to East Germany. Twenty years later, there were some forty million. Telephone contact between the two halves of Berlin, virtually unknown in 1970, had reached the level of ten million calls per year by 1988 … the reuniting of families and release to the West of political prisoners, redounded to the credit of Ostpolitik and reflected the Communists' growing confidence in the West German policy of 'stability' and 'no surprises'.*
>
> *The rulers of East Germany had particularly good reason to be pleased with these developments. In September 1973 the United Nations recognized and admitted East and West Germany as sovereign states; within a year the German Democratic Republic was diplomatically recognized by eighty countries, including the USA … Whereas the 1968 constitution of the GDR spoke of a commitment to unification on the basis of democracy and socialism, this phrase is absent in the amended constitution of 1974 …*

Tony Judt, *Postwar: A History of Europe Since 1945* (Vintage 2010) p.499

1. According to Judt, what were the results of *Ostpolitik* for the two Germanys?

Agreements between the United States and China

As you saw in the previous chapter, there were also several significant areas of improvement in relations between the USA and China:

- The USA dropped its objections to China taking its seat on the Security Council. Therefore, mainland China (the PRC) replaced Taiwan.
- Trade and travel restrictions between the two countries were lifted.
- Sporting events between the two countries took place, the most famous being the visit of the US table-tennis team to Beijing (so-called ping-pong diplomacy).
- Nixon visited China – the first American president to do so.

Détente between the United States and China was spurred on by the deterioration of relations between China and the USSR, and it also gave the USA more leverage and bargaining power in its arms agreements with the USSR. This became known as '**triangular diplomacy**'. The USA, however, did not abandon Taiwan and continued to stand firm in its support of Taiwan's independence from mainland China.

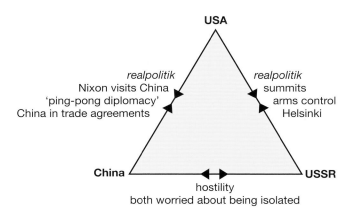

The 'high point of détente': the Helsinki Agreement

Kissinger, Brezhnev, Ford, and Gromyko outside the US Embassy in Helsinki, 1973.

At the Moscow summit of 1972, President Nixon agreed to participate in a **European Security Conference**. This was held in Helsinki in 1973. It was attended by 33 countries and produced a final agreement (**the Final Act**) on 1 August 1975. This took the form of three so-called baskets:

- **Basket 1:** This was the security basket. It followed Willy Brandt's *Ostpolitik* negotiations with the Soviet Union and recognized that Europe's frontiers were 'inviolable': that is, they could not be altered by force. Thus both East Germany and West Germany were now recognized by both sides of the Cold War divide.
- **Basket 2:** This was the co-operation basket. It called for closer ties and collaboration in economic, scientific, and cultural fields.
- **Basket 3:** This was the human rights basket. All of the signatories agreed to respect human rights and individual freedoms, such as freedom of thought, conscience, or religion, and freedom of travel.

Given the Soviet attitude towards human rights, Basket 3 was clearly the most controversial of the agreement. The West hoped that it would undermine Soviet control in the satellite states, and organizations were set up to monitor Soviet action against the principles set out in the **Helsinki Agreement**. However, for Brezhnev, the important aspects of the Helsinki Agreement were Baskets 1 and 2, and he was thus prepared to sign the agreement despite Basket 3.

Apollo–Soyuz Test Project

Another result of détente was co-operation in space. On 17 July 1975, three US astronauts and two Soviet cosmonauts met up when their spacecrafts docked 140 miles above the earth. Co-operation in what was seen as a key area of Cold War conflict – the space race – seemed symbolic of the improved international atmosphere.

Activity 4

Views on the Helsinki Agreement

Source A

❝ No one should try, on the basis of foreign policy considerations of one kind or another, to dictate to other peoples how they should manage their internal affairs. It is only the people of each given State, and no one else, who have the sovereign rights to decide their own internal affairs … A different approach is flimsy and perilous ground for the cause of international co-operation.

Leonid Brezhnev, speech at the Helsinki Conference, 31 July 1975

Source B

❝ In Moscow, there were heated debates in the **Politburo** over whether to sign the 'Final Act'. Although the Final Act enshrined the concepts of national sovereignty and non-interference, the critics argued that Basket III would legitimize the growing foreign interference in Soviet internal affairs. Foreign Minister Gromyko acknowledged that problem, but stressed that the package finally granted the Soviet Union what it had strived to achieve for thirty years – the recognition of the post-war frontiers. He won the day by making the point that Kissinger had made to him: 'No matter what goes into the Final Act, I don't believe that the Soviet Union will ever do anything it doesn't want to do.'

Gordon S Barrass, *The Great Cold War: A Journey Through the Hall of Mirrors* (Stanford University Press 2009) p.200

Source C

❝ Critics of the Helsinki Conference found it difficult to reconcile many provisions of the Final Act with the Soviet invasion of Czechoslovakia in 1968, the Brezhnev Doctrine justifying that invasion and the dismal record on human rights in the Eastern bloc countries. The West seemed to gain nothing more than vague promises of good behaviour from the Soviet Union. When the Eastern bloc governments made no real improvements in their handling of human rights issues, disillusionment with détente set in rapidly in the West.

John Mason, *The Cold War* (Routledge 1996) p.54

Source D

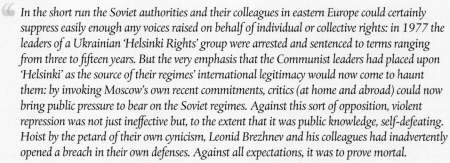

❝ In the short run the Soviet authorities and their colleagues in eastern Europe could certainly suppress easily enough any voices raised on behalf of individual or collective rights: in 1977 the leaders of a Ukrainian 'Helsinki Rights' group were arrested and sentenced to terms ranging from three to fifteen years. But the very emphasis that the Communist leaders had placed upon 'Helsinki' as the source of their regimes' international legitimacy would now come to haunt them: by invoking Moscow's own recent commitments, critics (at home and abroad) could now bring public pressure to bear on the Soviet regimes. Against this sort of opposition, violent repression was not just ineffective but, to the extent that it was public knowledge, self-defeating. Hoist by the petard of their own cynicism, Leonid Brezhnev and his colleagues had inadvertently opened a breach in their own defenses. Against all expectations, it was to prove mortal.

Tony Judt, *Postwar: A History of Europe Since 1945* (Vintage 2010) p.503

1. Read Sources A and B. What was the attitude of the Soviets towards:
   a. Basket 1 of the Helsinki Agreement?
   b. Basket 3 of the Helsinki Agreement?
2. Compare and contrast the points made in Source B with those made in Source A.
3. According to John Mason (Source C), what impact did Basket 3 have on the détente process? What do you think Kissinger would have said about this?
4. According to Tony Judt (Source D), what was the impact of Basket 3 on the Soviet Union?

Review question

5. What do you consider to be the most important achievements of détente?

Why did détente between the USA and the USSR come under pressure?

Activity 5   ATL Thinking skills

"LET'S HAVE ANOTHER ROUND"

An American cartoon from 1975.

1. What is the message of this cartoon?

Political factors that undermined détente

Détente came under pressure for a number of reasons. Firstly, many in the United States felt that the arms agreements were benefiting the Soviets – that the USSR was building up a strategic superiority based on its ICBMs – and that SALT I was effectively allowing the USSR to win the Cold War. Secondly, actions in the Middle East and Africa seemed to indicate that the Soviet Union was continuing to expand its influence.

- When the **Yom Kippur War** started in October 1973, the USA suspected that the USSR had known in advance about Egypt's surprise attack on Israel. Following the agreement mentioned earlier, which the USA and the USSR had signed promising to inform each other of any conflict that might threaten world peace, the attack on Israel and its aftermath, in the words of Anatoly Dobrynin, 'definitely damaged the trust between the leadership of both countries'.
- The Soviet Union was also involved in the civil war in Angola, supporting the **Popular Movement for the Liberation of Angola** (**MPLA**) with military aid. Soviet aid, along with aid given by Cuba, was key to the success of the MPLA.
- The Soviets and Cubans were also involved in supporting Ethiopia against Somalia in 1977. The scale of Soviet intervention was worrying to the Americans and it seemed that the Soviets were involved in some grand scheme of expansion in several key areas of the world. In fact, it was more a case of the Soviets randomly assisting Marxist rebels throughout the world. As Dobrynin notes, this policy was a kind of 'ideological bondage' which did not in fact benefit the Soviet Union in the long term.

Thirdly, as already mentioned, there was disillusionment over the Soviet Union's attitude towards the human rights 'basket' of the agreement made at Helsinki. Under Jimmy Carter, who was elected president in 1976, the United States increasingly tried

CHALLENGE YOURSELF

Research skills ATL

Research the actions of the Soviet Union and Cuba in Africa in the 1970s. How did the USA respond to this intervention?

to link economic deals to improved human rights: for example, by allowing new trading agreements only if the Soviet Union would allow Soviet Jews to emigrate. This 'linkage' was deeply resented by the Soviet Union.

There were also critics of détente within the Soviet Union. When Israel struck back in the 1973 war, trapping Egypt's Third Army, the Soviets tried to negotiate a solution with the US within a détente framework, by using the UN Security Council to agree to a joint ceasefire. The Israelis ignored this, however, and Soviet attempts to get the USA to force Israel to abide by the ceasefire failed. Odd Arne Westad writes that:

> The Arab defeat in the Yom Kippur War was a reminder to the Soviets that the United States, in spite of détente, still considered itself to be more 'super' than the other superpower in the Third World. While the basic declaration of co-operation that the two powers had signed in May 1972 refuted 'any efforts to obtain unilateral advantage at the expense of the other, directly or indirectly', Yom Kippur had shown that Washington only co-operated with Moscow as far as its own interests went.

Odd Arne Westad, *The Global Cold War* (CUP 2006) p. 200

In addition, the Soviets were concerned that the US was still supporting anti-Communist governments in the 'Third World', such as the Chilean government.

All of these factors meant that by the end of the 1970s 'the complexities and contradictions of détente had become explosive' (James Fitzgerald, *The Cold War and Beyond* [Nelson 1992] p.136).

Economic factors that undermined détente

How does oil (both Western access to oil and the price of oil) impact on international relations today?

In the late 1960s, both superpowers saw that détente could benefit their respective economies. However, the US economy started to recover in the late 1970s, giving the US less incentive to pursue détente. Following the oil price crisis of 1973, when **OPEC** (Organization of the Petroleum Exporting Countries) launched a complete oil embargo against Israel's allies in the Yom Kippur War, Western economies took measures to make their economies more secure. This included finding new sources of energy and setting up the **G7** – a group of the main world economies – to work at creating economic stability at the international level. Between 1974 and 1978, the oil price once again stabilized, which laid a foundation for further economic growth, thus removing any economic motivations for détente from the US's side.

At the same time, however, the economy of the USSR was experiencing a decline. The inefficiencies of central planning and a rise in interest rates had a disastrous effect on the economy of the Soviet Union. In the 1950s the annual growth rate for the Soviet Union averaged 7 per cent, but by the 1970s it had fallen to 3 per cent. In addition, as mentioned above, Congress was increasingly linking trade agreements to improved human rights in the Soviet Union. The **Jackson–Vanik Amendment** passed by Congress in 1974 placed significant restrictions on US–Soviet trade. The Soviet Union thus pulled out of trade deals which would have given it the access it needed to US technology.

With the economic position of each superpower so different, and with the imbalance benefiting the US, America had less incentive to pursue a policy of détente. In addition, the oil crisis emphasized the importance of safeguarding oil reserves and thus preventing any Soviet expansion in the Middle East that might jeopardize these.

CHALLENGE YOURSELF

(ATL) Research skills

Research the oil crisis of 1973. Why did the Arab states use the 'oil weapon' and what impact did this have on Western economies? Why did the Soviet Union initially benefit from the crisis?

Why did détente collapse?

Détente was already struggling to survive by the late 1970s, but it collapsed completely when the Soviets invaded Afghanistan in 1979. The reasons for this invasion are discussed in more detail in chapter 13, but for the Americans it seemed to be final proof of the Soviets' 'real' intentions: that is, their determination to spread their influence beyond their borders and thus, as Carter put it, to be a serious threat to world peace. Carter responded to Soviet actions by refusing to approve SALT II, stopping all electronic exports to the Soviet Union, and forbidding US athletes from participating in the 1980 Moscow Olympic Games. He also pledged to increase defence spending in real terms for each of the next five years, and announced the **Carter Doctrine**, which committed the United States to intervention if the Soviets threatened Western interests in the Persian Gulf.

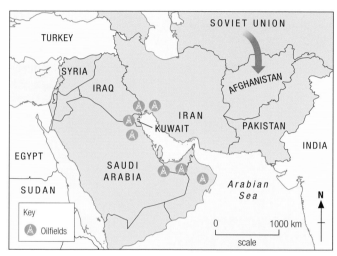

This map shows the countries and oil fields around the Persian Gulf.

Did détente fail? The historiography of détente

Writers in the mid-1970s, and of course the autobiographies of Richard Nixon and Henry Kissinger, stress the positive achievements of détente in terms of reducing tension and the threat of nuclear war. This view is supported by Post-revisionist historians such as Mike Bowker and Phil Williams in *Superpower Détente: A Reappraisal* (Sage 1988). They point out that détente was a necessary strategy to deal with the international situation and to find methods of managing competition 'in a way which prevented them from degenerating into hostilities' (p.257).

John Lewis Gaddis also points out that to call détente a failure is to misunderstand what détente was about in the first place. It was not ever intended to end the arms race, to reform the Soviet Union internally in the area of human rights, or to prevent Soviet–American rivalry in the developing world. It was intended to turn 'a dangerous situation into a predictable *system*', and indeed Soviet–American relations in the late 1960s and the 1970s were arguably less dangerous than were the first two decades of the Cold War.

Right-wing historians, however, interpret détente as a weak policy that allowed the Soviet Union to continue to strengthen itself and gain access to Western technology at the expense of American interests. One of the main supporters of this view is Richard Pipes, who views détente as nothing more than a 'trick' on the part of the Soviets. The collapse of the Soviet Union in the late 1980s is seen as a result of hardline policies towards the Soviet Union. Détente had failed because it had helped to keep the Soviet Union going.

The Carter administration and the Iran crisis

Jimmy Carter was a Democrat who was elected president in 1976 – the first president from the southern states since the American Civil War. He had some notable achievements during his presidency, such as the **Camp David Accords** on the Middle East, which brought peace between Egypt and Israel. However, he faced difficult issues in foreign policy, and was often inconsistent due to the fact that his two key advisers, Zbigniew Brzezinski (National Security Adviser) and Cyrus Vance (Secretary of State), had very different views on these issues – Brzezinski being much more hardline than Vance in his approach to the Soviets.

The most damaging event for President Carter was the takeover of Iran by radical Muslim fundamentalists led by Ayatollah Ruhollah Khomeini. This forced the US-backed Shah (king) to flee his country. The Shah had been a valuable anti-Communist ally in the Middle East and his fall was a major defeat for US foreign policy. When President Carter allowed the Shah to enter the United States for medical treatment, Iran retaliated by seizing the US Embassy in the Iranian capital, Tehran, and taking 52 diplomats as hostages. The intention was to hold the hostages until the Shah was returned to Iran for trial. When the United States tried to rescue the hostages in a covert military operation, the mission ended in failure. The hostages were later released at the beginning of the Reagan presidency.

TOK

Could it be argued that a key problem for détente in the longer term was that there had been no real **paradigm shift** in the way the USSR or the USA perceived each other? To what extent are **paradigms** cultural, or guided by religion or politics? Do we learn from history anything about our perceptions of a) other states and regions, and b) inter-state and cross-regional relations?

Activity 6

ATL **Communication skills**

1. Ronald Reagan, as the new president of the USA in 1980, wants your advice on Soviet–American relations. Write a report to Reagan. This will be in two parts.
   - The first part needs to give him a factual update on the current situation as it stands in 1980. You may want to use sub-headings in your report to cover arms control, Helsinki, human rights, Soviet actions in Africa, Afghanistan, and so on. How do you view the success of détente?
   - The second part needs to set out recommendations on how you think the US administration should now deal with the Soviets.

The Second Cold War

Ronald Reagan had been elected to power on a wave of anti-Communist feeling and a belief that the USA had to reassert its power in the world. Reagan also believed that détente had been a failure and a 'one-way street' that had been used by the Soviet Union to pursue its own aims – in particular, to continue with world revolution.

This map shows US involvement in Central America in the 1980s.

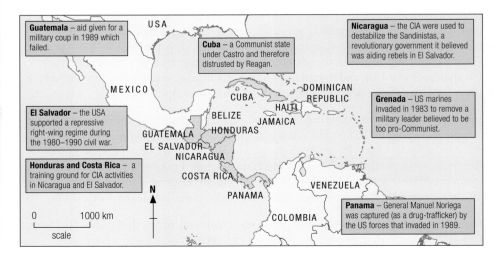

Guatemala – aid given for a military coup in 1989 which failed.

Cuba – a Communist state under Castro and therefore distrusted by Reagan.

Nicaragua – the CIA were used to destabilize the Sandinistas, a revolutionary government it believed was aiding rebels in El Salvador.

Grenada – US marines invaded in 1983 to remove a military leader believed to be too pro-Communist.

El Salvador – the USA supported a repressive right-wing regime during the 1980–1990 civil war.

Honduras and Costa Rica – a training ground for CIA activities in Nicaragua and El Salvador.

Panama – General Manuel Noriega was captured (as a drug-trafficker) by the US forces that invaded in 1989.

Reagan put his tough anti-Soviet policy into action in a number of ways:

- Defence spending was increased by 13 per cent in 1982 and over 8 per cent in each of the following two years. This was the largest peacetime build-up in US history.
- New nuclear weapons were developed, including the stealth bomber and Trident submarines.
- A new **Strategic Defense Initiative** was announced in 1983 ('**Star Wars**'). This was a research programme for setting up a space-based laser system that would intercept and strike Soviet missiles. It undermined the whole idea of MAD (mutually assured destruction – the 'balance of terror'), which had acted as a deterrence against either side using nuclear weapons.
- The Reagan Doctrine was announced. This gave assistance to anti-Communist insurgents as well as anti-Communist governments – for example, the **Contras**, a right-wing guerrilla group fighting against the left-wing government of the **Sandinistas** in Nicaragua. The USA also supported an unpopular right-wing government in El Salvador against a growing popular revolt by the left and, in 1983, US forces invaded the Caribbean island of Grenada and deposed its left-wing government (see map on page 180). In addition, aid was stepped up to the **Mujahidin** in Afghanistan.
- The US deployed Intermediate Range Missiles (**IRMs**) in Western Europe to counter the Soviet SS-20s.
- Reagan restricted trade with the Soviet Union, limiting Soviet access to US technology as well as access to US oil and gas.
- He used aggressive language towards the Soviets, calling them an 'evil empire' and 'the focus of evil in the modern world'.

The renewed tension in the Cold War was not helped by the situation in the Soviet Union, where ageing and infirm leaders prevented any kind of initiative or strong leadership. Brezhnev died in 1982 and was succeeded first by Yuri Andropov – who was already an ill man when he took over – and then Konstantin Chernenko in 1984, who himself only lived another year.

The most dangerous point in this 'Second Cold War' era was the shooting down by the Soviets of a Korean airliner that had flown into Soviet airspace. All of the 269 passengers were killed and there was outrage in the West. The Soviets claimed it was a CIA spy plane and refused to give any clarification as to the situation that had led to them shooting down a civilian Boeing 747. Reagan's administration condemned Moscow for what it called a 'callous and brutal attitude to human life'.

On 28 September 1983, Yuri Andropov denounced the actions pursued by the United States as 'a militarist course which poses a grave threat to peace', and concluded that 'one begins to doubt whether Washington has any brakes at all to prevent it from crossing the line before which any sober-minded person must stop' (Yuri Andropov, 'Statement' in the Soviet newspaper **Pravda**, 28 September 1983).

However, this bleak situation in the Soviet–American relationship was to change radically with the appointment of Mikhail Gorbachev as premier of the Soviet Union in 1985.

CHALLENGE YOURSELF

Research skills

Able Archer

Another dangerous point in the Second Cold War came in November 1983 when NATO was doing a military exercise called Able Archer. Tensions were so high that the USSR suspected that this was a cover for the USA carrying out a nuclear **first strike**.

Find out more about this near-catastrophe and how it was averted, and make notes.

Activity 7

The following sources all relate to the SALT talks.

Source A

 SALT was silent on the issue of multiple independently targeted re-entry vehicles (MIRVs) so the Russian advantage in missile numbers was matched by the US advantage in deliverable warheads. The agreement did not cover medium-range and intermediate-range missiles, nor bases in Europe. However, SALT was an important first step. It would eventually usher in a new era of détente between the superpowers. In 1972 the SALT I Treaty effectively froze the military balance between the Soviet Union and the U.S. They now realized that each side must be able to destroy each other, but only by guaranteeing its own suicide.

An extract from Jeremy Isaacs and Taylor Downing, *Cold War: An Illustrated History, 1945– 1991* (Little, Brown & Co. 1998) p.277

Source B

 The effort to achieve strategic arms limitation marked the first, and the most daring, attempt to follow a collaborative approach in meeting military security arrangements. Early successes held great promises, but also showed the limits or readiness of both superpowers to take this path … The early successes of SALT I contributed to détente and were worthwhile … There was remarkable initial success on parity and on stability of the strategic arms relationship but there was insufficient political will (and perhaps political authority) to ban, or sharply limit, MIRVs.

An extract from a book by Raymond L Garthoff, former American diplomat and member of the US SALT I delegation: *Détente and Confrontation: American Soviet Relations from Nixon to Reagan* (Brooking Institution 1994)

Source C

 The domestic political difficulties of the Nixon administration contributed to the failure to conclude a new SALT treaty … The main obstacle to progress on arms control, however, was the evident unwillingness of both superpowers to abandon the arms race with each other. Behind the public advocacy of détente and disarmament lay the reality that the freeze on missile numbers in SALT I had never been intended to prevent either side from continuing to develop and modernize its existing weapons.

An extract from a book by Joseph Smith, a lecturer in American diplomatic history at the University of Exeter in the UK: *The Cold War 1945–1991* (Wiley 1997) p.112

Remember to look back to chapter 5 at the guidelines for answering questions on sources, and the Hints for success box on page 160.

1. Compare and contrast the views expressed about SALT I in Source A and Source B.

2. With reference to their origin, purpose, and content, assess the values and limitations of Sources B and C for historians studying the SALT agreements.

3. Evaluate the success of arms control during the 1970s. Use these three documents and also the information in the rest of this chapter to answer this question. Refer to the documents directly in your answer.

Activity 8 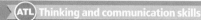 ATL Thinking and social skills

Essay planning

Planning essays is an essential way to revise topics as you approach examinations. In pairs or groups, plan out the following essays. Your plan should include:

- an introduction written out in full
- the opening sentence for each paragraph
- bullet points giving an idea of the information to go in each paragraph
- a conclusion written out in full.

1. *'Détente meant not friendship, but a strategy for relationships among enemies.' Examine the reasons for détente and what changes, if any, it brought to East–West relations.*

2. *To what extent did the Cold War become less confrontational between 1970 and 1980?*

3. *'Despite the claims of those who promoted détente, its achievements were limited.' To what extent do you agree with this statement?*

4. *Discuss how and why détente collapsed in the late 1970s and early 1980s.*

Activity 9 ATL Thinking and communication skills

Essay writing

Consider the following essay question:

> **To what extent did relations between the USA and the USSR change between 1970 and 1980?**

Introduction: In order to assess the extent of 'change', you need to set out what the relationship between the USA and the USSR was in the 1960s: that is, before détente. What were the aims of the USA and USSR in seeking détente? This could give a clue about the extent to which the relationship changed.

First section: Look at the ways in which the relationship changed; this will involve discussion on the achievements of détente and how these impacted on the relationship. Consider the viewpoint of pro-détente historians who argue that there was a positive change in terms of how superpower confrontation was managed.

Second section: Look at the areas in which it could still be argued that there was minimal change in the relationship. Where did confrontation still exist? Consider the Middle East, Africa, Afghanistan, and the issue of human rights.

Again, look at historians' views. You may also want to consider the speed at which détente collapsed – had there in fact been any substantial shift in how each side viewed the other?

Conclusion: Come back to the question and assess the change that had or had not taken place, based on the evidence that you have provided in the body of your essay.

Here are some questions you should consider while planning your essays:

- Does the essay specify dates? How does this affect your choice of information to be included?
- Does the essay title give clues as to the structure you should follow?
- Is there a quotation you need to refer to/explain/ come back to in your conclusion?
- Does the question require you to make a judgement?
- Where can you include historiography?

Each group should present its essay plan to the rest of the class. How much overlap of content is there between the different essay plans?

This is a straightforward essay in terms of structure, but you need to show a good understanding of the achievements and limitations of détente in order to assess how far the relationship between the USA and the USSR changed. You should show awareness of the historical debate over détente and quote specific historians where appropriate.

To access websites relevant to this chapter, go to www.pearsonhotlinks. com, search for the book title or ISBN, and click on 'chapter 12'.

13

Soviet containment 1945–1980

Key concepts: Continuity and significance

As you read this chapter, consider the following essay questions:

· Examine the nature of Soviet control over the satellite states.
· To what extent was the USSR successful in containing challenges to Soviet control?
· Discuss the reasons for and the results of Soviet intervention in Afghanistan.

Challenges to Soviet control in Eastern Europe

Between 1944 and 1948, the Soviet Union under Joseph Stalin established control over the countries on its borders. By 1949, Hungary, Czechoslovakia, East Germany, Romania, and Poland were on the eastern side of the 'iron curtain'. For each of these countries, the system established by Stalin meant tight Soviet control:

· The establishment of one-party rule, including installation of national leaders dependent on the USSR.
· Nationalization of private enterprise.
· The establishment of Soviet-style five-year plans. Heavy industry was encouraged and agriculture collectivized.
· Integration of the economy of Eastern Europe with the Soviet Union, to offset the weakness of industry and agriculture in the USSR. Each country had to produce what the USSR needed: for example, Poland produced coal, steel, and ships. The satellite states were not to co-operate economically with each other, however. This situation was one of exploitation of the satellite states for the economic advantage of the USSR, and it had disastrous effects on any attempts at economic modernization in the satellites.

This map shows the satellite states of the Soviet Union.

This economic and political system was backed up by:

· social and ideological controls (Cominform, secret police)
· censorship of all media
· suppression of religious freedom
· military presence of Soviet troops
· political purges.

However, from 1945 onwards there were attempts by the satellite states to resist this extreme level of Soviet control.

Timeline of Soviet control in Eastern Europe		
1948	**June**	Yugoslavia expelled from Cominform
		Purges begin in other satellite states to get rid of 'Titoists'
1953	**June**	Strikes break out in East Germany and Soviet troops restore order
1956	**Feb**	Khrushchev gives de-Stalinization speech

185

Timeline of Soviet control in Eastern Europe – *continued*		
1956	June	Polish workers' revolt suppressed by Soviet troops
	Oct	Soviet suppression of Hungarian Uprising
1968	April	Dubcek reveals plans for modernization of Czechoslovakia
		The Prague Spring
	Aug	Warsaw Pact forces invade Czechoslovakia
	Sept	Brezhnev announces Brezhnev Doctrine
		Albania leaves Warsaw Pact
1979	Dec	Soviet forces invade Afghanistan
1980	Aug	Strikes in Poland. Gdansk agreements recognize Solidarity
1981	Dec	Martial law imposed in Poland

This map shows Yugoslavia in 1945.

The challenge of Yugoslavia

The Yugoslavs had organized a successful resistance campaign against the Germans during World War Two and had liberated their country in 1945. Marshal Tito was one of the resistance leaders. He had been head of the Yugoslav Communist Party since 1937 and was elected leader of the new republic in 1945. Tito was popular because he had resisted the Germans. Therefore, in Yugoslavia the establishment of Communism was not due to Soviet influence. Moreover, Tito was not interested in being tied too tightly to Moscow, and wanted to be free to trade with the West as well as with the Soviets. In addition, the Yugoslavs were unhappy with Stalin's lack of support for Tito's claim to Trieste, for the Greek Communists, or for a Balkan Federation.

Tensions came to a head in 1948. Stalin expelled Yugoslavia from Cominform, which then declared that the Yugoslav party was 'in the hands of murderers and spies' and cut off economic aid. However, these actions failed to topple Tito, who was able to continue without Soviet support. His regime remained Communist, but Tito followed his own road to Communism, which also involved full contact and trade with the West and acceptance of aid from the International Monetary Fund (IMF). (See page 265 for Tito's involvement in the Non-Aligned Movement.)

Why was Tito able to survive?

Because of his resistance against the Nazis in World War Two, Tito was a popular leader. He was also the only leader to defend the idea of Yugoslavia as a multi-ethnic, federal state (within which the power of Serbia would be held in balance). Unlike the other satellite states, the government had not been installed by the Soviet Red Army (the Red Army left in 1944) and did not depend on Soviet support to remain in power. In addition, from 1950 Tito received both military and economic aid from the USA, which enabled him to maintain his independence from the Soviet bloc.

What was Stalin's reaction to Tito?

Having failed to get rid of Tito, Stalin took his revenge on suspected 'Titoists' by carrying out East European purge trials. Fabricated charges ensured that leaders, such as the Hungarian Foreign Minister Laszlo Rajk, were demoted, tried and either imprisoned or executed during the late 1940s.

Although this got rid of open Tito sympathizers, secret sympathizers remained. The exploitative and repressive nature of the regimes in the satellite states meant that Soviet rule was resented by ordinary people and never achieved any popular support. Thus on several occasions, from 1945 onwards, there were to be more challenges to Soviet control: East Germany in 1953, Poland and Hungary in 1956, Czechoslovakia in 1968, and Poland in the 1980s.

Challenge in East Germany, 1953

It was the combination of relaxation of controls with continuing repression which helped to trigger the East German riots of 1953. East Germany was facing a crisis at this time due to the mass exodus of East Germans to the West through Berlin. Beria, the deputy Soviet prime minister, suggested that the USSR should get rid of the unstable and expensive GDR by selling it to the West. This idea was not taken up, as his colleagues still believed that it was possible to work towards a unified Socialist Germany. However, the East German leader, Walter Ulbricht, was forced by the Soviet government to take a more conciliatory approach in his policy of forced collectivization of farms and socialization. Unfortunately, this softer approach came too late, and no attempt was made to reduce the high production targets that had been set for the workers by Ulbricht. This created a dangerous situation and, on 16–17 June, workers in Berlin and elsewhere in East Germany rose up in revolt.

 Activity 1

" *We, the working-people from the district of Bitterfeld demand:*

1. *The immediate resignation of the so-called German Democratic government which has come to power through manipulation of the elections*
2. *The creation of a provisional government consisting of the progressive working-people*
3. *Admission of all the big West German democratic parties*
4. *Free and secret direct elections within four weeks at the latest*
5. *Release of all political prisoners (the plain political ones, the so-called fiscal criminals, and those persecuted because of their religious confession)*
6. *Immediate abolition of all borders and withdrawal of the People's Police*
7. *Immediate normalization of the social standard of living*
8. *Immediate dissolution of the so-called National Army*
9. *No reprisals against even a single striking worker*

Demands of the East Berlin Strike Committee, 1953 (telegram sent to the government of the GDR)

1. From these demands, what can you learn about the actions and policies of the East German government?

This was the first time that anything like this had happened in the Soviet sphere of influence and the uprising was quickly suppressed by Red Army troops; however, the revolt was very embarrassing for the Soviet Union. Beria was arrested and executed for being a Western agent. The idea of having a friendly, neutral Germany was abandoned. Repression continued, and Ulbricht and Khrushchev now concentrated on building up the GDR as a separate state.

 What was the American reaction?

The United States felt that it had to do something to help the East Germans. It therefore called for a four-power foreign ministers' conference to discuss the future of Germany, but also continued to make provocative broadcasts from its radio stations in West Berlin to try to prolong the unrest in East Germany.

Challenges to Soviet control under Khrushchev

Khrushchev and de-Stalinization

In 1956, at the Twentieth Congress of the Communist Party, Khrushchev proclaimed his policy of de-Stalinization. Although for a time this did strengthen his position at home, it seriously weakened his authority over Communism elsewhere. It is ironic that Khrushchev got rid of Stalin's weapons of terror and yet he had to use more force than Stalin had ever done in order to keep control in Hungary.

Khrushchev's de-Stalinization speech

In 1956 Khrushchev gave a speech to the Twentieth Congress of the Communist Party in which he denounced Stalin. He criticized the excesses of Stalin's regime and denounced his crimes and the growth of the 'cult of personality'. This was shocking to the Communist world.

> Communists were not used to having mistakes admitted at the top, and certainly not on this scale. It was, as Secretary of State Dulles commented at the time, 'the most damning indictment of despotism ever made by a **despot**'.

John Lewis Gaddis, *The Cold War* (Penguin 2005) p.107

See chapter 7 for more details.

Khrushchev and Tito

As part of his attack on Stalin, Khrushchev claimed that Stalin had made a major error concerning Tito and Yugoslavia. He argued that had Stalin understood Tito and the national cause he represented, Yugoslavia would never have broken away from the East European bloc. He thus restored relations with Yugoslavia, visiting Tito in 1955 and 1956. However, Tito continued to maintain his non-aligned status in his relationship with the USSR.

Khrushchev and Poland

In revising the USSR's relations with Yugoslavia, Khrushchev did not intend to revise the USSR's relations with its other satellite states. However, many of the satellite states saw Khrushchev's approach to Yugoslavia as a sign that he also would accept them finding their own way with regard to Communism.

Protests began in Poznan in June 1956 and quickly spread. The Poznan demonstrators wanted better working conditions and the protest of around 100 000 people was put down with force when the Polish government sent in around 10 000 troops and 400 tanks. The government regained control, but more than 60 people had been killed and hundreds wounded.

However, the shock of this protest led to the reinstatement (without Khrushchev's approval) of Wladyslaw Gomulka, who had been imprisoned under Stalin. Gomulka implemented a rapid de-Stalinization programme. On 19 October 1956, Khrushchev flew to Warsaw and Soviet military forces moved into intimidating positions. However, Gomulka refused to be intimidated by Khrushchev, even threatening to arm the Polish workers to resist the Soviets. Importantly, however, Gomulka also told Khrushchev that he had no intention of taking Poland out of the Warsaw Pact. This calmed Khrushchev's fears. He agreed to allow Gomulka to remain in power. This was significant as it was the first time that the Soviet Union had compromised with another Communist state on its choice of leader. In fact, Gomulka turned out to be a trusted ally of Khrushchev, and the freedoms acquired by the Poles in 1956 were gradually taken away.

Cold War Crisis:

The Hungarian Uprising, 1956

Khrushchev, however, did not compromise over Hungary, and it was here that it became clear that Khrushchev was as determined as Stalin to maintain Soviet control over the satellite states.

News of the Polish success had spread to Hungary, where people lived under the repressive regime of Matyas Rakosi. Crowds took to the streets and demanded that Rakosi be replaced with the more moderate Imre Nagy. Khrushchev agreed to this, but riots continued. Khrushchev ordered the Red Army to restore order, but, surprisingly, it failed to do this, and Nagy was able to negotiate the withdrawal of Soviet forces on 28 October 1956. Shortly afterwards he announced that Hungary would leave the Warsaw Pact and become a neutral state. He was also planning to share power in Hungary with non-Communist groups.

This was something that Khrushchev could not tolerate and, aware that the attention of the West was focused on the Suez Crisis, Soviet forces launched a general offensive against the Hungarians. There was bitter fighting in the streets of Budapest. Over 2500 Hungarians and 700 Soviet troops were killed, and 200 000 Hungarians fled the country. However, the Soviets were successful in bringing Hungary back under their control. A new Hungarian government under Janos Kadar was created and Imre Nagy was later executed by the Soviets.

What actions did the USA take?

The Hungarian revolt had been encouraged by CIA broadcasts on **Radio Free Europe**, which led Hungarians to believe that they would get US support. However, the Americans made it clear to the Soviet leaders that the United States would take no action to save Nagy. It is true that US attention was being diverted by the Suez Crisis, but there is no evidence that President Eisenhower ever considered interfering in Hungary. This was because he believed (probably mistakenly) that Khrushchev might have been prepared to risk nuclear war rather than lose this satellite state.

Why did the Soviets act differently in Hungary and Poland?

In Poland, the Communist Party had retained control, while in Hungary it had lost control. Nagy's decision to declare Hungary a neutral state would have meant the exclusion of Soviet influence and a weakening of the defensive ring of states established on its Western borders since 1944. Khrushchev's actions in Hungary showed that de-Stalinization did not mean a softening of the USSR's fundamental attitudes. When the Communist Party was in danger of losing control over state machinery, or where its control of the Eastern bloc was challenged, it was prepared to use whatever pressure was necessary to pull the satellites back into line.

The Suez Crisis

This crisis occurred after President Gamal Abdel Nasser of Egypt took the decision to nationalize the **Suez Canal**. The British, French, and Israelis invaded Egypt to take back control of the canal, but faced condemnation from both the USA and the USSR as a result. Britain and France were forced to withdraw and Nasser retained control over the Suez. (See chapter 18 for more details.)

Activity 2	

Source A

❝ *We have almost no weapons, no heavy guns of any kind. The Hungarian people are not afraid of death. You can't let people attack tanks with their bare hands. What is the United Nations doing?*

… Civilized people of the world! Our ship is sinking. Light is fading. The shadows grow darker over the soil of Hungary. Help us!

An extract from radio messages sent by Hungarian rebels during the fighting

Source B

❝ *A Socialist state could not remain an indifferent observer of the bloody reign of Fascist reaction in People's Democratic Hungary. When everything settles down in Hungary, and life becomes normal again, the Hungarian working class, peasantry and intelligentsia will undoubtedly understand our actions better and judge them aright. We regard our help to the Hungarian working class in its struggle against the intrigues of counter-revolution as our international duty.*

From an editorial in *Pravda* dated 23 November 1956

1. What do the extracts in Source A tell you about Hungarian expectations regarding the involvement of the West?
2. Using the information in chapter 16, explain the UN response to events in Hungary.
3. In Source B, what was *Pravda*'s view of the uprising in Hungary? How might a Hungarian argue against this view?
4. What was *Pravda*? What are the values and limitations for the historian in using extracts from *Pravda* to understand the events in Hungary?

What were the results for Khrushchev and the Soviet Union?

Khrushchev's position in the USSR was strengthened by the events in Hungary and Suez. It also meant that the Soviets could now feel confident that there would be no American influence in their area of control. However, events also made clear that the Warsaw Pact (unlike NATO) was not based on voluntary participation, and that the USSR could not always rely on the loyalty of its satellite states.

Activity 3	ATL Thinking skills

Source A

This cartoon, entitled 'Trainer Khrushchev's Problem', by Leslie Illingworth was published in *Punch* (a British magazine) on 31 October 1956. (The countries on the podiums, from left to right, are: Jugoslavia, Czechoslovakia, Poland, Hungary, Albania, Bulgaria.)

Source B

> Across the rest of Eastern Europe and around the world, the Hungarian Revolution helped alter the international perception of the Soviet Union for good, especially in the Western communist parties. After 1956, the French communist party fractured, the Italian party broke away from Moscow and the British communist party lost two thirds of its members.

Anne Applebaum, *Iron Curtain: The Crushing of Eastern Europe* (Penguin 2013) pp. 488–489

1. Using your knowledge of events in Eastern Europe, explain the actions of the different bears in the cartoon in Source A.
2. What is the message of Source A?
3. According to Source B, what were the key effects of the Hungarian Uprising for the USSR?

Soviet leader Leonid Brezhnev.

Cold War Crisis:

Prague, 1968

In the 1960s the dissatisfaction felt by the Czech people at their repressive regime came to a head. Alexander Dubcek became First Secretary of the Communist Party in 1968 and this marked the beginning of what became known as the 'Prague Spring'. Aiming to create 'socialism with a human face', Dubcek introduced measures to modernize and liberalize the economy. There were also to be wider powers for trade unions, expansion of trade with the West, and freedom to travel abroad. In June he even abolished censorship and encouraged criticism of the government. Conscious of what had happened to Hungary in 1956, he was careful to assure the USSR that Czechoslovakia would stay in the Warsaw Pact and remain a valuable ally.

What actions did the Soviets take?

Soviet leader Leonid Brezhnev and the other leaders of the Warsaw Pact became increasingly worried at the events in Prague, and the USSR decided to resort to force. In August 1968, Soviet troops, together with other members of the Warsaw Pact, invaded Czechoslovakia. The Czech government decided not to resist in order to avoid a repetition of what had happened in Hungary in 1956. However, the Czech people tried to resist passively for a time; they organized strikes and peaceful anti-Russian demonstrations. Ultimately, however, the government was forced to abandon its reforms. The following year, Dubcek was replaced by Gustav Husak, who was subservient to Moscow and remained in power until 1987.

What were the results of the invasion of Czechoslovakia?

In order to justify his actions in Czechoslovakia, Brezhnev laid down what became known as 'the Brezhnev Doctrine':

> There is no doubt that the peoples of the socialist countries and Communist parties have and must have freedom … theirs must damage neither socialism in their own country nor the fundamental interests of other socialist countries … This means that every Communist party is responsible not only to its own people, but also to all the socialist countries and the entire Communist movement. Whoever forgets this in placing sole emphasis on the autonomy and independence of Communist parties, lapses into one-sidedness, shirking his internationalist obligations …

The Brezhnev Doctrine as quoted in *Pravda*, 26 September 1968

Thus the actions of one socialist country were recognized as affecting all. Therefore, collective action to deal with any threat to the socialist community was viewed as justified and necessary. It was now clear that any attempt at 'liberalism' by a state in the Eastern bloc would not be tolerated. As a result, reform plans throughout the region were abandoned, with disastrous economic consequences for the future of the Soviet bloc.

The invasion of Czechoslovakia seriously damaged the international reputation of Communism and the Soviet Union. Yugoslavia, Albania, and China condemned the Soviet action. In Western Europe, many Communists stopped looking to Moscow for guidance. However, it had no major impact on East–West relations. It slowed down the détente process, but did not throw it off course.

> *Moscow's goals in Czechoslovakia led most observers on both sides of the Iron Curtain to regard the intervention as a decisive Soviet victory. Relations with the West experienced some setbacks … Ultimately, however, the need to involve Moscow in negotiations with North Vietnam overcame American indignation …The invasion … created instant tensions with the East European nations that had not taken part in the operation. As for the nations remaining in the Soviet-led alliance, the invasion confirmed that autonomous political reforms would no longer be tolerated … [also] the invasion seriously damaged Moscow's ability to build a united front against the Chinese.*

Matthew Ouimet gave this overall assessment of the effects of the invasion of Czechoslovakia in *The Rise and Fall of the Brezhnev Doctrine in Soviet Foreign Policy* (University of North Carolina Press 2003) p.57

'Out, Out, Brief Candle!' by Herblock, 1968.

Activity 4 — ATL Thinking skills

"Out, Out, Brief Candle!"

1. What is the message of this cartoon?

Activity 5 — ATL Thinking skills

1. To what extent did the Soviet actions in Czechoslovakia have more impact on their relations with other Communist countries than with the West? Refer also to chapter 10, in answering this question.

The challenge from Poland in the 1980s

In the late 1970s, dissatisfaction with the poor economic situation in Poland resulted in industrial unrest, food shortages and strikes. The opposition to the government centred on the port city of Gdansk, and in 1980 the Gdansk shipyard workers went on strike. They were led by an unemployed shipyard worker named Lech Walesa, and were successful in securing economic and political rights, including the right to strike and form free trade unions. This led to the establishment of the independent trade union movement called **Solidarity**. By 1981, Solidarity claimed a membership of 10 million, and was seen as a threat to the USSR. The Red Army sent troops to the Polish border, but did not invade. Stanislaw Kania, the new leader of Poland, convinced Brezhnev that he could restore order himself, and it is also possible that American warnings against the use of force kept back the Soviet troops. However, reliable elements of the Polish army were used to seize control of the government in December 1981. The loyal General Wojciech Jaruzelski was installed as prime minister and declared martial law, banned Solidarity, and arrested thousands of activists. By 1983, the government was in firm control, but the economic problems, along with continued support for Solidarity, remained (see chapter 15).

The declaration of martial law in Poland along with the invasion of Afghanistan helped to weaken détente, which was already struggling to survive at this point.

Poland and Catholicism

The Catholic Church in Poland occupied a unique position in the Eastern bloc. Religious worship within the Soviet Union was only tolerated under certain limitations. However, attempts to curb the power of the church in Poland had boosted its support among the Polish people. In fact, after 1970, the leader of Poland, Edward Gierek, allowed religion to be taught in schools. Catholicism in Poland was given a further boost by the appointment of the Polish Pope John Paul II and his visit to Poland in 1979, which seriously undermined the whole concept of the Communist, atheist state. Gaddis writes, 'When John Paul II kissed the ground at the Warsaw airport on June 2, 1979, he began a process by which Communism in Poland – and ultimately everywhere else in Europe – would come to an end' (John Lewis Gaddis, *The Cold War* [Penguin 2005] p.193).

Lech Walesa addresses striking workers at a shipyard in Gdansk, 1980.

Activity 6

ATL Thinking and self-management skills

1. Copy out the grid below and summarize the Soviet containment of challenges to its control in Eastern Europe.

Country	Why protest/ challenge?	How did they challenge?	Soviet reaction	Western reaction	Containment successful?	Consequences for superpower relations

TOK

Many totalitarian and/ or authoritarian states view artists as a threat to their control. Discuss why poets, musicians, writers and painters are often persecuted by governments. Consider the extent to which artists 'tell the truth'.

Activity 7

 ATL Thinking skills

1. In pairs, read the following extract from Anne Applebaum's book *Iron Curtain*. Discuss what she means by 'every aspect of society' becoming a 'potential form of protest' under Soviet control. What does this suggest about the ability of the USSR to 'contain' dissent and challenges to its control after the 1980s?

> *Over time the nations of Eastern Europe began to have much less in common By the 1980s, East Germany had the largest police state, Poland the highest church attendance, Romanians the most dramatic food shortages, Hungarians the highest living standards and the Yugoslavs the most relaxed relationship with the West. Yet in one narrow sense they remained very similar: none of the regimes ever seemed to realize that they were unstable by definition. They lurched from crisis to crisis not because they were unable to fine-tune their policies, but because the communist project itself was flawed. By trying to control every aspect of society, the regimes had turned every aspect of society into a potential form of protest.*

Anne Applebaum, *Iron Curtain: The Crushing of Eastern Europe* (Penguin 2013) pp.492–493

To what extent were Soviet leaders following Stalin's structural legacy?

The system set up by Stalin in Eastern Europe – his 'legacy' – is outlined at the beginning of this chapter. Although Khrushchev attempted to carry out de-Stalinization and improve relations with Tito, there was no fundamental change in the relationship between the Soviet Union and the satellite states as established under Stalin. This was even more the case during Brezhnev's leadership:

- Power remained centralized in Moscow; economically the satellite states continued to develop their economies to suit that of the Soviet Union. After the Brezhnev Doctrine was introduced, all economic experiments in the Soviet bloc aimed at modernization and increased competitiveness came to an end.
- The leaders of the satellite states remained men who were loyal to Moscow.
- When any of the states attempted to resist or deviate from this situation, the Red Army was used ruthlessly to restore order and maintain the system; the Brezhnev Doctrine justified this as necessary for preserving socialism throughout the Eastern bloc.

Cold War Crisis:

The Soviet invasion of Afghanistan

The Brezhnev Doctrine was also used as a reason for invading Afghanistan in 1979. Although not part of the official Soviet sphere of influence, the USSR was anxious to prevent a situation developing in Afghanistan that might threaten Soviet security.

Why did the Soviets intervene in Afghanistan?

In April 1978, the People's Democratic Party (PDP) of Afghanistan seized power. This was a pro-Soviet organization and received economic assistance from Moscow. However, the PDP, headed by Hafizullah Amin from 1979, carried out social and economic policies that included land reform, women's rights and secular education. These reforms were resisted by both fundamentalist Muslims within Afghanistan and other factions within the PDP.

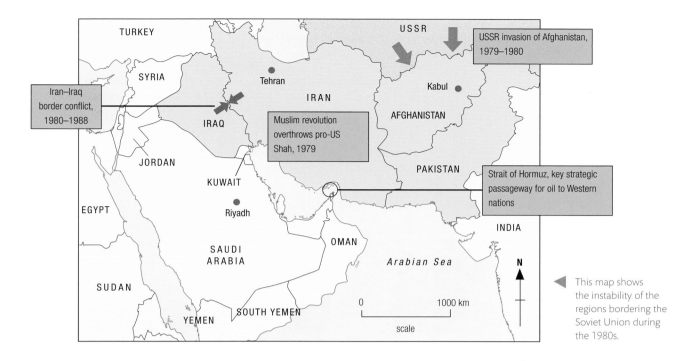

TURKEY

SYRIA

Tehran

IRAN

USSR

USSR invasion of Afghanistan, 1979–1980

Kabul

AFGHANISTAN

Iran–Iraq border conflict, 1980–1988

IRAQ

Muslim revolution overthrows pro-US Shah, 1979

JORDAN

KUWAIT

PAKISTAN

Strait of Hormuz, key strategic passageway for oil to Western nations

EGYPT

Riyadh

INDIA

SAUDI ARABIA

OMAN

Arabian Sea

N

SUDAN

SOUTH YEMEN

YEMEN

0   1000 km

scale

This map shows the instability of the regions bordering the Soviet Union during the 1980s.

Afghan Muslims began joining the Mujahidin, who declared a *jihad* or holy war against the Amin regime, which became increasingly dependent on Soviet aid. However, relations between the Soviets and Amin were strained, and Amin also began to initiate contact through the CIA with the US government. This triggered rumours that Amin himself had been recruited by the CIA. To the Soviets there seemed to be no alternative but to intervene militarily and replace Amin with the pro-Soviet Babrak Karmal.

The official Soviet reasons for invading Afghanistan included the following:

• The USSR did not want the 'Afghan Revolution' defeated and Afghanistan turned into a pro-Western state.
• The USSR believed that the victory of the 'counter-revolution' would result in a 'bloodbath' caused by religious **zealots** and vengeful **feudal** lords.
• The USSR believed that a victory for the counter-revolution's forces would allow for massive American military involvement in Afghanistan. This was a country bordering the USSR, and thus a threat to Soviet security.
• The USSR claimed that it would have 'ceased to be a great power' if it turned away from taking 'unpopular, but necessary, decisions'.

In a letter to Brezhnev, Yuri Andropov wrote:

66 *We have been receiving information about Amin's behind-the-scenes activities which may mean his political reorientation to the West ... In closed meetings he attacks Soviet policy and the activities of our specialists. Our ambassador was practically expelled from Kabul. These developments have created, on the one hand, a danger of losing the domestic achievements of the Afghan revolution, and, on the other hand, a threat to our positions in Afghanistan ...*

In addition, there were unofficial reasons for the invasion:

• The moderate Western response to the invasion of Czechoslovakia may have encouraged the Soviets in their decision to invade Afghanistan.

- Détente was already in difficulties, so the impact that the invasion might have on relations with the USA was not so much of a concern to the Soviet leadership as it might have been several years earlier.

From this point on, the new Karmal regime that replaced Amin was dependent on Soviet military strength to maintain its control against the popular revolutionary troops of the Afghan Islamist forces. However, the problem was, as Westad comments, that Afghan Communism had already 'self-destructed' well before the Soviet invasion:

> *The basic policy failure of the Soviet Afghan invasion was the belief that foreign power could be used to secure the survival and ultimate success of a regime that demonstrably could not survive on its own.*

Odd Arne Westad, *The Global Cold War* (CUP 2007) p.326

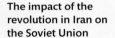

Mujahidin fighters in Afghanistan.

The impact of the revolution in Iran on the Soviet Union

In January 1979 the Shah of Iran (who had been backed by the USA) was removed in an Islamist uprising and replaced by the Ayatollah Khomeini – a Muslim fundamentalist. The implications of this for the United States have already been discussed (see chapter 12, page 180). However, this new regime threatened Soviet security as well. The Central Asian republics of the USSR, bordering Afghanistan, had significant Muslim populations, and the spread of Islamic fundamentalism could destabilize these areas.

Activity 8  ATL Thinking skills

> *On 3 July Brzezinski* had persuaded Carter to offer direct aid for the rebels in Afghanistan. Washington was 'well aware of Soviet concern over the situation. Beginning on September 10, intelligence reports to the president began to discuss the possibility that the Soviet Union might be forced to act' … 'We did not push the Russians into intervening,' Brzezinski confessed, 'but we did knowingly increase the chances that they would so.' Brzezinski planted the seeds of suspicion that would hopefully force Moscow to do precisely what it had set out to avoid: military intervention.*

* Zbigniew Kazimierz Brzezinski was Security Adviser to President Carter.

Jonathan Haslam, *Russia's Cold War* (Yale University Press 2011) pp.324–325

1. What does Brzezinski reveal about US intentions in Afghanistan?
2. What points does the historian Jonathan Haslam make about the Soviet invasion?

What was the American response to the Soviet invasion of Afghanistan?

The Soviets completely miscalculated the impact that their actions would have on the West. Generally, the invasion was seen in the West not as evidence of maintaining control in an already existing sphere of influence, as had happened in Czechoslovakia, but as evidence of Soviet expansionism. President Carter stated that the invasion might pose the most serious threat to world peace since World War Two and imposed stringent measures against the USSR (see also chapter 12, page 178). The Carter administration took the following actions:

- The 'Carter Doctrine' was announced – it pledged US intervention in the Persian Gulf if the Soviets threatened its interests there.
- Carter's National Security team decided to resist the Soviet invasion by 'proxy': that is, by providing the Mujahedin rebels with weapons.

After 1981, President Reagan's more aggressive stance towards the Soviet Union involved a more direct approach in Afghanistan. Reagan increased levels of aid, and, in the mid-1980s, began to send US supplies of arms to the Mujahidin and their Afghan allies, some via Pakistan:

 By 1985, a very complex web of foreign support for the Mujahidin was in place in which the United States worked and co-operated closely with conservative Arab governments and voluntary organizations to jointly fund and operate key initiatives.

Odd Arne Westad, *The Global Cold War* (CUP 2007) p.355

As the war of attrition continued to the end of Brezhnev's rule, and through those of Andropov and Chernenko, the impact of direct American aid probably gave the rebels the upper hand:

 … in Afghanistan, a large covert operation was mounted to arm the Mujahedin rebels through Pakistan. It was, however, only in Reagan's second term, after 1985, that the crucial Stinger anti-aircraft missiles were provided. Easily portable and fired by a single soldier, the Stingers turned the tide of the Afghan War by challenging the Soviet command of the air.

Martin Walker, *The Cold War* (Vintage 1995) p.287

The war in Afghanistan cost the lives of more than a million Afghans and 25 000 Red Army soldiers. It also cost the USSR in the region of $8 billion per annum. The reason that the Soviets ultimately pulled out was very much down to the political thinking of the new Soviet leader – Mikhail Gorbachev. He believed that this money was desperately needed for his domestic reforms. Also, the war itself did not fit in with his new philosophy for Soviet foreign policy – the USSR was no longer to foot the bill for supporting the cause of world Communism. Gorbachev announced his intention to pull Soviet troops out of Afghanistan in February 1988. By the following February, the USSR had completed its military withdrawal.

The impact of Afghanistan on the USSR

With its involvement in Afghanistan the US had aligned itself with Muslims. This meant the USSR was confronting the Capitalist world, Communist China, and now Islamist forces at a time when the Soviet Union was in economic decline.

Activity 9

Cartoon by Nicholas Garland in British newspaper *The Independent*, May 1988.

"... AND HE MARCHED THEM DOWN AGAIN."

1. What is the message of the cartoonist?

Afghanistan and its impact on détente

The view of the right wing in the United States is that the invasion of Afghanistan was a key example of how the Soviets were still pursuing the Marxist–Leninist expansionism embodied in their political doctrine. Thus the Soviets were responsible for the breakdown of détente.

The Post-revisionist view is that the Soviet Union was responding defensively to a genuine threat to its security. This threat was also in its sphere of influence. The US response was cynical, and intended to take advantage of the unstable situation caused by Islamic fundamentalism in Afghanistan. It was in fact changes in US foreign policy – as championed by Carter's adviser Zbigniew Brzezinski and then by Reagan's government – that led to the Second Cold War and renewed tension, not the Soviet invasion of Afghanistan.

What is the situation inside Afghanistan today? How can the Soviet invasion and American involvement in the 1980s be linked to the current instability in this region?

Activity 10  ATL Thinking skills

1. Examine the impact of the invasion of Afghanistan on the Cold War, between 1979 and 1985.

   To answer this question comprehensively, refer back to chapter 12.

Activity 11 ATL Thinking skills

Essay writing

Consider the following essay question:

> *To what extent was the Soviet Union successful in containing challenges to its control over the satellite states in the period 1945-1980?*

Essay planning hints

Introduction: For your introduction, you need to put the question into context: that is, explain briefly how the Soviet Union tried to control the satellite states and describe the main challenges to that control that took place up to 1980. Also identify your main line of argument – whether you think that they were or were not successful.

CHALLENGE YOURSELF

 ATL Research skills

Enquire into the Soviet–Afghan War from 1979. Consider the use of 'guerilla warfare' by the Mujahidin; Soviet strategies and tactics in Afghanistan; the role of Pakistan; the role of USA support for the Mujahidin; and the impact of '**stinger missiles**'.

To what extent do you agree that Afghanistan was the Soviet Vietnam?

Main body: You want to avoid a chronological run-through and description of the challenges. Keep to the question, which is to *analyse the success* of the Soviet Union in keeping control. How can you do this?

- You could consider looking firstly at where and in what ways the Soviet Union was successful in keeping control, and then where and in what ways it was not successful.
- You may also want to discuss what the cost of its 'successes' were for the satellite states (and future Soviet control), and what factors affected the Soviet Union's success or failure.

Also have a go at planning the following essay question:

> **Compare and contrast the causes of, and the results of, the Vietnam War and the Soviet Afghan war.**

Activity 12  **ATL** Thinking and self-management skills

1. The opening words of an essay are key for telling you what exactly you should be aiming to do in your essay, and what the focus of your key arguments should be.

Below are essay questions on the Cold War. The opening key words or phrases in each essay question have been italicized. In pairs, briefly discuss what each of the words/phrases is expecting you to do in the essay and how they might have an impact on how you structure the essay.

- *To what extent* was the Soviet Union successful in maintaining control over its satellite states in the period 1945–1980?
- *Examine* the significance of the Yalta and Potsdam conferences for the development of the Cold War between 1945–49.
- *Discuss the impact of* the Korean War on the development of the Cold War after 1950.
- *Examine the reasons for* the growing hostility between China and the Soviet Union up to 1970.
- *Examine the role of* ideology in the origins of the Cold War.
- *Compare and contrast* the part played by Vietnam and Afghanistan in the Cold War.
- *Discuss how and why* superpower rivalry dominated international politics after 1945.
- *Compare and contrast* the successes and failures of US and Soviet policies of containment.

 To access websites relevant to this chapter, go to www.pearsonhotlinks. com, search for the book title or ISBN, and click on 'chapter 13'.

14

Confrontation: The impact of the arms race on the Cold War

> **Key concepts:** Consequence and perspective

As you read this chapter, consider the following essay questions:

- Discuss the impact of the nuclear arms race on the development of the Cold War.
- Examine the impact of the concept of 'deterrence' on the development of Soviet–American nuclear strategy from the early 1960s.

66 *The major lesson of the Cuban Missile Crisis is this: that the indefinite combination of human fallibility and nuclear weapons will destroy nations.*

Robert McNamara in the television documentary *Fog of War*

The advent of nuclear weapons with the dropping of the first A-bomb on Hiroshima had a crucial impact on the Cold War. These new and terrifying weapons:

- started an arms race between the major powers, which became an integral part of the Cold War, helping to maintain and continue the hostility between the superpowers
- caused both sides to rethink military strategy and thus the way conflicts were handled during the Cold War
- put huge economic strains on both countries and thus played a role in the ending of the Cold War.

Key terms used in this chapter

Atom bomb or A-bomb: A nuclear bomb launched from a missile or plane.

Hydrogen bomb or H-bomb: A thermonuclear bomb (also referred to as nuclear) that is much more powerful than the A-bomb.

Strategic bombers: Planes capable of carrying and delivering nuclear weapons.

ICBM: Inter-continental ballistic missiles, which have a range of over 3000 nautical miles and carry nuclear warheads.

SLBM: Submarine-launched ballistic missiles. These missiles with nuclear warheads are carried on submarines.

ABM: Anti-ballistic missiles, which can be used to intercept and destroy nuclear weapons.

MIRV: Multiple independently targetable re-entry vehicle. This device is launched by a missile that allows several warheads to be used, each guided to a different target.

How did the nuclear arms race develop during the Cold War?

As you have seen, the decision of President Truman during World War Two to use the A-bomb to end the war in the Pacific has caused much debate. It has been viewed by some historians as the first act of the Cold War (see chapter 4), and can be seen as the trigger for the nuclear arms race between the USSR and the USA.

The A-bomb was regarded by the USA as a vital counter to the much larger conventional forces of the USSR. However, the Soviet Union was well on its way to developing its own A-bomb, which was tested successfully in 1949, several years earlier than the USA had expected. The arms race was on. The United States then stepped up its efforts to develop the hydrogen bomb, which was 1000 times more powerful than the bombs dropped on Hiroshima and Nagasaki. It achieved this in 1952, only to be followed by the USSR a year later.

TOK

Discuss the following questions:

- To what extent do scientists have the freedom to research what they want?
- How far is the development of scientific knowledge dependent on the decisions made by 'political authorities' or governments? What implication does this have for 'scientific truth'?
- How does history impact on scientific development?

CHALLENGE YOURSELF

(ATL) Research skills

Research the extent and type of nuclear testing that took place during the Cold War. What controversies exist regarding some of the testing that took place in the 1950s? How effective has the Test-Ban Treaty of 1963 been?

The 1950s also saw the development of inter-continental ballistic missiles (ICBMs). As was described in chapter 7, the US government became concerned that the USSR was moving ahead of it in terms of arms production and missile technology, and, after the launch of Sputnik, the Americans became even more concerned about a perceived 'missile gap'. U-2 flights over the USSR reassured Eisenhower that in fact there was no missile gap. Nevertheless, the United States continued with a massive build-up of ICBMs. This put pressure on the Soviet Union to respond, particularly when the reality of its inferior missile numbers was revealed by President Kennedy. By 1968, the Soviets had also developed ABM defensive missile systems. Meanwhile, the United States' development of MIRVs, which increased the chances of nuclear weapons reaching their intended targets, helped intensify the race, with the USSR instituting its own MIRV programme in 1975.

Timeline of the development of the arms race between the USA and USSR.

First in race			Second in race	
USA	1945	atom bomb	1949	USSR
USA	1952	hydrogen bomb	1953	USSR
USSR	1957	ICBM	1958	USA
USSR	1957	first satellite	1958	USA
USSR	1958	early warning radar	1960	USA
USA	1960	SLBM	1968	USSR
USSR	1968	ABM	1972	USA
USA	1970	MIRV	1975	USSR
USSR	1971	sea cruise missile launched	1982	USA

The build-up of arms after 1945						
Strategic bombers	1956	1960	1965	1970	1975	1979
USA	560	550	630	405	330	316
USSR	60	175	200	190	140	140
ICBMs	1960	1964	1968	1970	1974	1979
USA	295	835	630	1054	1054	1054
USSR	75	200	800	1300	1587	1398
SLBMs	1962	1965	1968	1972	1975	1979
USA	145	500	656	655	656	656
USSR	45	125	130	497	740	989
Warheads	1945	1955	1965	1975	1985	
USA	6	3057	31265	26675	22941	
USSR	0	200	6129	19443	39197	

Your conclusions should include evidence from the dates, the quantities of weapons produced, and which country was in the lead in each area.

Activity 1

(ATL) Thinking skills

1. Using both the timeline and the table of arms race statistics above, what conclusions can you draw about the characteristics of the arms race up to 1985? Give evidence from both documents to support your answer.

Why was the arms race so intense during the Cold War?

The development of the Cold War, and the increasing hostility between East and West, meant that both sides viewed the stockpiling of nuclear weapons as necessary to safeguard their interests. The continuing advances in technology continually made each side feel vulnerable; each felt it had to stay one step ahead of the other. As President Truman said when being advised on the dangers of developing the H-bomb: 'Can they do it? … If so, how can we not?' Secrecy in the 1960s, and the fear of falling behind in the case of the Americans, or the need to catch up in the case of the Soviets, fuelled the race. Therefore, until the 1980s, both sides continued to develop increasingly powerful and sophisticated weapons, as shown in the timeline on page 202.

What strategies were developed for using nuclear weapons?

Both sides had vast numbers of highly destructive nuclear weapons throughout the Cold War period. The question was, could they ever actually be used? Bernard Brodie, a leading American strategist at the time, was quick to see the military significance of nuclear weapons. In his book *The Absolute Weapon* (New York 1946) he explained that whereas before the invention of nuclear weapons the chief purpose of the military had been to 'win wars', from now on their chief purpose would be to 'avert them'. He claimed that the new weapons could have no other purpose. Thus, military victory in **'total war'** was no longer possible.

Leaders in both the USA and the USSR saw the danger of nuclear weapons. Stalin went so far as to say: 'Atomic bombs can hardly be used without spelling the end of the world' (quoted in Simon Sebag Montefiore, *Stalin: The Court of the Red Tsar* [Knopf 2004] p.601); and, following an early hydrogen bomb test, President Eisenhower commented that 'Atomic War will destroy civilization'. Khrushchev was also appalled by the prospect of military use of nuclear weapons, and his policy of 'peaceful co-existence' meant that war with the West was not now inevitable, though this did not stop him threatening it!

Despite the obvious dangers of nuclear weapons, both sides believed that there had to be a strategy that could be devised in which they could be used, otherwise what was the point of having them?

Eisenhower and massive retaliation

Although many of Eisenhower's advisers were working towards the idea of some kind of limited nuclear warfare, Eisenhower himself put forward the idea of massive retaliation – that the United States would fight with every weapon at its disposal if attacked, despite the devastating consequences that this would have. Dulles went as far as to say, at a NATO council meeting in April 1954, that '[nuclear] weapons must now be treated as in fact having become conventional'. Although this policy was criticized by many, it could be argued that Eisenhower – who was highly conscious of the dangers of war – was trying through this threat of all-out nuclear war to ensure that no such conflict would take place.

The Baruch Plan

As you will read in chapter 16, there was an attempt to use the United Nations to control the spread of nuclear power. US representative Bernard Baruch presented a proposal to the United Nations Atomic Energy Commission (UNAEC) in June 1946 for the creation of an international Atomic Development Authority, which would oversee the development and use of atomic energy and manage any nuclear installations that had the ability to produce nuclear weapons. However, in the increasingly hostile atmosphere of the cold war, the Soviets opposed any plan that would involve inspection of their nuclear programme, or the giving up of any of their power to the UN (which they already perceived as being pro-US).

Investigate the impact of the nuclear arms race, both in terms of the results of testing new weapons, and in terms of the dumping and disposal of obsolete weapons, on the environment. Which regions seem to be most impacted? What lessons can be learned about the testing and disposal of these types of weapons?

Others also realized that the concept of a 'limited nuclear war' was highly problematic. George Kennan, in his Reith Lectures for BBC Radio in 1957, argued:

> ❝ *It is a thesis which I cannot accept. That it would prove possible, in the event of an atomic war, to arrive at some tacit and workable understanding with an adversary as to the degree of destructiveness of the weapons that would be used and the sort of target to which they could be directed seems to me a very slender and wishful hope indeed.*

> **GF Kennan, *Russia, the Atom and the West* (OUP 1958) p.59**

The role of internal, domestic factors in the arms race

It is also important to note that within both countries there were pressures to keep the arms race going. In the Soviet Union, the military resisted cuts on spending for arms, and in the United States, the so-called military–industrial complex (see page 69) wielded a huge influence on the government by encouraging the continued manufacture of armaments.

Europe and nuclear weapons

The British governments of the 1950s also moved to a position of 'nuclear deterrence'. They supported Eisenhower's 'New Look' policy and had no objection to nuclear-capable US bombers being stationed on British soil. The British exploded their first plutonium bomb in the Australian desert in August 1952. The French also had an atomic weapons policy; they exploded their first bomb in 1960. Neither wanted these nuclear weapons to be part of a European defence programme; both kept the nuclear weapons under their own national control rather than a collective European command. This meant of course that the US had to keep its presence in Europe.

McNamara and 'counterforce'

President Kennedy was determined to widen the options beyond massive retaliation. As has already been discussed (see chapter 6), he formed a policy of flexible response. Part of this was developing a nuclear strategy which could be fought in a more limited way than the idea of massive retaliation. Kennedy's Secretary of Defense, Robert McNamara, developed a '**counterforce strategy**' in which the objective would be to destroy the enemy's military forces, but not cities and thus not civilian populations. Clearly, there were problems with this strategy:

- the issue of successfully hitting a target accurately at this early stage of missile development
- hitting a military target without affecting a city when so many military facilities were located near to cities
- ensuring that the Soviets also followed the same 'no cities' rule.

The USSR was angered by this new policy as it implied that the United States would make '**pre-emptive strikes**' in a crisis situation:

> ❝ *A strategy which contemplates attaining victory through the destruction of the [Soviet] armed forces [by nuclear strikes] cannot stem from the idea of a 'retaliatory' blow; it stems from pre-emptive action and the achievement of surprise.*

> **VD Sokolovsk, 'A Suicidal Strategy', *Red Star*, 19 July 1962**

Public opinion in the United States also was not favourable to this policy as it seemed to make nuclear war more, not less, likely.

The impact of the Cuban Missile Crisis: mutually assured destruction (MAD)

During the Cuban Missile Crisis, the risk of events spiralling out of control highlighted the problems of a counterforce strategy as described above.

 What had appeared to be 'rational' behaviour in Moscow had come across as dangerously 'irrational' behaviour in Washington, and vice versa. If a common rationality could be so elusive in peacetime, what prospects would there be for it in the chaos of a nuclear war? McNamara himself recalls wondering, as he watched the sun set on the most crucial day of the crisis, whether he would survive to see it do so again. He did survive, but his conviction that there could be a limited, controlled, rational nuclear war did not.

John Lewis Gaddis, *The Cold War* **(OUP 2005) p.80**

So, the idea of targeting military objectives was changed. McNamara now believed that both sides should aim to target cities with the objective of causing the maximum number of casualties possible. The belief here was that if no one – Soviet or American – could survive a nuclear war, then there would not be one.

This idea became known as 'mutually assured destruction', or MAD, and it went back to the idea first proposed by Bernard Brodie in 1946 that the existence of nuclear weapons meant that there could never be a total war between the superpowers. Historian Richard Crockatt sums it up:

 By a curious logic, vulnerability, the nightmare prospect envisaged by the Eisenhower administration, had come to be seen as the guarantor of national security, however fragile that might be.

R Crockatt in *The Fifty Years War* **(Routledge 1995) p.148**

Both the Soviet Union and the United States came to accept MAD. They continued to build up their nuclear weapons, but at this point both also saw the need for agreements on how to manage them. For this reason, the Cuban Missile Crisis was followed by:

- the Test-Ban Treaty in 1963, which stopped nuclear weapons testing in the atmosphere
- the Nuclear Non-Proliferation Treaty in 1968, which required nations possessing nuclear weapons not to pass on relevant information or technology to non-nuclear countries
- the Strategic Arms Limitation Interim Agreement in 1972, which restricted the number of land- and sea-based ballistic missiles.

There was also now tacit agreement on Eisenhower's idea of 'open skies', which allowed satellite reconnaissance in order to minimize the possibility of surprise attack. The Anti-Ballistic Missile Treaty of 1972 also banned defences against long-range missiles. This was to ensure that MAD remained the key strategy. If defences were allowed, then one or both superpowers might believe that they stood a chance of using nuclear weapons and this would take away the 'stability' that came from MAD (see chapter 12 for more discussion on these arms limitation agreements, which formed part of the détente process).

It was this understanding – the fact that nuclear weapons could not be used – that helped to keep the Cold War going for so long. The arms race, Gaddis argues, 'exchanged destruction for duration'.

CHALLENGE YOURSELF

 Research skills (ATL)

Research the nuclear disarmament movement. Which individuals and organizations have protested against nuclear weapons from the 1950s through to today? What forms has protest against nuclear weapons taken?

The impact of Reagan and Gorbachev

US President Ronald Reagan changed this way of thinking – this 'stability' in the area of nuclear relations. Firstly, he stepped up the arms race with the biggest arms build-up in the history of the United States. There were new developments, such as the stealth bomber and the neutron bomb, and, in 1983, **cruise missiles** were first shipped to Europe. However, it was the Strategic Defense Initiative (**SDI**, or 'Star Wars') that upset the Soviet Union the most. This aimed to set up a space-based missile system that could intercept and destroy missiles before they reached the United States. It was criticized by the Soviets, as well as by many of the United States' allies. This was because it would have undermined the 'assured destruction' required for MAD and given the USA a first-strike capability, thus destabilizing the international situation. The Soviets, whose economy was on the verge of collapse, also knew that they could not compete with this new round of nuclear technology expansion. Indeed, some historians believe that it was the threat of SDI that led directly to the success of arms talks between Soviet leader Mikhail Gorbachev and President Reagan.

However, equally important was the changed thinking of Gorbachev, the new Soviet premier. He argued that as nuclear war was not possible, security must therefore be gained by political rather than military means, and that negotiation and co-operation were as important as the continued build-up of the military. He put forward the idea of '**reasonable sufficiency**', which meant that the Soviet Union should have only enough weapons to defend itself, rather than enough to launch a pre-emptive strike or fight a preventative war. This change in the Soviet mindset, along with the good relationship between Gorbachev and Reagan, would lead to an end to the arms race, as will be discussed in the next chapter.

The role of conventional weapons

The fact that nuclear weapons could not be used, except as a last resort, meant that both sides needed to keep large conventional forces, which remained central to military strategy. Indeed, the Korean War and the Vietnam War were fought with conventional arms, and highlighted the importance of staying ahead in this area as well. The USSR still retained the lead in conventional forces. By the mid-1970s, the Warsaw Pact countries had nearly twice as many men and three times as many tanks in Europe as their counterparts in NATO.

The space race

Another arena of Cold War competition, which went alongside the arms race, was the space race. Following the successes of the USSR in this area in the 1950s, Khrushchev claimed that the 'economy, science, culture and the creative genius of people in all areas of life develop better and faster under Communism'. However, the space race was also part of a race for military superiority, as space race technology was linked to technology in the weapons race. As you have read in chapter 7, the space race heated up when the USSR put the first satellite, Sputnik, in space. This caused hysteria in the USA, not just because the Soviets had beaten the Americans in the race, but because it now proved that they could launch ballistic missiles that could reach the US. Satellites were also important for surveillance of the other side's military installations.

The USSR continued its lead in space exploration by succeeding in sending the first person into space: cosmonaut Yuri Gagarin orbited Earth in Vostok 1 on 12 April 1961. Less than a month later, Alan Shepard became the first American in space. The space race reached its peak on 20 July 1969 with Apollo 11 and the US landing of

Following the end of the Cold War, most people believed that the world would be a safer place, now that there was no threat of the superpowers using their stockpiles in a nuclear showdown. However, new threats regarding the use of nuclear weapons have emerged. What are these threats?

Research online the Bulletin of the Atomic Scientists and their Doomsday Clock, which shows how close the world is to nuclear war; how many minutes to 'midnight' does this clock now show and why?

the first humans on the moon. This followed JFK's determination (stated in 1961) to 'beat the USSR to demonstrate that instead of being behind by a couple of years, by God, we passed them'. Conversely, a key event symbolizing détente was the April 1972 agreement on a co-operative **Apollo–Soyuz Test Project**, resulting in the July 1975 meeting of a US astronaut crew with a Soviet cosmonaut crew while orbiting the earth.

Activity 2

 Thinking skills

1. Explain the meaning of the following:
   a. massive retaliation
   b. counterforce
   c. assured destruction
   d. mutually assured destruction
   e. SDI

2. 'It's not mad! Mutual Assured Destruction is the foundation of deterrence' (Robert McNamara speaking on the CNN *Cold War* television series). Explain in your own words why McNamara believed that MAD acted as a deterrent to nuclear war. Do you agree with McNamara's view that MAD made the world a safer place? Or, do you believe that 'the lack of superpower war owed much to plain luck' (Theo Farrell in 'Counting the Costs of the Nuclear Age', *International Affairs* 75, 1, p.125).

Activity 3

ATL Communication skills

Essay writing

Write the following essay using the frame below to help you.

> ***Discuss the impact of the nuclear arms race on the Cold War.***

Essay frame

Introduction: Give some context: for example, the dates and scope of the nuclear arms race. Indicate the key points of your argument and set out your judgement – for instance, that the nuclear arms race had a profound impact on the nature and length of the Cold War.

First paragraph: Firstly, nuclear weapons had a key impact on the development of military strategy as both sides tried to work out how nuclear weapons could be best used. You could consider the following evidence to support this point:

- Eisenhower's strategy of massive retaliation, followed by counterforce under Kennedy.
- the move to MAD and the acceptance that nuclear weapons could not be used.

Second paragraph: Linked to the first point, it could be argued that the nuclear arms race helped to create stability. You could consider the following evidence to support this point:

- Aware of the dangers of MAD, both sides avoided head-to-head confrontations; conflict was confined instead to proxy wars such as in Vietnam, where conventional weapons were used (though still to devastating effect).
- It meant that both sides kept out of the other's sphere of influence, ensuring for example that the US did not interfere in Hungary in 1956, or Czechoslovakia in 1968, as the risk of a nuclear showdown was too great.
- After the Cuban Missile Crisis, both sides worked to reduce the dangers of a nuclear war through measures such as the hotline and the Non-Proliferation Treaty.
- These factors extended the length of the Cold War (refer to Gaddis's quote on page 205).

Third paragraph: However, nuclear weapons led to a massive arms race, which was a dominant feature of the Cold War and led to a huge economic drain of resources for both countries. You could consider the following evidence to support this point:

- The economic impact helped lead to various arms treaties, such as SALT I, that put limits on the production of some categories of nuclear weapons.
- Ultimately, it contributed to the economic decay and collapse of the USSR, thus – ironically – ending the Cold War.

Fourth paragraph: The obsession with getting ahead in the arms race also led to destabilizing effects. You could consider the following evidence to support this point:

- There was an ongoing competition to develop more powerful and lethal weapons (give examples).
- The secrecy surrounding this competition contributed to a growth in tension; fear of a missile gap on the part of the USA; the impact of the U-2 flight incident; the discovery of missiles on Cuba.

CHALLENGE YOURSELF

Research skills (ATL)

Research the key events of the space race. What factors allowed the Soviets to get ahead in this area? What factors allowed the Americans to take the lead by the end of the 1960s and get the first man on the moon? Why do you think that this area of Cold War conflict was followed with such interest by the populations in both East and West?

- Before 1962, the concept of massive retaliation and the use of brinkmanship, such as in Cuba, led to dangerous confrontations. In the 1980s, during the Second Cold War, there were other close calls, such as the Able Archer incident of 1983.
- China also engaged in the nuclear arms race from the late 1960s, adding to international tension.
- In the early 1980s USSR deployed SS-20s to Eastern Europe and NATO responded, raising tension in Europe.

Conclusion: You may want to highlight what you think is the most important impact of the nuclear arms race. Do you agree that it acted as a deterrence and created stability overall?

Activity 4 **ATL** Thinking skills

Cartoon analysis: identifying the message of a cartoon

When analysing the meaning of a cartoon you need to answer several questions:

- Which political figures are shown in the cartoon? Make sure you can recognize the political figures of the time.
- What event/issue is the cartoon is referring to? Look carefully at the date and use your knowledge of the period.
- Are there symbols or other items in the cartoon that have significance?
- Are there any labels or writing on the cartoon that help explain what is going on? What about the title?
- Do you have any knowledge about the cartoonist, or the country from which he or she comes, that might help to explain his or her point of view?

The following cartoons were all drawn for the Montreal newspaper *The Gazette* by a Canadian cartoonist called John Collins, and all are connected with the nuclear arms race.

'International Downhill Race', cartoon by John Collins, 1962.

'Emerging from the Ice Age', cartoon by John Collins, 1963.

'Fifty Years of Progress', cartoon by John Collins, 1968.

1. Annotate a copy of each cartoon with arrows to show clearly who or what is being shown in each case. Look carefully – there are several images in each cartoon that will need annotating.
2. Using your contextual knowledge, identify what was happening in the Cold War regarding the arms race at the date the cartoon was drawn.
3. Now, using the information from the last two questions, explain what the message of the cartoon was in each case. Make sure you use the titles of the cartoons in your answers, as these are key to helping to understand the messages.

Issues to consider when looking at the value of cartoons as source material

*   Cartoons show a point of view about an event or person.
*   A cartoonist usually draws a point of view that other people will understand and appreciate, and so this makes a cartoon useful for showing one current view or perception of what is happening.
*   In order to help work out how representative the cartoonist's view is, you can look at the publication in which it appears. If it is published in a newspaper or magazine with a large and or/wide readership, this will make it more useful in showing contemporary perceptions.
*   A Soviet cartoon will be useful for showing the nature of Soviet propaganda.

Issues to consider when looking at the limitations of cartoons as source material

*   A cartoon is only one point of view (of either a section of society or a particular country) and might not be the view of the majority of people.
*   The situation in the cartoon can be exaggerated in order to make a point.
*   You need to consider how much knowledge the cartoonist would have about an event or issue.
*   A Soviet cartoon will represent the views of the Soviet leadership only, and will be making a propaganda point.

Don't forget to refer directly to the details of the specific cartoon and the cartoonist you are analysing when answering a question on its value and limitations.

Now consider the following question:

How useful do you think John Collins' cartoons are to historians studying attitudes to the arms race?

 Look for two points that the cartoon is making. For the first cartoon, your opening sentence could read: 'The first message of this cartoon is that the arms race is a race that is very fast (possibly out of control) ...' Then go on to explain details in the cartoon that support this message. Continue with a second point: 'In addition, the cartoon is saying that there doesn't seem to be any way to stop the arms race. This is shown by the fact that ...'.

 To access websites relevant to this chapter, go to www.pearsonhotlinks. com, search for the book title or ISBN, and click on 'chapter 14'.

15 Confrontation and reconciliation:
The collapse of the Soviet Union and
the end of the Cold War

Key concepts: # Change, causation and perspective

As you read this chapter, consider the following essay questions:

- To what extent was Gorbachev forced to end the Cold War?
- Examine the role of the American administration and a renewed arms race in the fall of the Soviet Union.
- 'Economic problems within the USSR and its sphere of influence dictated the changes in policy under Gorbachev.' To what extent do you agree with this statement?
- Discuss the role of 'people power' and nationalism in the fall of the USSR.

> *The end of the Cold War baffles us; almost nobody expected it.*
>
> **Melvyn Leffler, 2004**

When Mikhail Gorbachev resigned as president of the USSR on Christmas Day 1991, the Soviet Union ceased to exist. The Cold War was finally over; the collapse of the Soviet Empire meant that the Cold War was definitely at an end. This monumental turning point in modern world history had occurred, amazingly, with little bloodshed. Perhaps just as astonishing was that no one had predicted this rapid collapse of the 'other' superpower. The United States and British intelligence services were as surprised as the East German border guards when the iconic symbol of the Cold War, the Berlin Wall, was torn down in November 1989. However, even before this happened, relations between the Soviet Union and the United States had changed dramatically.

Timeline of key events leading to the end of the Cold War		
1979		Invasion of Afghanistan
		Solidarity movement set up in Poland
1982		Brezhnev dies, succeeded by Andropov
1984		Andropov dies, succeeded by Chernenko
1985	**March**	Chernenko dies, succeeded by Gorbachev
		Perestroika reform era begins
1986		*Glasnost* era begins
	April	Chernobyl nuclear disaster
1987	**Dec**	Washington Summit – Intermediate Nuclear Forces Treaty is signed
1988	**Jan**	Law on State Enterprises – Soviet state no longer responsible for debts on economic enterprises
	Oct	Electoral law – new multi-candidate elections established in USSR and used in the elections for the new Congress of People's Deputies
	Dec	Gorbachev's speech to UN – outlines Warsaw Pact troop reductions and a withdrawal of Soviet forces from Afghanistan
1989	**Feb**	Soviet withdrawal from Afghanistan
	July	Commission on Economic Reform set up to consider ways to reform Soviet economy
	Oct	Anti-Soviet movements begin in Warsaw Pact countries. Gorbachev maintains he will not intervene

Timeline of key events leading to the end of the Cold War – *continued*		
	Nov	Fall of the Berlin Wall
		Malta Summit. Gorbachev and Bush declare the 'end of the Cold War'
1990	Feb	Article 6 of USSR constitution is dropped – ends monopoly of the CPSU (Communist Party of the Soviet Union) within the USSR
	March–May	Baltic republics (Estonia, Latvia, and Lithuania) declare independence
1991	Jan	Vilnius Massacre in Lithuania
	June	Boris Yeltsin elected president of Russia
	19–21 Aug	Coup against Gorbachev by hardliners is unsuccessful
	23 Aug	Yeltsin outlaws CPSU in Russia
	24 Aug	Gorbachev resigns as General Secretary of CPSU and dissolves the party
		Minsk Agreement ends the USSR – replaced by Commonwealth of Independent States (CIS)
	25 Dec	Gorbachev resigns as president of the Soviet Union
		George Bush acknowledges the end of the Cold War
	26 Dec	The Supreme Soviet recognizes the dissolution of the Soviet Union
	31 Dec	All Soviet institutions cease operation

What was the impact of Mikhail Gorbachev?

For the Soviet Union, Stalin's 'legacy' meant that politically the Soviet Union remained an authoritarian, one-party state, and that economically it was focused on producing military hardware rather than housing, transport, food, consumer goods, and healthcare. Mikhail Gorbachev is reported to have said 'We can't go on living like this' on the eve of his succession as General Secretary to the Politburo. Not only was he the youngest leader to have this position since Stalin, but he was also the first university-educated leader.

Gorbachev introduced two key reforming ideas – *perestroika* and *glasnost*. *Perestroika* (restructuring) aimed at restructuring the economy and *glasnost* (openness) was the principle that every area of the regime should be open to public scrutiny. This represented a radical change in politics in the Soviet Union. It involved greater **'democratization'**, with more people involved in the Communist Party and in political debate.

Through these strategies, Gorbachev intended to make the Soviet system more productive and responsive, and he realized that part of this process also had to involve a reduction in military spending. He knew that, if his reforming ideas were going to work, the Soviets could not rise to the challenge of matching Reagan's SDI system. He decided to abandon the arms race and attempt a negotiated reduction in arms with the USA. It was not just for economic reasons that Gorbachev wanted arms control:

> He called for a new thinking in international affairs, and he said that there could be 'no winners' in a nuclear war. Gorbachev declared the world to be interdependent and likened all its people 'to climbers roped together on the mountainside'.

John Mason, *The Cold War* (Routledge 1996) p.62

The **Chernobyl** disaster, in which an explosion destroyed a reactor at the Chernobyl nuclear power plant in Ukraine, only heightened Gorbachev's awareness of the dangers of nuclear power. As Anatoly Chernyaev, an aide to Gorbachev, put it, 'Gorbachev knew even before that catastrophe about the danger of nuclear weapons. That explosion showed that, even without war and without nuclear missiles, nuclear power could destroy humankind' (quoted in the CNN television series *The Cold War*).

Reagan was also interested in disarmament and had previously put forward to the Soviets an arms control proposal known as '**zero option**', which would eliminate all intermediate-range missiles in Europe. Gorbachev, unlike his predecessors, was prepared to discuss this option. This resulted in the two leaders meeting together in four summits to discuss arms control:

- **Geneva Summit, November 1985:** No substantial progress was made but the two leaders established a personal rapport and they agreed that 'a nuclear war cannot be won and must not be fought'.
- **Reykjavik Summit, October 1986:** Talks ended without agreement, mainly because of disagreement over SDI. Gorbachev said that SDI should be 'confined to the laboratory', but Reagan refused to make any concessions. However, the talks also covered the most sweeping arms control proposals in history, and Gorbachev declared that it had 'been an intellectual breakthrough' in relations between the United States and the Soviet Union.
- **Washington Summit, December 1987:** At this summit, agreement was reached. An Intermediate-Range Nuclear Force Treaty (**INF Treaty**) was signed, which actually agreed to abolish weapons: land-based missiles of intermediate and shorter range. This was an important first step in reducing the nuclear stockpiles of the two superpowers. Agreement was also reached for the first time on inspection of the destruction of missiles.
- **Moscow Summit, May 1988:** Again there was disagreement over SDI, but arms reductions negotiations continued. Standing in **Red Square**, Reagan confessed that he now no longer believed in the 'evil empire'.

Activity 1  ATL Thinking skills

> *Mikhail Gorbachev and Ronald Reagan made many mistakes at the summit. But their personal chemistry, the relations forged between their advisers, and the tenacity with which both sides kept talking all show that summitry can make a difference when properly managed. The encounters that began in frosty Geneva in November 1985 helped ensure that the Cold War ended not with a bang, or a whimper, but a handshake.*

David Reynolds, *Summits: Six Meetings that Shaped the Twentieth Century* (Allen Lane 2007) p.369

1. What key points about the importance of the 'summits' are made by Reynolds?

Other foreign policy initiatives put into action by Gorbachev were reassuring to the West. By 1988, Gorbachev had announced his plans to withdraw from Afghanistan, and he pulled back Soviet aid to its 'allies' in the developing world.

The 'thawing' of the Cold War continued under the new US president, George HW Bush. At the Malta Summit between the US and Soviet leaders in 1989, Soviet Foreign Minister Eduard Shevardnadze announced that the superpowers had 'buried the Cold War at the bottom of the Mediterranean'.

What was the role of Ronald Reagan?

Clearly, Gorbachev's willingness to tackle the issue of nuclear weapons, along with his new style of politics and doing business with the West, were key to explaining the breakdown of the Cold War. However, many historians also give Reagan credit for this, and argue that it was his approach to the Soviet Union in the early 1980s that was crucial for pushing the Soviet Union into arms negotiations. An article critical of the '**Reagan victory school**' describes this view below:

> As former Pentagon officials like Caspar Weinberger and Richard Perle ... and other proponents of the Reagan victory school have argued, a combination of military and ideological pressures gave the Soviets little choice but to abandon expansionism abroad and repression at home. In their view, the Reagan military build-up foreclosed Soviet military options while pushing the Soviet economy to the breaking point. Reagan partisans stress that his dramatic Star Wars initiative put the Soviets on notice that the next phase of the arms race would be waged in areas where the West held a decisive technological edge.

D Deudney and GJ Ikenberry, 'Who Won the Cold War?', *Foreign Policy* 87 (Summer 1992) p.124

This 'Reagan victory school' view is therefore critical of the 'détente' approach to relations with the Soviet Union, as explained below by Patrick Glynn:

> The Jimmy Carter–Cyrus Vance approach of rewarding the Soviet build-up with one-sided arms control treaties, opening Moscow's access to Western capital markets and technologies, and condoning Soviet imperial expansion was perfectly designed to preserve the Brezhnev-style approach, delivering the Soviets from any need to re-evaluate (as they did under Gorbachev) or change their policies. Had the Carter–Vance approach been continued ... the Cold War and the life of the Soviet Union would almost certainly have been prolonged.

Patrick Glynn, letter to the Editor, *Foreign Policy* 90 (Spring 1993) pp.171–173

Activity 2 · (ATL) Thinking skills

Read the two sources above again.

1. Identify three reasons from the first source to explain why Reagan's policies could be seen as responsible for ending the Cold War.
2. What criticisms does Patrick Glynn have of détente?

Other historians, such as Michael McGuire, also claim that Reagan played an important role, but believe this role was more connected to his views on eliminating nuclear weapons, which helped at the different summits to convince Gorbachev of the possibilities of halting the nuclear arms race. Reagan's character and willingness to engage with Gorbachev was also important. As Rozanne Ridgway, US Assistant Secretary of State, put it in the CNN series *The Cold War*, there was probably no other politician around at that time who would have 'moved forward, as Reagan did, to engage Gorbachev'.

This is supported by historian Robert J McMahon:

> To his great credit, Reagan proved willing first to moderate, and then to abandon, deeply held personal convictions about the malignant nature of Communism, thereby permitting a genuine rapprochement to occur.

From RJ McMahon, *The Cold War: A Very Short Introduction* (OUP 2003) p.162

Activity 3    **ATL** Thinking skills

1. Who do you believe played the more important role in bringing about a new relationship between the United States and the Soviet Union – Gorbachev or Reagan? (We discuss this question further in chapter 17.)

2. Explain what Zubok means in the quotation below. To what extent do you agree with his assertion?

> It was Ronald Reagan's luck that his presidency coincided with generational change in the Kremlin and the exit of the Old Guard. Mikhail Gorbachev was the first Soviet leader since Stalin to reappraise drastically the relationship between ideology and Soviet security interests.

Vladislav M Zubok, A Failed Empire: The Soviet Union in the Cold War from Stalin to Gorbachev (UNC Press 2007) p.341

Long-term factors in the ending of the Cold War

What was the role of the Soviet economy?

Although the actions of Gorbachev and Reagan are important for explaining how events turned out as they did, it is also important to look at the long-term forces that were at work in pushing the Soviet Union into ending the Cold War. By the time Brezhnev died in 1982, both the political and economic policies of the Soviet Union were in crisis.

Under Brezhnev, the Soviets spent even more resources on foreign policy. Although involved in important arms treaties with the USA, it was under Brezhnev that the USSR achieved **'parity'** with the USA in the nuclear field and, in some areas, surpassed it. This was achieved at a high price: by the mid-1980s, about 25 per cent of the USSR's gross domestic product (GDP) was being spent on the military; in comparison, the USA was spending 4–6 per cent. In addition, the cost of maintaining the USSR's empire proved a drain on resources; ventures in Africa and Afghanistan were extremely costly. Cuba received $4 billion in Soviet aid and subsidies; Vietnam received $6 billion. The members of the Warsaw Pact were also given $3 billion worth of oil subsidies.

Brezhnev's era is also remembered as a period of stagnation and decline in the USSR. This is due to the serious lack of spending not only on consumer goods, but on the domestic economy as a whole. Brezhnev left his successors an economy that was still based on the 'command economy' structure of Stalin's day. It was falling behind in modern technology and industrial output was declining. A large proportion of the agricultural workers lived below the poverty line and grain was imported from North America. Workers had little incentive to work harder or produce better goods. Labour morale was low; there was high absenteeism and chronic alcoholism. When Gorbachev took over, he inherited an economy in serious trouble. Between 1967 and 1980, the annual growth rate for Soviet industrial output declined from 5.2 to 2 per cent. The economy was also hit by a fall in oil and gas prices. It could thus be argued that Gorbachev was forced to take the actions that he did in both internal reform and negotiations with the West. Given this situation in the Soviet Union, some historians argue (in direct contradiction with the historians of the 'Reagan victory school') that keeping the Cold War going through containment and détente played a role in bringing about the end of the Cold War rather than prolonging it.

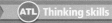
> The West did not, as is widely believed, win the Cold War through geopolitical containment and military deterrence. Nor was the Cold War won by the Reagan military build up and the Reagan Doctrine … Instead, 'victory' for the West came when a new generation of Soviet leaders realized how badly their system at home and their policies abroad had failed. What containment did was to successfully stalemate Moscow's attempts to advance Soviet hegemony. Over four decades it performed the historic function of holding Soviet power in check until the internal seeds of destruction within the Soviet Union and its empire could mature. At this point, however, it was Gorbachev who brought the Cold War to an end …

Raymond L Garthoff, 'Why Did the Cold War Arise and Why Did it End?' in Michael J Hogan (ed), *The End of the Cold War: Its Meaning and Implications* (CUP 1992) p.129

1. Explain the meaning of the following phrases used in the extract:
   a. geopolitical containment
   b. Soviet hegemony
   c. military deterrence
   d. internal seeds of destruction

2. What is the overall message of this document regarding the reasons why the Cold War ended?

3. Compare and contrast what Raymond Garthoff says about the reasons for the end of the Cold War with those given by Patrick Glynn on page 214.

The impact of Gorbachev's reforms

Meanwhile, the impact of Gorbachev's internal reforms was the collapse of the Soviet Union. Gorbachev had not intended this to happen – through *perestroika* and *glasnost* he had wanted to revive the Soviet economy and to modify the Soviet system. However, the economic reforms which encouraged **private ownership** (see interesting fact box) led to chaos. There was no effective system in the Soviet Union to cope with a market economy. In addition, the liberalization coincided with a fall in the world's oil prices. Economic growth by 1991 had dropped to −15 per cent.

At the same time, *glasnost* allowed for openness and discussion, which opened a floodgate for criticisms of both the old Soviet system and of Gorbachev's reforms. The old system was now openly criticized for its obvious failings to compete with Capitalism, while the new reforms were criticized for their failure to solve the country's many problems. In this new open atmosphere, with the faults of the Soviet Union laid bare, it was hard to defend the legitimacy of the existing system.

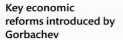

Key economic reforms introduced by Gorbachev

The Law on Co-operatives of 1987 permitted private ownership of businesses in the service, manufacturing, and foreign trade sectors. Workers were allowed to leave collective farms.

The Enterprise Law in July 1987 transferred decision-making from the central ministries to the enterprises and managers in state-owned companies, who were now given much more power.

The Law on Joint Ventures allowed foreign ownership of companies.

> **Cold War Crisis:**

What was the role of ideological challenge and people power in ending the Cold War?

> What no one understood, at the beginning of 1989, was that the Soviet Union, its empire, its ideology – and therefore the Cold War itself – was a sand pile ready to slide. All it took to happen was a few more grains of sand. The people who dropped them were not in charge of superpowers or movements or religions: they were ordinary people with simple priorities who saw, seized, and sometimes stumbled into opportunities. In doing so they caused a collapse no one could stop.

John Lewis Gaddis, *The Cold War* (Penguin 2005) p.238

In the late 1980s, a resurgence in nationalist movements began to develop in most of the satellite states. The reasons for this were:

The Velvet Revolution, Czechoslovakia, 1989.

1. The continued deterioration of living standards; as in the Soviet Union, the state-controlled industries in the satellite states were inefficient both in terms of quality and quantity of goods produced. Consumer goods were in short supply, along with food, clothes, and housing. Meanwhile, people in East Germany and Czechoslovakia, who were on the borders of West Europe, could see images of Capitalist living on West German television, and it looked decidedly superior to what they were experiencing in the East. The economic slow-down of the Soviet Union further impacted on the satellite states.

2. The growing disillusion with the Communist Party, which had shown itself as corrupt, with its leaders more interested in preserving their own privileges than in making life better for the workers. By the 1980s, the regimes of Eastern Europe were led by men who had no interest in reform, and were out of touch with the people they ruled. They maintained their positions through a repressive police network.

3. The implications of Gorbachev's reforms of *glasnost* and *perestroika*. Gorbachev also made it clear that he was unwilling to use force to maintain control over the satellite states.

In a speech to the United Nations on 7 December 1988, Gorbachev announced that the Soviet Union would cut by half a million men its commitment of troops to the Warsaw Pact. 'It is obvious', he argued, 'that force and the threat of force cannot be and should not be an instrument of foreign policy … Freedom of choice is … a universal principle and it should know no exceptions.' This was a clear signal to the people and governments of Eastern Europe. Gorbachev had made it clear that the Brezhnev Doctrine would not be applied, and that the satellite states could determine their own internal affairs. This is sometimes called the 'Sinatra Doctrine' (doing it 'their way'). As David Reynolds writes:

> By 1989 Gorbachev's insistence that the values of humanity took precedence over those of class and nation persuaded him that the Eastern Europeans must be allowed to go their own way peacefully. Unlike Khrushchev in 1956, Brezhnev in 1968, or the Chinese Communist regime that very year in Tiananmen Square, he refused to sanction the use of force when reform got out of hand and turned into revolution.

David Reynolds, *Summits: Six Meetings that Shaped the Twentieth Century* (Allen Lane 2007) p.369

Thus, 1989 saw an amazing series of revolutions in the satellite states, resulting in the whole Soviet system, including Stalin's legacy, being swept away.

CHALLENGE YOURSELF

Research and communication skills

Research the governments that existed in the eastern satellite states by the 1980s:

- East Germany under Erich Honecker
- Romania under Ceausescu
- Czechoslovakia under Husak

In groups, find out about the economic situation, standards of living, and methods of control over the lives of the citizens. Prepare a presentation to give to the rest of the class.

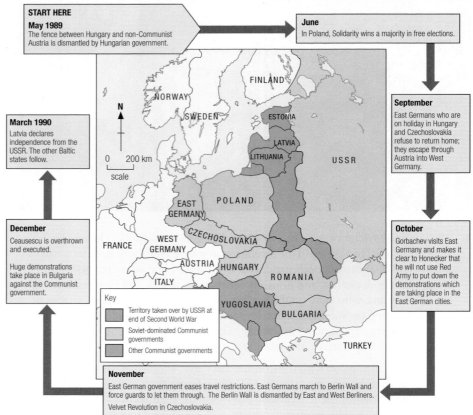

The events of 1989

START HERE

May 1989
The fence between Hungary and non-Communist Austria is dismantled by Hungarian government.

June
In Poland, Solidarity wins a majority in free elections.

March 1990
Latvia declares independence from the USSR. The other Baltic states follow.

September
East Germans who are on holiday in Hungary and Czechoslovakia refuse to return home; they escape through Austria into West Germany.

December
Ceausescu is overthrown and executed.

Huge demonstrations take place in Bulgaria against the Communist government.

October
Gorbachev visits East Germany and makes it clear to Honecker that he will not use Red Army to put down the demonstrations which are taking place in the East German cities.

November
East German government eases travel restrictions. East Germans march to Berlin Wall and force guards to let them through. The Berlin Wall is dismantled by East and West Berliners.
Velvet Revolution in Czechoslovakia.

Key

Territory taken over by USSR at end of Second World War

Soviet-dominated Communist governments

Other Communist governments

0   200 km
scale

The process by which the Soviet Union collapsed began in May 1989 when Hungarian Prime Minister Miklós Németh decided that his government could not afford to maintain the automatized border control along the boundary against Austria; he believed it was no longer necessary and was 'anachronistic' as Hungarians were allowed to freely travel anyhow. This gave an escape route for East Germans, many of whom took their holidays in Hungary with the intention of travelling from there to the West. Indeed, thousands of Hungarians and East Germans then crossed over to Austria in order to travel to West Germany.

Events in Poland

In Poland, the union movement called 'Solidarity' had been suppressed in 1981 by General Jaruzelski. He had then declared a state of martial law. Nevertheless, there continued to be popular support for Solidarity due to the combination of economic stagnation, which the government failed to solve, and support from the Catholic Church. In response to Gorbachev's reforms, Solidarity was legalized in 1988, and some attempt to introduce reforms was made. Solidarity won the first free elections in Poland in 1989. Jaruzelski remained president, but the Solidarity leader Lech Walesa became prime minister. The Communist Party had been defeated by a huge popular vote, and the government was the first in the Eastern bloc since the 1940s not to be controlled by Communists. Gorbachev had not intervened to support the old Communist regime, and, in the absence of internal or external support, the Polish Communist Party collapsed.

An American cartoon from 1989 showing events in Eastern Europe (Tony Auth, *The Philadelphia Inquirer*).

1. What is the aeroplane supposed to represent? What is significant about the way the cartoonist has drawn the aeroplane?
2. Who are the passengers supposed to represent?
3. What is enabling Poland to jump out of the aeroplane?

Events in East Germany

Erich Honecker, a hardline Communist, had been the leader of East Germany since 1971. Although it was considered one of the more 'successful' countries in the Eastern bloc, living standards were well below those enjoyed by their fellow Germans in the West. Honecker used sport as a focus for national identity, but this did not create the sense of an East German society, and many people still looked forward to the day when Germany would be reunified. Evidence of the insecurity felt by Honecker's regime was the extremely repressive nature of the East German secret police, the **Stasi**. The Stasi kept files on 5.5 million people. The regime was unpopular, but Honecker was particularly hated. By the mid-1980s there was growing pressure on the government to remove him.

Honecker hoped to consolidate Communist control in East Germany during the celebrations for the 40th anniversary of the GDR. However, people criticized the harsh and repressive East German system and openly demanded reforms. Thousands of East German holidaymakers in Hungary crossed into Austria via the now-open border. These 'escapes' were a return to the days before the building of the Berlin Wall – there was a mass exodus of East Germans (on one day alone 125 000 crossed to the West). More alarming still for the regime were groups like the **'New Forum'** that decided to stay and resist rather than flee to the West.

Honecker wanted to use force to control the swell of anti-Communist Party feeling. Gorbachev, however, made it clear that he would not intervene if there were a full-scale revolt. Demonstrations in East German cities continued to grow and a new leader, Egon Krenz, was put in place by the Politburo. In order to try to stem the flow of people from East Germany, the government announced on 9 November 1989 the easing of travel and emigration restrictions. Although this was not actually intended to signify an immediate opening of the checkpoints through the Berlin Wall, the lack of clarity in the official statement meant that thousands of East Berliners immediately descended on the checkpoints. The East German guards were taken by surprise and, lacking direction from above, had to go ahead and open the barriers that night. Within 24 hours, the Berlin Wall had ceased to be the symbol of Cold War division and instead its destruction by the people – both East and West Berliners – had become the symbol of the ending of the Cold War. When free elections were held in 1990, parties in favour of unification with West Germany won a majority of seats. East and West Germany were finally reunited on 3 October 1990.

People power brings down the Berlin Wall in November 1989.

▼

Events in Hungary

Reform in Hungary came more from within the Hungarian Communist Party itself. Reformers, encouraged by the new policies emerging from Moscow, sacked the hardline leader, Janos Kadar, and then dominated the government. On 23 October 1989, Matyas Szuros declared the Third Hungarian Republic and became interim president. Hungary's first free elections were held in 1990.

Events in Czechoslovakia

The changes that took place in Czechoslovakia, and which led to the downfall of the Communist regime, have become known as the **'Velvet Revolution'** as there was very little violence. People power can be seen as the clear driving force here. The government was forced to respond to mass demonstrations calling for reform. The campaign was co-ordinated by an organization called the **Civic Forum** and, in 1989, a leading dissident playwright, Vaclav Havel, was elected president by the federal parliament. The Warsaw Pact nations, including the USSR, issued an official statement condemning the 1968 invasion of Czechoslovakia as 'illegal' and promising never again to interfere in each other's internal affairs.

Events in Romania

In comparison to the Velvet Revolution in Czechoslovakia, events in Romania were far more violent. Romania's leader was President Nicolae Ceausescu and his regime was one of the most repressive in Eastern Europe. However, in December 1989, inspired by news of events in Hungary and by the killing of demonstrators by the Romanian army in Timisoara, there was an uprising against Ceausescu and his wife. When the Ceausescus appeared at a rally in the Romanian capital, Bucharest, one week after the army had killed 71 people in Timisoara, they met with a hostile reception. The army now refused to take action against the demonstrators. Ceausescu and his wife tried to flee, but were arrested by the army and then executed on Christmas Day, 1989.

> *At the beginning of 1989 the Communists had been in complete – and seemingly permanent – control of Eastern Europe. At the end of the year, they were gone. Democratic coalitions, promising free elections in the immediate future, had taken place in East Berlin, Prague, Budapest, Warsaw and even Bucharest … As a result, the Warsaw Pact had been, in effect, dismantled. The Soviet Union had withdrawn inside its borders. The Cold War in Europe was over.*
>
> **Stephen Ambrose sums up the events of 1989 in *Rise to Globalism* (Penguin 2011) pp.365–366**

Activity 6 — ATL Thinking skills

'The Pace of History Quickens', *The Philadelphia Inquirer*, November 1989.

1. Explain what is happening in the cartoon.
2. What is the message of the cartoon regarding events in Eastern Europe?

The end of the USSR

Abroad, Gorbachev's policies brought admiration, and in 1990 he was awarded the Nobel Peace Prize. At home, however, failure to bring about an improvement in the country's economic situation meant that he became increasingly unpopular. Events in Eastern Europe brought about calls for independence from the republics of the Soviet Union. Thus, during 1991, the Soviet empire disintegrated. In August, the Baltic states of Estonia, Latvia, and Lithuania claimed their independence, as did the other republics that had been part of the USSR (see the map below).

This break-up of the USSR intensified hostility towards Gorbachev in the Soviet Union and, in August 1991, there was an attempted coup by Communist hardliners against him. This was defeated by Boris Yeltsin, who was already president of Russia at this time and an opponent of Gorbachev due to his much more radical views on how to deal with the economy, the structure of the Soviet Union, and the position of the Communist Party. Although Gorbachev was restored as a result of Yeltsin standing up to the hardliners, he had now lost authority. He was humiliated by Yeltsin on his return and on 25 December 1991 Gorbachev resigned as president of the USSR. The **Commonwealth of Independent States** was established and the Soviet Union formally ceased to exist.

The former republics of the USSR, which became independent states in 1991.

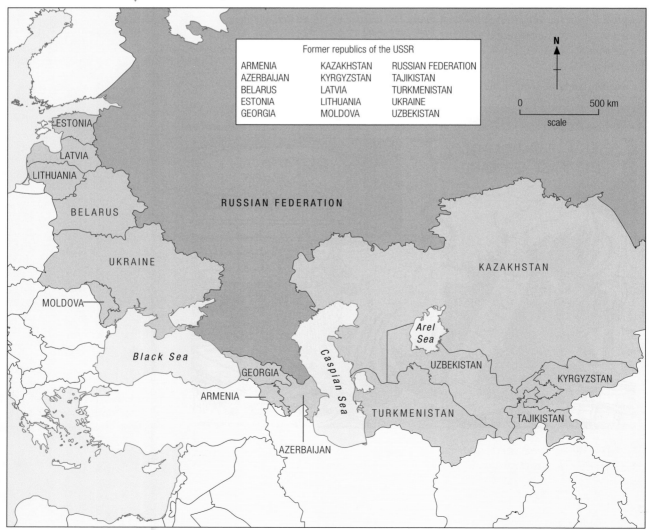

Former republics of the USSR		
ARMENIA	KAZAKHSTAN	RUSSIAN FEDERATION
AZERBAIJAN	KYRGYZSTAN	TAJIKISTAN
BELARUS	LATVIA	TURKMENISTAN
ESTONIA	LITHUANIA	UKRAINE
GEORGIA	MOLDOVA	UZBEKISTAN

What was the impact of the collapse of the USSR and the end of the Cold War?

The collapse of the Soviet Union had a huge impact on international politics as well as the economic situation of countries that had been dependent on the Soviet Union for aid.

For many in the United States, it seemed that they were the 'winners', and international politics became '**uni-polar**', with the USA as the only country now capable of having a military alliance around the world. Capitalism seemed to have triumphed. Communism remained the official ideology in only a few states – Cuba, North Korea, Vietnam, and China. Yet even in China and Vietnam, changes in economic controls allowed free-market forces to have an impact.

For Cuba, the drying up of Soviet economic aid, along with the US trade embargo, brought about an economic crisis. Similarly, other regimes in Africa formerly supported by the Soviet Union suffered economically. In other states that had been the focus of superpower conflict and fighting, such as Afghanistan, conflict continued:

❝ *Indeed, many of the Third World countries that had been the focus of excessive superpower interest in the 1970s and 1980s were dubbed 'failed states' in the 1990s as civil strife continued unabated and often with relatively little attention from the rest of the world.*

Jussi Hanhimaki and Odd Arne Westad, *The Cold War* (OUP 2004) p.630

The 11 September 2001 attacks on the United States led to a new focus for US foreign policy: the War on Terror. Islamic extremism was identified by the US government as the new global enemy.

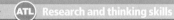

Activity 7 — **(ATL) Research and thinking skills**

1. Research the role of Boris Yeltsin both in the coup against Gorbachev and as president of the Russian Federation in the 1990s.

2. Draw a spider or flow diagram to show the factors that brought about the end of the Cold War. Distinguish between short- and long-term factors on your diagram.

3. A former US Secretary of State said: 'The Cold War did not have to end with a whimper; it could have ended with a bang.' What factors do you feel prevented the Cold War ending with a 'bang'?

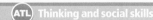

Activity 8 — **(ATL) Thinking and social skills**

1. Plan and film a documentary on the collapse of the Soviet Union. Work in groups. You will need to decide on:

   a. a title for the documentary

   b. who you are going to interview – you will have to take on different roles for the interviews

   c. what images you will want to include

   d. if you are going to include references to all the countries involved or if you are going to focus on just one or two countries

   e. if you are going to portray a particular viewpoint with regard to Gorbachev's actions or if you are going to try to maintain a 'neutral' approach.

Activity 9

Research and thinking skills

1. At which point do you think that it could be said that the Cold War was over? In pairs, discuss the implications of each of the following dates and decide which one most appropriately represents the end of superpower hostility.

   • President Reagan in Moscow, December 1988, when he said that he no longer believed in the 'evil empire'.
   • Malta Summit, 2/3 December 1989, when Gorbachev recognized the US as a 'European power' and Eduard Shevardnadze said that the Cold War was 'buried at the bottom of the Mediterranean'.
   • A reunified Germany joins NATO, 3 October 1990, symbolizing the end of the reunification process. Condoleezza Rice called it 'VE Day two'.
   • Warsaw Pact disbanded, 25 February 1991 – there were no longer 'two opposing camps'.
   • Resignation of Gorbachev, 25 December 1991 – there was no longer a Communist Party and the USSR was disbanded.
   • President Bush's Christmas Day address, 1991 – Bush stated that the 'confrontation is over'.

Activity 10

Research and social skills

Below are a couple of research and/or discussion questions on the post-Cold War era.

1. What has been the impact of the collapse of the Soviet Union:

   a. on the European Union
   b. on Yugoslavia
   c. on NATO?

2. How has the relationship between Russia and the West developed since 1989? Is there now 'a new Cold War'?

Activity 11

Thinking skills

Essay writing

Consider the following essay question:

> ***To what extent was Gorbachev responsible for bringing about the end of the Cold War?***

Essay planning hints

Introduction: Put the question into context. Explain when the end of the Cold War took place. Set out the key factors you will be discussing and your main line of argument.

Main body: Don't forget to start with the factor that is given to you in the question – in this case, Gorbachev. Your first paragraph should thus deal with the role of Gorbachev in bringing about the end of the Cold War, both in terms of his relations with the United States and his attitude towards the satellite states, and how these relationships ultimately led to the collapse of the Soviet Union.

You then need to look at other factors:

• the impact of Reagan
• problems within the Soviet Union (you particularly need to emphasize the economic situation here)
• people power

There are plenty of opportunities for you to bring historiography into this essay – include references to the historians and extracts that are mentioned in this chapter. You should also distinguish between the long- and short-term causes.

Conclusion: You need to decide how far the actions of Gorbachev were the most important factors in the ending of the Cold War. Was he key? Or do you come down on the side of the Reagan victory school? Or maybe you take the view that the economic situation would have led to the collapse of the Soviet Union anyway?

Now try planning these questions:

• ***'Economic problems within the USSR and its sphere of influence dictated the changes in policy under Gorbachev.' To what extent do you agree with this statement?***
• ***Examine the role of the American administration and a renewed arms race in the fall of the Soviet Union.***

TOK

After the fall of the USSR and the end of the Cold War, Soviet archives were opened up to historians for the first time. These archives provided new evidence for researchers to better understand the situation in the USSR and the motives, perspectives, and decisions made by its regime during the Cold War.

In pairs, discuss the following question and feed back to the class.

How far does this mean that historians in the 1990s were more able to find the 'truth' about the Soviet Union during the Cold War than their predecessors?

You should attempt to offer examples to support your ideas.

To access websites relevant to this chapter, go to www.pearsonhotlinks. com, search for the book title or ISBN, and click on 'chapter 15'.

16

The impact of Cold War tensions on the United Nations

Key concepts: Significance and consequence

As you read this chapter, consider the following essay question:

- Examine the impact of the rivalry between the USA and the USSR on the working of the United Nations.

Timeline of United Nations and the Cold War

1941	**Aug**	Atlantic Charter agreed by Roosevelt and Churchill
1943	**Nov**	Tehran Conference
1944	**Aug**	Dumbarton Oaks Conference
1945	**Feb**	Yalta Conference
	April	San Francisco Conference
1946	**Feb**	UN's first Secretary General, Trygve Lie, takes office
1948	**April**	Berlin Crisis
1950	**June**	North Korea invades South Korea
	July	UN resolution authorizes Korean force under US 'Unified Command'
	Aug	Soviets return to Security Council
	Nov	'Uniting for Peace' resolution passed by General Assembly
1953	**April**	Dag Hammarskjöld, second UN Secretary General, takes office
	July	Armistice signed in Korea
1956	**July**	Nasser nationalizes Suez Canal
	Oct	Soviets crush Hungarian Uprising
		US draft resolution calls for withdrawal of Israel from Suez
	Nov	United Nations Emergency Force established and sent to Suez
1958	**June**	UN Observation Group sent to Lebanon
	Sept	Death of Hammarskjöld; U Thant of Burma succeeds him
1962	**Oct**	Cuban Missile Crisis
1967	**May**	UNEF withdrawn from Suez
1971	**Oct**	People's Republic of China replaces Taiwan as 'China' in UN
1975	**April**	Civil war breaks out in Lebanon
1978	**March**	Israel invades Lebanon
1979	**Dec**	Soviet invasion of Afghanistan
1982	**June**	Israel re-invades Lebanon
1988	**April**	UN mission to Afghanistan and Pakistan established
1989	**Nov**	Berlin Wall comes down
1990	**March**	UN completes mission in Afghanistan and Pakistan
1992	**Jan**	Boutros Boutros-Ghali of Egypt becomes Secretary General
	March	UN protection force established for the former Yugoslavia
	April	United Nations Operation in Somalia established
1995	**March**	UN withdraws from Somalia
	Nov	Dayton Agreement on Bosnia signed

This timeline reflects the events covered in this chapter and is not a comprehensive catalogue of the UN's involvement in international crises in the second half of the 20th century. Some significant themes are not covered here, such as much of the UN's involvement in the Middle East during the Cold War.

The United Nations was the body set up at the end of the Second World War to replace and improve upon the League of Nations. Its key function was to maintain peace and international security. It would also be the body through which nations would be protected from the aggression and unwanted influence of more powerful nations through the principle of *collective security*.

The United Nations had been planned in the Atlantic Charter of 1941. The subsequent Allied meetings at Tehran (1943) and at Yalta and Potsdam (1945) continued to develop the plans for this new international organization. The Allies wanted to build a safer world and to prevent a world war ever happening again.

The key aims of the new United Nations organization were to:

• maintain international peace and security
• develop friendly relations among nations
• achieve international co-operation in solving problems
• act as the centre for collective action (Article 1 of the United Nations Charter).

So, the first purpose of the United Nations was essentially the same as that of its ill-fated predecessor, the League of Nations: keeping peace. However, the Allies attempted to redress what they saw as the main reasons for the League's failure to maintain peace: that is, the lack of commitment to peacekeeping from member states, particularly in providing military back-up. This problem had been exacerbated by the need to attain a unanimous decision to act on any resolution.

The basic idea of 'collective security', where member states work together to stop aggressor states and potential conflict, was to be the key working principle of the United Nations. The main advocates for the new organization were Roosevelt and Churchill. Indeed, the charter itself was generally an Anglo-American document.

The United Nations system

The Allies wanted to promote the idea of the 'equal rights of men and women and of nations large and small' and to establish the conditions under which 'justice and respect for obligations arising from treaties and other sources of international law can be maintained'. There were six main areas in the United Nations' structure.

The General Assembly was to be a forum for discussion and decision-making for all member states. Each state, no matter how small, was given a vote. However, the Security Council of the United Nations was the most powerful body of the organization. The General Assembly could be invited by the Security Council to make recommendations when it was considering a dispute, but this was not required.

The Security Council was to be a sort of executive body, and would preside over the most important and critical issues, including the use of military intervention to resolve a dispute. Force would only be considered when absolutely necessary. There were

Diagram showing the structure of the United Nations

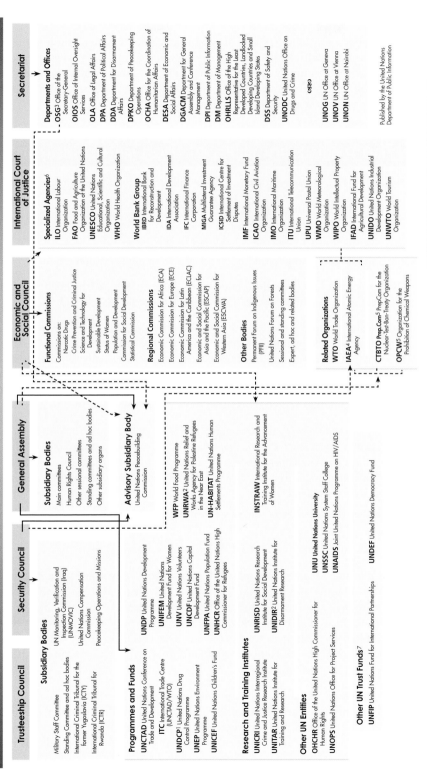

Principal Organs

Trusteeship Council

Security Council

General Assembly

Economic and Social Council

International Court of Justice

Secretariat

Subsidiary Bodies

- Military Staff Committee
- Standing Committee and ad hoc bodies
- International Criminal Tribunal for the former Yugoslavia (ICTY)
- International Criminal Tribunal for Rwanda (ICTR)

Subsidiary Bodies
- UN Monitoring, Verification and Inspection Commission (Iraq) (UNMOVIC)
- United Nations Compensation Commission
- Peacekeeping Operations and Missions

Subsidiary Bodies
- Main committees
- Human Rights Council
- Other sessional committees
- Standing committees and ad hoc bodies
- Other subsidiary organs

Advisory Subsidiary Body
- United Nations Peacebuilding Commission

Functional Commissions
Commissions on:
- Narcotic Drugs
- Crime Prevention and Criminal Justice
- Science and Technology for Development
- Sustainable Development
- Status of Women
- Population and Development
- Commission for Social Development
- Statistical Commission

Specialized Agencies[6]
- ILO International Labour Organization
- FAO Food and Agriculture Organization of the United Nations
- UNESCO United Nations Educational, Scientific and Cultural Organization
- WHO World Health Organization

World Bank Group
- IBRD International Bank for Reconstruction and Development
- IDA International Development Association
- IFC International Finance Corporation
- MIGA Multilateral Investment Guarantee Agency
- ICSID International Centre for Settlement of Investment Disputes

- IMF International Monetary Fund
- ICAO International Civil Aviation Organization
- IMO International Maritime Organization
- ITU International Telecommunication Union
- UPU Universal Postal Union
- WMO World Meteorological Organization
- WIPO World Intellectual Property Organization
- IFAD International Fund for Agricultural Development
- UNIDO United Nations Industrial Development Organization
- UNWTO World Tourism Organization

Departments and Offices
- OSG[3] Office of the Secretary-General
- OIOS Office of Internal Oversight Services
- OLA Office of Legal Affairs
- DPA Department of Political Affairs
- DDA Department for Disarmament Affairs
- DPKO Department of Peacekeeping Operations
- OCHA Office for the Coordination of Humanitarian Affairs
- DESA Department of Economic and Social Affairs
- DGACM Department for General Assembly and Conference Management
- DPI Department of Public Information
- DM Department of Management
- OHRLLS Office of the High Representative for the Least Developed Countries, Landlocked Developing Countries and Small Island Developing States
- DSS Department of Safety and Security
- UNODC United Nations Office on Drugs and Crime

- UNOG UN Office at Geneva
- UNOV UN Office at Vienna
- UNON UN Office at Nairobi

Regional Commissions
- Economic Commission for Africa (ECA)
- Economic Commission for Europe (ECE)
- Economic Commission for Latin America and the Caribbean (ECLAC)
- Economic and Social Commission for Asia and the Pacific (ESCAP)
- Economic and Social Commission for Western Asia (ESCWA)

Other Bodies
- Permanent Forum on Indigenous Issues (PFII)
- United Nations Forum on Forests
- Sessional and standing committees
- Expert, ad hoc and related bodies

Related Organizations
- WTO World Trade Organization
- IAEA[4] International Atomic Energy Agency
- CTBTO Prep.Com[5] Prep.Com for the Nuclear-Test-Ban-Treaty Organization
- OPCW[5] Organization for the Prohibition of Chemical Weapons

Programmes and Funds
- UNCTAD United Nations Conference on Trade and Development
  - ITC International Trade Centre (UNCTAD/WTO)
- UNDCP[1] United Nations Drug Control Programme
- UNEP United Nations Environment Programme
- UNICEF United Nations Children's Fund
- UNDP United Nations Development Programme
  - UNIFEM United Nations Development Fund for Women
  - UNV United Nations Volunteers
  - UNCDF United Nations Capital Development Fund
- UNFPA United Nations Population Fund
- UNHCR Office of the United Nations High Commissioner for Refugees
- WFP World Food Programme
- UNRWA[2] United Nations Relief and Works Agency for Palestine Refugees in the Near East
- UN-HABITAT United Nations Human Settlements Programme

Research and Training Institutes
- UNICRI United Nations Interregional Crime and Justice Research Institute
- UNITAR United Nations Institute for Training and Research
- UNRISD United Nations Research Institute for Social Development
- UNIDIR[2] United Nations Institute for Disarmament Research
- INSTRAW International Research and Training Institute for the Advancement of Women
- UNU United Nations University
- UNSSC United Nations System Staff College
- UNAIDS Joint United Nations Programme on HIV/AIDS

Other UN Entities
- OHCHR Office of the United Nations High Commissioner for Human Rights
- UNOPS United Nations Office for Project Services

Other UN Trust Funds[7]
- UNFIP United Nations Fund for International Partnerships
- UNDEF United Nations Democracy Fund

Published by the United Nations Department of Public Information

NOTES: Solid lines from a Principal Organ indicate a direct reporting relationship; dashes indicate a non-subsidiary relationship.
1 The UN Drug Control Programme is part of the UN Office on Drugs and Crime
2 UNRWA and UNIDIR report only to the GA
3 The United Nations Ethics Office and the United Nations Ombudsman's Office report directly to the Secretary-General
4 IAEA reports to the Security Council and the General Assembly (GA)
5 The CTBTO Prep.Com and OPCW report to the GA
6 Specialized agencies are autonomous organizations working with the UN and each other through the coordinating machinery of the ECOSOC at the intergovernmental level, and through the Chief Executives Board for coordination (CEB) at the inter-secretariat level
7 UNFIP is an autonomous trust fund operating under the leadership of the United Nations Deputy Secretary-General. UNDEF's advisory board recommends funding proposals for approval by the Secretary-General.

initially to be four permanent members of the Security Council – the USA, the UK, the USSR, and China – later rising to five, with the inclusion of France. It was hoped that all other states would be guided by their decisions.

The Soviets were willing to accept apparent Security Council domination by pro-Western states (with Jiang's Taiwan representing China, as the West refused to recognize the legitimacy of Mao Zedong's PRC), as each permanent member had the power of 'veto'. Veto power gave each Security Council permanent member the power to block a decision agreed on by the other four.

The main principles of the United Nations

According to its charter, the UN has the following main functions:

• to be a forum for discussion and decision
• to meet as a syndicate for action
• to employ non-forcible measures to improve the world
• to spread moral values and higher standards in international relations.

However, the ideological differences between the USA and the USSR predictably led to differences in the superpowers' interpretations of the UN's key ideas.

Firstly, both superpowers were concerned over issues of sovereignty. Neither the USA nor the USSR wanted its sovereign rights subordinated to the UN. Their powers of veto in the Security Council meant that they could usually block anything they considered against their country's best interests. But at the same time, this meant that the veto could also prevent them doing what they wanted to do. Therefore, the United Nations could only act when its most powerful members agreed to it.

> *Any restraint shown by the superpowers tended to be self-restraint, induced by the existence of nuclear weapons and the fear of mutual assured destruction … Indeed the UN often became just another Cold War battleground … It was inevitable that the effectiveness and credibility of the organisation would, therefore, decline, since the paralysis of the Security Council meant that it was used less and less.*

Stephen Ryan, *The United Nations and International Politics* (Macmillan 2000) p.49

Three key principles of the UN Charter

The **Collective Security Principle** underpinned most of the key principles of the **UN Charter**. Members were to take 'effective collective measures' to prevent and remove threats to peace and to suppress aggressive acts. Any call to action had to come from the Security Council. However, with the Security Council dominated by the USA and the USSR, both with their powers of veto, it was clear that the Cold War blocs and not an independent United Nations would dominate what was interpreted as a threat to peace or an aggressive act.

The charter did not allow for intervention in 'domestic matters' and this could be viewed as an important omission, as it allowed for the development of spheres of influence in the Cold War. This meant that the tension between the superpowers would have a significant impact on many nations around the world. The respective superpowers asserted that any 'suppression' of groups seen as anti-American or anti-Soviet in their sphere of influence was legitimate. There was also no clear directive for action in self-defence if one member state attacked another.

The **Regional Principle** allowed for the development of regional arrangements or agencies for dealing with threats to peace in a region, as long as they worked in line with UN principles. With Security Council authorization, these could be used to enforce UN resolutions. However, regional groupings were often developed within the superpower blocs.

The **Association Principle** set down that all 'peace-loving states' could be members of the United Nations. This principle, however, led the USA and the USSR into dispute, as they did not agree on which states qualified as genuinely 'peace-loving'. There was opposition to countries perceived as being in the Capitalist or socialist blocs. For example, between 1946 and 1961 the Soviet Union used its veto 96 times to block the memberships of Ceylon, Ireland, Italy, Jordan, and Spain. The USA and its Western allies did likewise over the memberships of Albania, Bulgaria, Hungary, and Romania. In addition, the USA stopped the membership of Vietnam until 1976, and backed the representation of China by Taiwan at the UN until 1971. Thus, from the very outset, the Cold War had a direct impact on the membership of the UN.

With the development of the Cold War in Europe, the early optimism, particularly in the West, for the potential of the United Nations, soon ended. This new international organization was going to be hindered in its work by the bi-polar tension between the United States and the Soviet Union. The balance of power was held by the superpowers in the UN, and its role in the Cold War was to reflect this.

The American perspective and expectations

Indeed, the superpowers had very different expectations of the United Nations. American hopes for the new institution, according to historian DJ Whittaker, 'now strike us as very optimistic, even evangelistic' (*United Nations in the Contemporary World* [Routledge 1997] p.29). The former isolationists had no practical experience as leaders in peacetime. The United States primarily believed that the international collective represented by the UN would support US values. The UN was to promote only moderate and constructive change. Revolutionary and violent change was to be suppressed. The foundation for peace would be built on fostering US-style economic objectives in a global free market.

President Harry S Truman declared to the opening conference of the UN in San Francisco:

> *The powerful nations have a duty to assume responsibility for leadership toward a world of peace … By their own example the strong nations of the world should lead the way to international justice.*

The Soviet perspective and expectations

In contrast, the Soviet delegates set out to use the UN to promote their ideological beliefs, which were both politically and economically opposed to the US model. They saw the United Nations' role as purely to prevent another great war. The Soviets aimed to encourage revolutionary change, but, perhaps paradoxically, they also wished to retain the balance of power. Economic and social change could not be based on a global free market, but on freeing people from exploitation. The Soviets were suspicious of the UN Charter and of the International Court of Justice, as some key clauses appeared to support Capitalist principles. Ultimately, the USSR viewed the UN's role as far more marginal than expressed in the initial hopes of the United States.

The UN and nuclear weapons: the Baruch Plan

At the onset of the UN, it was presumed that it would be responsible for atomic weapons control. In June 1946, the United States representative to the UNAEC, Bernard Baruch, presented the **Baruch Plan**. This said that the United States would agree to destroy its weapons on the one the condition that the UN would control all atomic development and that this would not be subject to veto in the Security Council. The Baruch Plan was passed by the UNAEC, but not agreed to by the Soviet Union, which abstained on the proposal in the Security Council. Although the powers continued to discuss this until 1948, agreement had broken down by 1947, and the United Nations was never used for this purpose.

Activity 2

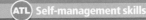

1. In pairs, draw up a bullet-point list of the key differences between the USA and the USSR in their interpretations of the UN Charter and the role of the United Nations.

The impact of the emergence of Cold War tension on the UN

The post-war 1940s saw the development of the Cold War between the USSR and the USA. It soon became evident that the Cold War would have a defining impact on the role and operation of the United Nations. As Senator William Fulbright commented about the first years of the UN, it was 'a history of retreat from false hopes and of adjustment to the reality of a divided world'.

Inevitably, the potential of the United Nations as a viable world force for peacemaking and peacekeeping was made very difficult, if not impossible, by the fact that at its core were two superpowers working against one another. It was unlikely that there would be much co-operation between the Americans and the Soviets, and this would have a dramatic impact on the ability of the UN to pursue its charter meaningfully. Given the different views of the UN held by the USA and the USSR, it is not surprising that, as Gaddis writes, 'the United Nations functioned more as a debating society than as an organization capable of defining principles and holding states accountable to them' (John Lewis Gaddis, *The Cold War* (Penguin 2005), p.159).

The United Nations took a back seat in the developments in Europe during 1945–1949. There was no 'collective' response to the Soviet occupation of Eastern Europe. The UN did not interfere when Truman declared his 'doctrine' for Greece and Turkey. There was no UN alternative to the economic aid offered by the Americans to rebuild Western Europe and bolster their political influence there. The USSR's intervention in Czechoslovakia in 1948 received mere condemnation from the UN. When the first real crisis of the Cold War developed in Germany, and the superpowers were on the brink of war over Berlin in the blockade of 1948–1949, the UN was powerless to intervene. As DJ Whittaker suggests, by the end of the 1940s it was clear that 'Europe's collective security depended then on a pull-back from the brink by major contestants without any prospect of UN intervention' (*United Nations in the Contemporary World* [Routledge 1997] p.19).

This also meant that the role of the UN in ensuring the security and independence of nations around the world was hampered by superpower rivalry. In addition, it seemed unlikely that the UN could prevent superpower influence over – and possible direct intervention in – countries around the world.

Therefore, as the Cold War developed in the late 1940s, there was a very real danger that the UN would be at best marginalized or, at worst, become irrelevant as all major disputes increasingly became the focus of superpower hostility. The United Nations found that the only way of avoiding irrelevance was in pursuing the 'mediation principle'; in other words, 'peacekeeping' would give the United Nations a role in the Cold War.

'Bicycle Built for Two' by John Collins, published in the Montreal Gazette in 1947.

1. What is the message of the cartoonist
2. What does Gaddis mean when he says that the UN functioned more as a 'debating society'? (see page 232)

The UN and the global Cold War: the 1950s

By 1950, the Cold War was poised to take on global dimensions. As hostility increased between the superpowers, the apparent viability of the UN decreased further; international relations were increasingly determined by individual countries aligning with one or other of the superpowers. As professor of politics Norrie Macqueen suggests, the 'idea of [an] independent "disinterested" global body seemed … unworkable'.

In April 1950, US NSC-68 (see chapter 5) stated that the USSR was a 'slave society' and claimed that the spread of Communism must be resisted by force. The rise of McCarthyism led to accusations in the United States that Americans working for the

UN were in fact working for the Soviets – spying against the USA. Nevertheless, the United States had the majority of support in the UN at this time, and many saw the UN's role as a tool of American foreign policy. Indeed, this attitude to the UN was made clear by an aide of Truman's in 1948, who wrote in a memo: 'The United Nations is a God-given vehicle through which the United States can build up a community of powers … to resist Soviet aggression and maintain our historic interests.'

The Soviets also saw the UN as being turned into a tool of the Western Capitalists, a key example of which was the American refusal in 1949 to recognize Mao's new People's Republic as the legitimate Chinese government. The USSR was boycotting the United Nations as a result of this when the Korean War broke out in 1950.

Activity 4 — ATL Thinking skills

'Tank Trap' by John Collins, 1950.

1. What is the message of the cartoonist?
2. Does the cartoonist support the idea that the UN was a 'tool of American foreign policy'?

The impact of Cold War tensions on the UN's first decade

There were notable achievements of the UN in the early years of the Cold War, such as the Declaration of Human Rights (1948) and the Convention on Genocide (1948). However, it was limited by the Cold War in its impact on international crises.

The American-led mission in Korea had ultimately broadened the conflict into a war with China. It had also gone beyond the UN's principal mandate (see chapter 5). The success of the independent UN 'peacekeeping' in Suez was limited, as it was only possible because both superpowers had backed the campaign (see chapter 18 for events in the Suez crisis).

The UN had failed to act during the Soviet invasion of Hungary. It also failed to act against American interference in the internal affairs of sovereign states in the 1950s. Using covert operations, the USA was involved in the overthrow of the Iranian government in 1953, and the coup in Guatemala in 1954.

The UN and the Cold War: the 1960s

In the 1960s, African states began to emerge from colonial domination. Many African nationalist movements became embroiled in the ideological battle between the East and the West. These former colonies often needed support in setting up their new independent administrations and infrastructures, and were economically vulnerable after the withdrawal of their European colonizers. The Congo was one such country, but the involvement of the UN in the Congo highlighted the dangers of the UN becoming embroiled in a conflict that also became a Cold War battleground.

Throughout the 1960s, the United Nations continued to engage in 'peacekeeping' missions around the world. The UN's work was generally in areas the superpowers did not find strategically important. It was clear that the UN could only function with authority when the interests of the USA and the USSR were not threatened.

When the USA attempted to force regime change in Cuba in 1961, with the invasion of the Bay of Pigs (see chapter 9), the UN did not get involved. As had been the case with Soviet aggression in Eastern Europe, the UN avoided becoming engaged in the superpowers' spheres of influence. However, because the Cold War had gone 'global', this philosophy extended to any country or region where the superpowers had identified interests.

Activity 5  Thinking skills

> [during the Cuban Missile Crisis] *the great power tussles of the Cold War were waged in a very new kind of arena, in which rhetoric and political rationalizations of the great powers could be tested and judged by an increasingly informed and concerned audience. First there was the presence of the ever-expanding United Nations, a court of world opinion which both US and Soviet Union took seriously enough to invest heavy diplomatic and financial resources. Second, there was television.*

Martin Walker, *The Cold War* (Vintage 1994) p.161

1. Martin Walker suggests that the UN's importance in the 1960s during the Cold War was as a 'court of world opinion'. Explain what he means.
2. What is Walker implying about the relevance of the UN when he compares it to 'television'?

TOK

In small groups discuss the impact of the Cold War on the UN. Try to develop lines of argument that a) hold the USSR responsible for the UN's limitations, b) hold the USA responsible for the UN's limitations, and c) hold a neutral position on responsibility. Consider whether it is possible to write a historical account that is free from bias.

The UN and détente, 1968–1979

The emergence of the period of détente meant a relaxation of tension between the superpowers. Some of the ways in which détente was brought about – fear of mutually assured destruction, for example – meant that both the USA and the USSR were more ready to look for agreement between each other when conflicts arose rather than inciting an escalation of tension. Therefore, during détente, the USA and USSR were more ready to work with the UN and its idea of 'peacekeeping'.

In addition, by the late 1960s not only had relations between the superpowers changed, but the UN had too. The balance of power shifted from Western domination to a majority of newly independent and/or 'non-aligned' states. By the end of the 1960s, the Americans no longer could be confident of having things their own way in the General Assembly. The Soviets had always been suspicious of Western influence in the UN, and were now more comfortable with the new balance of power.

It could be because of these changes that during this period UN forces had a number of limited successes. The UN was involved in achieving a ceasefire in Kashmir when fighting broke out in 1965 between India and Pakistan, and again in Cyprus when it was invaded by Turkish forces in 1974.

However, as had been the case in the Hungarian Uprising a decade before, the UN proved impotent in the face of superpower aggression. Soviet forces invaded Czechoslovakia in 1968. The USSR had sent forces in to crush what it perceived to be a move away from Soviet control by the Czech leadership (see chapter 13). Once again, the Security Council had attempted to pass a resolution condemning this action, but this was, of course, vetoed by the USSR. The Soviets claimed to the UN that the Czechs had requested their assistance – the Czechs denied this. The UN was powerless to stop the Soviet Union.

The UN was again powerless when the United States attempted to force regime change in Chile. In October 1970, the democratically elected Marxist government of Salvador Allende took office. The CIA had been involved in covert attempts to undermine Allende in the election campaign, but he had still been elected. President Nixon then authorized the CIA to 'unseat him'. For the next three years the CIA attempted to destabilize the Allende government. Finally, in September 1973, a military coup successfully took control in Chile. Salvador Allende was dead, possibly by suicide. The Chilean government was under the leadership of an anti-Communist General, Augusto Pinochet. The UN had not responded.

The UN and the Second Cold War

In the 1980s, when the USA and the USSR resumed the rhetoric and hostility of the pre-détente period of the Cold War, the UN's dependence on the superpowers was again revealed. Unable to reach agreement on responses to crises in the Security Council, peacekeeping missions ended.

> In the 1950s and 1960s peacekeeping had provided the UN with a means of sealing off superpower involvement in local conflicts peripheral to their main interests. In the 1970s, when cold war gave way to détente, it had offered the superpowers themselves a tool for the management of relationships with troublesome clients. Now, in the 1980s, with bi-polar competition sharpened once again and the Second Cold War underway, no third phase of UN peacekeeping emerged to meet the new situation.

Norrie Macqueen, *The United Nations Since 1945: Peacekeeping and the Cold War* (Longman 1999) p. 66

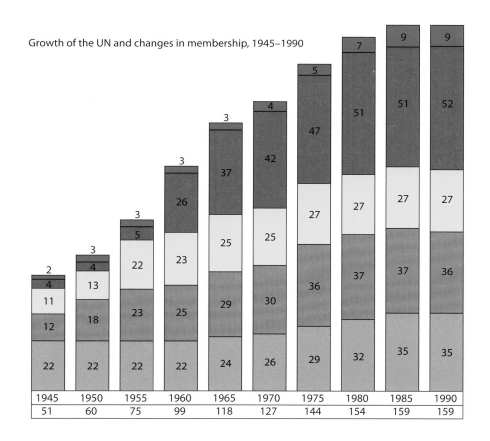

Growth of the UN and changes in membership, 1945–1990

Key
- Oceania and Indonesia
- African States
- European States
- Asian and Middle Eastern States
- American and Caribbean States

1945	1950	1955	1960	1965	1970	1975	1980	1985	1990
51	60	75	99	118	127	144	154	159	159

Graph showing growth and changes in UN membership since 1945. The bottom of each column shows the year and total number of member countries.

It could be argued that the UN's key function of responding to potential conflict situations was only possible when the Cold War was not played out in the Security Council. This meant that the UN's key function of protecting smaller nations from the aggression of bigger nations was significantly limited. Where the superpowers' interests were at stake, or if the superpowers wanted to expand their spheres of influence, the UN was rendered impotent.

The UN and the end of the Cold War

Given the ineffectiveness and relevance of the United Nations during the Cold War, it is understandable that many saw that the UN would be able to play a much more constructive role in the new world order post 1990. The UN would no longer be held to ransom by the opposing forces of the East and West, crippling its ability to respond to crisis; genuine 'collective security' seemed a real possibility.

Indeed, the UN began to launch new peacekeeping missions on an unprecedented scale. More missions were launched in the decade following 1988 than in the three decades following the end of World War Two. However, the end of the Cold War's dominance did not mean the end of superpower influence on the UN. It soon transpired that the post-Cold War world was dominated by self-interested states, disinclined to involve themselves in any collective action that was not directly in line with their own foreign policy objectives.

Activity 6

Source A

The really serious problem, which had been brewing since the end of the Cold War and the emergence of the USA as sole superpower, was about the future relationship between the UN and the USA. Tension began to mount as soon as the Bush administration took office in 2001: within its first year the new government rejected the 1972 Anti-Ballistic Missile treaty, the 1997 Kyoto Protocol … Tensions reached a climax in March 2003, when the US government, aided and abetted by UK, decided to attack Iraq … The challenge for the UN in the coming years is how best to harness and make use of the power and influence of the USA instead of being impeded or stampeded by it.

Norman Lowe, *Mastering Modern World History* (Palgrave 2005) p.189

Source B

A President can't subordinate his decision making to a multilateral body. He can't sacrifice one ounce of our sovereignty to any organization.

Statement by Vice President George HW Bush, August 1988

1. What key issues does Norman Lowe highlight in Source A as future problems for the post-Cold War United Nations?
2. What is Vice President George Bush's view of the UN in Source B?

 This quotation is from a speech made by Mikhail Gorbachev to the United Nations on 7 December 1988.

We are entering an era in which progress will be based on the common interests of the whole of humankind. The realization of this fact demands that the common values of humanity must be the determining priority in international politics … This new stage requires the freeing of international relations from ideology.

What, if any, are the 'common interests of the whole of humankind'? Can we learn lessons from history regarding what would be in the interests of 'the whole of humankind'?

The UN and the Cold War: Conclusion

In the 1950s, the view of the Soviet Union towards the UN was that the organization was virtually another Western alliance system. The 'Uniting for Peace' resolution perpetuated this perception, as the balance of power in the General Assembly was in the United States' favour. The decolonization movements of the 1960s, and the emergence of newly independent states in Africa and Asia, shifted the balance of power in the UN and gave the Soviet Union renewed interest in the potential of the organization.

However, ultimately, the impact of the Cold War on the role of the United Nations was more significant than the impact the UN had on the development and course of the Cold War. There were times when states were able to stand up to the dominance of the superpowers – for example, the Non-Alignment Movement – but even this did not really empower the UN as an independent organization.

The UN's success was dependent on the support of the superpowers, or, in certain cases, their indifference. Often the UN had little choice but to remain 'passive' in the face of Soviet or US aggression. In addition, when the UN did get involved in 'peacekeeping' operations, this often had a negative impact on relations between the USA and the USSR. Peacekeeping missions often aggravated the tensions between the Soviets and the Americans.

There was a generally accepted view that Cold War tensions had held the UN hostage and frustrated its ability to function effectively. However, this perception may have been an exaggeration, as during the post-Cold War era the UN has had similar problems in controlling the domination of the USA, and has shown itself limited in achieving collective security through military action. Perhaps the Cold War was a 'smoke screen' and the fundamental weakness of the United Nations is, and always was, the unwillingness of states to hand over some degree of sovereignty to an international organization.

Activity 7

 Thinking and social skills

1. Discuss whether the limitations of the UN due to Cold War tension left nations vulnerable to superpowers' influence and intervention.

 How effective has the UN been in the post-Cold War world? To help you answer this, consider what international conflicts are currently taking place. What is the role of the UN in these conflicts? Has the end of a bi-polar world allowed the UN to be more effective?

 To access websites relevant to this chapter, go to www.pearsonhotlinks. com, search for the book title or ISBN, and click on 'chapter 16'.

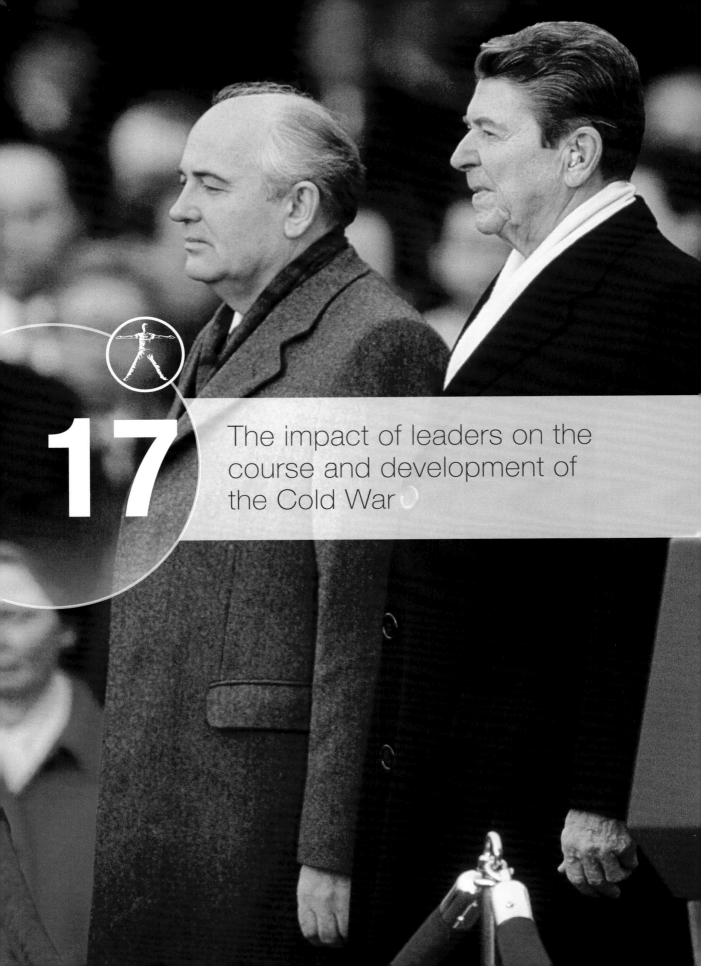

17

The impact of leaders on the
course and development of
the Cold War

Key concepts: Change, continuity, and significance

As you read this chapter, consider the following essay question:

- Compare and contrast the role of two leaders from different regions in the course and development of the Cold War.

In this chapter we will be considering the roles of leaders from different regions in the course and development of the Cold War. For most of these case studies you will need to review material from other sections and chapters in the book so that you can engage in the activities.

The impact of leaders on the course and development of the Cold War: Truman and Stalin

> Roosevelt believed that Russians would come and bow down to America and beg, since Russia is a poor country, without industry, without bread. But we looked at it differently. For the people were ready for sacrifice and struggle.

Former Soviet Foreign Minister Vyacheslav Molotov, June 1976

Activity 1

> **ATL** Thinking skills

Source A

> So-called revisionist historians were writing that President Franklin D Roosevelt's subtle treatment of the Soviet Union had been reversed by his successor, Harry S Truman, who saw foreign affairs as a checker game instead of the chess game it really is; that the United States under Truman's direction had tried to oust the Soviet Union from Eastern Europe, giving little or no consideration to Russia's security needs in an area close to its borders; that the Americans had dropped two atomic bombs on the Japanese in order to alert the Russians to US power; that the government had striven to keep the Russians aware of the Americans' monopoly of atomic power and, largely for such a purpose, advanced a system of international control of atomic weapons – the Baruch Plan – that was almost bound to fail. Meanwhile, the United States government had used every economic device at hand, such as cutting off lend-lease to the USSR, reneging on the reparations agreements concluded at the end of the war, and refusing to consider seriously the Russians' pressing need for a postwar loan. Then, early in 1946, the Americans had seized upon an admitted Soviet reluctance to get out of northern Iran and, in a confrontation at the United Nations, virtually forced the Russians out. The next year, 1947, had marked a rapid increase in American–Russian antagonism, for President Truman intervened in the Greek civil war with the Truman Doctrine and in order to gain support scared hell out of the country, to use a phrase attributed to Sen. Arthur H Vandenberg. (Somewhat later, beginning in 1950, the administration would get what it deserved for this tactic, at the hands of a senator who took a free ride on the anticommunist bandwagon.) The Truman Doctrine inspired the administration to sponsor the Marshall Plan, a program worthy in itself but which had the unfortunate effect of dividing Europe; the president, the revisionists believed, probably had this divisive effect in mind, for in his memoirs he described the Truman Doctrine and Marshall Plan as being two halves of the same walnut. All the while, through a series of moves, the administration was creating a new state in Europe, West Germany, for the purpose of enlisting German industry and eventually a German army to protect the free world against world communism.

Robert H Ferrell, *Harry S Truman and the Cold War Revisionists* (University of Missouri Press 2006) p.2

In pairs, with reference to their origin, purpose and content, assess the values and limitations of Sources A and B for historians studying the role of specific leaders in the breakdown of the Grand Alliance. Take note of the content of the sources: where can you see emotion in their accounts? How do historians assess the reliability of their sources? Are their methods similar to the process you have just completed?

TOK

Source B

❝ *Even Old Bolsheviks … began to talk in the language of imperialist expansion, planning to create Soviet spheres of influence and to gain access to strategic sea routes. In January 1944, Maisky [Soviet ambassador to London] wrote to Stalin and Molotov, commissar for foreign affairs, that the USSR must position itself in such a way after the war as to make it 'unthinkable' for any combination of states in Europe and Asia to pose a challenge to Soviet security. Maisky suggested annexation of Southern Sakhalin and Kurile Islands from Japan. He also proposed that the USSR should have 'a sufficient number of military, air, and naval bases' in Finland and Rumania [Romania], as well as strategic access routes to the Persian Gulf via Iran. In November 1944, Litvinov sent a memo to Stalin and Molotov that the postwar Soviet sphere of influence in Europe (without specifying the nature of that 'influence') should include Finland, Sweden, Poland, Hungary, Czechoslovakia, Rumania, 'the Slav counties of the Balkan peninsula, and Turkey as well.' In June and July 1945, Litvinov argued that the USSR should penetrate into such traditional zones of British influence as the zone of the Suez Canal, Syria, Libya, and Palestine.*

The former general secretary of the Comintern, now the head of the new party's department for international information, Georgy Dimitrov, regarded the Red Army as a more important tool of history than are revolutionary movements. In late July 1945, when Stalin and Molotov negotiated with Western leaders in Potsdam, Dimitrov and his deputy, Alexander Panyushkin, wrote to them: 'The countries of the Middle East acquire increasing importance in the current international situation and urgently need our intense attention. We should actively study the situation in those countries and take certain measures in the interests of our state.'

Vladislav M Zubok, A Failed Empire: The Soviet Union in the Cold War from Stalin to Gorbachev (University of North Carolina Press 2007) p.8

1. Read Source A and discuss what evidence there is to support the revisionist view that President Truman was responsible for the breakdown of the Grand Alliance.

2. Read Source B. What does this suggest about the motives behind Stalin's actions in the post-war period?

3. Can you find evidence in chapters 2 and 3 to support the idea that Stalin pursued the objectives outlined in Source B?

Activity 2

ATL Self-management and thinking skills

Essay writing

Consider the following essay question:

> **Compare and contrast the roles of Stalin and Truman in the development of the origins of the Cold War.**

In a compare-and-contrast essay, it is important not to just write about each leader separately. You need to think about areas of comparison and areas of contrast, and focus on these to guide your structure.

Look at the ideas for a plan below. What extra detail could you add as evidence to support each point? How would you split up each section into paragraphs? How and where could you use quotes from the historians in chapters 2 and 3, and from the sources above?

Write a full introduction and full conclusion.

Comparisons

- Both Stalin and Truman pursued ideological confrontation: for example, the Truman Doctrine and the 'two camps' doctrine.
- Both created spheres of influence in Europe.
- Both intervened in Asia to establish spheres of influence.
- Both used their military capability to confront the other.
- Both focused on Germany as a key strategic territory.
- Both broke the agreements made at Yalta and Potsdam.

- Both engaged in an arms race.
- Both pursued 'containment' of the other in Europe and other regions.

Contrasts

- Truman used the economic strength of the USA to gain political influence in Western Europe; Stalin used conventional military strength to gain political control in Eastern Europe.
- Truman relied initially on the ability to threaten the use of nuclear weapons to contain the Soviets whereas Stalin relied on conventional forces.
- Truman responded to Western Europeans, particularly the British, asking for economic assistance (that is, Marshall Aid), whereas the Eastern Europeans were forced by Stalin to join COMECON.
- Truman broke agreements on Germany economically speaking, with the introduction of a new currency into the western sectors, whereas Stalin broke the political agreements.

The impact of leaders on the course and development of the Cold War: Khrushchev and Mao

Mao and Khrushchev meeting in Beijing in 1958.

You will need to review the material on Sino-Soviet relations in chapter 10, and the material on Sino-Soviet relations in chapter 11, before considering the following comparative activities.

Activity 3

Look at the cartoon below and answer the questions that follow.

'The Mantle of Lenin' by John Collins, 1963.

1. What is the message of the cartoonist?
2. Using your own knowledge, explain in what ways and for what reasons the two Communist powers' leaders are 'moving in different directions'.

Activity 4

Source A

> *Neither economic nor political reforms in the Soviet Union would have been possible without the reduction of military spending to a necessary minimum. And this in turn demanded the establishment of a new modus vivendi [way of working] in relations with the United States and other Western countries. Khrushchev and his advisers formulated this task and attempted to accomplish it. It is impossible to agree with domestic and foreign scholars who believe that Khrushchev's foreign policy was a chain of utter improvisations and adventures. From a historical perspective the reduction of tensions that he began helped the world to hold out without any major cataclysms up until the mid-1980s ... Just as Khrushchev tried to combine a domestic reform with a relaxation of international tension, the formula for Gorbachev reforms was 'perestroika plus new thinking.' The second stage of Russian reform also put an end to the Cold War.*

William Taubman, Sergei Khrushchev and Abbott Gleason (eds), *Nikita Khrushchev* **(Yale University Press 2000) p.317**

Source B [on Mao's rapprochement with the USA]

❝ It weakened the Soviet international position, making the USSR more anxious to reach agreement with the United States on issues already under negotiation. China tied down a million Russian troops on the Manchurian–Siberian border, thereby correspondingly reducing Soviet military pressure elsewhere. Thus, in the new triangular relationship, the United States distinctly held the balance.

Immanuel Hsu, *The Rise of Modern China*, 5th ed. (OUP 1995) p.800

1. What does Source A suggest about the significance of Khrushchev's policies on the Cold War?
2. What does Source B suggest about the impact of the rapprochement between Mao and the USA on the Cold War?

Activity 5  **ATL** **Communication skills**

Essay writing

In pairs or small groups, discuss and then plan the following essay question:

> **Compare and contrast the roles of Khrushchev and Mao in the course and development of the Cold War.**

You can use the following suggestions as a basis for your essay plan and add other themes, supporting details, and evidence.

Comparisons

- Both increased tension and caused periods of 'crisis' with the USA.
- Both attempted to lead the Communist world.
- Both leaders caused divisions between Communist states.
- Both leaders ultimately attempted to improve relations with the USA: Khrushchev with Eisenhower; Kennedy and the summit meetings, visits and treaties; and Mao with the rapprochement with the USA under Nixon, and 'ping-pong diplomacy'.
- Both leaders developed their technological capability: Khrushchev stepped up the arms race in an attempt to establish parity with the USA; Mao developed his own nuclear weapons in the 1960s, enabling China to position itself as another superpower the USA had to take seriously.

Contrasts

- Khrushchev fostered a move away from the ideological position of conflict with the West towards 'peaceful co-existence', which Mao condemned as 'revisionist'.
- Khrushchev was weary of nuclear confrontation and moved back from the 'brink' during the Berlin Crisis and the Cuban Missile Crisis, whereas Mao appeared willing to provoke a nuclear strike during the Taiwan crises and pressured the Soviets to support him with their weapons systems.
- The USSR remained focused on supporting revolutions based on Soviet interpretations of Marxism, whereas Mao supported revolutions based on subsequent 'Maoist' interpretations, which emphasized the revolutionary role of the peasant: for example, in their respective support for regimes in Vietnam and Cambodia.
- Khrushchev used the UN to challenge the USA and influence other nations whereas Mao joined the Non-Aligned Movement in an attempt to maintain China's independence and gain international influence.

What conclusions can you draw about the roles of Khrushchev and Mao in the course and development of the Cold War?

The impact of leaders on the course and development of the Cold War: Brezhnev, Brandt, and Nixon

Brezhnev, Brandt, and Nixon all played key roles in the period we call 'détente'; each contributed to the easing of tensions during this period and to substantial international agreements. However, the actions of Brezhnev in particular helped to cause the end of détente.

Activity 6

ATL Thinking skills

Source A

❝ The task at hand, as the Nixon administration saw it, was to get beyond Vietnam without suffering geopolitical losses, and to establish a policy toward the communists that was geared to the relevant battlefields. Nixon saw détente as a tactic in a long-run geopolitical struggle; his liberal critics treated it as an end in itself while conservatives and neoconservatives rejected the geopolitical approach as so much historical pessimism, preferring instead a policy of unremitting ideological confrontation.

Henry Kissinger, *Diplomacy* (New York 1994) pp.744–745

Source B

❝ If Willy Brandt was willing to risk a breach with the conventions of West German politics, it was in large measure because of his experience as Mayor of West Berlin. Indeed, it is no coincidence that some of the most enthusiastic proponents of Ostpolitik in all its forms were former mayors of Berlin … To these men it was obvious that the Western Allies would take no untoward risks to overcome the division of Europe – an interpretation confirmed by the West's passive acceptance of the Warsaw Pact invasion of Czechoslovakia. If West Germans wanted to break the central European stalemate, they would have to do it themselves, by dealing directly with the authorities in the East.

Tony Judt, *Postwar: A History of Europe Since 1945* (Vintage 2005) p.497

Source C

❝ For a while, it could be said, two parallel tracks of Soviet foreign policy were being formed, roughly at the same time. The one that had central importance for the leadership was the policy of détente towards the United States and Western Europe, mostly carried out by the Foreign Ministry. But at the same time political advisers who generally supported the détente process put down the foundations for a more activist approach to the Third World. The Soviet system of decision making … meant that it took a very long time before the Politburo realized that one policy could endanger the other. For most leaders, including Leonid Brezhnev himself, the two were both correct responses to a changing world, based on the best of Soviet political theory … And if the Soviet Union were to make use of its power in the future to support other friends in the Third World, it would still be a 'little interventionist' compared to the United States, as Brezhnev saw it.

Odd Arne Westad, *The Global Cold War* (CUP 2005) p.206

1. Identify what each source says about the aims of each leader during the 1970s.
2. Using your knowledge of this period from chapter 12, what impact did these aims have on the direction of the Cold War during the 1970s?
3. How successful was each of these leaders in achieving these aims?

Activity 7

ATL Social skills

Essay writing

In pairs, or small groups discuss the following question:

> **Compare and contrast the roles of Nixon and Brezhnev in the course and development of the Cold War between 1968 and 1974.**

You can use the following suggestions as a basis for your essay plan and add other themes, supporting details, and evidence. How did each of these points impact on the development of the Cold War?

Comparisons

- Both men worked towards an improvement in relations at the end of the 1960s.
- Both men were receptive to the idea of arms control talks and reducing the danger of nuclear war.

In small groups discuss the role of leaders of nations in global developments today. Try to consider the role of a leader from your own region and the roles of leaders from other regions. How significant are individual leaders in fostering a) international co-operation, and b) international confrontation and crisis?

- Both men were prepared to agree to the treaties concerning Germany and human rights (Helsinki).
- Both men continued to work in what they saw as the best interest of their own countries, regardless of détente.
- Both continued to support their 'client' states even at the cost of escalating tension, as was seen in the Yom Kippur War.

Contrasts

- Nixon also worked to create détente with China whereas Brezhnev remained hostile to China.
- Brezhnev continued to support revolution in the 'Third World', which would ultimately help turn the USA against détente and thus undermine it.

What are your conclusions regarding the impact of each man? Who do you think had the greatest impact on events during this period?

Now try to answer this essay question:

> *Compare and contrast the roles of Brandt and Nixon in the course and development of the Cold War between 1968 and 1974.*

The impact of leaders on the course and development of the Cold war: Reagan and Gorbachev

Ronald Reagan and Mikhail Gorbachev signing the INF (Intermediate-Range Nuclear Forces) Treaty in 1987.

As you will have read in chapter 15, both of these men have been credited with having a major impact on the development of the Cold War, and helping to bring about the end of the Cold War, in different ways.

1. Historians differ in their interpretation as to the role of each man, as you can see from the following sources. Read the sources and then in pairs discuss the conclusions reached in each source concerning the roles of Reagan and Gorbachev.

Source A

> *Reagan's armament program, accompanied as it was by a boom in the US economy, had a demoralising effect on the Soviet elite [who saw that] the attempt to out-arm and out-perform the West was hopeless. A new way had to be found, and its direction lay in internal reform of a fundamental nature.*

Paul Johnson, 'Europe and the Reagan Years', in *Foreign Affairs* **68 (1988)**

Source B

> *Mikhail Gorbachev broke the Cold War's ideological straitjacket that had prevented Moscow and Washington from resolving their differences. Though politically weakened, Gorbachev conceded nothing to US military superiority. Never did he negotiate from a position of weakness. In doing so, he faced greater political, even physical risks. After considering all of this, it is difficult to avoid the conclusion that without Gorbachev, the end of the Cold War could have played out very differently.*

Norman A Graebner, Richard Dean Burns, and Joseph M Siracusa in *Reagan, Bush Gorbachev: Revisiting the End of the Cold War* **(Greenwood 2008) p.146**

Here is a summary of the key points that we have looked at for each of these leaders, regarding their impact on bringing the Cold War to an end.

Gorbachev

- He pursued a foreign policy based on co-operation rather than confrontation.
- He believed that negotiations should take place to reduce nuclear weapons and end the arms race. His nuclear policy was now 'reasonable sufficiency'.
- His actions towards the West were conciliatory and reassuring: for example, withdrawing Soviet troops from Afghanistan, agreeing to several face-to-face meetings, and ultimately signing the INF Treaty.
- His actions within the Soviet Union inadvertently brought about the end of the Cold War; his economic reforms caused the collapse of the Soviet Union from within.
- He abandoned the Brezhnev Doctrine and did not use force against the protests in the USSR's satellite states; this allowed the peaceful collapse of the satellite empire.

Reagan

- His military spending of the early 1980s forced the Soviets to compete with the USA; due to the economic weakness of the USSR, they could not keep up, and this was a factor that forced Gorbachev to seek both internal economic reform and negotiation.
- Reagan's policy of SDI undermined the concept of MAD and left the USSR vulnerable. This again forced the USSR to the negotiating table.
- Reagan's hardline approach to Soviet actions in Afghanistan made it difficult for the USSR to continue this war.
- Reagan also exposed the weaknesses of détente, which was a policy that favoured the USSR.
- He was committed to **anti-nuclearism**.
- In negotiating with Gorbachev, he proved to be a good negotiator who was also prepared to reverse his views on the 'evils' of Communism.

Activity 9

 ATL Thinking skills

Consider how the information in this section could be used in answering the following question:

> **Compare and contrast the roles of Reagan and Gorbachev in the course and development of the Cold War.**

Comparisons

- Both men saw the dangers of nuclear weapons – they even discussed the zero option of getting rid of nuclear weapons altogether.
- Both men worked together in the various summits to come to an agreement on nuclear weapons.
- Both were prepared to reverse their previous positions in order make compromises.

Contrasts

- Reagan started out with a very hardline position against the Soviet Union and by increasing spending on weapons; Gorbachev started out by being conciliatory.
- Gorbachev's actions were determined more by events within the USSR; he needed to reduce spending on weapons. Reagan on the other hand was prepared to keep up spending on the military if necessary.
- Gorbachev's actions had a larger impact as they led to the collapse of the USSR and thus, ultimately, the end of the Cold War (though some historians would argue that this was still determined by Reagan's actions).

Activity 10

ATL Communicaton and social skills

1. In pairs or small groups, discuss whether Reagan or Gorbachev had the most impact in bringing the Cold War to an end.

In the next chapter, you will have the chance to compare the impact of Nasser and Castro.

 TOK

With reference to your study of the Cold War, discuss as a class how far you agree with the following assertion:

'History is shaped by the actions of individuals.'

To access websites relevant to this chapter, go to www.pearsonhotlinks.com, search for the book title or ISBN, and click on 'chapter 17'.

18

The impact of Cold War tensions on nations

Key concepts: Consequence and significance

As you read this chapter, consider the following essay questions:

- Examine the impact of Cold War tensions on two nations.
- Compare and contrast the impact of Cold War tensions on two countries, each chosen from a different region.

The Cold War dominated international politics for nearly 50 years. As you have read, the impact that it had on the lives of governments and citizens within the Soviet Union and the US was profound. However, the tensions of this bi-polar world also affected the domestic and foreign policies of many other countries.

In this chapter we will consider the impact of Cold War tensions on Cuba, Egypt, West Germany, and China. You will need to have studied at least two case studies, each from a different region, to be able to answer questions on this topic.

The impact of Cold War tensions on individual states: Cuba

> Over 600 plans to assassinate Castro were devised. Nearly 3500 Cubans have died from terrorist acts, and more than 2000 are permanently disabled. As an ex-CIA agent has said, 'no country has suffered terrorism as long and consistently as Cuba'.

S Balfour, *Castro* (Longman 1990) p.90

Before you read the following on the impact of Cold War tensions on Cuba, you should review chapter 9 and consider the following questions:

1. Why did the USA oppose Castro's revolution in Cuba?
2. What were the results of the failed Bay of Pigs invasion?
3. To what extent were the policies and actions of the USA responsible for Castro's relationship with the USSR?
4. Explain the impact of the Cuban Missile Crisis on a) the USA, b) the USSR, and c) Cuba.
5. Assess the impact of Cold War tensions on Cuba up to 1963.

As you have read, Cuba was embroiled in Cold War politics from the moment that Castro took power and started carrying out social and economic reforms. The continued hostility towards Cuba throughout the Cold War kept Castro allied with the USSR, though the events of the Cuban Missile Crisis meant that he also followed a more independent path and attempted to carry out his own foreign policy. The continued actions of the USA in attempting to get rid of Castro also impacted Cuba domestically as it fostered a sense of 'siege' and led to state censorship and an intolerance of any political dissent within Cuba.

Impact of Cold War tensions on the nature and direction of Cuba's revolution

Castro gave a clear idea of his plans for Cuba when, after a failed attack against Batista in July 1952, he was arrested. At his trial he gave a now-famous speech in which he claimed 'history would absolve' him, and set out the **five revolutionary laws** that would be his manifesto:

Fidel Castro in 1959.

- return power to the people
- give land rights for those holding or squatting on smaller plots
- allow workers to have a 30 per cent share of profits
- allow sugar plantation workers to have a 55 per cent share of profits
- bring an end to corruption.

He also promised pensions, hospitals, public education, nationalization of utilities, and rent controls. When he finally entered Havana in 1959, following the defeat of Batista after a guerrilla war, he was ready to implement the five revolutionary laws.

However, in the context of the Cold War, these policies, which Castro believed would bring social and economic justice to Cuba, were viewed with suspicion by the USA, who saw them as Communist in nature. An example of this is the Agrarian Reform Act of July 1959, which sought to break up the large land holdings and redistribute them to the peasants that worked on them. In fact, Castro did not have a clear plan for his revolution; he even visited the USA to get help for his far-reaching reforms, but the Americans were convinced that he was in fact a Communist and refused aid. The actions of Castro in getting rid of US monopolies and breaking up large estates, many of which were owned by Americans, only confirmed the US's views; they imposed economic embargoes on the country, reducing the amount of sugar that was bought, before ultimately imposing a total blockade (see the timeline on pages 111–113). In addition, Operation Mongoose involved the CIA carrying out acts of sabotage against the Cuban economy.

These actions encouraged Castro to turn to the USSR to ensure Cuba's economic survival. The USSR could see the potential to expand their sphere of influence into the Americas region through Cuba: Castro's Cuba would be valuable anti-US propaganda, and in February 1960 the deputy premier of the USSR, Anastas Mikoyan, opened a trade exhibition in Cuba. The USSR agreed to buy Cuba's surplus sugar and offered a good guaranteed price for the next decade. The Peoples Republic of China also signed a five-year contract to buy sugar. In addition, the USSR began to deliver crude oil to Cuba at cheaper prices than the country had paid the USA. Thus, the Soviet Union had saved the Cuban economy and its offer meant Castro could plan his economy. Nevertheless, it also meant he had to maintain sugar production and was economically dependent on the USSR.

However, Castro only began to call the revolution 'socialist' following US air raids on Cuba on 16 April 1961, in the prelude to the Bay of Pigs invasion (see chapter 9). From the time of the Bay of Pigs invasion through to the end of the Cuban Missile Crisis the following year, Castro openly claimed he had always been a Marxist. It was clear that he needed the military support and commitment of the USSR to protect the Cuban revolution from US intervention.

The US failure at the Bay of Pigs increased nationalist sentiment in Cuba and the perceived threat and 'siege' conditions imposed by its superpower enemy enabled Castro to consolidate his control.

The impact of the Cold War on Cuba's economy

Castro believed that the Soviet command economy would be a good model for Cuba. With hostile economic sanctions imposed by the USA, Castro drew parallels with the way that Stalin had industrialized the then-isolated USSR in the 1930s. He thought that this could be emulated and would enable him to create a fairer society.

However, despite investment from the Soviet Union, sugar production fluctuated, with poor harvests in 1968 and 1969. Castro attempted to inspire higher productivity

The Cuban Communist Party

The Cuban Communist Party (**PSP**) had initially been hostile to Castro's revolution, claiming it was directed by 'bourgeois concepts'. Although some of the PSP began to support Castro's regime after 1959, many members of the PSP believed that he needed to promote more 'orthodox' Communists into the government. Castro would ultimately purge the PSP so that the remaining Communists were obedient to the regime.

by initiating a 'battle for sugar', and this campaign did increase yields. In addition, in the 1970s Cuba's economy was greatly helped by the increase in global sugar prices. However, this did not prevent Cuba from developing a huge debt to the USSR. This heavy debt led Castro to seek more and more Soviet economic advice. In July 1972 Cuba joined COMECON (see chapter 3) and Castro then went to Moscow to finalize a 15-year economic agreement with Brezhnev that gave Cuba even more subsidies, including an increase in price for sugar, deferment of debt, and $350 million of investment. Cuba was now in what some historians have called its 'Brezhnev years' as Soviet advisers recommended the setting up of the System of Direction and Planning of the Economy, and the adoption of Cuba's first 'five-year plan'. The impact of superpower rivalry meant the Soviets were determined to support Castro's regime.

As Cold War tension decreased between the superpowers, so the Soviet interest in supporting Cuba declined. Indeed, the economic relationship between Cuba and the USSR changed as Mikhail Gorbachev introduced his wide-ranging reforms. Gorbachev wanted to reduce Soviet support for Cuba and visited Havana in April 1989. He told Castro that he would cut subsidies and informed him that Cuba would now have to pay in US dollars for goods purchased from the USSR.

The impact of the end of the Cold War on Cuba's economy was dramatic. As revolutions swept across Eastern Europe and Communist regimes fell, their agreements with Cuba came to an end. The Soviets had cut oil supplies by 60 per cent by 1991, and when the Communist regime fell in the USSR its economic support for Cuba ceased. Without superpower assistance the Cuban economy almost collapsed with a fall in GDP of 35 per cent by 1993. There were gas, oil, electricity, and water shortages. Castro responded in July 1993 by making the US dollar legal tender in Cuba and permitted 'self-employment' for the first time. Castro, despite the real crisis in the economy, maintained much of his Cold War rhetoric and his opposition to Capitalism.

The impact of the Cold war on the nature of Castro's government

The hostility of the US and the continual threat of US intervention meant that Castro was able to strengthen his control; he was able to stress the idea that Cuba was threatened by imperialist forces and that it was essential for Cubans to remain united and to follow Cuban laws and directives. The defeat of the USA at the Bay of Pigs, and his survival of other US attacks, allowed Castro to appeal to nationalism and to unite the country behind him. The emphasis on the need for unity against such outside threats comes through in his speeches and in Cuban propaganda.

Activity 1

Source A

> The writers and artists in this congress are those who have stayed at home and are producing and working in our country. I do not know how many writers and artists have left since the revolution reached power. I am sure that the ones that left are not good writers or artists. The reactionary writers and the mercenary artists have left our country with the intention of not returning. There are doctors, architects, and professors who have left. A doctor that leaves the country when for the first time medicine is being given to the poor, when hospitals are being built for the poor, when medical service is free, when there is no immorality, when there are no criminal deals based on health of the people – he who is capable of leaving his country under those circumstances without caring for the lives that are lost certainly is not the most decent and honourable. The crime of a doctor leaving is more sensational, but the same thing is true

of the lawyer, the engineer, the writer, and the artist who leaves the country. That was part of the plan of action against the Cuban revolution. What shall we think of a professor who leaves when all the children are given an opportunity for an education and when 300 000 Cubans are working to wipe out illiteracy? The enemies of our revolution did not think it sufficient to try to leave our people without economic resources, markets, quotas, sources of supplies for our factories, raw materials, replacement parts; so they have done all they could to leave our country without doctors engineers, professors and artists.

Speech given by Fidel Castro in August 1961 to the Writers and Artists Congress in Havana

1. Read the source above and discuss the impact of Cold War tensions on Cuban society and culture.
2. Research Cuban propaganda posters from the 1960s and 1970s. What kinds of messages do these convey to the Cuban people? How might such messages inspire unity in Cuba and support for the regime?

Impact of Cold War tensions on Cuban Foreign Policy

As you have read, US hostility to the Cuban revolution and the resultant Soviet support meant Castro was always dependent to a large degree on the USSR. However, following the Cuban Missile Crisis, where Castro was left feeling used and a 'pawn' in the superpower game, he attempted to follow a more independent path and looked to the Non-Aligned Movement (see the interesting fact box on page 265). However, ultimately, he was forced to follow the USSR's foreign policy, due to Cuba's economic dependency on the Soviet Union by the late 1960s.

Latin America

When Fidel Castro came to power in Cuba in 1959, many Latin American countries saw his revolution as a victory over American imperialism. Castro's foreign policy aims quickly became focused on giving Cuban support to groups 'struggling against imperialism around the globe'. Specifically, Castro wanted to export his revolution across Latin America – he thought Cuba could act as the example for how smaller nations could successfully use guerrilla warfare against oppressive regimes and US influence; he wanted to create 'many Vietnams'. This was not only in line with Marxist–Leninist ideology in terms of fostering class struggle and liberating the exploited masses, but if revolution spread in the region it could end Cuba's US-imposed isolation. Cuba trained and helped to arm revolutionary groups in Latin America, and Che Guevara helped to organize these movements. Although these revolutions did not succeed, the USA was concerned with Cuban provocation in its sphere of influence.

Cold War tension focused US attention on the region when revolution swept through Nicaragua in 1979. A coalition of leftists (including Marxists and Liberals), called the Sandinistas, overthrew the government of Anastasio Somoza in a guerrilla war. There was international support for the revolution and even the US president at the time, Jimmy Carter, believed Somoza had been a corrupt and inhumane leader. Cuba sent 2500 advisers to the new Sandinista regime, which set out similar objectives to those Castro had in 1959. It wanted to have an economy based on social and economic justice. However, the new regime was challenged by a right-wing group called the 'Contras', and when Ronald Reagan became president in 1981 he changed US policy on Nicaragua. Reagan began to give material assistance to the Contras (see page 181). Cuba also sent advisers to the Caribbean island of Grenada at this time, but had to withdraw support when Reagan authorized an invasion in 1983 and accused the new regime in Grenada of attempting to set up a 'Soviet–Cuban' colony. This US invasion caused alarm in Nicaragua, and it then demanded Castro

The Argentinian Che Guevara was an iconic figure for the left. He had played an active role in the Cuban Revolution, and once Castro's regime was established he encouraged it to align with the USSR. Guevara wanted to export revolution to the developing world and left Cuba in 1965. He was active in the Congo, training guerrilla forces, before joining rebel forces in Bolivia. He was captured by Bolivian forces and executed on 9 October 1967.

withdraw all Cuban advisers. Nicaraguans now feared Cuban involvement could trigger a full-scale US invasion. The US had contained the spread of Communism in the region with military force.

Africa

Castro was a proponent of **internationalism** and a staunch anti-imperialist. Cuba therefore wanted to encourage **decolonization** movements in Africa. Following the overthrow of the government in Portugal in 1974, former Portuguese colonies were given independence. In Angola a civil war broke out between different groups vying for control after independence. One group, the FNLA, was supported by the USA, and another group, the MPLA, was backed by the USSR. Castro believed that Cuba could offer practical advice and experience on how to fight 'imperialists', and sent 17 000 troops to Angola. However, these forces were transported to Africa by the Soviet Union, and, therefore, the Cubans could not claim to be acting totally independently. Ultimately, the MPLA won the civil war in 1976 and the new government signed a **Treaty of Friendship** with the USSR.

Castro also gave support to leftist forces in Mozambique, who took control in 1977, and sent another 17 000 troops to fight in Ethiopia against Somalia in the Ogaden War. Ethiopia won and became a pro-Soviet socialist republic.

Cubans had played an important role in the victory of the pro-Soviet forces in Africa during this period. However, these victories were seen as the expansion of Soviet interests, and also helped to sustain US hostility towards Cuba, strengthening American resolve to undermine the Castro regime.

Nevertheless, Angola launched Castro onto the world stage. In September 1979, Castro was elected leader of the Non-Aligned Movement. That October he travelled to New York to address the UN General Assembly and demanded international redistribution of wealth and income in favour of the poor countries of the world. CIA analyst Brian Latell observed that: 'Those months in the fall of 1979 were the apogee of his power. How can you be a loyal, dependable Soviet ally and accept about $6 billion of Soviet assistance annually, and at the same time be the leader of the non-aligned nations? Well, Castro was able to carry out that exquisite, seemingly impossible balancing act.'

Activity 2 · ATL Thinking and communication skills

1. Add details to this mind map to show the impact of the Cold War on Cuba:

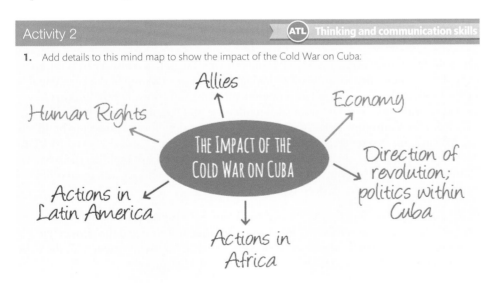

The impact of Cold War tension on Egypt

Gamal Abdel Nasser Hussein become president of Egypt in 1956 and, as with Castro, his polices for Egypt became affected by Cold War politics. He also believed that he could pursue an independent course in the Cold War; however, he quickly drew suspicion from the US and, as with Castro, was forced more closely into an alliance with the USSR.

Egyptian President Gamal Abdel Nasser

The Muslim Brotherhood was a transnational Islamist organization founded in Egypt in 1928.

Impact of Cold War tensions on the direction of Nasser's domestic policy

Nasser was not a Communist and wanted to pursue 'Islamic modernization'. In June 1956 he introduced a new constitution to Egypt in which Islam was declared the state religion and Egypt part of the 'Arab nation'. Nasser reshaped the structure of government – he could now lead as president for six years. The **National Union**, which was set up in 1957, replaced all political parties. Full democracy worried Nasser, as he believed that the poor would be drawn to either the Muslim Brotherhood or the Communists, and the middle classes would elect a government that supported their propertied interests.

Women could vote for the first time at the National Assembly in 1957, and the government passed measures to prevent child labour, improve working conditions, and provide healthcare. Nasser attempted to make the court system more secular and was criticized for this by the Muslim Brotherhood.

Nasser was one of the leaders who attended the first conference of the Non-Aligned Movement. He was impressed with the views and arguments presented and decided that he would pursue a neutral position in the Cold War.

By following this non-aligned philosophy Nasser triggered a crisis in the Middle East. He initially courted the Americans and managed to persuade them to fund the construction of the **Aswan Dam** project. He also joined the Baghdad Pact in 1955, a NATO-style alliance which was aimed at preventing the spread of Soviet influence in the Middle East. However, he was repeatedly disappointed by the refusal of the USA to sell arms to Egypt, and so decided to assert his independence from the West by buying arms from Czechoslovakia. This was condemned by the US; the Secretary of State, John Foster Dulles, believed that the move was as dangerous as the North Korean invasion of South Korea in 1950.

The USA was also alarmed by Nasser's land reforms. Egypt had a history of Western capital investment; Britain and France had invested in the building of the Suez Canal in the 1860s and had competed for imperial influence and control of the country. However, with Nasser showing socialist tendencies and seeming to now be seeking help from the Communist bloc, the USA withdrew funding for the project to build the Aswan Dam. Nasser responded by nationalizing the Suez Canal on 4 August 1956. Although the income from the canal would not cover the cost of building the Aswan Dam, this move brought him great public support at home and acclaim from other Arab states and the wider African region.

In the ensuing crisis over the Suez Canal (see chapter 19 for details on this crisis), Nasser balanced the superpowers against one another and emerged the winner. He kept the canal, humiliated the colonial powers, checked his involvement with the USA and the USSR, and emerged as the leader of Arab nationalism.

The impact of the Cold War on Egypt's economic policy

The Suez crisis helped push the Middle East as a whole further into Cold War conflict. Eisenhower issued his doctrine in 1957 stating that any Middle Eastern country could request American economic assistance or aid from US military forces if it was being threatened by armed aggression from another state. However, because Israel was an ally of the US, and because he faced hostility from the West for his reforms, it was inevitable that Nasser should draw closer to the USSR.

Buoyed by the success of nationalizing the Suez Canal, Nasser embarked on more confiscations of foreign businesses. Capitalism, it was argued, was not appropriate for Egypt as it was inherently associated with the imperialist powers. A National Planning Committee was set up to organize the 'Egyptianization' of all foreign banks, companies, and agencies; this would end Egyptian dependence on foreign capital. In 1958 a five-year plan was set up, which focused on increasing industrial output. It also attempted to bring about more land reform. The amount of land one farmer could own was limited in favour of co-operatives that the state would invest in. But landowners resisted these reforms, meaning that there was no significant increase in productivity, and only a very small percentage of peasants gained land from the redistribution plans.

Nasser did not want the state to fund all his projects and tried to encourage some private investment in his schemes. However, his attempts to develop a **mixed economy** had limited results, and Nasser moved towards more nationalization in the 1960s.

Nasser never had total government control of the economy and, although major companies were nationalized, two thirds of businesses remained privately owned. The planned expansion of industry did not happen and this, coupled with population growth, led to shortages in goods. Egypt was increasingly dependent on imported products and there was high **inflation**.

Nasser's most important domestic project was to complete the construction of the Aswan Dam. The USSR provided more than £500 million in aid to Egypt. The first stage of the building of the dam was completed in 1964 and the Soviet leader, Khrushchev, went to the opening ceremony and committed to give Nasser another £100 million to set up his second five-year plan. To foster Soviet economic support, Nasser promised to release all Communist political prisoners. Khrushchev awarded Nasser the award of the highest Soviet decoration, the star of the Hero of the Soviet Union with the Order of Lenin.

Many Egyptians studied in Soviet universities and military academies: including a future president, Hosni Mubarak, who completed training as a pilot in the USSR. Although Nasser forbade Communist proselytizing of Egyptians by Soviets in either Egypt or the Soviet Union, this was hard to stop when Egyptians were training abroad.

However, Nasser was also economically dependent on the USA. Egypt imported 50 per cent of its grain from America. The relationship was negotiated when President Kennedy was in office, but when President Johnson succeeded him relations became more tense. In 1966 there were acute grain shortages in Egypt and the USA sent its surplus to India. Nasser was outraged and asserted that relations with the US could not improve while Lyndon Johnson was president.

As with other charismatic leaders that opposed the West, the CIA and the British and French intelligence agencies plotted to assassinate Nasser. These plots failed and

Nasser died naturally of a heart attack in 1970. His successor, Anwar Sadat, moved away from the Soviets and instead attempted to get support and aid from the USA.

Impact of Cold War tensions on Egyptian Foreign Policy

❝ *The Cold War seriously exacerbated the conflicts that erupted in the region between 1945 and 1990. This in turn intensified the wars that scarred the Middle East during most of this period, and that still persist there.*

Rashid Khalidi, *Sowing Crisis: The Cold War and American Dominance in the Middle East* **(Beacon Press 2009) p.162**

Nasser's foreign policy was nationalist and promoted the idea of an '**Arab League**' to consolidate Arab interests in the Middle East. He wanted to address the 'Palestinian issue' and was hostile towards the state of Israel to this end.

Activity 3  (ATL) Thinking skills

1. Read through this source and explain the significance of Truman's March 1947 speech about the Middle East.

❝ *President Harry S Truman's address of March 12, 1947, to a joint session of Congress about these developments, which came to be known as the Truman Doctrine, was a key turning point in the Cold War as a whole. It was also the culmination of the sequence of events that began with these 1945 great-power confrontations over Iran, Turkey, and the Balkans. This speech focused on the crises involving Turkey and Greece in particular, and warned of the dangers developments there posed to the Middle East. Truman told Congress that if the United States did not extend military and financial aid to both countries in confronting domestic communist forces and the Soviet Union (although the latter was never mentioned by name in the speech) 'confusion and disorder might well spread throughout the entire Middle East'. This address, delivered less than two years after World War II ended, marked a notable evolution in the position of the United States in two respects. The first was vis-à-vis the Soviet Union, which was now being described publicly by the president as a rival and potential enemy. Truman's address was one of the first major landmarks of the Cold War, and showed clearly that a full-blown direct and indirect confrontation between East and West was already well under way in the Middle East. Second, this speech constituted the first time an American president had designated the Middle East as an area that was crucial to the national security interests of the United States. It thus signified that American power had become global and extended to areas never before considered vital to decision makers in Washington or to the American public. In consequence, Turkey and Greece, and later on other Middle Eastern states, became dependent on the United States, and in some measure became client states of this nascent superpower.*

Rashid Khalidi, *Sowing Crisis: The Cold War and American Dominance in the Middle East* **(Beacon Press 2009) p.41**

As you have read, Nasser supported the ideas of the Non-Aligned Movement, and the 1956 Suez Crisis demonstrated that the superpowers could not always push the smaller states around, nor could they always get what they wanted.

The very fact that the nature of the Cold War led the Soviets and the USA to believe that they 'needed' to bring neutral states over to their sides in itself gave these countries a weapon to wield against the superpowers. As Gaddis comments, 'Tails were beginning to wag the dogs.'

Activity 4

1. What did Gaddis mean (in the quote above) when he said that: 'Tails were beginning to wag the dogs'?

Source A

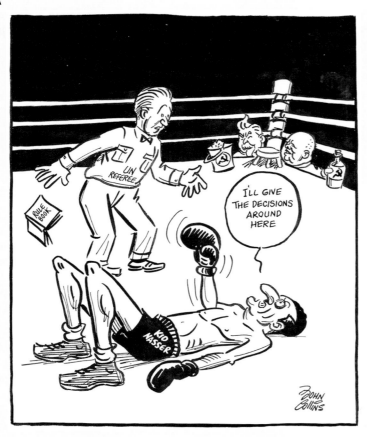

'The Voice from the Floor', by John Collins, 1956.

Source B

> The pressure to join American-sponsored alliance systems continued nonetheless, and played a large role in the polarization in the Arab world that, as we saw earlier, developed into what Malcolm Kerr called the 'Arab Cold War,' between a camp headed by Nasser's Egypt and another headed by King Faisal and Saudi Arabia. The same East–West polarization later affected the Arab–Israeli conflict, and, again as we have seen, both this conflict and the regional conflicts of the Arab Cold War eventually came to track closely with the Cold War itself, with the superpowers aligned with one or another side in each of these confrontations. Arab states, including Egypt and Syria, that resisted pressures to join superpower-dominated alliance systems and tried to remain non-aligned were stigmatized by John Foster Dulles's moralistic foreign policy as little better than communist dupes. Earlier, under the influence of chief communist ideologist Andrei Zhdanov's 1947 'two camps' theory, which appeared to presage a division of the world as rigid as that described by Kennan's famous Foreign Affairs article two months earlier, the Soviet Union initially seemed to take an equally dim view of non-alignment as between the communist and capitalist camps.

Rashid Khalidi, *Sowing Crisis: The Cold War and American Dominance in the Middle East* (Beacon Press 2009) p.181

2. What is the message of Source A?
3. According to Source B, what was the superpower view of the attempts by Arab states to pursue non-alignment?

Following the Suez crisis, the Cold War intensified in the Middle East with the Eisenhower Doctrine, which increased US support for Israel. This led to an increase in support from the USSR for Arab states, including Egypt. Tension grew in the region, particularly on the Israeli–Syrian border, where military clashes took place regularly in 1966 and the first half of 1967. On 13 May a Soviet intelligence report falsely claimed that Israeli troops were massing on the Syrian border. As a result, Egyptian troops moved into the Sinai in order to reassure Syria and to deter Israel. Nasser also increased tension by asking the UN forces that had been protecting the Sinai to leave, thus effectively removing the buffer between Israel and Egypt. On 22 May, Nasser closed the Straits of Tiran, and continued to raise the tension through aggressive speeches that threatened Israel.

On 28 May, Jordan and Egypt formed a defence pact and put their armed forces under join command. Iraq joined the pact a day later. Syria already had a pact with Egypt.

Faced with this overwhelming threat, Israel launched a pre-emptive strike on 5 June, which wiped out the Syrian, Jordanian, and Egyptian air forces on the first day. Israel went on to push the Egyptians out of Gaza and the Sinai, as well as capturing the old city of Jerusalem and occupying all of Jordan west of the Jordan River (the **West Bank**); in the north, the Israelis gained the Golan Heights. Israel achieved this in just six days.

Map showing the land gained by Israel in the Six-Day War.

This war was a disaster for Nasser and it meant that he needed the Soviet Union even more, as Egypt's forces had to be rebuilt. However, when Anwar Sadat took power in 1970, he reduced Soviet influence in the country. He expelled Soviet advisers and realigned Egypt with the West. He believed that Egypt should now open negotiations with Israel so that it could get back the Sinai; this would also allow Egypt to reduce its defence burden and hopefully gain American economic aid. However, all peace initiatives that he proposed were rejected by Israel, and the US – preoccupied with détente – failed to put pressure on Israel or help Sadat in his bid for peace.

Thus Sadat started planning for another war against Israel with the aim of persuading Israel to make peace on terms acceptable to the Arabs.

The resulting war of 1973 saw both Egypt and Syria achieve stunning successes in pushing back Israeli forces from the Sinai and the Golan Heights in the first few days. Although Israeli forces, with the help of massive US aid, were able to ultimately push back, the confidence of the Arab states was restored and the idea that Israel was invincible was smashed. The intervention of the superpowers ultimately forced a ceasefire in the war. The US changed its attitude and helped to bring about a peace agreement at Camp David between Egypt and Israel.

Nasser and the Yemeni Civil War

Nasser also got involved in a civil war in Yemen, which became his 'Vietnam'. In 1960 Yemen was divided in to two regions: a British protectorate and a theocracy ruled by Imam Ahmad. The Imamate was not opposed to more Arab unity, as proposed by Nasser, but condemned his social reforms as 'ungodly'. When the Imam died in 1962 a revolt broke out in which the Imam's son and heir was presumed killed, and the Yemen Arab state was proclaimed – and recognized by both the USSR and the USA. However, the son was still alive, and raised an army with the help of Saudi Arabia. Nasser sent in 15 000 troops in an attempt to back the Yemen Arab state. However, even with Soviet military assistance, the Egyptians had to fight hard just to keep the major cities in republican hands. Some historians argue that his involvement in this war contributed to Nasser's defeat in the Six-Day War.

Activity 5

> **ATL** Thinking skills

Essay writing

Attempt this essay question:

> *Compare and contrast the impact of Cold War tensions on two nations, each chosen from a different region.*

Use Cuba and Egypt as case studies for your response to this question. Suggested ideas for comparisons and contrasts are bulleted below. Remember to:

- Support each idea with precise evidence from your reading.
- Write an introduction that focuses on the question. You also need to give clear context here; state what your case studies will be (that is, Egypt and Cuba), and point out the fact that Cuba remained under the same leader and government for the whole Cold War, whereas in Egypt there was a change of leadership and thus government policy.
- Develop a clear line of argument: are there more similarities or more differences in how these countries were impacted by the Cold War? What is the most important similarity? What is the most important difference?

Similarities

- Both countries found themselves the focus of superpower interest in the 1950s due to their geographical locations.
- The Cold War affected the nature of their regimes – pushing them closer to the Soviet Union in both cases in the 1950s and 1960s.
- Both powers sought to avoid being caught up directly in Cold War politics by joining NAM.
- However, both were also forced to rely on the Soviet Union for economic aid and military aid at different times.
- Both attempted to spread their revolutionary ideas further afield and to support similar governments.
- Both faced hostility from the USA and assassination attempts by the CIA.
- Both countries were the focus of Cold War crises, in which they faced or experienced invasion.

Differences

- Cuba was affected more dramatically by the Cold War; the USA was more active in trying to get rid of Castro by invasion and sabotage as well as assassination.
- Connected to this point, Castro aligned himself more politically with the USSR by declaring himself a Marxist–Leninist.
- Cuba was a flashpoint of Cold War tensions in the missile crisis of 1962, when the island again faced invasion and even annihilation.
- The proximity to the US and the continued attempts of the US to get rid of Castro meant that the Cuban regime was more isolated, and as a result paranoid and repressive.
- Egypt never faced the hostility from the USA that Cuba faced; whereas the US had a complete embargo against Cuba, Egypt traded with the US – increasingly so under Sadat.
- Cuban foreign policy was more directly aimed at spreading socialist revolution, whereas Egyptian foreign policy, apart from the involvement in Yemen, was focused on the struggle against Israel and promoting Arab nationalism. Under Sadat, it was focused on getting a peace deal with Israel.

> As with comparison essays on leaders, you should avoid writing about the countries separately. Try to pick out points of comparison and then points of contrast so that you can talk about both countries in each paragraph. This will mean that you are being analytical rather than descriptive.

The impact of Cold War tension on Germany

Germany was profoundly affected by the Cold War. Its division in 1949 was a result of Cold War politics and its reunification came about when the Cold War had ended. Its capital city, moreover, remained the centre of tension throughout the war, the peak of which was in 1961, prior to the building of the Berlin Wall. The end of the Cold War is symbolized by the extraordinary events of November 1989 when the wall came down.

The impact of the Cold War on the division of Germany, 1945–1949

Before you read the following on the impact of Cold War tensions on Germany, review chapters 2, 3, and 8. Answer the following questions.

- How was Germany dealt with at Yalta and Potsdam?
- What were the different aims of the superpowers regarding Germany?

Consider how historians construct history, and discuss the extent to which this is a collaborative process. Do historians tend to work individually with their source material? What are the advantages and disadvantages of this methodology? How does this compare to the methods used in social or natural sciences?

261

- Why did tension develop between the respective zones leading up to the Berlin Blockade?
- What were the results of the Berlin Blockade?
- Why was the Berlin Wall built?

Although the division of Germany decided upon at Yalta was only meant to be temporary, Western- and Eastern-controlled zones were treated differently from the start and Cold War tensions were to lead to the country's permanent division.

The Allies had agreed to treat Germany as a single economic unit, but, as you have read, each side was allowed to extract reparations from its zone, with the USSR receiving extra reparations from the West in recognition of its losses in World War Two. Almost at once, the Soviets began to dismantle factories and to remove machinery and other valuable assets from their zone of control:

> *One thousand two hundred enterprises were hastily dismantled in a fortnight, possibly out of fear that the Allies would call a halt in favour of a systematic policy. Electricity cables and toilets were ripped out of private homes on 'orders' from Moscow. For the United States it was clear that the Russians had no intention of feeding the cow they wished to milk. This was not only morally indefensible, it was bad economics too.*
>
> **L Kettenacker, *Germany Since 1945* (OUP 1997) p.13**

In contrast to this, the British and Americans focused on dealing with food shortages and making their zones self-sufficient. They introduced a new currency in 1947, lifted price controls, and introduced incentives into the economy. All of this, along with Marshall Aid, helped to restart the economy.

Politically, zones also started to develop along different lines as well. In the West, non-Nazi parties were established. As you have read in chapter 3, the USSR hoped that all Germans could be won over to a socialist regime, but when it became clear that this was not going to happen, Stalin moved towards the idea of a separate state.

The Berlin Blockade (see chapter 3) was a symbol of the hardening of Cold War divisions between East and West and this made the division of Germany inevitable. Even as the blockade was continuing, plans were being drawn up for a state of West Germany – the Federal Republic of Germany – which officially came into being on 23 May 1949. The Soviets responded by setting up the German Democratic Republic on 7 October 1949. Thus the first obvious impact of the Cold War on Germany was its division into two states, with devastating effects for many German families, who remained divided throughout the Cold War. The two countries that emerged in 1949 – the DDR and FRG – reflected the ideologies of the opposing superpowers and, like the superpowers, they carried out media and propaganda wars against each other throughout the Cold War.

The impact of the Cold War on the constitution of the FRG

The Federal Republic of Germany was set up as a liberal democracy. The Basic Law ensured that power was shared between branches of government and between the federal **Länder** (states of Germany) in order to prevent another Nazi-style government ever emerging again. It also committed West Germany to the protection of human rights and to the reunification of Germany. Konrad Adenauer became chancellor, leading a CDU/CSU coalition, though West Germany did not immediately get full sovereignty, as the Allies retained the power of veto. The Ruhr was kept under international control and France retained control of the Saar coal-mining region.

The impact of the Cold War on the economy of the FRG

Under Adenauer, West Germany experienced an economic miracle, which was in part due to the Cold War.

- Marshall Aid, though not as key to German economic recovery as was once thought, nevertheless created a sense of confidence in investment. It also strengthened Adenauer's political position and thus created a sense of national stability that encouraged economic growth.
- The Korean War led to demand for German steel and manufactured goods, which further boosted the economy.
- The fact that Germany was not allowed a military force meant that it could concentrate its spending on rebuilding the country.
- The political stability of these years – combined with a strong, growing economy – attracted East German skilled workers who escaped to the West via West Berlin.

The strength of the economy helped lead to the FRG's independence in 1955. By this time, Adenauer had been able to reassure the Western powers that West Germany was no longer to be feared, and indeed the FRG signed the Treaty of Paris in 1951. This created the **European Coal and Steel Community**, which later led to the formation of the **European Economic Community** (EEC). It also joined the International Monetary Fund.

The impact of the Cold War on West German politics up to 1969

The impact of the Cold War also dominated West German politics. Many Germans considered reunification of Germany to be a priority in the early years and Adenauer faced criticism for becoming more involved in Western alliances and institutions. However, Stalin's proposal in 1952 for uniting Germany was rejected by the Allies, and Adenauer agreed that Stalin's intention was to split Germany from the West and keep a German state under Soviet influence. Indeed, Adenauer believed that the best path for West Germany lay in winning the support of the Western world and becoming friends again with the French. However, he faced criticism for this policy, as it seemed to suggest that he was not interested in unifying Germany. This criticism intensified when, following the end of the occupation, West Germany became a fully independent state, which led to Germans arguing that this reduced chances of unification. Nevertheless, Cold War tensions contributed to the longevity of Adenauer's position as chancellor (14 years), as Germans voted for the stability that he represented. Given the strong anti-Communist sentiment of the 1950s, the CDU/CSU coalition was more attractive than more left-wing parties such as the SPD.

The impact of the Cold War on West Germany's foreign policy

West Germany's geographical position bordering the Eastern bloc, and thus its importance for America in the conflict against the Soviet Union, meant that West Germany's foreign policy would be dictated by events in the Cold War.

West Germany had no army in 1949. However, from 1950, Adenauer began to argue for the creation of an 'armed security police', which could maintain internal security as well as contributing to the defence of Western Europe. With the outbreak of the Korean War showing the dangers of one side of a divided country attacking the other, this suggestion seemed reasonable, given that the FRG faced an armed DDR. Indeed,

West German political parties

The main political parties of the FRG were:

- the Christian Democratic Union (CDU), which consisted of various Christian and Conservative parties
- the Christian Social Union (CSU)
- the Social Democratic Party (SPD)
- the Free Democratic Party (FDP)

The CDU and the CSU merged into one political party in a conscious attempt to join Catholics and Protestants together to prevent the fragmentation of parties which had occurred during the Weimar Republic.

the US supported the idea of West Germany joining NATO. However, it was not until 1954 that France could be persuaded to allow this to happen.

The Soviet Union responded by setting up the Warsaw Pact, which further confirmed the division of Europe and of Germany. In 1955, Adenauer made a threat that became known as the **Hallstein Doctrine**, which stated that the FRG would break off diplomatic relations with any country that established diplomatic relations with the GDR. Hostility between the two Germanys reached a high point during the Berlin Wall crisis.

However, with the election of Willy Brandt in 1969, there was a change in attitude towards the GDR. As you have read in chapter 12, influenced by the wider forces pushing the superpowers towards détente, Brandt pursued his own form of détente with East Germany – *Ostpolitik* – by signing the **Basic Treaty**, which recognized the existence of the two states. They agreed to co-exist, to exchange 'representatives', to ease travel restrictions between the two Germanys, and to accept the status quo of European borders. Opponents to his policy argued that recognizing the existence of East Germany meant accepting the division of Germany. However, Brandt saw calls for unification as unrealistic and argued that his policy was based on realism. Indeed, it brought a relaxation of tension and stability to this area of Europe.

However, the wider Cold War atmosphere in the late 1970s and 1980s again influenced West Germany's foreign policy under the new chancellor, Helmut Schmidt. When the USSR began deploying **SS-20** intermediate-range nuclear missiles in Europe, Chancellor Schmidt supported the setting up of similar weapons in West Germany. The gains of *Ostpolitik* thus came under pressure as the détente between the US and the Soviet Union collapsed.

Nevertheless, with the fall of the Berlin Wall, West Germany – under Chancellor Helmut Kohl – seized the initiative by putting forward a plan for the reunification of Germany and then leading the way in the unification process. Germany was unified in October 1990.

The impact of Cold War tension on China

The fact that China became a Communist country had little to do with the actual Cold War – Mao's CCP and his struggle for power emerged before the Cold War had started. Moreover, his actual success in the civil war owed little to Stalin's help (see chapter 10). However, once Mao had taken power in 1949 and made China a Communist country, China was inevitably affected by the wider struggle between the Soviets and the Americans, as well as by its own conflict with the USSR.

CHALLENGE YOURSELF

 **ATL** Research skills

1. As you have read, both Germanys developed along the ideological and economic lines of the two superpowers. Research East Germany and compare its development in terms of politics, human rights, and economy in comparison with West Germany.

2. Germany was not the only country that faced division due to Cold War politics. Research either Korea or Vietnam. Examine the impact of the Cold War on the development of both the North and the South of each of these countries. What comparisons can you draw with Germany?

Activity 6	 **ATL** Thinking skills

Source A

> *During the early 1960s, [Mao] began seeing the Soviets as returning to a pre-revolutionary state, in which their cultural affinity with the West was determining their international political positions. The Soviets were part of the self-centred and complacent Western culture, while revolutionary China fought on against imperialism, helped by other Third World countries. The so-called 'three worlds theory' placed the United States and the Soviet Union within the First World as hegemonic superpowers, while the other industrialized countries, over which the two superpowers exerted their hegemony, constituted a Second World. China and the poor countries of the South made up a Third World, which were making revolution against the superpowers and would become the future centre of international development.*

Odd Arne Westad, *The Global Cold War* (CUP 2007) p.162

Source B

" *During the early years of the Cultural Revolution … the rhetoric of China's foreign policy grew defiantly revolutionary. In 1965 Lin Biao had declared that just as the rural revolutionaries had surrounded and strangled China's cities in 1948 and 1949, so now would the impoverished Third World countries surround and strangle the superpowers and the rest of the advanced capitalist nations … but the rhetoric was not backed by any overt military actions and turned out to be largely meaningless. Lin Biao's formula was, however, used to justify China's reaching out to a wide range of radical opposition groups abroad … visionary statements appeared in China's press of the inherent oneness of her people with the oppressed of the world. Chairman Mao's Red Book of his quotations was translated into scores of languages, with millions of copies distributed around the world.*

Jonathan D Spence, *In Search of Modern China* (WW Norton 1990) pp.627–628

1. Using these two sources, identify China's position regarding international interventions.

2. Using the sources and your own knowledge, explain how China's ideological conflict with the Soviet Union over the correct nature of Communism affected its domestic and foreign policies.

Activity 7

1. Both China's domestic and foreign policies were inextricably linked to what was happening regarding its relationships with the USSR and the USA, as part of the Cold War. Re-read chapters 10 to 11 and use the information in these chapters, along with the timelines on pages 289–291, to complete this task.

Identify how each of the following impacted on China. Consider the impact both on China's domestic and foreign policies.

- the Treaty of Friendship, 1950
- the Korean War
- Khrushchev's policy of peaceful co-existence
- the Non-Aligned Movement
- Taiwan
- the United Nations
- events in Albania
- the Cuban Missile Crisis
- the nuclear arms race
- the Vietnam War
- Gorbachev's reforms and the collapse of the USSR
- US policy of détente.

The Non-Aligned Movement

The purpose of the Non-Aligned Movement was to ensure 'the national independence, sovereignty, territorial integrity and security of non-aligned countries' in their 'struggle against imperialism, colonialism, neo-colonialism, racism, and all forms of foreign aggression, occupation, domination, interference, or hegemony as well as against great power and bloc politics' (Fidel Castro, 1979).

The 'Non-Aligned Movement' was founded in 1961 and was mainly the work and initiative of the Indian Prime Minister Jawaharlal Nehru. It set out to represent states that did not want to be aligned with one or other superpower.

It was successes such as Tito's Yugoslavia – which had refused to align with either superpower and had apparently not only survived but had benefited as a result of its independence from the USA and the USSR – that provided inspiration for Nehru of India and Zhou Enlai of China. Both leaders wanted to resist the bi-polar superpower domination.

To be considered non-aligned, countries could not join in alliances or defence pacts with the main world powers. Not only would this allow them to retain a degree of autonomy from superpower domination by not committing to either side in the Cold War, but it would also enable them to go one step further and attempt to manipulate the bi-polar divide to their own advantage. They would do this by ensuring that they left 'openings' to ally with either the USA or the USSR, and thus would continue to be courted by both. On the other hand, if pressure from one superpower got to be too much, they could threaten to ally with the other.

As a group or 'bloc' the Non-Aligned Movement had more influence in the General Assembly of the UN by the 1960s. The key political content of the movement at this time was:

* to encourage solidarity of member states
* to warn superpowers against spreading the Cold War in the 'Third World'
* to apply pressure against using war as a means of settling disputes
* to counter imperialism
* to stand committed to restructuring the world economic order.

The non-aligned heads of state sent letters to both Kennedy and Khrushchev, warning them against the threat of war and urging a 'peaceful solution' during the Berlin Crisis in 1961. Many of the non-aligned states represented countries that had shifted the balance of power away from the United States in the General Assembly of the UN. This meant that in the 1960s the Non-Aligned Movement (NAM) had to be taken seriously by both superpowers.

Although it continued to grow, it was as early in the movement's development as 1962 that the idea of a 'bloc' began to collapse. In 1962, the Sino-Indian border war broke out. War between two of the movement's most powerful members – India and China – undermined its credibility. Indeed, India moved closer to the Soviets during the dispute with China. This was a big blow to the idea of 'solidarity' and of course to the key Bandung principle of 'peaceful resolution'.

In 1970, a non-aligned conference was organized in the Zambian capital, Lusaka. However, by this time, much of the early belief and enthusiasm for NAM had evaporated. Many of the post-colonial regimes in Africa failed in the 1970s, and these countries moved away from non-alignment and towards the USSR. Cuba's leading role in NAM was questioned by some states, as its relationship with the Soviets clearly meant it had a degree of 'alignment' with a superpower.

The Americans did not want to support NAM as its members often assumed an anti-colonial stance in the UN, and this could lead the United States into conflicts with its European allies. The USA wanted to focus on preventing the spread of Communism, and thus wanted the NAM states to be clearly aligned with it in the Cold War. The USA could not accept that many 'Third World' countries wanted to back Communist or socialist regimes. For example, Henry Kissinger viewed Salvadore Allende's victory in Chile in the 1970s as being caused by an 'irresponsible electorate' rather than the result of a genuinely informed choice by the Chileans.

Many states chose to align with the Soviets as they needed economic development, and the USSR promised aid and support. The Soviet Union also offered support for the political movements that were attempting to realize modernization. For example, whereas the United States wanted to resist the revolutionary forces in Vietnam, Khrushchev offered arms and money. Therefore, many NAM leaders, even when they were more nationalist than Communist, turned to the Soviets for assistance – as Castro had done in the early 1960s.

In 1979 the members of NAM turned against each other over the Soviet invasion of Afghanistan. Those non-aligned states that were allied or friendly to the USSR were in support of the invasion; however, other states, including many Muslim countries, were strongly opposed to it.

By the end of the 1980s, the 'Third World', as Odd Arne Westad commented, had ceased to exist as 'a meaningful political or economic concept'. Dramatic economic and political changes, which had begun in the 1970s, had moved many African, Asian, and Latin American countries in very different directions. For example, some Southeast Asian countries had embarked on rapid economic development, whereas most of Latin America was, in contrast, stagnating economically. In Africa, the **Balkans**, and certain parts of South Asia, ethnic and religious differences became more important than ideological ones. Political Islam was on the rise and often usurped secular politics.

Jonathan Fryer, an expert on international affairs, puts it this way:

> *it was a movement that basically set itself up as something which it is not, rather than something which it is … In other words, it was meant not to be associated with Washington and not to be associated with Moscow. It is very much a child of the Cold War.*

To access websites relevant to this chapter, go to www.pearsonhotlinks. com, search for the book title or ISBN, and click on 'chapter 18'.

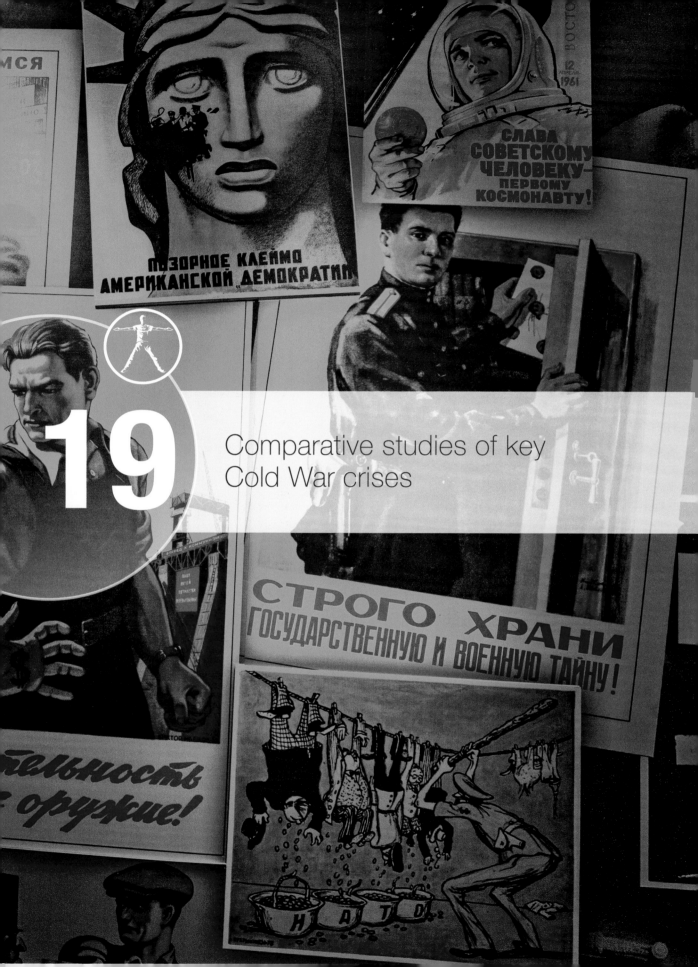

19

Comparative studies of key
Cold War crises

Key concepts: Continuity, significance, and perspective

As you read this chapter, consider the following essay question:

- Compare and contrast the causes, impact, and significance of two Cold War crises, each chosen from different regions.

What makes an event in the Cold War a 'crisis'?

When you are writing about Cold War crises, here are some points that you need to consider:

- A crisis was a clear escalation of tension or rivalry between the superpowers.
- A crisis involved the superpowers (in some cases one of the superpowers may have been only indirectly involved).
- Many Cold War crises brought the superpowers to the brink of war before tension de-escalated.
- A 'crisis' will always be a relatively short period of time; this means that in a question on a conflict that lasts for some time, such as the Korean War or the Soviet–Afghan War, then the 'crisis' will only be the initial period and not the ensuing war.

As you have read, there were many 'crises' between 1945 and 1985. These crises took many forms and created various degrees of tension between the superpowers.

It is important that you know in detail the causes, the key events, and the results of these crises and that you are able to compare them and discuss their relative effects on superpower relations. It is also important that you can compare crises from different regions.

Case Study comparison: Berlin Crisis of 1948–1949 and the North Korean invasion of 1950

Berlin Crisis of 1948–1949

The Berlin Blockade was the first major crisis of the Cold War. Review chapter 3 along with the sources below. Then, in pairs, consider the discussion questions before attempting the essay.

Causes of the Berlin Crisis

Activity 1   ATL Thinking skills

1. What was the role of each of the following in causing the 1948 crisis?
   - the Yalta and Potsdam Conferences
   - the issues of reparations
   - the actions of the Western powers
   - the actions of Stalin

The impact of the crisis

The crisis had several key effects:

- the permanent division of Germany into two states
- the setting up of NATO
- the continuation of Berlin as a divided city within the Soviet zone
- the containment of Communism.

The significance of the crisis

- It illustrated the policy of containment in action and showed that the West, by 1948, was not prepared to see the Soviets expand any further.
- It was a propaganda disaster for Stalin, who had to back down.
- However, it showed that Stalin was not prepared to escalate the conflict and risk war.
- It brought about the final stage in the division of Europe: economically, politically, and militarily.
- Berlin remained a source of tension between the superpowers.

The invasion of South Korea by North Korea, 1950

What were the causes of the Korean War?

As you have read in chapter 5, the causes of the Korean War were very much 'a comedy of errors' (Gaddis).

Activity 2 〉 (ATL) **Thinking and social skills**

1. Discuss, in pairs, the following question:

   What was the role of each of the following in causing the invasion?

   - Kim Il Sung
   - Stalin
   - Mao
   - the USA

What was the impact of the crisis?

Review the effects of the crisis for each of the countries involved (see pages 67–68).

What was the significance of the crisis?

The Korean War was significant for setting the pattern of 'proxy' wars that was to be used throughout the Cold War. It also showed how the US was prepared to use force to follow through its policy of containment.

Activity 3 〉 (ATL) **Thinking skills**

1. Read the sources below and highlight the key points that each author makes regarding the significance of this war.

Source A

> *The onset of the Korean War, coupled with the 'loss' of China, played a major role in accelerating the US policy of containment. As Randall B Woods put it, 'Had it not been for the fall of China and the Korean War, the cold war as a fifty-year phenomenon involving the expenditure of billions of dollars and the destruction of millions of lives might never have happened.' The North Korean attack against South Korea on 25 June 1950 provided the*

Truman administration with all the proof that it needed that Stalin was on the move; the involvement of China in late November silenced critics of NSC68 and ushered in a new, more dangerous world.

Joseph M Siracusa, *Into the Dark House* (Regina 1998), p.xiv

Source B

The Korean War altered the nature of the Soviet–American confrontation, changing it from a systematic political competition into an ideologically driven, militarized contest that threatened the very survival of the globe … [Agreeing to the] invasion of the South proved to be Stalin's most disastrous Cold War gamble. It postponed détente with the United States for twenty years. It intensified a confrontation that continued for forty years at enormous cost to the major antagonists ... The war shifted the balance of forces within the United States ... allowing them to divert the attention and energies of the American people from needed reform to the hunt for Communists at home and abroad. It allowed ... [the creation of] a military-industrial complex that consumed the productive power of the American economy and fuelled conflict all over the world.

Warren I Cohen, *America in the Age of Soviet Power, 1945–1991* (CUP 1995), pp.58–66

2. Using the information in chapter 5 and the sources above, draw up a mind map to show the significance of the Korean War on the development of the Cold War.

Activity 4 Communication skills

Essay writing

Now plan the following essay.

> *Compare and contrast the causes, impact, and significance of the Berlin Crisis of 1948–1949 and the North Korean invasion of 1950.*

Here are some points to get you started:

Similarities of causes

- Both crises originated from the post-war settlement and superpower rivalry.
- Both crises were initiated by Stalin.
- Both crises had been precipitated by US involvement/action.
- Both involved an attempt to remove Western influence.
- In both cases it seemed Stalin underestimated the reaction of the West, which encouraged him to go ahead.
- Both cases involved the US implementing its policy of containment.

Differences of causes

- In the case of Korea, Stalin was acting under pressure from Kim Il Sung rather than alone.
- Stalin believed that the West would not intervene in Korea; he knew that there would be a stronger reaction regarding Berlin.
- The role of Mao was significant in causing the North Korean crisis; it was not just a USSR–USA confrontation as in Berlin.

Similarities of impact

- Both crises led to the permanent division of each country.
- Both crises led to the US stepping up its military commitment and thus the intensification of hostilities between East and West.
- Both crises had a negative impact on the citizens of the respective countries.

Differences of impact

- The loss of life and destruction in Korea was vast; there was no substantial damage or loss of life in the Berlin Crisis.
- The impact of the Berlin Crisis was to secure the status quo in Europe, whereas the impact of the Korean War was to globalize the Cold War.
- Berlin had a negative outcome for Stalin whereas events in Korea were seen as more positive for the USSR in the short term.

Each paragraph of your essay should include references to both crises. Do not write about each crisis separately and then rely on a comparative paragraph at the end.

Similarities of significance

- Both crises had a profound effect on the development of the Cold War.
- Both showed the two sides attempting to avoid head-to-head confrontation.
- Both demonstrated the superpowers' commitment to consolidating their spheres of influence.
- Both contributed to the establishment of alliance blocs, NATO and SEATO respectively.

Differences of significance

- With Germany, the West used peaceful means to achieve its end, whereas in Korea it showed it was prepared to use force.
- The Berlin Crisis highlighted the US's policy of containment of Communism in Europe that had developed by 1947, but Korea started a new era of global containment for the US.
- The significance of Korea was more far-reaching for the future actions of the US and also for the globalization of the Cold War.
- Korea had more long-term negative consequences for the Soviet Union in terms of the increased scale and militarization of the Cold War.
- Korea established the People's Republic of China as a regional power.

Case Study comparison: the Suez Crisis, 1956 and the invasion of South Korea by North Korea, 1950

Now consider how the Suez Crisis of 1956 can be compared to the Korean Crisis.

Cold War Crisis:

The events of the Suez Crisis, 1956

You have already read in chapter 18 of how Nasser upset the West by buying weapons from Czechoslovakia and then nationalizing the Suez Canal in retaliation for the US cancellation of loans for the building of the Aswan Dam. This was the main cause of the Suez Crisis. As it was a vital waterway for British and French shipping, neither the British nor the French could tolerate Egyptian control of Suez, and so the British initiated a secret plan with the Israelis and the French to take back control.

Following this plan, the Israelis attacked through the Sinai, and within a day were close to the canal zone. The British were then able to demand that both sides withdraw to a zone of 8 kilometres on either side of the waterway. When the Egyptians rejected this, British and French aircraft attacked the Egyptian airfields and landed troops at Port Said, saying that they were doing so to protect lives and shipping. However, their actions caused a storm of protest across the world, and the Americans refused to support Britain. At the United Nations, both the Americans and the Soviets demanded a ceasefire, and prepared to send a UN force. This pressure forced Britain, France, and Israel to withdraw, while UN troops moved in to establish a police force on the frontier between Egypt and Israel.

What was the impact and significance of the Suez Crisis?

1. Study the three sources below. What do they tell you about the impact and significance of the Suez Crisis?

Source A

Punch cartoon by Leslie Illingworth, 1956. Russia holds down Hungary while other student leaders write out 'I must not bully' in class.

Source B

Anglo-French prestige in the Middle East was in ruins after the Suez incident, but the US moved to replace it on 5 January 1957, when the President presented the Eisenhower Doctrine to Congress. Egypt and Syria objected to American involvement in the Middle East and to resist it they drew nearer to the USSR, thus giving further justification to Washington. The USSR boosted its aid to Egypt and sent Soviet officers to train the Syrian force.

Colin Brown and Peter Mooney, *Cold War to Détente* (Heinemann 1999) p.154

Source C

One of the key reasons why the United States had reacted so angrily to the invasion was Soviet attempts at using the Suez Crisis to increase their influence among Arab nationalists and to portray their own crushing of the Hungarian rebellion in a better light ... In deciding to pull the rug from under London's and Paris's actions in Egypt the Eisenhower administration knew that they were effectively ruining both the power and the will that the European countries had to defend their colonial possessions in the future. America would replace them as the major Western force all over the Third World, with a policy based on its own strategic and economic priorities.

Odd Arne Westad, *The Global Cold War* (CUP 2007) p.126

Activity 6

 Thinking and social skills

1. In pairs, plan the following essay:

   Compare and contrast the causes, impact, and significance of the North Korean invasion of 1950 and the Suez Crisis of 1956.

   Points to consider in your comparisons:
   - the role of Nasser and Kim Il Sung in causing the crisis
   - the role of the UN and whether it was a success or failure
   - the reaction and involvement of the US and its allies
   - the reaction and involvement of the USSR
   - the significance of each event for US policy and thus the wider Cold War
   - the significance of each event for Soviet policy.

Case Study comparison: the Berlin Crisis, 1958–1961 and the Cuban Missile Crisis, 1962

The Berlin Crisis

Review chapter 8 along with the sources below. Then, in pairs, consider the discussion questions in activities 7 and 8.

What were the causes of the Berlin Crisis?

Activity 7

 Thinking and social skills

Source A

 The presence in Berlin of an open and, to speak to the point, uncontrolled border between the socialist and capitalist worlds unwittingly prompts the population to make a comparison between both parts of the city, which, unfortunately, does not always turn out in favour of Democratic Berlin.

Ambassador Pervukhin in a report to Moscow in December 1959

Source B

In [the Berlin Crisis] it was Ulbricht who drove the process, with Khrushchev scrambling to keep up. Requirement of alliance solidarity ... pushed a reluctant Soviet leader to confront the United States and its own allies in the summer of 1961. Both superpowers now had to face explicitly the question that had been implicit in 1958–59; would Berlin be worth a nuclear war? Fortunately, they managed to agree that it would not be and, despite grave misgivings on the part of each of their German clients, to devise a mutually tolerable if draconian solution.

John Lewis Gaddis, *We Now Know* (OUP 1997) p.143

Discuss the following questions in pairs.

1. What do Sources A and B reveal as the causes of the Berlin Crisis?
2. What other factors can you add from your own knowledge?
3. How and why did Khrushchev escalate the crisis over Berlin in a) 1958 and b) at the Vienna Summit?

What was the impact and significance of the Berlin Crisis?

Activity 8 · ATL Thinking and social skills

Source A

❝ Both the East Berliners and the East Germans must have been as aware of the truth as were their compatriots in the West: East Germany needed to build a wall to keep its people in. Also despite all his threats to sign a peace treaty with East Germany and hand over responsibility for access routes, Khrushchev did not do so; his diplomacy and blustering had failed. The West had been unable to prevent the building of the Wall. They had successfully defended the status of West Berlin but the Potsdam Agreement had made the three major Allies joint trustees of the whole of Berlin. Their trusteeship had failed. The building of the Wall divided a city, family and friends, brought grief to separated Berliners and a loss of face to the Allies. The Berlin Wall was a defeat for both sides in the Cold War.

Colin Brown and Peter Mooney, *Cold War to Détente* (Heinemann 1999) p.78

Discuss the following questions in pairs:

1. According to Brown and Mooney, what was the impact (result) of the Berlin Crisis? What do they see as the *significance* of the crisis?
2. Review the sources on the impact of the Berlin Wall on page 108. How do these authors differ from Brown and Mooney in their interpretation of the significance of the building of the wall?

The Cuban Missile Crisis, 1962

What were the causes, impact, and significance of the Cuban Missile Crisis?

Activity 9 · ATL Thinking skills

First, review chapter 9, then read the sources below and answer the questions.

Source A

❝ Khrushchev had two clear motives. The first was to defend Cuba against the constant possibility of either an American-inspired or openly American invasion. There was a degree of honour involved here. Dean Rusk recorded Anastas Mikoyan saying: 'You Americans must understand what Cuba means to us old Bolsheviks. We have been waiting all our lives for a country to go Communist without the Red Army, and it happened in Cuba. It makes us feel like boys again.'

Khrushchev's second motive was to create a nuclear balance. The Soviets were very much more advanced at intermediate-range nuclear missiles than in the more complex field of ICBMs. It would take almost a decade to establish parity in ICBMs; but parity could be achieved overnight through the back door, by installing medium-range missiles in Cuba. If Kennedy was seriously considering the possibility of a first strike, then parity through Cuba might be the way to save the Soviet Union.

Martin Walker, *The Cold War* (Vintage 1994) p.169

Source B

❝ During the crisis Kennedy and his advisers came up with four possible explanations for Khrushchev's actions: (i) Cuba was to be a 'lever' for Soviet ambitions in Berlin ... (ii) the move was part of internal Kremlin power struggles; (iii) Khrushchev was trying to compensate for Soviet strategic inferiority; (iv) Khrushchev seriously feared a coming US invasion of Cuba and was seeking ways to avert it.

Of these, only (iii) and (iv) were true, in some degree – and it is symptomatic of the near-tragedy of errors in October 1962 that most of the men in the White house were much more disposed to believe and act on the assumption of (i) or (ii).

Tony Judt, *The Crisis: Kennedy, Khrushchev and Cuba in Reappraisals* (Vintage 2009) p.320

1. According to Walker, what were the immediate causes of the crisis?
2. How far does Judt agree with Walker regarding the causes of the crisis?
3. What point does Judt make about American perceptions of Khrushchev's motives?
4. From your own knowledge, what other factors pushed this event into becoming a crisis? (Consider the actions of Kennedy here.)

Source C

❝ *The significance of the crisis lies in the fact that the world has never been closer to a nuclear exchange. It was also a hinge, or a turning point, in the history of the Cold War. Among the experiences that shaped policy makers' approaches to any issue in the post-1962 period was a memory of the way in which crisis management was not crucial to the very survival of life on earth. As Defence Secretary McNamara later put it, the very idea of crisis management was shown to be a dangerous misperception. Crises, by their nature are unmanageable. Within months, a hotline had been created to facilitate communication between the White House and the Kremlin. Kennedy and Khrushchev moved in 1963 to complete and secure ratification of the partial test ban treaty that had been the subject of years of complex negotiations … The outcome of the crisis, cemented the position of Cuba and West Berlin as outposts of their respective blocs and changed both sides' negotiating styles … the crisis bred new perspectives in both superpower capitals and helped contribute to the rise of détente. Although it changed the cold war confrontation, it did not end it …*

Mike Sewell, *The Cold War* (CUP 2002) p.88

5. According to Sewell, what was the *significance* of the crisis?
6. Do you agree that the Cuban Missile Crisis represented a 'turning point'? What evidence can you provide from international events post-1962 that would support this idea?
7. What were the other results of this crisis:
   a. for Kennedy
   b. for Khrushchev?

Activity 10 ▶ ATL Thinking skills

Essay writing

Now try the following essay question:

> *Compare and contrast the causes, impacts, and significance of the Berlin Crisis, 1958–1961 and the Cuban Missile Crisis, 1962.*

Here are some starting points:

Similarities of causes

- It could be argued that both were initiated by the Soviet Union under Khrushchev.
- Both involved the consolidation/defence of superpower spheres of influence.
- Both crises were precipitated by US economic policies towards Cuba and Berlin.
- In both cases, Khrushchev was under pressure from the local Communist leadership – Castro and Ulbricht – to take action.
- In both cases, the USSR presented its actions as defensive.
- There was a fear on both sides that, as tension escalated, it could lead to direct confrontation.

Differences of causes

- Putting missiles in Cuba was Khrushchev's idea, whereas with regard to Berlin, Ulbricht seized the initiative to build a wall.
- Khrushchev's bid to force the West out of Berlin, followed by the building of the wall, was an attempt to save the economy of East Germany, so was a more passive and defensive measure, whereas putting missiles in Cuba was more offensive.

- The Berlin Crisis was an attempt to push the USA out of the Soviet sphere of influence, whereas the Cuban crisis was an attempt by the Soviets to expand into the US sphere of influence in the Americas region.
- The US reaction to the construction of the wall was to merely condemn it, whereas it reacted strongly to the missiles going into Cuba and demanded their removal.

Similarities of impact

- Both brought the USA and USSR dangerously close to conflict, especially after the Vienna Summit (for Berlin) and after missiles were discovered (for Cuba).
- Both ultimately led to an easing of tension – though the arms race continued and intensified.
- The handling of both crises was criticized by other Communist countries.
- It could be argued that the outcome of both crises was a failure for Khrushchev but a victory for Kennedy.
- However, in both crises Khrushchev had gained something – the sealing of the escape route via East Berlin and the dismantling of the missile bases in Turkey.

Differences of impact

- The Berlin Wall resolved the issue that had led to the crises – the USA was content to let the wall remain and there was no longer pressure on the USSR over the human exodus. Although the wall was embarrassing, the fact that Khrushchev was forced to remove missiles from Cuba was deeply humiliating. The USSR lost a lot of credibility as a result of the crisis.
- The issue of missiles in Cuba was more dangerous; having missiles only 90 miles off the coast of the USA was an even greater issue for America than the question of Berlin.
- The Cuban Missile Crisis was far more damaging for the USSR in terms of its relationship with other Communist countries; the results were condemned by the PRC and led to a period of hostility and resentment from Castro's Cuba.
- Whereas the results of the Berlin Crisis led to the refocusing of superpower rivalry to other regions, the Cuban Missile Crisis led to a more tangible period of rapprochement as both sides wanted to prevent another crisis on this level. It led to the development of more direct lines of communication and it led to arms talks.

Similarities of significance

- Both showed that the two sides were prepared to pull back from the brink to prevent a nuclear war.

Differences of significance

- The Berlin Wall removed the issue of Germany – as a source of conflict – from the Cold War, but Cuba remained an ongoing problem for America.
- The Cuban Missile Crisis had a greater impact on the behaviour of the two superpowers and ultimately helped lead to arms agreements and to détente.
- The Cuban Missile Crisis further developed the Sino-Soviet split.

Case Study comparison: Hungary, 1956 and Afghanistan, 1989

What were the causes, impact, and significance of the Hungarian Uprising of 1956?

Activity 11　　　　　　　　　　　　　　　　　　ATL Thinking skills

Review chapter 13 on the Hungarian Uprising, then read the sources and answer the questions below.

Source A

66 What the Kremlin could not condone was the Hungarian party's abandonment of a monopoly of power, the 'leading role of the Party'. Such a departure from Soviet practice was the thin edge of a democratic wedge that would spell doom for Communist parties everywhere. That is why the Communist leaders in every other satellite state went along so readily with Khrushchev's decision to depose Nagy.

Tony Judt, *Postwar: A History of Europe Since 1945* (Vintage 2005) p.320

Source B

> The Hungarian uprising, a brief and hopeless revolt in a small outpost of the Soviet empire, had a shattering impact on the shape of world affairs. In the first place it was an object lesson for western diplomats. Until then the United States, while officially acknowledging the impossibility of detaching Eastern European satellites from Soviet control, continued to encourage the 'spirit of resistance' there. Covert actions and diplomatic support were directed, in the words of National Security Council Policy paper No 174 (December 1953) to 'fostering conditions which would make possible the liberation of the satellites at a favourable moment in the future'. But, as a later confidential document, drawn up in July 1956 to take account of that year's upheavals, was to emphasise, 'the United States is not prepared to resort to war to eliminate Soviet domination of the satellites'.

Tony Judt, *Postwar: A History of Europe Since 1945* (Vintage 2005) p.319

Use the sources along with your own knowledge to discuss the following:

1. What actions did Nagy take that upset the Soviets?
2. Why had Poland not been invaded?
3. How significant was the response of the West?
4. What was the impact of this crisis for the Hungarians and for the rest of the Soviet bloc?

What were the causes, impact, and significance of the Soviet invasion of Afghanistan in 1989?

Activity 12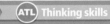

1. Review the reasons for the Soviet invasion of Afghanistan (chapter 13). How are these different to the reasons for the Soviet invasion of Hungary?
2. Read the source below by Crockatt on the significance of the invasion. What reasons does he give for the Western reaction to this invasion?

> The Soviet action would have been provocative in any circumstances. In the circumstances of détente, it was doubly so ... the intervention was in important respects an aberration from Soviet practice in the Third World. The scale of military involvement was unprecedented and, unlike the Angolan and Horn of Africa instances, the Soviets sought direct control of the Afghan government, despite the fiction of Kamal's independence. This suggests that Afghanistan was conceived to be a vital interest, akin to the United States' interest in, say, Mexico. Of course, outside observers could not be sure that this was not the beginning of a new pattern which might be extended elsewhere. The world reaction must be seen partly in that light.

Richard Crockatt, *The Fifty Years War* (Routledge 1996) p.287

Activity 13

Essay writing

1. Now try the following essay question:

    Compare and contrast the causes, impact, and significance of the Soviet invasion of Hungary in 1956 with the Soviet invasion of Afghanistan in 1989.

    Here are some suggestions for comparisons and contrasts.

    Comparisons of causes

    - Both were precipitated by actions of the USSR, who claimed that in both cases its security was threatened.
    - In both cases the USSR was prepared to use force to secure aims.
    - In both cases there was discontent/resistance to Soviet influence.

- The West had an influence in prolonging the crisis in both cases. In 1956 it gave hope to the rebels that help would come, encouraging them to keep fighting. In Afghanistan, the CIA was involved with the failed Afghan government, and, after the Soviets invaded, gave arms to the rebels.

Contrasts of causes

- Hungary was caused by a more moderate regime moving away from Soviet principles (supported by the Hungarians) whereas in Afghanistan the problem was a hard-line government that was sticking too closely to Soviet principles (and that was in opposition to the Afghans).
- The government in Afghanistan asked the Soviets to intervene, whereas the intervention in Hungary was an act of violence against the government.
- The Soviets acted to 'contain' a challenge to their control in Hungary within their sphere of influence, whereas Afghanistan was not in their established sphere of influence.

Similarities of effects

- The West condemned the Soviets in both cases as evidence of Soviet aggression.

Contrasts of effects

- Intervention in Hungary was a success for the USSR – it achieved its aims, whereas it failed to achieve its aims in Afghanistan.
- Linked to this, the Hungarian Crisis strengthened the Soviet's hold on its satellite empire, but its actions in Afghanistan weakened it severely.
- The invasion of Hungary only caused verbal condemnation by the West, but in the case of Afghanistan it led to military aid for the rebels, the Carter Doctrine, and the end of détente via a series of anti-Soviet measures.

Similarities of significance

- There was a high death toll in both crises – for Hungarians and Afghans.
- Both showed the determination of the Soviets to maintain stability within client states.
- Hungary undermined the 'thaw' and Afghanistan ended détente.

Contrasts of significance

- The West was not prepared to intervene when the Soviets used aggression within its existing sphere of influence, but was still determined to prevent the Soviets from moving outside of this sphere of influence.
- Linked to this, these events showed that the US would only intervene against the USSR if its own interests were threatened.
- The invasion of Hungary had a limited impact on superpower relations, whereas Afghanistan was a key factor in causing the Second Cold War.

2. Now re-plan this essay, substituting the Hungarian Crisis of 1956 with the Czechoslovakian Crisis of 1968.

3. Review chapter 6, focusing on the Taiwan crises in the 1950s. Plan the following essay question:

   Compare and contrast the causes and impact of the Taiwan crises (1950s) and the Cuban Missile Crisis (1962).

CHALLENGE YOURSELF

Research and social skills

Research the following case studies in Cold War crises.

- Lebanon (1958)
- US intervention in Chile (1973)

Make sure that you organize your notes into causes, impact, and results.

In pairs or small groups, identify the similarities and differences between the two case studies. Discuss whether each case study compares and contrasts more easily with a different case study you have explored.

Theory of Knowledge

Introduction

The Theory of Knowledge (ToK) course is part of the core of the IB Diploma programme and, along with the subject-specific courses, counts towards the Diploma. History is both one of the subject-specific courses in the IB Diploma and an area of knowledge in ToK. This chapter aims to discuss the key concepts of ToK, showing the interaction between the History course and its function as an area of knowledge within ToK.

There is a substantial overlap between history and ToK, as both emphasize the importance of critical thinking. Both ask the question, 'How do we know?' Both want you to understand that your cultural identity is rooted in the past.

ToK uses knowledge frameworks as a concept to differentiate between areas of knowledge. This table helps you see how a knowledge framework could apply to IB History.

Scope/ applications	• It is the study of the recorded past. • It helps us to understand that our cultural identities are rooted in the past.
Concepts/ language	• It discusses change and continuity. • It explores causation and consequences. • It recognizes the power of language in influencing thoughts and actions.
Methodology	• It has a clear, strong, and demanding methodology. • It has recognized ways of collecting evidence, questioning sources, and constructing theories. • It tests significance. • It asks, 'How do we know?'
Historical development	• It recognizes that current values affect our views of the past. • It changes over time in subject matter and interpretations.

Links to personal knowledge	• It acknowledges the influence of individual historians on shared knowledge. • It allows for a range of perspectives. • It recognizes the importance of a shared history to a person's identity.

You will find that an understanding of ToK will help you to evaluate sources in your History course. It will also help you to complete the reflection section of the internal assessment component of the History course.

You may also find that an understanding of history is useful in your ToK course. It will help you to analyse the real-life issue in your ToK presentation and will provide a strong area of knowledge, with great examples, to refer to in your ToK essay.

Ways of knowing

Both ToK and history ask the question, 'How do we know?' ToK answers this question by identifying eight possible ways of knowing. Your knowledge must come from somewhere and by analysing where it comes from, you are able to assess its reliability.

ToK identifies the eight ways of knowing as:

- Language
- Perception
- Reason
- Emotion
- Memory
- Intuition
- Imagination
- Faith

You can use these concepts in ToK to assist in:

- checking the reliability of a first-hand testimony
- analysing the way emotions influence the witness and the interviewer
- determining the possible bias in the language used
- assessing the fallibility of memory
- analysing the desire to see a rational explanation for events.

Activity 1

1. Discuss how each of the ways of knowing listed on the previous page is used by historians when developing their historical accounts.

2. What challenges do historians face when using the following ways of knowing in developing their historical accounts?

   a. reason

   b. emotion

   c. imagination

3. Historians often give names to specific periods of time in history. We have used the headings or titles given in the IB History guide, for example 'The Breakdown of the Grand Alliance' or 'Peaceful Co-existence'. Why do historians do this? Would people who lived through these events recognize these labels?

4. 'Historians seek to be detached, impassionate, impartial. In fact, however, no historian starts with his mind a blank, to be gradually filled by the evidence' (Historian AJP Taylor, in *The Times Literary Supplement*, 6 January 1956). What does Taylor mean by, 'no historian starts with his mind blank'?

You can also use the ways of knowing in history to assist in establishing the origin, purpose, and content of sources, in order to assess their value and limitations.

Language is one of the key ways of knowing, so here is an example exploring the use of language in the accumulation and communication of knowledge in history.

Activity 2

Read the source below in pairs and answer the questions that follow.

This source discusses the Berlin Blockade 1948–49.

> There is cause for satisfaction in our handling of the Berlin blockade from June 1948 to May 1949. The Russians had a strong case for terminating the four power occupation of Berlin, because the West had announced plans on June 7 for the creation of a West German government. Since the four power occupation of Berlin was based on the assumption that Berlin would be the capital of a united Germany, the quadripartite occupation did become an anomaly when the assumption was destroyed. Thereafter West Berlin became from the Russian standpoint only a listening post and spy center for the West in the center of East Germany, and an ideological thorn in her side. The announcement of a new currency for West Germany, imperatively needed, also created urgent problems for East Germany, since it would circulate in Berlin.

> These were real grievances, but from the Western standpoint they did not justify an attempt to starve out 2,000,000 West Berliners. The crisis was grave and it was met by the West imaginatively, boldly and resolutely. The advocates of sending an army of tanks to Berlin were silenced and the airlift did the job, dramatically lifting allied prestige to new heights. In this engagement of the Cold War the action of the West was a model of combined courage and restraint, and President Truman deserves his large share of the credit for it.

D. F. Fleming, *The Cold War and its Origins, 1917–1960*, vol. 2, Garden City, NY (Doubleday, 1961)

1. How has the historian used language in his account? Does his use of language affect how readers of this book might view the American role in the Berlin Blockade?

2. Review the material in chapters 2 and 3. Consider the language used in sources from the time, for example the Fulton speech (page 25), the X Article (page 34) and Vyshinsky's response to the Marshall Plan (page 32). How does the language in the sources affect their value and limitations?

3. Consider the extent to which language is a challenge to historians in their accumulation and communication of knowledge in history.

Activity 3

British historian EH Carr described how historians work:

> The facts are like fish swimming in a vast murky ocean, and what the historian catches will depend partly on chance, but mainly on what part of the ocean he chooses to fish in and what bait he chooses – these two facts of course being determined by the type of fish he wants to catch. By and large the historian will get the facts he wants.

EH Carr, 'What is History?' (from a lecture given in 1961)

1. With reference to Carr's quote above, what ways of knowing are used by a historian?

Areas of knowledge

History is one of the eight areas of knowledge identified by the ToK course. A full list of the areas of knowledge is:

- Mathematics
- Natural sciences
- Human sciences
- History
- The arts
- Ethics
- Religious knowledge systems
- Indigenous knowledge systems

281

You can use these areas of knowledge to understand why we approach different types of knowledge in different ways. We recognize that a work of art is not the same as a chemical formula or a historical interpretation. We test them using subject-specific criteria, acknowledging that a historical fact cannot be verified in the same way as a natural science fact. History uses a rigorous methodology to test its facts, but it is not the same method as used in the natural sciences.

Historians develop theories of causation based on evidence and supported with evidence that has been assessed for its reliability; they have their theories, arguments, and accounts 'tested' by other historians or experts in their field. Perhaps the way in which historians' work can be considered similar to science is that their accounts are open to peer criticism, correction, and revision.

Also, history, like the natural sciences, uses deconstructions, and **macro and micro scales**. For example, in accounts of the Cold War, a historian may focus on a turning-point event or consider the role of broader impersonal factors, such as ideology. Broader factors could then be applied to consider causal developments of a specific case study in crisis. However, historical evidence can also be viewed as different from scientific evidence in the way it is 'found'. Scientific experimentation, 'double-blind testing', and so on are not methodologies available to the historian.

Historians, like scientists, search for cause and effect. Some History examination essay questions will ask you to find a number of key causes and/or assess their relative importance. As for natural and human scientists, there can be challenges for historians when establishing the difference between correlation and causation.

There are also problems in terms both of scope and depth when examining causation. For example, how far back in time should we go to look for causes? How much detail is relevant? This is also a problem when examining the effects of a past historical episode in terms of how far forward we should look for relevant consequences.

Activity 6

It is also important to consider the role of 'accident' and 'chance' in history. Can you identify any events in the Cold War where there was an element of 'chance' in the factors that caused them? How useful is the consideration of 'accidental' causation to a historian? Discuss in pairs whether 'chance' is an acceptable causal factor in the natural sciences.

There is an interesting interplay between the arts and history. In one sense, the arts reflect the historical forces at play in society, but, in another sense, the arts influence history. Here are two examples exploring the complex relationship between the arts and history.

Case study 1

After the Bolshevik revolution in Russia and the establishment of the USSR, an artistic movement developed called Constructivism. Soviet Constructivists argued that art had been 'bourgeois' and separate from society. This movement wanted to use art to foster a new *Communist society* by creating a new proletarian culture. Art would focus on the key role of the industrial worker and this would change the way people understood, and functioned in, society. The artists attempted to produce 'industrial style' works of art that used geometrical shapes, straight lines, and often featured male and female workers.

Activity 4

Briefly research the impact of Marshall Aid money on one European country – a theme from chapter 3. While you are researching, consider the following:

- the language used by the historians
- information included or omitted by the historians
- details emphasized by each historian
- analytical concepts used by each historian and whether such concepts are liable to 'change over time'.

Activity 5

In pairs, review the different historical perspectives in chapter 4 and consider the extent to which history can be seen as 'changing' within new theoretical frameworks.

Activity 7

Investigate Constructivist art and the artists that led the movement. Discuss the extent to which the movement could be considered as influencing history. How could historians use art from this period to understand early Soviet society?

From 1929 Stalin was dictator of the USSR and artistic experimentation ended. Art was controlled by the state, which approved of only one style of artistic expression – Socialist Realism. The state wanted to have total control over artists, and Socialist Realism meant that all art had to glorify the worker, and show the 'reality' of revolutionary development. This meant that all visual art, music, theatre, films, and literature had to adhere to the Communist Party line of the proletariat as heroes leading society to a Communist ideal. Art would be bold and clear and depict happy working people. Therefore, artists were used by Stalin in the 1930s and 1940s for indoctrination and propaganda. Their work was used to justify the great sacrifices made by Soviet citizens. Indeed, Stalin described artists as the 'engineers of the soul'. In the USSR under Stalin, and during the early period of the Cold War, artists had to conform to survive.

'Builders of Communism', an example of Socialist Realist art from 1967.

Activity 8

From the case studies you have considered above, in small groups discuss:

a. how art influences history

b. how art reflects the historical forces in societies.

Activity 9

In small groups discuss the following questions.

1. Is history really more about highlighting and emphasizing the nature of humankind, and the human condition, in the way that the arts sometimes do?

2. Do historians paint pictures with their words, highlighting issues and events in ways that might mirror the power that artists can command with their images? If so, does the artistic method have any similarities to the methods employed by historians?

3. 'History has more in common with the arts than with the natural sciences.' To what extent to do you agree with this statement?

Historical development

Historical development is one of the criteria on the knowledge framework that ToK uses to differentiate between the areas of knowledge. Historical development is part of all the areas of knowledge, recognizing that our knowledge and the way we approach that knowledge changes through time. For instance, the way we approach natural sciences – and what we know about them – is quite different now to a hundred years ago.

You can use this concept to explore how our approach to history changes: that is, what subjects we study in history, how our views change as more information comes into the public domain, and how our current values influence our view of the past. Historians use reason to construct a logical interpretation of the past based upon the available information. Sometimes there is so much information that it is difficult to find a single thread of cause and effect in it. Sometimes there is too little information. Occasionally new information becomes known as official documents are released or research is completed.

Historians are human beings with roots in their own time, place, and background. Their interpretations have an emotional and cultural context, so it is not surprising that the interpretations change over time, as society's values change.

Indeed, there are challenges for historians both in terms of selection and bias. When writing a descriptive account of events, or even a chronological timeline, the historian might have to be selective, omitting some events that other historians might think relevant or significant. These additions and omissions create a personal interpretation of the events. A further step away from objectivity is taken when a historian then has to select or identify different themes, causes, and effects. The choice of language in which these selections are presented will also impact on objectivity when developing a historical account and will lead to bias. Historians face the challenge of assessing the values and limitations of their sources, as well as a potential lack of documents in some areas. Historians are also products of their own time and context.

Activity 10

Refer back to chapter 4 and the historiography of the origins of the Cold War. In small groups discuss the extent to which historians' perspectives changed over time due to:

a. the source material available to them at the time

b. where and when they were working

c. their own academic and/or political backgrounds

d. the effect of their own culture and societies.

Activity 11

Refer back to chapter 15. Discuss in pairs the different perspectives on the reasons for the end of the Cold War and the extent to which these perspectives changed over the period 1991–2010. Discuss how current events and issues may shape how we, as historians of that period, view the reasons for the end of the Cold War.

Activity 12

In small groups discuss the following questions.

1. The historian EH Carr, writing in his book *What is History?* (1961), asserted that: 'The belief in a hard core of historical facts existing objectively and independently of the historian is a preposterous fallacy, but one which it is very hard to eradicate'. How far do you agree with Carr's assertion? Why does Carr say this view is 'very hard to eradicate'?

2. The British novelist and social commentator George Orwell wrote in an essay entitled 'On Revising History' (4 February 1944): 'History is written by the winners'. To what extent does your group agree with this statement? Refer to examples from chapter 15, including the 'Reagan victory school' perspective on the reasons for the end of the superpower confrontation.

Personal and shared knowledge

ToK is interested in the links between shared knowledge and personal knowledge as they relate to history. You can use this concept to explore the role of key historians in shaping our shared knowledge, but you can also use it to investigate how our shared knowledge helps shape our own identities. One of the key concepts of IB History is that multiple interpretations are possible and one of the key concepts of ToK is that each individual should be encouraged to think critically for themself.

You can use the ToK concept of memory as a way into this topic. On a personal level, memory is important in creating our personalities; and on the cultural level, collective memory is important in uniting, but also in dividing, people. Here are a couple of examples exploring memory in history.

Over 60 years ago the British philosopher and historian RG Collingwood defended the study of history, saying:

> *What is history for? … Knowing yourself means knowing, first, what it is to be a man; secondly, knowing what it is to be the kind of man you are; and thirdly, knowing what it is to be the man YOU are and nobody else is. Knowing yourself means knowing what you can do; and since nobody knows what he can do until he tries, the only clue to what man can do is what man has done. The value of history, then, is that it teaches us what man has done and thus what man is.*

RG Collingwood, *The Idea of History* (OUP, 1946)

History helps us to understand ourselves in the present. Our own individual 'histories', are also important in helping us to understand the world we live in and our place within it. Significantly, history is used to argue and justify political positions, economic policies, the rationale for foreign policy initiatives, and relations between countries and regions. In fact, most other areas of knowledge rely to a certain extent on the use and application of history. For example, it would be difficult for a scientist to add to the body of knowledge in his or her subject in a meaningful way without knowing what had come before, and why and how something had been discovered or invented.

Activity 13

Investigate how your parents, grandparents, or extended family viewed key events and crises during the Cold War, or the dramatic events and personalities that led to the end of the Cold War. Compare and contrast their memories of events to those accounts you have read in this book. Do they have a different perspective on these historical events? Do the accounts from memory highlight specific elements and omit apparently important details? What can we learn from these personal memories?

Activity 14

In small groups consider how your own study of the Cold War is relevant to understanding global events today. In what ways has your understanding of crises, confrontation, and reconciliation between nations and regions been enhanced by studying superpower rivalry.

Activity 15

As a class discuss the following:

Can we draw lessons that are applicable today from our study of superpower rivalry and its impact in the 20th century?

Conclusion

There is a considerable overlap between history and ToK. The concepts of change, continuity, significance, causation, consequence, and perspectives are included in the IB History syllabus and they fit well into the knowledge framework in ToK.

You can use skills you develop in history to add depth and meaning to your ToK presentations and essays. You can use skills developed in ToK to help you evaluate sources and to write the reflection section of your historical investigation. You can use the methodology of history to address the real-life issues that you discuss in ToK. By collecting evidence, weighing the value and limitations of sources, and building a logical, consistent interpretation of the facts you will be able to construct sound, well-supported arguments. History is one of the key areas of knowledge in ToK.

For further information about the ToK course, consult the Pearson Baccalaureate: Theory of Knowledge 2nd edition book.

APPENDIX I

Basic timeline

This is for quick reference only. At the beginning of each chapter there is a more specific and detailed timeline. This timeline should be used to put key events into context, and to give you an idea of some of the 'turning point' years in the Cold War.

1944	November	Tehran Conference / Big Three meet
1945	February	Yalta Conference
	April	Roosevelt dies – Truman now president
	May	Germany surrenders, Victory in Europe
	June	UN formed
	July	Potsdam Conference
	August	Hiroshima and Nagasaki – Japan surrenders, victory in Pacific
1946	February	Stalin's 'two camps' speech
	March	Churchill's Fulton 'Iron Curtain' speech
	June	Baruch Plan proposed
1947	March	Truman Doctrine
	June	Marshall Plan proposed
	July	Kennan's 'X article'
	October	Cominform created
1948	February	Czech Coup – Marshall Plan implemented
	May	State of Israel created
	June	Berlin Blockade (and Yugoslavia expelled from Cominform)
	November	Truman re-elected
1949	January	COMECON founded
	April	NATO established
	May	Berlin Blockade ends
	September	USSR explodes atomic bomb
		FDR established
	October	GDR established
		Mao proclaims foundation of People's Republic of China
1950	April	NSC-68
	June	North Korea invades South Korea
1951	September	USA and Japan sign mutual security pact
1952	November	Eisenhower elected
1953	March	Stalin dies
	June	East German uprising
	July	Armistice in Korea
1954	January	Dulles announces massive retaliation policy
	May	Fall of Dien Bien Phu
	July	Geneva Conference on Vietnam
	September	SEATO established
	October	West Germany joins NATO
1955	May	Warsaw Pact signed
	July	Geneva Summit
	September	Nasser announces arms deal with USSR
	November	Baghdad Pact
1956	February	Khrushchev's 'de-Stalinization' speech – 'peaceful co-existence' promoted
	July	Suez Crisis
	October	Hungarian Uprising suppressed
1957	October	Sputnik launched by USSR

286

1958	July August	Revolution in Iraq Quemoy and Matsu blockaded
1959	January May September	Castro takes power in Cuba Dulles dies Khrushchev visits USA
1960	May November	U-2 spy plane shot down over USSR Kennedy elected Sino-Soviet split confirmed
1961	January August	USA breaks off relations with Cuba Berlin Wall built
1962	October	Cuban Missile Crisis
1963	August November	Partial Test-Ban Treaty signed in Moscow (USA, USSR, and UK) President Kennedy assassinated – Johnson now president
1964	August October November	Gulf of Tonkin Resolution USA goes to war in Vietnam Khrushchev deposed – replaced by Brezhnev China detonates A-bomb Johnson re-elected
1965	August	Fighting between India and Pakistan over Kashmir
1966	September	NATO headquarters moved to Brussels after French withdrawal from military command structure
1967	June August	Six-Day War between Israel and Arab states ASEAN established
1968	July August November	Brezhnev Doctrine Warsaw Pact forces invade Czechoslovakia Nixon elected
1969	November	Nuclear Non-Proliferation Treaty
1970	April	SALT talks begin
1971	October	UN admits China, expelling Taiwan
1972	February May November	Nixon visits China Nixon visits USSR SALT I signed Nixon re-elected
1973	October	4th Arab–Israeli War (Yom Kippur War)
1974	August	Nixon resigns over Watergate
1975	April August	Communists victory in Vietnam and Cambodia Helsinki Final Act signed
1976	February September November	SEATO disbands Mao dies Carter elected
1977	June December	USA plans to deploy cruise missiles USSR deploys SS-20s in Europe
1978	May	UN special session on disarmament
1979	January June November December	USA and China open diplomatic relations Carter and Brezhnev sign SALT II US hostage crisis in Tehran Soviet forces invade Afghanistan
1980	May August September November	Tito dies Mass strikes in Poland Iraq attacks Iran Reagan elected

1981	January	US hostages released in Iran
	April	Argentina seizes Falkland Islands
	November	Death of Brezhenev – replaced by Andropov
1983	March	Reagan promotes SDI
	October	US troops invade Grenada
	December	Soviets walk out of START talks
1984	February	Andropov dies – replaced by Chernenko
	November	Reagan re-elected
1985	March	Death of Chernenko – replaced by Gorbachev
	September	USSR criticize SDI at UN
	November	Reagan and Gorbachev summit
1986	April	Chernobyl disaster
1987	December	Summit in Washington – Reagan and Gorbachev present
1988	February	Gorbachev announces withdrawal from Afghanistan
	May	Summit in Moscow – Reagan and Gorbachev sign INF treaty
	November	Bush elected US president
1989	April	Soviet troops withdraw from Hungary
	June	Tiananmen Square massacre
	September	Hungary opens border with Austria
	October	Honecker forced to resign in East Germany
	November	Berlin Wall comes down
		Czech Communist Party resigns
	December	East German, Lithuanian, and Latvian parliaments abolish special position of Communist Party
		Ceausescu executed in Romania
		Havel new Czech president
1990	January	Bulgarian parliament abolishes special position of Communist Party
	March	Lithuanian parliament declares independence
		Estonian parliament votes for secession from USSR
	May	Latvian parliament declares independence
	June	Bush/Gorbachev summit in Washington
	July	NATO declares formal end of Cold War
	August	Iraq invades Kuwait
	October	German unification
	November	Gorbachev wins Nobel Peace Prize
		Signing of CFE Treaty and Paris Charter – ends economic and military division of Europe
1991	February	Warsaw Pact disbands
	April	UN forces expel Iraq from Kuwait
	June	Georgia declares independence from USSR
	August	Yeltsin becomes president of Russia
		Failed coup against Gorbachev – Yeltsin condemns hardliners
	September	Estonia, Latvia, Lithuania, Ukraine, and Belarus declare independence
	December	11,000 Soviet personnel are withdrawn from Cuba
		Ukraine votes for independence
		Russia, Ukraine, and Belarus declare USSR no longer exists
		Gorbachev resigns as president

APPENDIX II

China's relations with the USA and the USSR

Actions of China	Date	Actions of USA	Actions of USSR
Mao's Chinese Communist Party takes power People's Republic of China established	1949	USA refuses to recognize legitimacy of PRC	Soviets recognize the PRC as legitimate
The People's Liberation Army invades Tibet PRC warns USA/UN against threatening Chinese border in Korea	1950	USA condemns invasion of Tibet USA commits to protect Taiwan USA under UN flag sends forces to defend South Korea	Sino-Soviet Treaty signed USSR boycotts Security Council in UN due to non-recognition of China USSR condemns USA/UN action in Korea
Accepts truce in Korea PRC constructs 'Third Line' defences	1953	Accepts truce in Korea	Stalin dies
PRC shells Quemoy and Matsu islands off Taiwan	1954	USA threatens massive retaliation if Taiwan is directly threatened	
China attends the Bandung Conference Asserts the USA is the key danger to world peace	1955		
Mao sees Khrushchev's 'de-Stalinization' speech as attack on own personality cult Mao sees 'peaceful co-existence' as a betrayal of Marxist ideology Mao views Hungarian Uprising as failure for USSR	1956		Khrushchev makes 'de-Stalinization' speech Khrushchev champions idea of 'peaceful co-existence' Soviets crush Hungarian Uprising At conference of world's Communist parties Soviets angered by Deng Xiaoping's attacks on policies
At conference of world's Communist parties Mao condemns the Soviets as 'revisionists'	1957		
Mao launches the 'Great Leap Forward' Khrushchev visits China Mao gives up presidency of PRC PRC again shells Matsu and Quemoy – Taiwan crisis	1958	USA prepares for war with PRC over Taiwan	Khrushchev visits China
	1959		Soviets condemn Mao's 'Great Leap Forward'
	1960		Soviets withdraw scientists working on nuclear programmes in China
Chinese delegation leaves CPSU Congress in Moscow The PRC offers support to Albania	1961	Kennedy becomes president	USSR withdraws aid from Albania
Sino-Indian Border War PRC condemns USSR policy in Cuba Sino-Soviet border clashes	1962	USA allowed by India to fly U-2 spy planes over China US responds to discovery of Soviet missiles with blockade of Cuba	Soviets give MIG fighters to India in war with China Soviets establish nuclear missiles in Cuba Sino-Soviet border clashes
PRC condemns Soviets for abandoning role as revolutionary leaders by working with West in Test-Ban Treaty	1963	USA signs Test-Ban Treaty with USSR	USSR signs Test-Ban Treaty with USA

Actions of China	Date	Actions of USA	Actions of USSR
A-bomb tested by PRC	1964		
Mao launches Cultural Revolution PRC condemns American involvement in Vietnam as 'imperialism'	1966	USA does not want to involve the PRC in escalating war in Vietnam	
H-bomb tested by PRC	1967		
Mao condemns Soviet actions in Czechoslovakia	1968		Brezhnev leader of USSR Soviets crush Czech regime
Sino-Soviet Border War PRC threatens rocket attacks on USSR	1969		USSR attempts to exlude PRC from international Communist movement Sino-Soviet Border War USSR threatens rocket attacks on PRC
China launches first space satellite	1970		
Sino-USA talks begin PRC takes China seat in UN	1971	Sino-USA talks begin USA accept PRC as 'China' in UN	
US President Nixon visits PRC	1972	US President Nixon visits PRC	
	1973	USA troops begin withdrawal from Vietnam	
Jiang Jieshi dies PLA into Cambodia	1975	USA final withdrawal of all personnel from Vietnam	
Zhou Enlai dies Mao dies Hua Guofeng becomes CCP Chairman Anti-Soviet Gang of Four removed	1976		
Deng becomes CCP Secretary	1977		
Four Modernizations adopted	1978		Soviets sign military alliance with Vietnam Soviets support Vietnam in invasion of Cambodia
Pro-democracy movement begins Full diplomatic relations between PRC and USA established PRC invades Vietnam PRC condemns Soviet invasion of Afghanistan	1979	Full diplomatic relations between USA and PRC established USA condemns Soviet invasion of Afghanistan	Soviets invade Afghanistan
Gang of Four on trial	1980		
PRC issue Nine Principles on Taiwan	1981		
Margaret Thatcher visits PRC to discuss Hong Kong	1982		
Sino-British declaration in Hong Kong	1984		

Actions of China	Date	Actions of USA	Actions of USSR
Gorbachev visits PRC Tiananmen Square – pro-democracy demonstration crushed	1989	Moderate condemnation of actions in Tiananmen Square	Gorbachev visits PRC
	1990	USA gives PRC 'most favoured nation status'	Abandonment of the USSR Communist Party
	1992		
Deng Xiaoping dies Hong Kong returned to China	1997		

US presidential policies during the Cold War

	Truman	Eisenhower	Kennedy	Johnson	Nixon	Carter	Reagan
Key policy ideas/beliefs	Containment – the Truman Doctrine	Containment – the 'New Look', also massive retaliation Domino effect Eisenhower Doctrine Despite Dulles talking about 'roll-back', no attempt was ever made to liberate Communist territory	Containment – flexible response Domino effect	Containment Domino effect	'Peace with honour' in Vietnam Need for new relationships with both USSR and China to take account of the changed world situation and remove focus from Vietnam Idea of 'linkage' Nixon Doctrine	Wanted to continue détente and arms control Believed in an 'ethical' foreign policy Carter Doctrine	Re-assertion of US power Reagan Doctrine Reduction of nuclear weapons
How put into practice	Marshall Plan Western Military integration (NATO) NSC-68 – increase in military spending Setting up of military bases around the world Support to groups 'resisting Communism', e.g. in South Korea, Taiwan, Indochina	Continuation of all of Truman's actions But in addition: Increased reliance on nuclear weapons Use of covert operations by the CIA Economic aid and intervention in Middle East More prepared to negotiate with the USSR, e.g. Geneva Summit	Continuation of all of Truman's actions Continued with Eisenhower's policy of increasing reliance on nuclear weapons but also built up conventional forces Continued use of CIA Also prepared to negotiate with the USSR Introduced Green Berets as counter-insurgency force Wanted to give aid to developing countries (Alliance for Progress) Peace Corps – sending young Americans to 'Third World' countries to give aid	Continuation of all of Truman's actions plus USA's commitments in Middle East and Asia Stepped up involvement in Vietnam by sending troops Helped anti-Communist governments in Latin America, e.g. in Dominican Republic	Withdrawal from Vietnam by 1973 Détente with USSR through arms and trade agreements and summits Détente with China through summit and trade agreements	Linked arms control reduction to human rights issues (annoyed Soviets) After Soviet invasion of Afghanistan stopped exports to USSR and increased defence budget	Defence spending was increased New missiles developed Star Wars (SDI) Use of CIA covert operations Support to anti-Communist insurgents in Central America After 1985, involved in arms reduction talks with USSR in a series of summits

	Truman	Eisenhower	Kennedy	Johnson	Nixon	Carter	Reagan
Successes	Containment – successful in Europe. Marshall Plan rebuilds European economies. Berlin blockade resisted. West Germany created as democratic and economically stable country. In Asia, Japan emerging as powerful anti-Communist country. Communism in Korea contained	Containment – successful in Europe. West still in Berlin. Strengthened NATO. Korean War ended. Massive retaliation policy deterred Chinese actions against Taiwan. Lebanon and Jordan secured as allies in Middle East. Secured friendly government in Iran after CIA coup of 1953. Competent handling of Suez crisis. Attempted to control military spending. Achieved warmer relations with the USSR	Containment – successful in Europe. Safeguarded West's position in Berlin. Successful handling of Khrushchev at Vienna Summit. Skilful handling of Cuban Crisis. USA maintains its nuclear supremacy. Starts space programme. Arms agreements with USSR. Hot-line established	Containment – continues to be successful in Europe (though no major crises occur under Johnson)	Withdrawal of US troops from Vietnam. Improved relations with USSR and China – significant arms agreement with SALT I	Raised awareness of human rights issues around world. Camp David Agreement – peace treaty between Israel and Egypt. Panama Canal Treaty, which ended dispute about control over the Panama Canal through agreement to hand it over to Panama by 1999, as long as it remained neutral territory. Helsinki Agreement. USA formally recognizes Communist government in China	Star Wars helps bring USSR to negotiating table (according to some historians). INF Treaty signed with USSR reduces nuclear stocks. Cold War hostility greatly reduced through meetings with Gorbachev
Failures	Involved USA in Indochina – failed to appreciate complexity of Asian nationalism. Massive increase in military spending with implementation of NSC-68. China is now an enemy	Indochina: failure to take part in 1956 elections discredited US aims in Vietnam. Supported Diem – repressive ruler. CIA intervention in Iran and Guatemala condemned as examples of US imperialism. Reliance on covert operations made CIA too powerful. Embarrassment over U-2 flight	Economic aid to Latin America never achieved aims. Bay of Pigs – humiliation for USA. Significantly increased aid to South Vietnam – tied into supporting South Vietnam government after assassination of Diem	Intervention in Dominican Republic to support a Conservative junta against a counter-coup to restore the democratic government of Bosch, which led to complaints from Bosch that 'this was a democratic revolution smashed by the leading democracy in the world'. Vietnam – failed to stop escalation of the conflict. Tet Offensive seen as a major US failure.	Unable to secure financial support for South Vietnam, which fell to Communist rule in 1975. Invasion of Cambodia was a failure and helped lead to Pol Pot's victory. SALT agreement – not comprehensive. (Some critics would regard détente as a failure – see chapter 12)	Lacked ability to have a clear approach to Soviets due to divisions in own administration. SALT II never ratified. Ongoing hostage crisis in Iran (though this was resolved on Carter's last day in office)	In early 1980s his approach to USSR – 'evil empire' – raises tensions. Policy in Central America received a lot of criticism – USA seen as supporting narrowly based right-wing governments

	Truman	Eisenhower	Kennedy	Johnson	Nixon	Carter	Reagan
Legacy	Huge commitment to defence of democracy and anti-Communist governments worldwide Commitment in Indochina Huge expenditure on military	Left Kennedy a difficult legacy: unsolved problems in Cuba, Vietnam, Laos Also a crisis in US–Soviet relations following U-2 incident Also CIA planning invasion project for Cuba	Improved relations with USSR; new acceptance of danger of nuclear weapons and beginning of arms control agreements Germany removed as an issue Cuban crisis resolved Space programme established But USA in increasingly difficult position in Vietnam	Divided opinion over USA's role in the world; a questioning of USA's involvement in Vietnam	Significant arms agreements, but a continuing arms race PRC now in UN Increasing concern from many in USA that détente was benefiting the USSR	Belief that USA needs to assert itself in the world – hence election of Reagan	End of Cold War

FURTHER READING

Books

These books offer good overviews of the Cold War:

- *America, Russia and the Cold War 1945–2006*, Walter LaFeber (McGraw-Hill 1996)
- *The Cold War*, John Lewis Gaddis (Penguin 2005)
- *The Cold War*, John Mason (Routledge 1996)
- *The Cold War*, Martin Walker (Vintage 1994)
- *The Fifty Years War*, Richard Crockatt (Routledge 1995)
- *The Global Cold War*, Odd Arne Westad (CUP 2007)
- *International Relations Since 1945: A Global History*, John W Young and John Kent (OUP 2004)
- *Postwar: A History of Europe Since 1945*, Tony Judt (Vintage 2010)
- *Rise to Globalism*, Stephen Ambrose and Douglas Brinkley (Longman 1998)

These books contain more in-depth analysis and are useful for Individual Assignments, Internal Assessments, or Extended Essays with Cold War themes:

- *Alliance: The Inside Story of How Roosevelt, Stalin and Churchill Won One War and Began Another*, J Fenby (Pocket 2008)
- *Argument Without End: In Search of Answers to the Vietnam Tragedy*, Robert McNamara (Westview Press 2000). McNamara's documentary *Fog of War* is also worth watching for his perspective on different events in the Cold War
- *The Cold War*, Klaus Larres and Ann Lane, eds (Blackwell 2001)
- *Colossus: The Rise and Fall of the American Empire*, Niall Ferguson (Penguin 2004)
- *Eastern and Central European States 1945–92*, John Laver (Hodder and Stoughton 1999)
- *Europe and the Cold War*, David Williamson (Hodder & Stoughton 2001)
- *Inside the Kremlin's Cold War*, Vladislav Zubok and Constantine Pleshakov (Harvard 1996)
- *Iron Curtain: The Crushing of Eastern Europe 1944–56*, A Applebaum (Penguin 2013)
- *The Last Decade of the Cold War*, Olav Njolstad, ed. (Frank Cass 2004)
- *The Rebellion of Ronald Reagan: A History of the End of the Cold War*, J Mann (Penguin 2011)
- *Revolution 1989: The Fall of the Soviet Empire*, V Sebestyen (W&N 2010)
- *Seize the Hour: When Nixon Met Mao*, Margaret MacMillan (John Murray 2006)
- *Stalin's Wars*, Geoffrey Roberts (Yale University Press 2006)
- *Vietnam: The Ten Thousand Day War*, Michael Maclear (Methuen 1981)
- *We Now Know*, John Lewis Gaddis (OUP 1997)
- *Yalta: The Price of Peace*, SM Plokhy (Viking 2011)

This is a book of documents with commentary:

- *The Cold War: A History in Documents and Eyewitness Accounts*, Jussi Hanhimaki and Odd Arne Westad, eds (OUP 2003)

It is also a good idea to look at biographies, autobiographies, and memoirs by the central figures in the Cold War, such as Mao Zedong, Nikita Khrushchev, Henry Kissinger, Richard Nixon, Ronald Reagan, and Mikhail Gorbachev.

This book is good for thinking about Theory of Knowledge in the context of history:

- *The Landscape of History*, John Lewis Gaddis (OUP 2002)

Websites

To visit the following websites, visit www.pearsonhotlinks.com, enter the book title or ISBN, and click on the relevant weblink.

- The Cold War International History Project website – click on weblink 1.
- The website accompanying the CNN *Cold War* television series – click on weblink 2.
- The Spartacus Educational website. This has good summaries on key individuals and events – click on weblink 3.
- The BBC History website. This useful website also has audio links to speeches, and so on – click on weblink 4.
- The website of the Avalon Project at Yale Law School. This is good for documents – click on weblink 5.
- This National Security Archive contains many useful documents on the Cold War – click on weblink 6.
- The Miller Centre at the University of Virginia has many Cold War documents – click on weblink 7.
- The PBS website focuses on the key people and events associated with the nuclear arms race – click on weblink 8.
- Weblink 9 gives good information on sources from the Soviet archives.
- Weblink 10 is another PBS webpage with documents and information on the Vietnam War.

17th parallel: Temporary division of North and South Vietnam established by the Geneva Accords.

38th parallel: The latitude line chosen to divide Korea after World War Two. North of the line was put under Soviet administration and south of the line was put under American administration. It was intended to be a temporary division, but after the Korean War it became the permanent dividing line between North Korea and South Korea.

Able Archer: A NATO military exercise. Able Archer 1983 almost started a nuclear war with the USSR as the Soviets thought it was a cover for a first strike.

ABM: Anti-ballistic missiles, which can be used to intercept and destroy nuclear weapons.

A-bomb: Weapon with huge explosive power that results from the sudden release of energy.

Agent Orange: Herbicide used by US military in Vietnam. The aim was to defoliate forested areas and expose guerrilla fighters. It had huge health effects on those exposed to it.

Allied Control Council (ACC): Council set up to control the whole of Germany after World War Two: members were the UK, USSR, USA, and later France.

Allies (Allied powers): Name given to the grouping of the United Kingdom, the USA and USSR that fought on the same side in World War Two.

American–Japanese Security Treaty: Treaty first signed in 1951 (after the Peace Treaty of San Francisco) that made Japan a military protectorate of the USA.

anarchy: When there is no government or control in society, leading to disorder and confusion.

Anti-Ballistic Missile (ABM) Treaty: Treaty between the US and USSR on the limitation of anti-ballistic missile systems, which can be used to intercept and destroy nuclear weapons.

anti-colonialism: Against the idea of countries having colonies.

anti-nuclearism: Opposition to nuclear weapons.

apartheid: Racist system of 'apartness' which was introduced by the nationalist government of South Africa in 1948 to ensure white-dominated political rule.

Apollo–Soyuz Test Project: July 1975 joint US–Soviet space mission and symbol of détente. It marked the end of the space race.

appeasement: Achieving peace by giving concessions or by satisfying demands. It was the policy used by the UK towards Germany before World War Two (see Munich Agreement).

Arab League: Organization of Arab countries formed in 1945, which aims to draw closer relationships between states.

armistice: Agreement to end fighting.

arms race: Competition to gain weapons superiority that took place between East and West during the Cold War.

Association Principle: UN principle that all 'peace-loving states' could be members.

Aswan Dam: Dam across the Nile in Aswan, Egypt. It was built between 1960 and 1970 to prevent flooding, provide people with water, and generate electricity. It helped to improve the Egyptian economy.

Atlantic Charter: Policy statement issued in 1941 that set out Allied goals after World War Two, drafted by the US and UK.

Attorney General: In the USA, the top law enforcement officer and lawyer for the government.

Austrian State Treaty of 1955: This treaty was signed by the UK, France, the USA, and the USSR. At a conference, agreement was made to end the post-war occupation of Austria and to recognize the Austrian Republic.

backyard furnaces: Used by the Chinese during the Great Leap Forward, these were blast furnaces in the backyards of people's homes, used to make steel.

Baggage Train leaders: Men who had spent much of World War Two war in Moscow, and were considered by the Soviets to be 'trustworthy'. They would thus ensure that the post-war governments of their respective countries would be dominated by Moscow-backed, 'Stalinist' Communists.

Balkans: Region in southeast Europe; Albania, Bulgaria, and Yugoslavia were governed by Communists during the Cold War.

ballistic missile: A rocket that follows a flightpath to deliver warheads to a target.

Bandung Conference: This conference in August 1955 in the Indonesian city of Bandung was the first international gathering of independent Asian and African countries. It inaugurated the Non-Aligned Movement.

Baruch Plan: Proposal for an organization that would regulate atomic energy. The plan proposed that the United States would destroy its weapons on the condition that the UN controlled all atomic development and that this would not be subject to veto in the Security Council. The plan was not accepted by the Soviet Union.

Basic Principles Agreement: Laid down rules for the conduct of nuclear war and development of weapons, and committed the USSR and USA to work together to prevent conflict and promote peaceful co-existence.

Berlin airlift: After World War Two, the German capital city, Berlin, was located in the Soviet zone, but was also divided into four sections under the USA, UK, France, and USSR. The USSR closed all routes into Berlin in 1948 during the Berlin Blockade, but Britain, France, and the US supplied their sectors by carrying out airlifts of supplies for a year.

Berlin Blockade: This was one of the first major crises of the Cold War and lasted from June 1948–May 1949. After World War Two, the German capital city, Berlin, was located in the Soviet zone, but was also divided into four sections under the USA, UK, France, and USSR. In June 1948 the USSR closed all routes into Berlin in response to the introduction of the new currency into the Western sectors of the city. On 12 May 1949, Stalin abandoned the blockade, but the clash was to lead to the division of Germany into East and West and to the building of the Berlin Wall.

Berlin Crisis: This event lasted from 1958 in 1961. The USSR demanded that the Western powers in Berlin – the UK, USA, and France – withdrew from the city within six months. Tension continued to grow and more people moved from East to West Berlin. Khrushchev and Ulbricht closed the East German border in Berlin in August 1961. The initial barbed wire fencing was replaced by a concrete wall that separated East and West until 1989.

bias: Opinion taking into consideration only one side of an argument.

Big Five: The first five permanent members of the UN Security Council: the USA, the USSR, France, Britain, and China.

Big Three: Term used to refer to Roosevelt, Stalin, and Churchill at the Yalta Conference.

bilateral agreement: An agreement in which the parties exchange promises to do something for each other.

bill of rights: Document that sets out rights for individuals in a country.

Bizonia: The combined US and British zones of Germany in 1947.

bloc: A group of countries or people that share the same interest or aims and usually act together.

Bolshevik: A Russian Communist; a member of the left-wing Leninist Russian Social Democratic Workers' Party.

Bolshevik Revolution: This took place in Russia in October 1917 when the Bolshevik Party, under the leadership of Lenin, overthrew the provisional government, which had been in power since the abdication of the Tsar in February 1917. In the aftermath of the revolution, the Union of Soviet Socialist Republics (USSR) was established.

bourgeois: Relating to the 'middle classes' (bourgeoisie) or associated with the middle classes of a country. It is usually used in a negative way in the context of Marxist writings where the bourgeoisie are contrasted with the superior proletariat, or working classes.

boycott: When a group of people, or a country, refuses to take part in something, or do business/have contact with another group or government.

BRD: Bundesrepublik Deutschland, or West Germany. See **FRG**.

Bretton Woods system: Agreements about international economic relationships made between the UK, US, and other Allied countries in June 1944. It included the International Monetary Fund (**IMF**) and the World Bank. The USSR was originally involved but withdrew in 1945.

Brezhnev Doctrine: The doctrine expounded by Leonid Brezhnev in November 1968 affirming the right of the Soviet Union to intervene in the affairs of Communist countries to strengthen Communism.

brinkmanship: Pushing dangerous events to the brink of disaster in order to achieve the most advantageous outcome. This tactic was used during the Cold War.

Brussels Pact: This was signed in 1949 between Belgium, France, Luxembourg, the Netherlands, and the UK. It was designed to organize a system of European mutual defence and was thus a precursor to NATO, which was set up later in 1949.

Camp David: The country retreat of the US president in Washington, DC.

Camp David Accords: Agreements signed by Anwar Sadat and Menachem Begin (the Israeli leader) in 1978 at Camp David, which led to the Israel–Egypt Peace Treaty.

Capitalism: An economic system where a great deal of trade and industry is privately owned and runs to make a profit.

Carter Doctrine: This doctrine committed the United States to intervention if the Soviets threatened Western interests in the Persian Gulf.

catalyst: Something that speeds up or causes the action of a process or event.

censorship: Control by the government of the content of films, newspapers, books, and so on, and by this action suppression of anything considered a threat to the power of the state.

Checkpoint Charlie: The name the Western Allies gave to the crossing point in the Berlin Wall between East and West Berlin.

Chernobyl: City in Ukraine, under Soviet authority, which was the site of a nuclear power plant disaster in 1986.

Chinese Civil War: After World War Two ended in 1945, renewed civil war – ongoing since the 1920s – broke out between Mao Zedong's Communist followers and the Nationalist Party, the Guomindang, led by Jiang Jieshi. The war ended when Mao declared the creation of the People's Republic of China (PRC) in 1949.

Chinese Communist Party (CCP): The ruling political party of the PRC, founded in 1921. In 1949 it defeated the Guomindang and has been in power since.

Chinese People's Liberation Army: The military of the PRC, under the Chinese Communist Party's leadership.

CIA: The Central Intelligence Agency, the main intelligence-gathering agency in the USA.

Civic Forum: Political movement established in 1989 during the Velvet Revolution that called for reform in Czechoslovakia.

clique: Small, exclusive group of people that is apart from the main group.

Collective Security Principle: A UN principle of member states working together to stop aggressor states and potential conflict.

collectivization: Process by which all private farmland in the Soviet Union was put into large collective farms controlled by the state.

colony: A state controlled by another country.

collusion: Secret understanding, often for a dishonest purpose.

COMECON: The Council for Mutual Economic Assistance, economic organization from 1949 to 1991 under the leadership of the USSR and including Eastern Bloc countries and other socialist states.

Cominform: Communist Information Bureau set up in September 1947. This was the first official forum of the international Communist movement and increased Stalin's control over the Communist parties of other countries.

Comintern: The Communist International, an international Communist organization begun in Moscow in 1919. It aimed to spread Communist revolution.

Committee of National Liberation: Group which later came to be known as the Lublin Committee, who stated that they were a coalition of democratic and patriotic forces who wished to work with the Soviet Union.

Commonwealth of Independent States (CIS): A free association of sovereign states of republics that were formerly part of the Soviet Union; formed in 1991.

communiqué: Official form of correspondence, such as a news report.

Communism: Political viewpoint that all businesses and farms should be owned by the state on behalf of the people. Only one leader and party is needed, and goods will be distributed to individuals by the state. Everyone will thus get what is needed and everyone will be working for the collective good.

Comsymp: A person sympathetic to Communist causes.

Conservatism: Political viewpoint that believes in maintaining the existing or traditional order. Conservatives believe in respect for traditional institutions, limiting government intervention in people's lives, and gradual and/or limited changes in the established order.

constitution: Set of rules that lay down how an organization or a country should be governed.

containment: US policy towards Communism by which it would resist Communism anywhere in the world where it was perceived to be a threat. This would involve the USA fighting in both the Korean War and the Vietnam War.

Contras: Right-wing group who challenged the Sandanista regime in Nicaragua.

conventional arms: Weapons that are not of mass destruction, such as biological and nuclear.

Council of Foreign Ministers: Organization agreed at Potsdam in 1945. It consisted of the foreign ministers of the UK, USSR, China, France, and the United States, and had the job of drawing up peace treaties with various countries, sorting out territorial questions, and making a peace settlement for Germany.

counter-insurgency: Type of military campaign which is used during an occupation or a civil war to put down rebellion.

counterforce strategy: Policy of Kennedy's Secretary of Defense, Robert McNamara, in which the objective would be to destroy the enemy's military forces, but not cities and thus not civilian populations.

coup/coup d'état: Violent or illegal seizure of power by a small group or clique.

covert: Secret or hidden.

cruise missile: Guided missiles that are designed to deliver a large warhead over long distances with high accuracy.

Cuban Missile Crisis: Thirteen-day confrontation in 1962 between the United States and the USSR over Soviet missiles in Cuba. This was the closest the Cold War came to nuclear conflict.

Cuban People's Party: Party joined in 1947 by Castro, who was attracted to this new party's campaign against corruption, injustice, poverty, unemployment, and low pay.

cult of personality: The creation of a heroic and all-powerful leader by use of media, propaganda, especially in totalitarian states.

cultural genocide: Destruction of the culture of a nation, race or religious group. It follows from the word genocide, which is usually used to denote the physical destruction of a national, racial, religious or ethnic population.

Cultural Revolution: Launched in May 1966, Mao's programme to initiate a revolution at the very heart of traditional Chinese 'culture' in order to eliminate liberal and bourgeois thinking and behaviour.

Curzon Line: Demarcation line between Poland and Russia, proposed in 1919 after World War One.

Czech Coup: Events of 1948 in Czechoslovakia, which was seen by the Soviets as moving towards the West. Twelve non-Communist politicians were forced to resign and a Communist-led government was installed. Truman used the events to implement the Marshall Plan in Europe.

DDR: see **GDR**.

decolonization: Process by which colonies or lands that had been controlled by European powers regained their independence after 1945.

deconstructions: Taking things apart in order to look at them in more detail.

defoliants: Chemical sprays that destroy plants; Agent Orange was a defoliant used in the Vietnam War to destroy the jungle.

demilitarization: Reduction of a nation's army, weapons, and/or military vehicles to an agreed minimum, often as part of a peace treaty.

demobilization: When an army disbands and goes home.

democracy: Greek term, meaning 'rule of the people'; a form of government in which citizens choose the government through free and fair voting systems and elections.

Democratic Party: In US politics, one of the two main political parties, the other being the Republican Party. It promotes social–liberal, left-wing policies; a mixed economy; civil rights; welfare state systems; and equality. Other democratic parties have similar ideals.

democratization: The transition to a more democratic political system.

despot: A ruler or other person who holds absolute power – typically one who exercises it in a cruel or oppressive way.

de-Stalinization: Process of Soviet political reform after Stalin's death in 1951, which included the changing or removal of gulags, his cult of personality, and the bodies and institutions that he had set up to support his power.

détente: Meaning 'relaxation', or 'thawing out', this is the easing of strained relations, especially in a political situation. It a US term used mainly to refer to the easing of Cold War tensions between the USA and USSR from 1969 to the 1980s.

deterrence: The idea that possession of nuclear weapons by a country will deter other states from attacking with nuclear force due to the effects of retaliation and the threat of mutually assured destruction (MAD).

developing world: Countries in which there is a lower standard of living and less-developed industry than, for example, many Western countries such as the USA.

diplomatic isolation: Sometimes called international isolation, a penalty applied by an international organization, such as the UN or a group of countries, towards a nation, group, or government, in effect cutting it off – isolating it – from the worldwide community.

disarmament: The reducing, limiting, or abolishing of weapons.

dollar imperialism: Term used by Molotov (Soviet Foreign Minister) to express the belief that the USA was using the Marshall Plan to create a sphere of influence in the West and would extend this to the Eastern bloc.

domestic: Concerned with what is going on inside a country itself, as opposed to its international relations.

domestic policy: Policy that concerns laws, government programmes, and administrative decisions, such as taxes, social welfare and legal rights, within a country's borders.

domino effect: Belief that if one country fell to Communism, then all countries in the area would also fall to Communism, like a row of dominoes falling over after one is knocked.

DPRK: Abbreviation for North Korea – the country's official name being the Democratic People's Republic of Korea.

East Germany: see **GDR**.

economic sanctions: Sanctions imposed against a country in an attempt to force it to change its policies. It usually relates to trade, meaning that certain goods will not be sent to, or traded with, the country in question.

EEC: The European Economic Community, an international organization created by the Treaty of Rome in 1957. Its aim was to bring about economic integration. In 1993 it was renamed the European Community (EC).

egalitarianism: The idea of equality for all people.

Eisenhower Doctrine: 1957 policy that the United States would assist any country in the Middle East to fight against Communism.

embargo: Partial or complete prohibition of commerce and trade with a particular country or a group of countries.

European Coal and Steel Community: International organization to unify European countries after World War Two established by the Treaty of Paris 1951 and signed by Belgium, France, West Germany, Italy, the Netherlands, and Luxembourg. The ECSC was a precursor of the European Union (EU).

European Security Conference: Conference in Helsinki in 1973 and the high point of détente. It was attended by 33 countries.

ExComm: The Executive Committee of the National Security Council (commonly referred to as simply the Executive Committee or ExComm); a body of US government officials that convened to advise President Kennedy during the Cuban Missile Crisis in 1962.

expansionist: Policy of expanding or increasing power or territory.

fallout shelter: Place built to protect people from a nuclear attack.

fanaticism: Extreme opinions, usually referring to politics or religion.

fascism: A political ideology that favours limited freedom of people, nationalism, and/or use of violence to achieve ends, and an aggressive foreign policy. Power is in the hands of an elite leader or leadership.

FBI: Federal Bureau of Investigation, a US government agency that investigates crime and is an intelligence agency. It was established in 1908.

feudalism: A way of structuring society around the loan of land in exchange for labour. A class- or caste-based system of power and privilege.

Final Act: The final agreement of the European Security Conference held in Helsinki in 1973, which took the form of three 'baskets'.

first strike: Refers to the ability to launch the first nuclear strike in a nuclear war.

five revolutionary laws: Fidel Castro's manifesto for Cuba, which promised that there would be a return of power to the people; land rights for those holding or squatting on smaller plots; workers to have a 30 per cent share of profits; sugar plantation workers to have a 55 per cent share of profits; and the end of corruption.

five-year plan: Five-year plans for the development of the national economy of the Soviet Union were a series of nationwide economic development plans. Other Communist countries followed similar plans.

flexible response: President Kennedy's method of containing Communism – by expanding the available means of fighting against it.

foreign policy: Strategies chosen by a nation to guard its national interests and to maintain and manage international relations with other countries.

Formosa: Historical name for Taiwan.

Formosa Resolution: A bill of 1955 that said America had a commitment to defend Formosa (Taiwan) and which ended the first Taiwan crisis.

Four Modernizations: Deng Xiaoping's policies for modernization in agriculture, defence, and technology.

free market: Economic system often associated with Capitalism, in which the prices for goods and services are set by sellers and consumers and not by the government or other authority.

free trade: Policy in international markets, in which governments do not restrict imports or exports.

FRG: The Federal Republic of Germany, or West Germany (in German: *BRD, Bundesrepublik Deutschland*).

G7: A group consisting of the finance ministers and banks of seven major, advanced economies: Canada, France, Germany, Italy, Japan, the UK, and the USA. The UN is also included.

Gaither Report: 1957 report to President Eisenhower that recommended a significant strengthening of American military capabilities.

Gang of Four: Group that gained political power and influence during the Chinese Cultural Revolution (1966–1976).

GDR: Abbreviation for East Germany, the German Democratic Republic. In German it is called the *DDR* (*Deutsche Demokratische Republik*).

General Assembly: The main deliberative, policy-making and representative organ of the UN. All members have a vote in the General Assembly.

Geneva Accords: Peace agreement of 1954, after the French defeat at the Vietnamese battle of Dien Bien Phu, through which Indochina was freed from French colonial control, Vietnam was divided, and Laos and Cambodia became independent states.

Geneva Conference: Conference in Geneva in 1954 to end hostilities and create peace in Indonesia. It produced the Geneva Accords.

glasnost: Policy of 'openness' introduced by Mikhail Gorbachev when he became Soviet president in 1985.

GNP (gross national product): Annual total value of goods and services produced in a country.

Grand Alliance: Name given to the alliance of the USA, UK and the USSR during World War Two.

Great Leap Forward: Policy of Mao, begun in 1958, to develop rapidly China's agricultural and industrial sectors simultaneously, via grain and steel production. In the process, Mao would also create the 'proletarian class' required for revolution by the Marxist model.

Great Proletarian Cultural Revolution: Full name of Mao's Cultural Revolution, launched in May 1966. His declared aim was to initiate a revolution at the very heart of traditional Chinese 'culture' in order to eliminate liberal and bourgeois thinking and behaviour.

Great Society: US President Johnson's programme to improve civil rights, eradicate poverty, increase access to health and education, and create a cleaner environment.

Great Terror: Stalin's purges of all political opponents from 1936–1940, as well as millions of ordinary people, who were executed or sent to the gulags.

Green Berets: US military counter-insurgency force trained in guerrilla fighting.

Guantanamo Bay: US naval base on Cuba, located on land leased for American use since 1903. Since 2002 it has also been the site of a military prison for those suspected of terror offences in the wake of the War on Terror.

guerilla war: Form of warfare in which small groups of fighters use tactics such as launching sudden, unexpected attacks, raids, and ambushes.

gulag: A network of forced labour camps in the Soviet Union, or a camp in this network.

Gulf of Tonkin: Body of water off the coast of northern Vietnam and southern China. In August 1964 American ships were allegedly fired on by North Vietnamese patrol boats while patrolling and gathering intelligence in the Gulf of Tonkin, which President Johnson used to pass the Gulf of Tonkin Resolution.

Gulf of Tonkin Resolution: This authorized the US president to 'take all necessary measures to repel any armed attack against the forces of the United States and to prevent further aggression'. The Tonkin Resolution was used as the legal basis for the war in Vietnam.

Guomindang (GMD): This is the name of the Nationalist party led by Jiang Jieshi that fought against the Communists in the Chinese Civil War. After it lost to Mao Zedong's Communists in the Civil War, it set up a Chinese Nationalist government on the island of Taiwan.

Hallstein Doctrine: In 1955, Adenauer made a threat, which became known as the Hallstein Doctrine, by which the FDR (West Germany) would break off diplomatic relations with any country that established diplomatic relations with the GDR (East Germany).

H-bomb: A thermonuclear bomb (also referred to as nuclear) that is much more powerful than the A-bomb.

hegemony: Leadership by one state over a group of states.

Helsinki Agreement/Accords: Diplomatic agreement signed in Helsinki in 1975 in an effort to reduce tension between the Soviet and Western blocs.

Hiroshima: Japanese city that was the first city in history to be targeted by a nuclear weapon, in 1945.

historiography: Study of the writings of historians.

Ho Chi Minh Trail: This is the supply route between North Vietnam and South Vietnam that was used by the Vietcong. It ran through Laos and Cambodia in an attempt to avoid US bombing raids.

humanitarian: Concerned with improving the lives of people and reducing suffering.

Hungarian Uprising: Event in 1956 in Hungary, inspired by the Polish Uprising. The Hungarians lived under the repressive regime of Matyas Rakosi and demanded that the more moderate Imre Nagy replace him. When Nagy announced that Hungary would leave the Warsaw Pact and become a neutral state, the Soviets brought Hungary back under their control and set up a Hungarian government under Janos Kadar.

ICBM: Inter-continental ballistic missile, which as a range of over 3000 nautical miles, and carries nuclear warheads.

ideological: Conforming to an ideology, which is a set of beliefs shared by a group of people. It is a means of explaining how society works or ought to work. For example, the Soviet ideology was based on Marxism and the American ideology was based on Capitalism and liberal democracy.

imperialism: Policy of gaining colonies (control over other countries) and thereby creating an empire. The United States was accused of imperialism during the Cold War: in this case not by ruling directly over other countries, but by influencing them economically and ideologically.

IMF (International Monetary Fund): International organization formed in 1944, and based in Washington DC, comprised of 188 countries who work to ensure economic growth around the world as well as to secure financial stability, facilitate trade, retain high employment and reduce poverty.

inauguration: Ceremony during which a US president officially takes office after having been elected.

Indochina: Vietnam, Cambodia, and Laos.

Indo-Pakistan War: Military confrontation between India and Pakistan in 1971. It lasted for 13 days and concerned the liberation of Bangladesh.

Industrial Revolution: In modern history, the process of change from an agrarian economy to one dominated by industry and machine manufacture.

industrialization: Process in which a society transforms from an agricultural society into an industrial one, based on the manufacturing of goods and services.

INF Treaty: Intermediate-Range Nuclear Force Treaty (INF Treaty), agreement made at the Washington Summit, December 1987, by which it was agreed to abolish land-based missiles of intermediate and shorter range.

inflation: Economic term for an increase in the general price level of goods and services over a period of time.

Interim Treaty: Agreement of SALT I placing limits on the numbers of ICBMs and SLBMs.

internationalism: Movement advocating greater economic and political co-operation among nations for the theoretical benefit of all.

IRMs: Intermediate range missiles, used by the US in Western Europe to counter the Soviet SS-20s during the Second Cold War.

isolationist: When a country keeps out of conflicts in foreign affairs and does not get involved in military alliances. After World War One, the United States took an isolationist position.

Jackson–Vanik Amendment: A 1974 American legal provision that restricted US trade with Communist bloc countries.

Jesuit: A member of a Roman Catholic monastic order called the Society of Jesus.

jihad: An Islamic term signifying a struggle. It has two meanings: one is an inner spiritual struggle and is often called the 'greater jihad' and the other, 'lesser jihad', is a defence of Islam in the form of a holy war. One who fights in the lesser jihad is called a *mujahid* (plural *mujahidin*).

junta: Group of military officers who rule a country after taking power by force.

Katyn Forest Massacre: Mass executions of Polish citizens by the Soviet Secret Police, the NKVD, in 1940.

Khmer Rouge: Followers of the Communist Party in Cambodia/Kampuchea formed in 1968. It ruled from 1975–1979 under Pol Pot and orchestrated genocide and the deaths of around a third of the population of Cambodia.

Kommandantur: The four-power governing body for Berlin after World War Two.

Korean War: War between North and South Korea from 1950–1953 concerning divisions made to the country after World War Two. The USA and UN fought on the side of the South and China, and the Soviets fought for the North.

KPD: Communist Party of Germany.

Länder: The states of Germany. (Singular is *Land*.)

League of Nations: International organization set up after World War One which was intended to maintain peace and encourage disarmament.

left wing: Political ideas or positions that promote social equality, reduce inequality, and that usually show concern for the disadvantaged.

Leninism: The Communist ideas and politics, economics, social thinking, and policies of Vladimir Lenin.

liberalism: Political worldview or way of thinking founded on ideas of the liberty and equality of every person.

Little Red Book: A book of selected statements and writings by Mao Zedong published from 1964–c.1976. It had a bright red cover, hence the (Western) name.

London Conference of Ministers: This was a meeting of British, French, American, and Soviet representatives in 1947. As agreed at the Potsdam Conference, ministers continued to meet to discuss post-war issues. At the London Conference, there was a marked deterioration in relations between the West and the Soviets.

Lublin Committee: A group set up in Lublin, Poland, in July 1944, who stated that they were a coalition of democratic and patriotic forces who wished to work with the Soviet Union.

Lushan Conference: A meeting of the top leaders of the Communist Party of China held between July and August 1959.

macro and micro scales: Looking at a situation close up (micro) and in broader context (macro).

Mafia: An organized crime syndicate that will often practise drug trafficking, fraud, and loan sharking, whose members are bound by a code of silence. Although there are such organizations in many countries, the Mafia usually refers to the Italian–American or Sicilian Mafia.

Manchu Dynasty: Also called the Qing dynasty, this was the last imperial ruling dynasty of China.

Maoism: Political theory based on the thought of Mao Zedong; a form of Marxism–Leninism, which was the ideology of the Chinese Community Party. It stressed the revolutionary potential of the peasant class.

marshal: The highest military rank of the USSR, created in 1935 and abolished 1991.

Marshall Plan: The American initiative to aid Europe, in which the United States gave $17 billion (approximately $160 billion in current dollar value) in economic support to help rebuild European economies after the end of World War Two.

martial law: Military rule established in a country, usually as a temporary measure during a political crisis.

Marxism–Leninism: Stalinist term for his political ideology and that of the Communist Party of the Soviet Union and Comintern. It is based on Marxism and Leninism, but with emphasis on the Leninist doctrine of class struggle and liberation of the exploited masses from imperialism.

massive retaliation: A military term for retaliation that is much greater in force than the original attack.

McCarthyism: Term that means making accusations of actions such as subversion or treason without having proper evidence, or by using unfair methods. The term comes from the hunts for those believed to be Communists, or Communist sympathizers, led by Senator Joseph McCarthy in the USA in the 1950s.

MIG fighter: A Soviet jet fighter plane.

military coup: The sudden seizure of a government by the military.

military–industrial complex: Term first used by Eisenhower in 1961 to refer to the network of individuals and institutions involved in the production of weapons and military technologies.

MIRV: Multiple Independently Targetable Re-entry Vehicle, launched by a missile that allows several warheads to be used, each guided to a different target.

missile gap: The missile gap was the Cold War term used in the US for the perceived superiority of the number and power of the USSR's missiles in comparison with its own.

mixed economy: Economic system that includes private and public ownership, and/or private and state ownership.

modus operandi: Particular way of working or dealing with a task.

Molotov Plan: A series of bilateral trade agreements that aimed to tie the economies of Eastern Europe to the USSR.

monolithic: Describing a single huge organization. The Americans believed that all Communist states were part of one massive organization controlled by the Soviets.

monopolize: To have or to take the greatest share of something so that others are prevented from a fair share.

Monroe Doctrine: A 19th-century American policy that stated efforts by European nations to colonize land in North or South America would be viewed as acts of aggression. It was named after President James Monroe.

Moscow Conference: 1945 conference at which the United States and the Soviet Union dealt with how Japan and Korea were to be governed post-World War Two.

most favoured nation status: This is granted to a country as part of a trade agreement with another country in favour of better trading conditions.

Mujahidin: the people engaged in a *jihad*, especially as guerrilla warriors, such as during the Soviet invasion of Afghanistan in the 1980s.

Munich Agreement: This 1938 agreement was signed between the United Kingdom, Germany, France and Italy. It forced Czechoslovakia to give an area called the Sudetenland (which contained German speakers) to Germany. This was part of the UK policy of appeasement. The then-prime minister of Britain, Neville Chamberlain, believed that by giving Hitler what he and Nazi Germany were asking for, a European war could be avoided.

My Lai: Village in South Vietnam that was the scene of a massacre by the US Army in 1968.

Nagasaki: Japanese city that was the second target of a nuclear bomb during World War Two.

napalm: Gel made from petrol that readily catches fire. It was used by US forces during the Vietnam War. It sticks to the skin and causes terrible burns.

National Union: Egyptian premier Nasser set up the National Union in 1957 to replace all political parties.

nationalism: The belief that nations will benefit from acting independently rather than collectively; emphasizing national rather than international goals.

nationalization: When a government takes over private industry or land so that it is owned by the state.

NATO: The North Atlantic Treaty Organization, a military alliance founded in 1949. Its members agree to mutual defence if one is attacked: its website says that 'NATO's essential purpose is to safeguard the freedom and security of its members through political and military means.' During the Cold War, rival nations joined the Warsaw Pact.

Nazi: A member of Hitler's German Nazi (National Socialist) Party. The term is now often used to describe someone with far-right views.

Nazi–Soviet Pact: see **Non-Aggression Pact**.

New Course: A Soviet economic policy to improve the standard of living in East Germany.

New Forum: A political resistance movement in East Germany formed in the lead up to the collapse of East and West Germany.

New Look: The name given to the USA's national security policy during Eisenhower's presidency. It stresses the deterrence effects of weapons and preventing the extension of Soviet Communism outside of the areas where it was already established.

Nixon Doctrine: 1969 doctrine in which Nixon moved away from US policies followed in Asia since Truman. It stated that nations were responsible for their own defence.

NLF: The National Liberation Front; the political arm of South Vietnamese groups of Communists (the Vietcong).

Non-Aggression Pact 1939 (Nazi–Soviet Pact): This was the agreement signed between the Soviets and the

Germans in August 1939, in which they agreed not to attack each other. Secret clauses of the agreement provided for joint military action against Poland.

Non-Aligned Movement: Group of countries that pursued a neutral position in the Cold War.

NSC-68: A report by the US National Security Council, produced in 1950, which warned that all Communist activity could be traced back to Moscow. It encouraged military and economic aid to be given to any country perceived by the USA to be resisting Communism.

nuclear arms race: Competition for supremacy in nuclear warfare between the United States, the Soviet Union, and their allies during the Cold War.

nuclear holocaust: Term used for what would happen if there was a nuclear war, such as total destruction and great loss of human life.

nuclear parity: When opposing forces possess equal-strength nuclear offensive and defensive systems.

Nuclear Non-Proliferation Treaty: Treaty of 1968 that prevented signatories from transferring weapons, or knowledge of how to make them, to non-nuclear powers.

OAS: Organization of American States; an inter-continental organization founded in 1948 to ensure regional solidarity and cooperation among its members. Members include South and Central American countries, Canada, and Caribbean islands, as well as the USA.

Oder–Neisse Line: The border between Germany and Poland drawn up after World War Two.

OPEC (Organization of the Petroleum Exporting Countries): International organization with its base in Vienna, founded 1960, to ensure the stabilization of oil markets.

open-door policy: The economic policies of Deng Xiaoping, which from 1978 opened up China for foreign business investment.

Open Skies: Eisenhower's proposal that the USA and Soviets would exchange plans of military installations and allow aerial surveillance of each other's installations.

Operation Barbarossa: The code name for Nazi Germany's invasion of the Soviet Union in World War Two.

Operation Overlord: The code name for the Allied operation that invaded Nazi-occupied Europe in World War Two.

Operation Rolling Thunder: The name of a sustained US bombing campaign against North Vietnam from 1965–1968.

Orthodox view: The position also known as the 'Traditional view', which generally holds that the Soviet Union was responsible for the Cold War. This was the position taken by historians writing in the 1950s and early 1960s.

***Ostpolitik*:** Policy followed by West German Chancellor Willy Brandt, in the 1970s, which aimed to improve West German relations with East Germany.

pacifist: Someone who does not believe in fighting in a war.

Panmunjom Armistice: The armistice that ended the Korean War in 1953.

paradigm: Philosophical or theoretical framework or model.

paradigm shift: A radical change in a belief or theory.

paranoia: Abnormal tendency to be suspicious of and lack trust in other people.

Paris Peace Accords: Intended to establish peace in Vietnam, the accords ended direct US military involvement and temporarily stopped the fighting between North and South Vietnam. A peace agreement was signed in 1973.

Paris Peace Talks: Negotiations that led to the Paris Peace Accord, which ended the Vietnam War, beginning in 1972.

Paris Summit: A 1960 summit that aimed to establish better relations between the USA and Soviets, but which collapsed due to Gary Powers' U2 spy plane being shot down over Russia.

parity: The state of having similar capability to another – in Cold War terms, the USSR having nuclear parity with, or the same capability as the United States.

peaceful co-existence: Theory developed and applied by the Soviets at times during the Cold War, which said that Socialist states could co-exist with Capitalist ones.

Percentages Agreement: An agreement made in 1944 between Stalin and Churchill about how to divide various European countries (regarding the influence and control the Western powers and the USSR would want to have) after World War Two.

***perestroika*:** Soviet leader Mikhail Gorbachev's policy of 'restructuring' the economy of the Soviet Union.

Perimeter speech: Speech made by Dean Acheson in 1950 in which both South Korea and Taiwan were publicly excluded from the American defensive perimeter in the Western Pacific.

ping-pong diplomacy: A term that refers to the exchange of table tennis players between the USA and PRC in the 1970s. It marked a thaw in relations.

Platt Amendment: 1902 amendment to a treaty outlining US–Cuban relationship. The Platt Amendment outlined the role of the United States in Cuba and the Caribbean.

polemic: Speech or piece of writing which contains very forceful arguments for or against something.

Polish Peasant Party: Sometimes called the Polish People's Party, this party existed in Poland from 1945–1949, led by Stanislaw Mikolajczyk.

Polish Revolt: Event in Poland in June 1956 when workers in the industrial city of Poznan revolted and the Polish Communist Wladyslaw Gomulka, who had been imprisoned under Stalin, was brought back to political prominence as First Secretary. This took place without Khrushchev's approval, but he agreed to allow Gomulka to remain in power.

Politburo: The highest policy-making authority of the Soviet Communist Party, founded in 1917 and which ended in 1991 with the break up of the USSR.

Popular Movement for the Liberation of Angola (MPLA): Political party founded in the 1950s that has ruled Angola since 1975 and independence from Portugal.

Post-revisionist: School of thought which stresses that neither the USA nor the USSR can be held solely responsible for the origins of the Cold War. Gaddis is one of the key figures of this group.

Potsdam Conference: Conference in Germany in 1945 between the UK, USA, and Soviet Union. The delegates (Stalin, Truman, and initially Churchill, who was replaced by Attlee) met to discuss how to deal with the defeated Nazi Germany and other post-World War Two issues.

Prague Spring: A time of political liberalization in Czechoslovakia in 1968 with the election of Dubcek as First Secretary. It ended with an invasion by Warsaw Pact countries, who feared Dubcek's moves.

Pravda: Russian political newspaper that began in 1912 and which was an official state-backed newspaper until the demise of the USSR. It is still published. *Pravda* means truth in Russian.

pre-emptive strike: A surprise attack launched in order to prevent the enemy from attacking first.

private ownership: Non-governmental ownership of property.

Proletariat: The working class; wage earners who must earn their living by working.

propaganda: Information, usually biased or misleading, that promotes a political cause or idea. In war, it is used to create a false image of an enemy or cause.

proxy: The authority to represent another.

PSP: Abbreviation for the Cuban Communist Party (*Partido Socialista Popular*).

puppet regime/puppet state: Terms used for a government or rule that is actually being controlled by an outside power.

purges: Term used to describe the mass killings carried out in the USSR by Stalin from the mid-1930s.

quagmire theory: A theory used to explain the United States' involvement in the Vietnam War. It suggests that successive presidents became increasingly involved in the war, and the US became more and more stuck in Vietnam.

quarantine: A state or area of forced isolation.

Radio Free Europe: Also called Radio Liberty, a broadcasting organization that provides news, information, and analysis to countries in Eastern Europe, parts of Asia, and the Middle East. It was founded as an anti-Communist news source during the Cold War in 1949. Its coverage of the Poznam riots of 1956 inspired the Hungarian Uprising.

rapprochement: A rapprochement, from the French *rapprocher*, 'to bring together', is the re-establishment of cordial relations between countries.

reactionary: Political term for someone who is opposed to progress or reform, or who wants to put things back to the way they were.

realpolitik: Approach to politics which is based on practical concerns and the actual circumstances of the time rather than on ideology.

reconnaissance: When one side checks out or surveys the strength of the other side – for example, using aircraft.

Red Army: Soviet army created by the Communist government after the Bolshevik Revolution of 1917.

Red Scare: The promotion of fear of a potential rise of Communism or radical leftism.

Red Square: A city square in Moscow, Russia.

Reagan victory school: This view credits President Reagan's policies with ending the Cold War.

reasonable sufficiency: Gorbachev's idea that the Soviet Union should have only enough weapons to defend itself, rather than enough to launch a pre-emptive strike or fight a preventative war.

re-education: Chinese Cultural Revolution process sending anyone considered bourgeois (such as intellectuals, artists, and musicians) to camps to be re-educated through forced labour, which would give them empathy for the labourer and common worker.

regime change: When there is a change in the government of the country.

Regional Principle: UN principle allowing for the development of regional arrangements or agencies for dealing with threats to peace.

reparations: Payments that are imposed on countries that have been defeated in a war by the victors, in order to pay for the costs of the war incurred by the victors.

repatriation: Sending someone back to his or her own country.

republican: Someone who advocates a republic – a form of government that is not a monarchy or dictatorship.

Republican Party: American political party founded by anti-slavery activists in 1854. Policies are usually conservative rather than liberal and include free market Capitalism and opposition to unions. A supporter is a Republican.

Revisionist: Perspective on the Cold War that holds US policies responsible.

revisionists: Critical term used by Communist governments to describe those they believed had deviated from the true Marxist path.

right wing: Groups or individuals who favour free market Capitalism and place an emphasis on law and order, limited state interference, and traditional values in society; those who believe that things are better left unchanged.

roll-back: A 1952 US presidential election campaign term that meant liberating countries held by the Soviets in Eastern Europe. Roll-back never happened – under Eisenhower, the US administration developed a policy of containment it called the 'New Look'.

Russian Civil War: This war followed on from the Russian Revolution and involved many different groups, all vying to determine Russia's political future. The two main groups were the Red Army and the White Army, the former were Bolsheviks in favour of socialism and the latter were against it. By 1921 the Bolsheviks were in control and Russia became a Communist state.

Russian Revolution: This refers to a number of revolutions that took place in Russia after the end of Tsarist rule in 1917 and which led to the creation of the Communist Soviet Union.

Russo-Polish War: This 1921 war was started by the Poles to gain land from the new Soviet Bolshevik state. After the Poles' initial progress had been checked by the Red Army (which nearly captured Warsaw), the Curzon Line was proposed as the frontier between the two states. However, this was never ratified and the Poles were actually able to get much more Russian territory through the Treaty of Riga. The Soviet Union only reacquired this land as a consequence of the Nazi–Soviet Pact and its invasion of Poland in 1939.

saboteurs: People who secretly and deliberately damage something.

salami tactics: Term used by Hungarian Communist leader Matyas Rakosi, commenting on how the USSR secured Communist control in Eastern Europe – 'like slicing off salami, piece by piece'.

SALT I/II: Strategic Arms Limitation Talks (SALT), two rounds of talks and treaties between the USA and Soviet Union about arms control. They took place in Helsinki between 1969–1979.

Sandinistas: Members of a socialist party in Nicaragua that established a revolutionary government from 1979–1990. A CIA-funded militia, the Contras, was formed in 1981 to overthrow the Sandinista government.

satellite empire/state: A political term that designates a country that is nominally independent but that is under the heavy political, economic, and military control of another country.

SCAP: Supreme Commander of the Allied Powers; a post given to General MacArthur after Japan's 1945 defeat that allowed him great powers to devise and execute policies there.

SDI: Abbreviation for **Strategic Defense Initiative**.

search-and-destroy missions: Key part of US strategy in Vietnam. US soldiers would look for the Vietcong (often by helicopter) and then destroy their bases or the areas in which they believed that the Vietcong were hiding.

SEATO: The Southeast Asia Treaty Organization, an international organization for collective defence in Southeast Asia, signed in September 1954 in the Philippines.

Second Cold War: Period in the 1980s when the USA and the USSR were again hostile towards each other.

Secretary General: The chief officer and head of the United Nations.

Secretary of State: Senior official in the US government, mainly concerned with foreign affairs and policy.

Security Council: One of the six principal organs of the UN, which is charged with the maintenance of international security and peacekeeping.

self-immolation: Act of suicide by setting oneself on fire.

Seventh Fleet: A US military naval fleet that took part in the wars in Korea and Vietnam.

Shanghai Communiqué: An important diplomatic document issued by China and the USA during Nixon's visit in 1972. It pledged that the two countries would pursue a good relationship.

show trial: Public trials used in the Soviet Union in the 1930s for propaganda purposes to show to the world that key political opponents of the ruling elite were indeed guilty.

Siberia: A vast territory in Russia and the site of many gulags and labour camps.

single polar: One source of influence, where only one country dominates. This is as opposed to bi-polar or multi-polar.

Sino-Soviet Treaty of Alliance: The first treaty between the USSR and China, 1950.

Six-Day War: Also known as the 1967 Arab–Israeli War. The war was fought in 1967 by Israel against Egypt, Jordan, and Syria.

SLBM: Submarine-launched ballistic missiles – missiles with nuclear warheads that are carried on submarines.

socialism: Political theory of social organization stressing shared or state ownership of production, industry, land, and so on.

Solidarity: Polish trade union founded in 1980 by Lech Walesa; the first non-Communist-controlled union.

space race: 20th-century (1955–1972) competition between the USA and USSR for supremacy in space flight.

sphere of influence: Area over which a country has influence. For example, Eastern Europe was within the Soviet Union's sphere of influence after 1945. Both the Soviet Union and the United States tried to increase their spheres of influence during the Cold War.

Sputnik: The first artificial satellite, launched by the Soviets in 1957, which began the space race.

SS-20: A Soviet nuclear warhead.

Stalinism: Political viewpoint/government policies based on those of Joseph Stalin, including one-country socialism, industrialization, collectivization, a cult of personality, and purges.

Star Wars: see **Strategic Defense Initiative**.

Stasi: The Ministry for State Security, the official state security service – secret police – of East Germany.

State Department: The United States Department of State, responsible for the USA's international relations.

status quo: The existing condition or state of affairs.

stinger missile: A surface-to-air missile that can be fired from ground vehicles or helicopters, developed in the USA.

Strategic Arms Limitation Interim Agreement: See **SALT I/II**.

strategic bombers: Planes capable of carrying and delivering nuclear weapons.

Strategic Defense Initiative: Reagan's aim to set up a space-based missile system that could intercept and destroy missiles before they reached the United States (also known as 'Star Wars').

strategic hamlets program: A plan by South Vietnam and the United States to combat Communist insurgency by population transfer during the Vietnam War.

Suez Canal: An artificial waterway in Egypt that connects the Mediterranean with the Red Sea, opened in 1869. Use of the canal cuts around 7000 miles off a voyage from Europe and Asia. It is a key route for oil supplies. In 1956 the Suez became a point of crisis when Nasser nationalized it to raise funds for building the Aswan Dam.

Suez Crisis: An invasion of Egypt in late 1956 by Israel, Britain, and France to regain control of the Suez Canal (which was of vital importance to shipping) and remove Egyptian President Nasser. The French, Israeli, and British actions caused a storm of protest; UN – and US and Soviet – pressure forced their withdrawal and a UN peacekeeping force was sent to the region to restore order.

summit: Conference or meeting of high-level leaders, usually called to shape a programme of action.

superpowers: Term given to USSR and USA (and eventually the People's Republic of China) after the end of World War Two. It signifies their immense economic, political, and military power compared to other countries.

Tehran Conference: Meeting held between Stalin, Roosevelt, and Churchill to discuss key areas of World War Two.

Test-Ban Treaty: A treaty concerning nuclear weapons testing. The Limited Test-Ban Treaty, 1963, prohibited nuclear weapons tests in the atmosphere, in outer space, and underwater. The Comprehensive Nuclear-Test-Ban Treaty (CTBT) banned all nuclear explosions in all environments.

Tet Offensive: A large military campaign of surprise attacks during the Vietnam War, begun in 1968 by Communist forces against targets in South Vietnam.

Tiananmen Square: A large city square in Beijing, scene of pro-democracy protests in 1989.

total war: War in which the government of a country uses all the economic and human resources it has in order to win.

trade embargo: government order imposing a trade barrier on any regulation or policy that restricts international trade.

Treaty of Friendship: A generic name for any treaty establishing close ties between countries.

Treaty of San Francisco: US–Japan treaty signed in 1952 that enabled the United States to maintain military bases in Japan.

Treaty of Versailles: Peace treaty with Germany at the end of the First World War, signed in 1919.

triangular diplomacy: Term employed by Henry Kissinger to describe the relationship he was trying to establish between Washington, Moscow, and Beijing.

Trotskyist: Someone supporting the ideas of Leon Trotsky. Trotsky had been a rival to Stalin for the leadership of the Soviet Union after the death of Lenin. Stalin used the term Trotskyist in the 1930s to attack his political opponents.

Truman Doctrine: Truman's doctrine that the United States would provide political, military, and economic assistance to all democratic nations under threat.

Tsar: An emperor of Russia before 1917.

Tsarist: The Russian Tsarist government hinged on the supreme authority of the Tsar and the ministers, governors, and bureaucrats who implemented his orders.

'two camps' Doctrine: Soviet doctrine developed by Andrei Zhdanov, which said that the world was divided into 'two camps': the imperialistic US-led camp and the democratic Soviet-led camp.

U-2: A single-engine, ultra-high altitude reconnaissance plane operated by the United States Air Force and used by the CIA.

UN Charter: The foundational treaty of the UN, signed in San Francisco in 1945.

unconditional surrender: A surrender in which no guarantees are given to the surrendering party.

unequal treaties: A series of treaties signed with Western powers and China in the 19th and 20th centuries.

uni-polar: Term used after the Cold War meaning that international politics became 'uni-polar', with the USA as the only country now capable of having a military alliance with other countries around the world.

United Nations: Intergovernmental organization founded in 1945 to promote international relations and co-operation. It now has almost 200 members.

Velvet Revolution: Non-violent transition of power in Czechoslovakia in 1989 that ended Communist rule.

veto: Right to reject or forbid a decision.

Vienna Summit: Meeting of President Kennedy and Nikita Khrushchev in 1961 to discuss Cold War issues associated with the relationship between their countries, including Berlin.

Vietcong (VC): A political organization and army in South Vietnam that was on the side of the USA in the Vietnam War.

Vietminh: A national independence movement in Vietnam founded in 1941, to gain independence from French rule, and revived by Ho Chi Minh against the Japanese and French hold over Vietnam.

Vietnam War: War from 1955–1975 between North (supported by the USSR and China, and Communist allies) and South (supported by the USA and non-Communist allies) Vietnam.

Vietnamization: A policy introduced by Nixon during the Vietnam War to end the USA's involvement by training the South Vietnamese in combat.

Warsaw Ghetto: The Warsaw Ghetto was the largest of all the Jewish ghettos in Nazi-occupied Europe during World War Two.

Warsaw Pact: A defence treaty between eight Communist European states during the Cold War, formed in 1955.

Warsaw Uprising: A major World War Two Polish resistance operation to liberate Warsaw from the Nazis.

West Bank: A disputed territory to the west of the Jordan River, occupied by Israel in the 1967 Arab–Israeli War.

West Germany: see **FRG**.

White Paper: Government report outlining policy.

Whites: Anti-Communists who fought the Bolsheviks in the Russian Civil War.

'X article': An article written by George Kennan that outlined the US's Cold War policy of containment toward the Soviet Union.

Yalta Conference: Yalta was called to help the Allied powers decide what would happen to Europe, and in particular Germany, at the end of World War Two. At Yalta, in early 1945, one of the main decisions was to split Germany into four zones of occupation after the war.

Yom Kippur War: Also known as the 1973 Arab–Israeli War; this war, led by Egypt and Syria, aimed to expel Israeli forces occupying Sinai. (Yom Kippur is a Jewish festival.)

Zaibatsu: Elite and powerful Japanese families that controlled industry and finance.

Zealot: A fanatically committed person.

zero option: The name given to an American Reagan administration proposal for the withdrawal of Soviet missiles from Europe, later used to talk about the elimination of all nuclear weapons.

Zhongnanhai: An imperial garden in central Beijing. It serves as the central headquarters for the Communist Party of China and the State Council of the People's Republic of China.

Italic page numbers indicate an illustration, be it a picture, table or map. Bold page numbers indicate an interesting fact box.

Improve your learning

Take a look at some of the interactive tools on your
The Cold War: Superpower tensions and rivalries 2nd ed eText.
Note that the examples below may be from a different title, but you will find
topic-appropriate resources on your eText.

Worksheets

A variety of research activities
with questions for you to
work on together outside the
classroom, giving you practice
of essay-writing skills.

BACCALAUREATE
Causes and Effects of
20TH Century Wars

Chapter 8 – The Second V

Worksheet: The Roles of Individuals

How important were individuals in determining the course
the impact of the following individuals on the outcome of
that you would like to research). Consider specific decisi
hese actions impacted on the defeat of Germany and

Winston Churchill
eral Zhukov
oosevelt

pter 8: Cross-Regional War: The Second World

Put the following developments in chronol

Drag and drop the events into the correct order and then click Submit.

Hitler's armies reverse the defeats of the Italians i

Italy enters the Second W

The British sink half the

Revision Quizzes

These include a variety of
exercise types e.g. check
whether you can put events
in the correct order.
Get immediate feedback:
great for revision practice.

al War: Ch...

r 1 Example question 3: Com...

r violence by Japanese soldiers. [6 n...

Work through the stages of planning an answer to this

Sources

Source 1

Inventing Japan 1853–1964 (2004) by Ian Buruma

For years, the Japanese had been told that the
Chinese were inferior and the Japanese a ...
race. Contempt for the Chinese goes ba...
Meiji prints in which the Japanese are ...
...igorous and the Chinese are coweri...
...tins; Government propaganda, p...
...tic Japanese press, told sold...
...ly war.

...the name of...

...correct answers.

...his is a typical example of Question 1b in Paper
...question is asking you to do?

☐ Demonstrate understanding of the source's messag...

☐ Consider the successes and failures of Mussolini's fore...

☐ Give an account of the similarities and differences bet...
expressed in the source and your own knowledge on ...
foreign policy.

...ook at Source 1. What event is it referring to?

...lini's declaration of aims for f...

Exam Practice Activities

Practice with source analysis
helps to get you ready for
the exam.

HITLER

1889–1945

Adolf Hitler (1889–1945): Austrian-born German politician and
leader of the Nazi Party. As Chancellor and dictator of Germany,
his expansionist regime led to World War Two, one of the most
deadly conflicts in the history of humanity. Hitler's political and foreign
policy aims were outlined in his book *Mein Kampf* (My Struggle), which
included strong anti-Semitic views. His aggressive foreign policy,
which sought to find 'lebensraum' or living space for Germans, caused
the outbreak of the Second World War. Hitler ewar also led to the
Holocaust, where millions of Jewish people were killed.

Biographies

To help you remember who the
key figures are, these posters
include the significant facts on
each person.